Leopold Zunz

The Prayer Rites of Synagogal Worship and their Historical Development

Edited and translated by Stefan C. Reif

Studia Judaica

Forschungen zur Wissenschaft des Judentums

Herausgegeben von
Charlotte Fornrobert, Elisabeth Hollender,
Alexander Samely und Irene E. Zwiep

Band 125

Rethinking Diaspora

Edited by
Stefan C. Reif, Simha Goldin, Andreas Lehnardt,
Nahem Ilan, and Roni Stauber

Volume 6

Leopold Zunz

The Prayer Rites of Synagogal Worship and their Historical Development

Edited and translated by
Stefan C. Reif

An English Translation of the German Edition
of Berlin 1859

Prepared with the assistance of Renate Egger-Wenzel

DE GRUYTER

ISBN 978-3-11-221519-7
e-ISBN (PDF) 978-3-11-114250-0
e-ISBN (EPUB) 978-3-11-114303-3

Library of Congress Control Number: 2023932390

Bibliographic information published by the Deutsche Nationalbibliothek
The Deutsche Nationalbibliothek lists this publication in the Deutsche Nationalbibliografie; detailed bibliographic data are available on the internet at http://dnb.dnb.de.

This volume is text- and page-identical with the hardback published in 2023.
Typesetting: Integra Software Services Pvt. Ltd.
Printing and binding: CPI books GmbH, Leck

www.degruyter.com

For Avigail Shulamit,
my first great grandchild

Contents

An Introduction to Zunz the Liturgist —— 1

The Prayer Rites of Synagogal Worship and their Historical Development —— 23

Annotations —— 195

Appendices —— 201
Pp. 184–93 Appendix I —— 201
Pp. 194–201 Appendix II —— 211
Pp. 202–3 Appendix III —— 219
Pp. 204–10 Appendix IV —— 221
Pp. 211–21 Appendix V —— 227
Pp. 222–25 Appendix VI —— 237
Pp. 226–28 Appendix VII —— 241
Pp. 229–30 Appendix VIII —— 245
Pp. 231–33 Appendix IX —— 247

Pp. 246–49 Geographical Index —— 249

An Introduction to Zunz the Liturgist

Why an English translation?

It is widely recognized in the world of scientific Jewish scholarship that Leopold (Yomtov Lipman) Zunz (1794–1886) was a pioneer in the historical examination and critical analysis of Hebrew literature. With his publications, he set the tone for many studies of the past century and a half and nowhere is this truer than in the area of Jewish liturgy. His 1859 publication *Die Ritus des synagogalen Gottesdienstes geschichtlich entwickelt*[1] was, as its title indicates, a study of the historical development of synagogal worship, and its place in Zunz's overall scholarly agenda will shortly be traced. Before this is done, however, it seems appropriate to explain why I have chosen to offer an English translation of this relatively short but singularly important opus.

Whoever has, since 1859, engaged in the effort to understand how the rabbinic prayer-book originated, and to unravel the complex twists and turns in its historical journey through the ages, will have made use, either directly or indirectly, of the data and expositions provided by Zunz.[2] Those who have turned for guidance to the original German of *Die Ritus* will have soon entertained the thought that neither the content nor the language is easily understood. One probable reason for this is that the German is by now of course antiquated, but is also related to tendency of the leading proponent of *Wissenschaft des Judentums* to avoid spelling things out when he had doubts, and to canter through vast swathes of the liturgical countryside often with no more than a side glance at the textual flora and exegetical fauna. Though anxious to cover ground quickly, he nevertheless sought to write something about almost everything and, more often than not, left the reader with important information but also a hankering after more detail as well a desire for closer analysis. He also chose to interchange, somewhat freely, present and past tenses, and I have tried, wherever possible, to follow him in this.

Given such considerations it is then hardly surprising that, although more than 160 years have passed since its appearance, no sound English translation of *Die Ritus* has been published, many scholars having doubtless been daunted by

1 Published by Springer in Berlin.
2 Obvious examples are Ismar Elbogen, *Der jüdische Gottesdienst in seiner geschichtlichen Entwicklung* (Frankfurt am Main: Kaufmann, 1931. Reprint: Hildesheim: Olms, 1962); Ezra Fleischer, *Eretz-Israel Prayer and Prayer Rituals as Portrayed in the Geniza Documents* (Hebrew; Jerusalem: Magnes Press, 1988); and Naphtali Wieder, *The Formation of Jewish Liturgy in the East and the West. A Collection of Essays*. 2 vols. (Hebrew; Jerusalem: Ben-Zvi Institute, 1998).

https://doi.org/10.1515/9783111142500-001

the challenge of undertaking such an obvious desideratum. When the Hebrew edition of *Die Ritus* appeared in 2016,[3] edited by Avraham Fraenkel and translated by Ze'ev Breuer, the long wait for the volume's availability to be extended appeared to be over. Fraenkel had gone to enormous trouble to provide and update all Zunz's sources, to clarify his sometimes less than clear references, to identify the current provenances and classmarks of the manuscripts Zunz used, and to correct those few instances in which the German-Jewish Homer had nodded. Breuer had transformed nineteenth-century academic German into broadly readable modern Hebrew. The world of learning owed them both a significant debt of gratitude for what was undoubtedly a major contribution to the contemporary study of the Hebrew prayers as they developed over a period of two millennia.

Why then the English translation and introduction that are here being offered? A number of reasons suggest themselves. First of all, Fraenkel neither set *Die Ritus* in the overall contexts of the scientific analysis of Jewish liturgy, nor explained Zunz's motivations for authoring the work, and it seems to me that these lacunae require to be addressed.[4] Secondly, Breuer's treatment at times amounts not to a literal translation but rather to a paraphrastic version that may provide the overall sense but is not wholly faithful to Zunz's original version. My concern is that those many scholars, especially in Israel, who have no competence in German will cite *Die Ritus* in its Hebrew version and build on this foundation, even if it is not always a sound one. This has occurred not infrequently when translations of classic works in European languages have become standard refence tools in modern Hebrew. There are numerous instances when my rendering does not quite match Breuer's and needs to be offered to the English readers for their consideration.

One should of course add that there are English-speaking scholars in current academia who are unacquainted with German and less than comfortable with modern Hebrew but whose work would nevertheless benefit from reading this classic study by Zunz. My aim in this volume has been to link *Die Ritus* with Zunz's other works and their scholarly intent by way of this brief introduction and to provide as literal and as faithful a translation as has been possible, without the result reading more like German than like English. I have even therefore reproduced Zunz's footnotes in the highly abbreviated form that he used although I have added as an appendix to this introductory essay a bibliographical list that explains these when they may not be obvious even to a learned reader and owes a great

3 *Minhagey Tefillah U-Piyyuṭ bi-Qehillot Yisrael*; English title: *Leopold Zunz: Rites of Synagogue Liturgy* (Jerusalem: World Union of Jewish Studies, 2016).

4 Some of the remarks made below are included in my forthcoming article "To what Extent is Genizah Research on Jewish Liturgy a Continuation of the Work of Leopold Zunz?", in a *Festschrift* for a colleague, the details of which (for obvious reasons) I am not yet at liberty to reveal.

deal to Fraenkel's important bibliographical efforts. Unlike Fraenkel, who relegated some of Zunz's original comments to the footnotes and expanded those footnotes to include post-Zunzian scholarship until the present, I have, in order to avoid any confusion on the part of current readers of English, adhered strictly to the original source. Those seeking updates on Zunz and identifications of the manuscrips he used are referred to Fraenkel's expanded footnotes and lists. For ease of reference for those wishing to compare the English with the German, I have, as Breuer and Fraenkel before me, indicated the original pagination without following it in my own text. Zunz's square brackets are reproduced but when I have felt the need to make a small addition of my own for clarity, I have done so in curly brackets. I have also employed such curly brackets to surround some bibliographical additions that I regarded as essential for the guidance of the reader. Much fuller information is to be found in Fraenkel's various lists at the end of his volume.. I have not included here Appendix 10 on pp. 234–45 of Zunz's volume because these additional notes relate not to the text of *Die Ritus* but to his *Die synagogale Poesie*.[5]

To that end, I have worked closely with my wife Renate, who is a native German speaker and who has, in her own scholarly work, often had to grapple with nineteenth-century German.[6] She has prevented many a misunderstanding and we have struggled together to produce an English version of precisely what Zunz had to say. I am most grateful to her for her generous devotion to this project. It would be highly remiss of me if I did not also acknowledge how very much I owe to both Fraenkel and Breuer. Without the former's careful bibliographical research it would have taken me much longer to master Zunz's volume, and without the latter's important Hebrew text I might often have been at an initial loss to explain complex sentences in the original.

Manuscript research

A nineteenth-century development that proved highly productive for historians of the medieval world was the expansion of the Hebrew and Jewish manuscript collections in the major academic libraries of North America and Europe. Through the agency of travellers, explorers and booksellers, as well as academic researchers themselves, hundreds of codices, many of them dating from the fourteenth to the sixteenth centuries were added to the literary treasures that had already been

5 *Die Synagogale Poesie des Mittelalters* (Berlin: Springer, 1855).

6 See, for example, the major reference tool she has recently published: Egger-Wenzel, Renate, *A Polyglot Edition of the Book of Ben Sira with a Synopsis of the Hebrew Manuscripts*, CBET 101 (Leuven: Peeters, 2022).

amassed during the explosion of learning that had characterized the periods of the Protestant Reformation and the various reactions to it.[7]

It had, for some centuries, often been the case that Jews—and not necessarily those who had apostatized—could be found useful for teaching Hebrew and expounding Jewish texts at centres of higher education. Because they were religiously disqualified, they could not be appointed to official positions, but they made their contributions, and it was not unusual for others to claim the benefit. This trend took on a new form in the second half of the nineteenth century. Jewish scholars were invited to compile the catalogues of Hebraica and Judaica at leading universities. For example, Moritz Steinschneider described the printed books and Adolf Neubauer the manuscripts at the Bodleian Library in Oxford, while Solomon Marcus Schiller-Szinessy prepared a catalogue of the Hebrew manuscripts at Cambridge University Library. Once the religious tests were removed, Neubauer was appointed to a readership at Oxford in 1884, and Schiller-Szinessy to a similar post in Cambridge in 1879.[8]

Zunz's academic heroes

These latter developments and the wider acceptance of the scientific study of Jewish sources that Zunz had promoted took place in his later years, when he had recognized that his plans for Jewish studies at German universities had not proved attractive to those—non-Jewish and Jewish alike—with the potential to change things. Zunz in his youth may have regarded his Berlin professors August Wilhelm Böckh (1785–1867) and Friedrich August Wolf (1759–1824) as his heroes but they, for their part, were impressed neither by his ethnicity nor by his academic plans. Böckh was on the committee that rejected Zunz's suggestion for a chair in Jewish History and Literature at the Humboldt University in Berlin, on the grounds that this would only encourage the Jews to remain separate instead of effecting their ultimate, and obviously much preferred, assimilation.[9] Wolf's view of the "Hebrew nation" was that it had "not raised itself to a level of culture that would permit it

7 For an invaluable introduction to all these collections, see Benjamin Richler, A *Guide to Hebrew Manuscript Collections* (second, revised edition; Jerusalem: Israel Academy, 2014).
8 For much of the background, see Stefan C. Reif, "Sources", *Cambridge History of Judaism*, vol. 5, *The Medieval Era: The Islamic World*, ed. P. Ackerman-Lieberman (Cambridge: Cambridge University Press, 2021), 35–63.
9 Ismar Schorsch, *Leopold Zunz. Creativity in Adversity* (Philadelphia: Pennsylvania University Press, 2016), 169.

to be considered a scholarly people."[10] On the other hand, according to Zunz, they showed no personal malice to Jews and, as Leon Wieseltier has put it, "anyone at all familiar with developments in early nineteenth-century philology will recognize in Zunz's organization of Jewish studies the lofty, meticulous, scholarly ambience of F. A. Wolf and August Wilhelm Boeckh".[11]

Antisemitism

If inspiring savants such as Böckh and Wolf could at least tolerate Jews, as long as they behaved as true Germans believed they should, there were some Christian hebraists who expressed intense animosity to Jews and Jewish learning in general and to Zunz in particular. When the distinguished orientalist Paul de Lagarde died in 1892, Adolf Neubauer acknowledged his eminence, his minute method and the "great gap in many branches of learning" left by his demise, and also made reference to his joviality in company. At the same time, he decried his haughtiness and arrogance towards his academic colleagues. He also noted that he had been a member of the Prussian Conservative Party and had exceeded Heinrich Ewald (a Protestant theologian and biblical exegete at Göttingen whom Neubauer had met in Oxford) in antisemitic prejudice.[12] Perhaps, like his friend and colleague, Archibald Sayce, Neubauer had heard how de Lagarde had had all his Hebrew books bound in pigskin, in order, as he put it, "to keep the dirty fingers of the Jews from off them".[13]

Elisabeth Hollender has chronicled a debate between Lagarde and Jewish scholars that was set off by a doctoral dissertation by Lagarde's pupil Ludwig Techen on two Göttingen *Maḥzor* manuscripts. Techen attacked the methodology of Zunz and other Jewish scholars, referring to "Zunz's penchant to cast subjective, unimportant and worthless material into bombastic language." Techen's Jewish critics pointed to the impudence of a novice who knew little Hebrew and nothing about Jewish liturgy. De Lagarde came to Techen's defence in "Lipman Zunz und seine Verehrer",

10 Quoted from the German by Theodore Dunkelgrün, "The Philology of Judaism: Zacharias Frankel, the Septuagint, and the Jewish Study of Ancient Greek in the 19th Century", *Classical Philology and Theology: Entanglement, Disavowal, and the Godlike Scholar*, edited by Catherine Conybeare and Simon Goldhill (Cambridge: Cambridge University Press, 2020), 65–66.

11 Leon Wieseltier, "Etwas über die jüdische Historik: Leopold Zunz and the Inception of Modern Jewish Historiography", *History and Theory* 20.137.

12 Adolf Neubauer, "Paul de Lagarde", *Journal of the Royal Asiatic Society for 1892*, 384–86 and "Jede Zeit hat ihren Eisenmenger", *Ben Chananja* 6: 109 (1862).

13 Archibald H. Sayce, *Reminiscences* (London: Macmillan, 1923), 53.

and, after a second round, in "Juden und Indogermanen". The latter contained a section of unrestrained antisemitic invective, but even in de Lagarde's scholarly arguments there is an undertone of antisemitism and contempt.[14] Neubauer too entered the debate and, in his obituary of de Lagarde, took the opportunity of defending Leopold Zunz against de Lagarde's unjustified and derisory dismissal of one of his translations.[15]

When, in 1873, Zunz published the fifty-three pages of his essay "Bibelkritisches", comprising a philological study of selected books of the Hebrew Bible,[16] Ewald mocked this Jewish attempt to compete with Christian biblical scholarship that had centuries of research to its credit. Earlier, in 1860, as Schorsch records, Ewald had "dismissed in one fell swoop the scholarly value of Zunz's recently published two volumes on liturgy". For Ewald, Zunz was no more than "an utterly one-sided Jew lost in the biases of his hatred".[17] In sum, the German patriotism and the religious commitments of many Christian scholars in Germany meant that they could not easily accommodate themselves to Jewish attempts to become genuine Germans, to offer a Jewish perspective on historical study of the Bible, and to present rabbinic literature as a genuinely cultural achievement of interest and of value to the wider world of learning. Most of them saw the German Protestant culture of their day as the epitome of philosophical accuracy and theological truth and, try as Zunz might, he could not persuade them that Jewish history and literature might also, at least to some degree, constitute the key to an important part of human thought, religious teaching and poetic achievement.

Doctrinal science

While Zunz in his younger years held the view that sound, scientific study of Jewish literature would surely convince the German academic establishment that Jews and Jewish Studies could become an integral part of university establishments, there were co-religionists of his who were also outstanding scholars but who felt less inclined to await the beneficence of European centres of higher education. They not only wished to prepare Jewish students for careers in the rabbinate and the teaching profession but were also of a mind to educate them to think, research

14 Elisabeth Hollender, "Verachtung kann Unwissenheit nicht entschuldigen: die Verteidigung der Wissenschaft des Judentums gegen die Angriffe Paul de Lagardes 1884–1887", *Frankfurter Judaistische Beiträge* 30.169–205 (2003).

15 See n. 12 above.

16 "Bibelkritisches", *Zeitschrift der Deutschen-Morgenländischen Gesellschaft* 27: 669–89 (1873).

17 Schorsch, *Zunz*, 195 and 218.

and write in a modern critical fashion rather than in the style of the traditional yeshivot, but always to the benefit of their religious communities.

To that end, rabbinical and teaching seminaries were founded, ranging in religious commitment from reform to orthodox, in France as early as 1829, in Breslau in 1854, in London in 1855, in Vienna in 1860 and 1893, in Berlin in 1872 and 1873, in Cincinnati in 1875, in Budapest in 1877, and in New York in 1886 and 1896. The teachers in such institutions were among the nineteenth century's most brilliant, inspiring and productive scholars of Hebraica and Judaica and included, in Europe, such names as Zecharias Frankel (1801–1875), Michael Friedländer (1833–1910), Meir Friedmann (1831–1908), Eisik Hirsch Weiss (1815–1905), Abraham Geiger (1810–1874), Julius Guttmann (1880–1950), David Kaufmann (1852–1899), Wilhelm Bacher (1850–1913) and Israel Lewy (1841–1917).[18] Somewhat surprisingly, Zunz was averse to such an approach to Jewish learning. As Schorsch has succinctly written, "[David] Kaufmann's profile was not prone to endear him to Zunz. Zunz disliked Frankel and Graetz in equal measure and derided their brand of scholarship as *Glaubenswissenschaft* (his term [meaning "the science of doctrine"]) whose parameters and conclusions were dictated by tenants of faith." Zunz felt that rabbinical seminaries "fell short of his hard-fought-for ideal of institutionalizing critical Jewish scholarship as a *bona fide* field of research within the German university."[19] Meanwhile, such Jewish seminaries were producing a large number of scholarly publications of the highest standard while the universities were hesitantly contemplating the degree to which they could allow the newly emancipated Jewish scholars serious recognition within the existing academic frameworks. Neubauer in Oxford was recognized by a number of his colleagues as the best candidate for the directorship of the Bodleian Library in 1882 but they were overruled. Schiller-Szinessy in Cambridge was a candidate for the Regius Chair of Hebrew in that same year but could not make progress with his application since he was religiously disqualified by the fact that he could not take up a Canonry at Ely Cathedral that was linked to the professorship.[20]

---

18 David N. Myers, *Re-Inventing the Jewish Past: European Jewish Intellectuals and the Zionist Return to History* (Oxford: Oxford University Press, 1995), 25–29; Shmuel Feiner, *Haskalah and History: The Emergence of a Modern Jewish Historical Consciousness (*Oxford: Oxford University Press. 2002), 133–37; and Reimund Leicht and Gad Freudenthal (eds.), *Studies on Steinschneider. Moritz Steinschneider and the Emergence of the Science of Judaism in Nineteenth-Century Germany* (Leiden: Brill, 2002).

19 Schorsch, *Zunz*, 224.

20 See Reif, "A Fresh Look at Adolf Neubauer as Scholar, Librarian and Jewish Personality" in a forthcoming *Festschrift for Haggai Ben-Shammai*, eds. P. Ackerman-Lieberman and M. Frenkel; Reif, *Hebrew Manuscripts at Cambridge University Library: A Description and Introduction* (Cambridge: Cambridge University Press, 1997), 28.

Synagogal pedigree

From his earliest publications, Zunz expressed an animosity to traditional talmudic study, believing that it could never attain the levels of historical analysis and dispassionate assessment that he thought were characteristic of his university education and his personal research. He opted to see his people's ideas, language and literature not so much as a reflection of narrow religious commitment but rather as the well-rounded products of a *Kulturvolk* that were deserving of recognition as such by contemporary European civilization. As he saw it, his religion was not one of fanaticism, antiquated ritual and vulgar demonstration, but the sound basis of all education, ennobling thought and behaviour. His research was centered on a passion for archives, bibliography, philology, as well as Hebrew language, history and literature, that was driven by intense industry as well as a meticulous concern for the tiniest detail. This did not demand a disengagement from the communal and political but was designed to contribute, in one way or another, to the emancipation of the Jews, both within their own communities and in the wider world.

Zunz saw the need to comb manuscript and printed editions for a huge mass of evidence. He made use of many editions and consulted numerous manuscripts, as in 1855 when he visited London and Paris and examined 100 printed books and 180 manuscripts. In 1863 he made a trip to Italy to consult its rich collections of hebraica, about which he wrote on his return, bewailing the fact that many of the catalogue entries displayed non-Jewish ignorance of Jewish history and literature.[21] Zunz regarded it as essential for scholarship to be generative, and wished to apply the new academic disciplines to Jewish liturgy, because that subject was especially important to him. He saw the synagogue as an "expression of Jewish nationhood, the guarantor of its religious existence", liturgy as reflecting Jewish historical experience and religious development, the sermon as an ancient educational process that had continued through the ages, and the liturgical poets as the composers of great poetry.[22] As Schorsch has put it, "Zunz invested it [i.e. the synagogue] with a noble pedigree. By reshaping the synagogue as the locus of midrash and piyut, he foregrounded the spiritual and responsive nature of Judaism."[23]

---

21 These remarks are largely based on Schorsch, *Zunz*, 15, 57, 96, 130, 140 and 214.

22 See Schorsch, *Zunz*, 57, 80–84, 196, 201–8; and also Schorsch, "Schechter's Indebtedness to Zunz", *Jewish Historical Studies* 48: 9–16 (2016) where he notes (p. 11) that Zunz had recovered the names of about a thousand Jewish liturgical poets.

23 Schorsch, *Zunz*, 244.

Liturgical science

It was with these thoughts in mind that he wrote his study of Jewish homiletics in 1832[24] and his three studies of synagogal poetry between 1855 and 1867.[25] The first presented Jewish liturgical poetry as worthy literature and translated many examples. The second (*Die Ritus*) linked the poems with the development of the various medieval rites. The third dealt with the lives and works of the poets and, as Schorsch tells us, "Zunz referenced 5,964 piyyutim and nearly 1,000 paytanim, despite the daunting fact that the majority of both were either unpublished or unknown." [26]

On the basis of these works, Schorsch's outstanding analysis, and a fresh look at *Die Ritus*, it is possible to reconstruct some broad aspects of Zunz's methods and achievements, especially as they relate to liturgy. He made many insightful assessments of the development of the various rites, referring broadly to their origins, influences and development. Contrary to the scholarly fashion, he paid attention to Ashkenazi as well as Sefardi trends and achievements, although it has immediately to be added that he did not see the original Ashkenazi rite as reflected in the customs of the Polish communities of the early modern period and of his own day.[27] He had little to offer on the rites of the Near East, including the land of Israel and Babylonia, but he was aware of this, writing that "the synagogues in Persia, Kabul and Bokhara still await reports by suitably qualified travellers."[28]

Methodology

Apart from some occasional notes, the founder and master of *Wissenschaft des Judentums* generally gave no detailed textual variations within the specific prayers in the different rites, but he did provide footnotes that listed the sources from which he had derived his data. Zunz sometimes referred to the non-liturgical aspects of synagogal activity, expressing himself in favor of some, while he was critical, or

24 *Die gottesdienstlichen Vorträge der Juden, historisch entwickelt : ein Beitrag zur Alterthumskunde und Biblischen Kritik, zur Literatur-und Religionsgeschichte* (Berlin: Asher, 1832).

25 *Die synagogale Poesie des Mittelalters* (Berlin: Springer, 1855); *Die Ritus des synagogalen Gottesdienstes geschichtlich entwickelt* (Berlin: Springer, 1859); *Literaturgeschichte der synagogalen Poesie* (Berlin: Asher, 1855, with an addendum in 1867).

26 On the total research agenda that lay behind these publications, see Schorsch, *Zunz*, 195–96.

27 See Schorsch, *Zunz*, 33, 43, 135–36, 143, 155, 204–5.

28 *Ritus*, 57: "Die Synagogen in Persien, Kabul, Bokhara warten noch eines kundigen Reisebeschreibers." See also Schorsch, *Zunz*, 200.

simply descriptive, of others. He was strongly of the opinion that study should be motivated by rigorous scientific and historical considerations, not the apologetic ones that had been employed by some of his predecessors. That was one of his complaints about the work of Abraham Geiger.[29]

He approved the idea of reforming the prayers but not radically; for example, he was in favour of maintaining *brit milah* (circumcision) and *tefillin* (phylacteries).[30] He certainly regretted the way in which, already in the seventeenth century, the dynamic development of liturgy had been stymied. In that connection, he expresses himself with cynical humour about cantors, rabbis and entertainers: "the last remnant of freedom with regard to determining the divine worship was lost, and all that remained for choice were the cantorial melodies, the casuistry of the visiting rabbi, and the entertainment of the wedding guests by the buffoon."[31] He saw a need to introduce vernacular sermons but questioned the observance of Tish'ah Be-Av, a view that apparently brought him into conflict with one of the communities that engaged him.[32] His idea that genuine scholarship had to be generative was to be applied not only in academia but also in the communal, religious and political fields. For him, the study of manuscripts and editions stood at the centre of Jewish Studies, and he deeply regretted that the desperate need for that discipline to be adopted in the universities remained unfulfilled. With a somewhat naïve optimism, he saw scientific study as leading to freedom, knowledge and love.[33] In sum, Zunz provided a wealth of raw material and many useful tools with which to rake, comb and utilize it.

Insights

We may now turn to some specific remarks made in *Die Ritus* that demonstrate just how prescient he was in a number of areas. In his assessment of the rabbinic prayers of the first few centuries of the current era, Zunz argues that there are elements of the *'amidah* (which he always cites as *tefillah*, as in mishnaic Hebrew) that go back to the first century, that there was no uniformity about benedictions and prayers, nor indeed about the use of Psalm verses, or prophetic readings. He also suggests that attendance at the synagogue was not universally practised, that

29 See Schorsch, *Zunz*, 93, 123, 138–41.
30 See Schorsch, *Zunz*, 116–17.
31 *Ritus*, 156.
32 See Schorsch, *Zunz*, 51–52, 78, 82, 116–21.
33 See Schorsch, *Zunz*, x, 2–3, 63, 87, 130, 168–70, 242–43. On Zunz's detailed political agenda, see Schorsch, *Zunz*, 156–81. Se also *Ritus*, 178.

local custom was much influenced by the authority of local teachers, and that the structure of the *'amidah* on Yom Kippur was not yet fixed in the third century, here and there being concluded with *ne'ilah* (without the evening service).[34] In the matter of the introduction of a special formula before the recitation of *Kol Nidrey* he is careful, as a critical historian, to distinguish the motivation for such a custom from its justification.[35]

He recognizes that the Geonim of the post-talmudic period inherited liturgical variety and attempted to standardize it by their influence and authority. He suggests that many customs reflect culture, convention, climate and language, and that Jews influenced, and were influenced by, other cultures. Despite his commitment to the promotion of Jewish liturgy as an impressive literary and cultural achievement, Zunz has no hesitation in pointing to the Christian precedents of some Jewish customs. Among these, he counts the commemoration of martyrs and benefactors, the role of a godfather at a circumcision, and the nomenclature of the "great sabbath" for the Sabbath immediately preceding Passover. In his view, commercial circumstances in the Christian countries led the Jews to read the afternoon service together with that of the evening.[36]

He traces the tensions between the prayer-leaders and the halakhic authorities, pointing out the degree to which the preferences and propensities of the former had a major effect on the development of the prayers, despite the disapproval of the latter. The power of the prayer-leaders had originally been considerably limited but "grew with the development of communal worship, with the deteriorating knowledge of the Hebrew language, and with the flourishing of poetry and grammar, and the increasing pleasure of singing." Zunz is unsure whether some prayers and benedictions had any written form in talmudic times, but he is of the view that, even if they did, such texts were certainly not available to congregants who used their memories, or were guided by the prayer-leader.[37]

He describes the innovative prayer-books of the Geonim Amram (the earliest available version of which he dates no earlier than 1100) and Sa'adya, and also traces to the geonic period the insertion of supplicatory texts into the *'amidah* to mark the Ten Days Of Repentance. He notes that the blowing of the shofar evolved from an individual ritual to that of an expert officiant and that it was done on the Sabbath in various communities. He explains how the authority of the Babylonian teachers of the geonic period gradually waned and how this led to the development

---

34 *Ritus*, 2–3, 95.
35 *Ritus*, 97.
36 *Ritus*, 3–4, 8–10.
37 *Ritus*, 5–8, 15.

of numerous rites in the Jewish communities of the Islamic and Christian worlds.[38] He then describes all of these, paying special attention to the French, German, Spanish, Provençal, Italian, Romaniote and North African prayer orders, and listing in remarkable detail their overall trends and the numerous variations within these. Although he stresses the limited size, changing nature and the lack of data about the communities of the land of Israel ("no longer the homeland of a nation" or "the seat of permanent communities"), he nevertheless goes on to describe some of the liturgical characteristics that he could locate.[39]

As to the emergence and dissemination of numerous sub-rites, he remarks: "Although names of rites are borrowed from the countries where they originated, it should not be assumed that all parts of that country followed the same rite. In the Middle Ages, the borders of states were often casual, liable to change, and unable to exercise any dominant influence, so that regions that were far from each other followed the same rite, while those that were closer together may have differed." He reports that the medieval English community spoke and wrote French and that Meir of Rothenburg regarded England and France as one country. He therefore suggests that their liturgical rites were probably similar if not identical.[40] He lays out the process by which the meaning of a word such as *maḥzor* could evolve from describing a calendrical cycle or a set of biblical texts into a term for the prayers and lectionaries of the whole year and later into the more specific sense of a volume of festival prayers. He also explains how philosophical speculation about the nature of God led to the adjustment of some texts. Where God was once simply described as existing in the past and in the future, such speculation led to the insertion of another expression describing his existence in the presence too.[41]

Poetry

Zunz is anxious to demonstrate the degree to which poetry was composed, embellished and incorporated into synagogal usage, and the manner in which, at times, it became so popular that it vied for precedence with the statutory prayers. He provides lengthy, and at times highly complex, lists of the poets and their works, revealing many previously unknown names and works, and he identifies which liturgical poems were recited in which communities and at which periods. He also notes the personal and communal occasions on which such poems were in use.

---

38 *Ritus*, 12, 16–19, 57.
39 *Ritus*, 83.
40 *Ritus*, 62.
41 *Ritus*, 19–20, 38–39, 182–83.

He traces the chequered history of these compositions and notes the crests and troughs in their waves of popularity as they made a powerful impact in the sea of Jewish literature. He explains how they were tailored to the needs of Sabbaths, festivals and rites de passage, and how penitential poetry especially grew and flourished when daily Jewish life was peppered with hatred, persecution, and physical violence.[42]

The increasing recitation of laments was "the one freedom that they had under oppression" and a contrast could be drawn between "the glorious past and the miserable present". He also reports on the challenging need of some complex, allusive and supra-learned texts for serious exegesis. At the same time, he is perfectly aware that some items had more impressive literary, linguistic and exegetical credentials than others, and he compares Jewish liturgical midrash with the paintings of the ancient world. He takes note of the gradual abandonment of many poems in the late middle ages and the particular animosity towards the genre within the Jewish European enlightenment of the modern period. Such an animosity was also displayed by non-Jewish intellectuals who were simply ill-equipped to appreciate the contents of many poems and preferred to mock them rather than to master their interpretation.[43] Zunz is decidedly outspoken about where such animosity could lead : "the motive for their studying was hatred and they were interested in the *Maḥzor* only for the curses that would lead to auto da fé's and atrocities."[44] Although he himself has criticism of the less impressive synagogal poetry, he nevertheless describes the genre as "a rich literature on which thousands of poets and thinkers had laboured for a millennium".[45]

Zunz explains how poems were expanded, abbreviated and wrongly attributed, and he is scathing in his description of how their texts became corrupted: "In the course of the centuries the compositions of the synagogal poets suffered not only the errors of the copyists and distortions, that were the fault of the commentators, but also losses and alterations. Even the arbitrary, though not always appropriate, use amounted to an injustice to the author. . .Inattention on the part of the community and lengthy singing on the part of the prayer-leader may also have been the occasion for similar changes while other distortions. . .bordered on sloppiness." The artistic and spiritual achievements of the medieval poets had been blurred by their transmission to the new generations "in the form of a torso, or even only a relic."[46]

---

42 Zunz deals with such matters throughout *Ritus* but see especially 9, 23, 28–29, 49–50, 78, 80, 82–83, 85–139.

43 *Ritus*, 88, 131, 162–71.

44 *Ritus*, 176.

45 *Ritus*, 170.

46 *Ritus*, 139–44.

Bias

While Zunz is fairly well-balanced in his assessments of most areas of Jewish liturgical expression, there is no denying the fact that he had, like many nineteenth-century Jewish rationalists in central Europe, a major psychological block about the appreciation of mysticism. He saw its encroachment on the prayers as a sop to the ignorant, as well as a promotion of the esoteric, and in his view superstitious elements savaged the divine service. He mocks the numerical contortions of the twelfth- and thirteenth-century Ashkenazi mystics such as Eleazar of Worms, but reserves his most critical remarks for the "super-piety and exaggerated worship" of the Lurianic kabbala, which he designates as outrageous and incomprehensible. For him, the public service of God had been brushed aside by a concern for superstition, angelology and the worship of spirits.[47]

There is another area in which Zunz betrays what is in our contemporary eyes a somewhat prejudiced view. He offers no sympathy at all for the Karaite movement and, unlike in his numerous other assessments , he chooses to follow a traditional rabbinic line rather than to offer a more balanced historical analysis. To be fair to him, the material available to later scholarship was not yet accessible but, that said, he might have attempted to look at developments as a disinterested historian, rather than as a polemicist. He sees the Ananite movement as motivated by a desire to adopt "the opposite of everything that was customary in Israel" and the Karaites as "the enemies of an authentic tradition, which they had forged into an artificial one." He also makes the questionable claim that, although later Karaism borrowed from the Rabbanites, there was never any borrowing in the opposite direction.[48]

Book science

The history of the book is another branch of modern scholarship that hardly existed in the first half of the nineteenth century but in this case Zunz does demonstrate some remarkable prescience. He traces not only the physical development of the prayer-book as *Siddur* and *Maḥzor* and the existence of increasingly larger volumes but also notes the emergence of smaller booklets dealing with more specific topics such as the growing commitment to, and greater use of, penitential prayers (*seliḥot*). He is aware of the expansion of the liturgical codex by the addition of notes, glosses

47 *Ritus*, 24, 28–29, 147–52.
48 *Ritus*, 156–62.

and ultimately commentaries, as well as the inclusion in an enlarged liturgical codex of many lectionaries, calendars, rules and regulations. With his usual eagle eye, he also identifies in this connection the mutual impact of the liturgical and the social. An example is his citation of a report that boys carried home from the synagogue what were apparently such weighty tomes.[49]

He also anticipates later historians of printing by identifying the revolutionary effect that this novel medium had on the content of the prayers. While it had in earlier times been the prayer-leader or the halakhic expert who had vied for control of the texts, it became the editors and proof-readers who constituted the newest authorities. As Zunz expresses it: "Once the art of book-printing had made manuals and prayer-books accessible to everyone, the publisher took the place of the concerned prayer-leader. Printing set the borders, rich manuscript collections became a sterile possession; the items that were included became the decisive ones, the standard nature of the texts that everyone possessed produced uniformity: *minhag* was based on the printed editions."[50]

Censorship

An earlier and more malignant influence on the text of the prayer-book also attracts the attention of the author of *Die Ritus*. Inspired by the campaigns of the Counter-Reformation, there was a drive by the Roman Catholic Church to eliminate all religiously competitive literature. Zunz explains how censorship of the Jewish prayers—in a project led by the Dominicans and manned by baptized Jews—targeted "words, idioms, lines, biblical verses, stanzas and whole sections", sometimes leaving only a few vowel-points in splendid isolation. Confiscation, banning and burning were also among the tools employed and the Jews were often so fearful of the censors that they themselves made drastic alterations to the prayers, even resorting to furnishing spurious explanations for spurious items.[51]

Further in the matter of campaigns against the Jewish prayer-book, Zunz cites numerous examples to illustrate his claim that "the baptized Jew, Christlieb, surpasses all his predecessors in his insolent stupidity." He also refers to the decision of the Westphalian Consistorium, supported by Mendel Steinhart, to delete certain prayers and *piyyuṭim*. . .the first time that such a step was taken by the German rabbinate." Interestingly, although one of Zunz's primary intentions was to provide

49 *Ritus*, 19–20, 22–23, 33–34.
50 *Ritus*, 145–46.
51 *Ritus*, 148–49, 222–25.

favourable reports of numerous aspects of Jewish liturgy and liturgical poetry for non-Jews, as well for Jews, he does not shy away from denouncing Gentile scholars who are wholly antagonistic to everything they find in these sources. They mock the content, declare the recitation to be meaningless, and express their animosity towards Jews and Judaism by way of abuse, as well as through statements and assessments that are abusive, ignorant and dishonest. One comment was that some of the prayers were understood only by a few and were "recited in the way that the Latin Psalms are recited by the nuns". It should also, however, be noted that Zunz has praise for such scholars as Franz Delitzsch whose comments were fairer, without, unsurprisingly, commenting on his active agenda for converting Jews to Christianity.[52]

Adjustments

Zunz appreciates that change in the prayers was also a feature of learned Jewish responses from as early as the post-talmudic period. The Geonim were anxious to remove what they regarded as theologically suspect items, to restore what they saw as forgotten texts, and to introduce what was to their minds consistency and accuracy. He makes reference to the enthusiasm of the medieval commentators for accurate manuscripts and to the drive on the part of some of the copyists for a liturgical Hebrew that was grammatically accurate according to their standards. Zunz notes the activities of various "correctors" such as Meir Benveniste of Salonika in the sixteenth century and Shabbethai Ha-Sofer of Przemysl in the seventeenth, and mentions the heated discussions in eighteenth-century Germany between Jacob Emden and Solomon Hanau about what constituted correct Hebrew. He argues that Isaac Satanow's efforts in this connection were exaggerated, unjustified, conjectural or downright faulty, while the cautious work of Wolf Heidenheim ("the Mendelssohn of the *Maḥzor*. . .the driving force behind a large number of publishers and exegetes") was superior and more valuable. His own partiality is exemplified by this comment of his: "At first secretly but then openly, grammar, poetry and philosophy vitiated the medieval forms, in particular the German-Polish divine service."[53]

Translation is also, of course, an attempt at clarification, and Zunz indicates that this was already done in the medieval period, referring to the use of the vernaculars, such as Arabic, French, German and Yiddish to ensure better understanding

52 *Ritus*, 171–72, 176–78, 223–24.
53 *Ritus*, 169–70, 173–75.

of the prayers. Keen social historian that he is, Zunz reports that Anschel of Posen "freely weaves into the translation of the *azharot* some gratuitous moral admonitions, such as 'do not shout aloud in the streets about your good deeds since they should not be known by anyone else but God'." He himself, when dealing with the modern period, cannot resist the temptation to praise, in what seems to the contemporary reader a somewhat naïve fashion, the pursuit of scholarly truth rather than the truest theology: "For about the past thirty years [before 1859], as Jewish self-confidence has increased, an unprejudiced view of ancient Jewish life has gained ground; it is the belief in what is true rather than in true belief that should prevail in matters both dated and modern."[54]

Social history

Zunz, though devoted to the historical summary and analysis of the various liturgical rites in all their complex and variant detail, is also keen to draw a degree of attention to tangential data that reveals him as a communal and social historian, and not merely a chronicler of the texts of the ritual. It is interesting for us today to note just a few of the scraps of evidence in their hundreds that tickled his archival fancy. With regard to the daily customs, Zunz notes that the reason for the communal reading of the biblical texts on Mondays and Thursday was that the working class did not have the required time to engage in such activity on a daily basis; that the separation of the fingers by the priests during their recitation of the priestly benediction was already reported in geonic times; and that in that same period only the beginning and end of the third paragraph of the *shema'* were recited at the evening service.[55]

In Spain, one looked downwards during the *qedushah*, and in Germany upwards. In the old French rite (but evidently not in the Spanish) those called to the Torah left their heads uncovered and in medieval Mainz unmarried men did not wear a *tallit*. With regard to Sabbath customs, he reports that in Regensburg the chanting of the *barukh she'amar* prayer took an hour; that communities in Crimea read the Book of Antiochus at *minḥah* on the Sabbath of Ḥanukah; and that the use of a box, rather than a bag, for the spices at the *havdalah* ceremony followed the twelfth-century practice of Ephraim of Bonn.[56] He also notes an example of how, in the early fifteenth century, a scholar in Bern reacted after his daughter had asked questions, presumably about

54 *Ritus*, 53–54, 63, 154–55, 168, 172.
55 *Ritus*, 14, 83, 123.
56 *Ritus*, 40, 67–68, 70, 82–83.

its contents, when he had lifted the Seder dish at the Passover eve celebration in his home. The father, Moses Cohen, decided that in that case there was no longer any need for the formal recitation of the *mah nishtanah* set of inquiries.[57]

The evidently more reserved congregational leaders of Mainz permitted banging during the Esther Megillah reading on Purim only at the names of Haman's sons, while in fourteenth-century Saragossa the reading of that book was done in Spanish for the women. The Passover Haggadah was translated into French for the women and children in thirteenth-century London. In Provence, the recitation of the book of Ecclesiastes was done in the Sukkah on the eighth day of the festival, while in Romaniote communities it was divided up among the four festive days of Tabernacles and read at the afternoon service. In Gerona everyone took a light when leaving the synagogue after Yom Kippur, while in Morocco and in Tetuan everybody brought salt into the synagogue on the second evening of Pesaḥ and then took a little of it home with them.[58] In Austria—as well as in Erfurt—they abstained from consuming the fat of an animal's belly while in the Rhineland they considered it permissible. The latter, on the other hand, would eat no duck while they did so in Styria. The Jews of Austria also ate lappish goose.[59]

With regard to the synagogal reading of the tractate Avot—as a typical example of his fastidious recording of detail—he goes to some length to explain the great variety of practices. In the daily prayers, in the Sabbath afternoon service, in the winter and summer, in the summer only, between Pesaḥ and Shavuot, or more extensively than that, one chapter at a time or two, in one, two or three cycles of readings—he traces examples of all of these customs and provides the relevant source for each.[60] As for the lists of *avinu malkenu* invocations that became so characteristic of penitential prayer in the Middle Ages, he correctly supposes that this list "was not yet to hand in the period of the Mishnah" and then traces the vast variety of formulations, numbers and applications, as well as fanciful interpretations, that occur during the geonic and medieval periods in the various sources and rites.[61]

Zunz characterizes the medieval German Rabbis as "pious and punctilious preservers of their traditions" while reporting that their French counterparts "attempted to make everything more difficult in the places where they were welcomed." Despite his aversion to Jewish conversion to Christianity, he still informs us of one community in Mallorca that converted. He also cites the theory that the reason for a fast

57 *Ritus*, 71–72.

58 *Ritus*, 41–42, 45–46, 53–54, 63, 69, 81.

59 *Ritus*, 71.

60 *Ritus*, 85–86.

61 *Ritus*, 118–20; see Reif, *Jews, Bible and Prayer: Essays on Jewish Biblical Exegesis and Liturgical Notions* (Berlin: de Gruyter, 2017), 322–23.

being held on 9 Ṭevet was that it had been "calculated that the birth of Jesus was on that day, and that, between the years 500 and 816, the 25 December fell on 9 Ṭevet twelve times."[62] Nor are economic matters ignored by Zunz. When mentioning that a twelfth-century collection of *seliḥot* sold for forty pfennings he set that price in context by informing his readers that the weekly rental of a horse at that time cost six pfennings and that three brothers needed only three pfennings for their daily bread, meat and wine.[63]

In sum

Later scholarly interest in locating and examining every scrap of manuscript text and in setting each of them in some sort of historical, literary and linguistic context undoubtedly owes much to the pioneering efforts of Zunz. Also inspired by him is the concern to see Judaism not just as a set of religious laws and talmudic texts but also more broadly as a total civilization. The kind of mastery of philology and bibliography that Zunz promoted and in which he excelled had become second-nature to much of Jewish scholarship in the period leading up to the Genizah discoveries.

Liturgy for the great champion of *Jüdische Wissenschaft* was not simply what the eastern European Jews referred to as "davenen" but was also a source for the better understanding of Jewish history and spirituality, and this precedent was followed by the scholars of the Genizah period. The history and characteristics of each of the rites that had occupied Zunz were also of interest to his scholarly successors. His initiative in treating Jewish liturgical poetry as impressive literature worthy of close attention set the tone for the intensive and extensive efforts of Genizah scholars in that area of study. Interestingly, it was not until recent decades that the statutory prayers that occupy a central place in rabbinic liturgy began to receive even a semblance of equal attention from critical scholarship.[64]

Heaps?

Zunz's obsession with the minutest data at times threatens to obscure for the reader of his liturgical *magna opera* any clear view of the larger historical picture. In spite of Zunz's hesitations about the nature of Graetz's scholarship, the younger

62 *Ritus*, 126.
63 *Ritus*, 33, 44, 72.
64 See Reif, "To What Extent" (n. 4 above).

Jewish historian had more than a little justification when he complained that "Dr Zunz's more bewildering than illuminating heaps of notes and lists of names hardly facilitated my work."[65] Graetz was inclined to stress the national element in Jewish history that had a political and social side to it, while for Zunz national meant cultural. As twentieth-century developments clearly demonstrated, Graetz's view became the dominant one. Regarding Zunz's "heaps of notes", another point that needs to be made is that the manner in which he cited his sources was so abbreviated and so allusive (perhaps also elusive)—and even at times inconsistent—that only a Jewish reader learned in traditional rabbinic literature would have found it simple to access the relevant texts. That being so, Zunz was clearly not making his case about the cultural value of Jewish liturgy directly to the non-Jews but was evidently hoping to educate his fellow Jews in this connection. To his mind, such a modern Jewish education would give his coreligionists the confidence to believe in themselves as a cultured and scholarly people and thereby to convince the intellectual and influential Gentiles of central Europe of the accuracy of that assessment. Zunz believed, still at least in mid-life, that the success of such a policy might bring welcome consequences for the Jews in the broader world of higher education.

There were also some distinctly funereal, even ultimately, pessimistic aspects to the Jewish *Weltanschauung* of Zunz and his loyal academic follower, Moritz Steinschneider. As Charles H. Manekin has argued, the latter may not have been quite so negative about the practice and future of Judaism as Gershom Scholem famously suggested in 1945, but in response to the rise of political Zionism he did, according to his student Gotthold Weil, state, in what was perhaps an offhand remark, that the history of the Jews had ended in 1848 and that what remained was to give its remains a decent burial.[66] Zunz's commitment to nineteenth-century liberalism may be seen to have clashed somewhat with his commitment to the future of the Jewish people. His mockery of Jewish mystical trends arose out of a less than balanced evaluation of Jewish spirituality, and his lenses were Euro-centered with little capacity for viewing Eastern Europe, or for looking beyond to what was in his day regarded as the "Orient".

My hope is that readers of English will now be able to utilize the rendering offered below to arrive at their own conclusions about the stature of Zunz, about his contributions to the study of Jewish liturgy, and about any shortcomings that they may feel he had.

---

65 Cited by Schorsch, *Zunz*, 186.

66 Charles H. Manekin, "Steinschneider's 'Decent Burial': A Reassessment", *Study and Knowledge in Jewish Thought*, vol. 1, edited by Howard Kreisel (Jerusalem: Bialik, 2006), 239–51.

Appendix: Bibliographical notes

The אורחות חיים of Aaron ben Jacob Ha-Kohen of Lunel is regularly referred to by the name of the author Aaron Ha-Kohen. The edition of Florence 1751 was used for the first part and manuscript evidence for the second part. In a note dedicated to the subject of the Kol Bo (pp. 179–80), Zunz cites, and expands on, the view of Karo that it represents a digest of the אורחות חיים reflecting the time, place and customs of a later compiler, with changes of order and of text, some of which assist in the reconstruction of the original אורחות חיים.

The מטה משה of Moses b. Abraham Mat (Cracow 1591) is cited on numerous occasions without reference to the author. The reference to an Amsterdam edition (p. 85 n. 6) may be erroneous.

The מנורת המאור of Isaac Abuab is consistently cited as Leuchter (Candelabrum in my translation) and its authorship is the subject of a lengthy analysis in Appendix IV. Zunz cites the comments of Zeraḥiah b. Isaac Ha-Levi on Alfasi as המאור.

The ספר חסידים of Judah b. Samuel of Ratisbon (Bologna 1538) is cited as Buch der Frommen (Book of the Pious in my translation) without reference to the author.

The צדה לדרך of Menaḥem b. Aaron ibn Zeraḥ is cited in transliterated form (Zedah laderech for Zunz, Ṣedah La-Derekh in my translation), only twice with a reference to the author (pp. 30 and 66) and presumably from manuscrpt evidence.

The שבלי הלקט of Zedekiah b. Abraham Anaw (Venice 1546) is cited as שבלי, usually without reference to the name of the author (but see p. 192).

The תמים דעים of Abraham b. David of Posquières (Lemberg 1812) is cited in its Hebrew name without reference to the author.

The תניא (Cremona 1565) is usually cited without reference to its authorship, which is declared (p. 31) to be that Zedekiah b. Abraham Anaw, the author of the שבלי הלקט.

The Prayer Rites of Synagogal Worship and their Historical Development

By Leopold Zunz

English Translation

https://doi.org/10.1515/9783111142500-002

Pp. 1–38

P. 1

In the history of Israel, there were developments known as Oral Law, but with a seemingly firm basis in the Pentateuch, that arose out of new ideas and reshaped circumstances, as well as out of harsh necessity and moral progress, but which freely diverged in a variety of directions. Both the Sadducean and Pharisaic doctrines on the one hand, as well as the authoritative rulings of the schools of Hillel and Shammai on the other, appeared to younger generations as two separate codes of law. Nevertheless, two centuries later the Mishnah in various ways was unable to unify the many applications of practice but had to be content with reporting a variety of opinions. In spite of numerous, simultaneously composed collections {of teachings}, the Mishnah did, however, remain the sole authority, while the Gemara split into eastern and western branches. Although the law was built on ancient legal structures and conventions, it could not avoid the influence of time and mutation. It is no less striking that worship, which is of later origin and more open to change, progressively underwent even more powerful diversification. Such growth involved a slow process, by which simple units of ritual gradually acquired more distinctive shape. The first

P. 2

elements of synagogal worship emerged from Temple cult, from communal custom related to sacrifices—*ma'amad*—from domestic and group devotion, and from Psalms and prayers that were composed for different times and special occasions. Those benedictions with which the *ma'amad* group greeted the morning and concluding prayers evolved into the *shema'* and the *tefillah*.[1] The *tefillah*, which around the year 100 was neither soundly edited nor universally obligatory, originally appears to have had only six units for the weekday and seven for Sabbath and festival, while ḥasidic and political origins are recognizable in the remaining units. Apart from what was legally prescribed, common usage—*minhag*—also determined, with respect to worship, form and practice on the one hand, as well as additions and innovations on the other. Already with regard to arrangements

1 Rapoport, Qalir {*Bikkure Ha-'Ittim* 10}; *gott. Vorträge* p. 367ff. Compare Brück *Pharisäische Volkssitten* pp. 84ff., 91ff., *Ceremonialgebräuche*, introduction pp. 38, 40.

established by the prophets, such as the celebrations on Tabernacles,[2] custom differed from institutional practice. Everything in the morning service before the *shema'*, as well as the recitation of Psalms,[3] and similarly the method of reciting the *hallel*,[4] were considered as custom, and every city chose its own system. The same applied to the confession of sins[5] on the day before the Day of Atonement. The concluding benedictions of the public fast-days were still flexible in the second century[6] while in the third century only a select group of the community came to the synagogue for the *musaf* service[7] so that they had to have their own prayer-leader.[8] In any case, visits to the synagogue, apart from on the Sabbath, were rare.[9] It took centuries before the prayer order that occurs in the Babylonian Talmud established itself. Nobody intended to fix a finalized form, that is, to make it immutable, nor were they capable of doing so.

The differences that existed in ancient times between the ritual of the Temple, and what was practised externally, between Palestine and the diaspora, partially evolved into the Western (Palestinian) custom and that of the East (Babylonia). With respect to the wording and

P. 3

recitation, there emerged over time a variety of views. Teachers of law and prayer-leaders ornamented the festival and fast-day prayers and these were disseminated by those who had heard them, with the result that some additions were popular in one place while others were preferred elsewhere. A benediction was transmitted in different recensions while the *tefillah* itself never attained an undisputed text-form.[10] The incorporation of biblical verses in the ancient world was optional and not fixed, as also the use of individual Psalms, and the choice of *hafṭarot*. The order of the Sabbath lectionaries followed two wholly distinctive systems, in which there were one-year, two-year[11] and three-year cycles. Even the accepted order in Europe

2 Sukkah f. 44a.
3 ס' יראים {of Eliezer b. Samuel}128.
4 Mishnah Sukkah 3.11.
5 Tosefta Yoma 4.
6 Ta'anit 17a.
7 Y. Rosh Ha-Shanah 4.8, compare Rapoport: *'Erekh Millin* p. 164.
8 Compare Ha-Manhig 16b, Kol Bo 71c,d.
9 *Gott. Vorträge* p. 339.
10 *Gott. Vorträge* p. 368 note b, 369 note d. Simeon Duran Responsa 2.161. Sa'adya's text has more than twenty variants.
11 ס' החנוך 557.

remained flexible for many centuries and the decision as to whether to separate the two practices, or to unite them, was regarded as a matter of custom.[12] It is even more remarkable that in the matter of the layout of the האזינו section, which has its own cypher in both Talmuds,[13] two groups[14] of ancient authorities have contradictory views. With regard to the content of the evening *tefillah*, the mishnaic teachers were already of different views; even Hai Gaon's view[15] is totally at odds with that of Eliezer ben Nathan.[16]

The dispersal into distant lands must also have encouraged the creation of diverse rites. As the connections became rarer and more difficult, so the custom of individual places became more strongly rooted, especially when the reputations of local teachers and leaders were instrumental in the choice and nature of ritual matters. Such a custom was accepted by major authorities and was championed by popular prayer-leaders even in the face of rabbinic disapproval. In the period of the Geonim, additions and

P. 4

changes had already created great variety and they, by way of their writings and their text-books, tried to standardize the ritual. However, by doing so they themselves contributed to a process of deviation, partly because in some matters they allowed the usage to be flexible, while in others they reported in their compositions that variations in rite seemed to be justifiable and could be explained as reflections of one custom or another. What is more, the legal decisions of the Geonim sometimes contradicted each other.

Levels of education and popular conventions also had an influence. Those who lived under Persians and Arabs, Syrians and Greeks, Gauls and Goths, in hot or temperate climates, undoubtedly experienced effects on their prayer content and system of ritual. Innumerable ideas and customs have their origin and progress in the co-existence with other peoples. Climate and convention, culture and language are also mirrored in divine service. The Jews borrowed from others a doctrine of

12 Notes {below} 1.
13 הזיולך (J. Megillah 3.7. Rosh Ha-Shanah 31a).
14 Soferim (12.8), 'Arukh s.v., Rashi (Rosh Hashanah loc cit., Aaron Ha-Kohen 24a), an early list (Even Shoshan עבור שנים 78b), Maimoniot (תפלה 13.5) dealing with the verse Deut. 32:36 (כי ידין); Palṭoi (Amram MS, Ha-Pardes 60b), Alfasi, Maimonides, Yehudah b. Nathan (שבלי הלקט 100) regarding the verse ibid. 32:40 (כי אשא); the latter is currently customary.
15 Ha-Manhig 23a.
16 אבן העזר § 169.

emanation, astrology, godfather,[17] rhyme, and requiem. The others obtained from the Jews ecclesiastical terminology, {and} liturgical convention such as jumping during prayer.[18] For a thousand years, there have been complaints about foreign elements being assimilated among the Jews. Among such condemnations, Alfasi condemns Arab ways of singing,[19] Parḥon[20] men's hairstyles and women revealing their own hair, Yehudah the Pious swearing by the devil, Caleb Apendopolou[21] the year-long mourning, del Bene[22] the reading of novels, Jacob Emden beautification and philosophy, and the {"}the Zion-protectors{"} the use of the organ and of German hymns. The fates of the Jews in various countries undoubtedly had an influence on the divine service.

P. 5

Furthermore, they determined the content and character of many prayers, so that one particular event often created a special commemorative day with its own liturgical expression.

It was not just Babylonia and Palestine that differed in individual matters of liturgy but also the centres of the leading scholars such as Nehardea, Pumbedita and Sura.[23] When, in questions addressed to them, the Geonim were made aware of an unusual custom, they were generally anxious to redirect the communities towards the Babylonian usage.[24] Nevertheless, their views were not always followed, even when they themselves were personally present.[25] It is not therefore surprising that Naṭronai[26] disapproved of phrases and sections in the statutory prayers that were later adopted by Sa'adya and in the rites of various countries. The more that the prayer-leaders inserted or recited, the greater became the differences between the rites, although it did take a long time for such additions to be

17 סנדק or סנדקוס Midrash Ps 35 in Yalquṭ Ps § 723, Roqeaḥ 108, Maimoniot מילה end and שבת 29, 25, Maharil 85a. Compare Pereṣ (סמק ms. 152 where there is an addition, compare ed. 157), Kol Bo 24b, 84d, ליקוטי פרדס 4b, הלכות נידה 61a, תשבי s.v., Jos{eph} Karo on Ṭur I 559. Aaron Ha-Kohen 36b.

18 Compare Vitringa *De Synag{oga}* p. 1111 with Tanḥuma 45a, Hekhalot ch. 9, Aaron Ha-Kohen תפלה § 83, Ha-Manhig 16b § 52.

19 *Syn. Poesie* p. 114.

20 *Lex{ikon}* entries צם and צמם {Solomon ben Abraham Parḥon on the 'Arukh}.

21 Appendix to אדרת, f. 29b.

22 {לבית דוד} כסאות f 27a.

23 Shabbat 116b. Pesaḥim 117b. Compare Isaac b. Sheshet Responsa 412.

24 המכריע {of Isaiah di Trani} 42.

25 Isaac Ghiyyat הלכות (in Geiger's {*Wissenschaftliche*} *Zeitschrift* 5, p. 398) and Ha-Manhig י"כ 64.

26 Siddur Amram f. 29.

permitted without objection on the part of the legal authorities, and even longer for them to be regarded as an essential component of the divine service. Before the seventh century, the only additions that seem to have occurred were alphabetical prose in Hebrew and Aramaic. The oldest poetic items, without rhymes, may belong to the period around the year 700. Once the *piyyuṭ* and the *pizmon* from Palestine and Syria arrived in the Arab and Byzantine countries, the local rites became more distinct from each other and the differences grew as composition and usage became freer. Around 980, the *piyyuṭ* of the festival divine service could no longer be identical in Egypt, Andalusia and France, and from the eleventh century the variations in rites became ever more historically recognizable. While the aggadic Qalirian *piyyuṭ* came from the Byzantine countries to the Germanic areas,

P. 6

the Spanish-Arabic *piyyuṭ* was transplanted in the communities of {North-}Africa and partially in the Mediterranean cities. The rites of the different countries fall into two separate groups: 1) Arabic or Spanish, and 2) the Palestinian[27] or Germanic ritual group. The first of these dominates Spain and the Islamic countries, while the second is prominent in the Christian countries, that is to say, those with Germanic populations—Goths, Franks and Lombards. The shape of the rites is obscured by the local situation, the changing population, and here and there by the intermixture of different elements, which is, for example, partially the case in Catalonia and Italy. In general, we can allocate Castile, Andalusia, Catalonia, Aragon, Mallorca, Provence, Sicily and the Arab countries to the Spanish group, while France, England, Burgundy, Lotharingia, Germany, Bohemia, Poland, Italy, Greece and, in earlier times Palestine, belong to the Germanic group.

Aggadah, as well as *piyyuṭ*, originated in Palestine. Just as the *sofer* had grown in power beside the priest, so in later times the prayer-leader increased in influence next to the sage.[28] Just as the sage had become more important than the prophet, so the prayer-leader was at the very least a psalmist. *Pizmon* and psalm went side by side and were of equal standing. The importance of the prayer-leader grew with the development of communal worship, with the deteriorating knowledge of the Hebrew language, and with the flourishing of poetry and grammar, and the increasing pleasure of singing. In earlier times, the prayer-leader stepped forward to the

27 Rapoport in *Kerem Chemed* 6 p. 247 § 27.

28 The authors of the *qerovah*'s or משוררים (Ha-Manhig 17b § 58) are called רבותינו הפייטנים (Maimoniot תפלה ch. 3).

ark only for the repetition of the *tefillah*. Later, this happened at the *qaddish* which precedes ברכו or at ישתבח, then at the *barukh she'amar*, and finally at the morning benedictions. Similarly, the early *piyyuṭ* begins with the *qerovah* and, later on, or only for the penitential festivals, with the *yoṣer*. Neither the prayers from the talmudic period, nor the allusions of the

P. 7

midrash,[29] were important enough to shape the characteristic differences between the rites. Only when the prayer-leader became more adventurous, and the poetic recitations multiplied, did the divergent rites become visible. Before 800, the Babylonian Geonim knew only the *pizmon*. Those of the ninth century still partly reject the *piyyuṭ*; the prayer-leader who knows *piyyuṭ* should not be accepted, and should even be removed; those who listen to *piyyuṭ* are certainly not scholars.[30] On the other hand, others tolerated it, and even approved it. It is possible that the poetic *qerovah* began to dominate in areas that saw the new Talmud of the Karaite Daniel, and various new prayers, which could not be accepted. The reason for this was that the *qerovah* was not popular in the academies. Be that as it may, it was the *piyyuṭ* at that time that precipitated the battle, as happens with all such novelties. Despite the disapproval expressed in the midrash[31] concerning their additions, the prayer-leaders inevitably acquired power[32] and Sa'adya, who could have put an end to their arbitrariness, finally bowed before them. One has, however, to admit that such opposition did eliminate unsuitable matters, as well as inappropriate personalities.

It may be maintained that, by the middle of the ninth century, the type of festival poetry used in the annual cycle was already well established and was, on the whole, no longer liable to variation: *seliḥah, hosha'na, qerovah, yoṣer*, had their specific design. The work of Yose, Yannai, Qalir and anonymous prayer-leaders made

29 Bereshit Rabbah ch. 12. Eliezer-Baraita ch. 4. Large Pesiqta 20, beginning and 37. Tanḥuma and Shemot Rabbah 124a [Zedner *Auswahl* {*historischer Stücke*, 1840} p. 17]. {Midrash} Death of Moses [*gott. Vortr*{*äge*} p. 146]. The passage in Midrash Yonah p. 99 is from the New Year's *musaf*. Other passages in the Mekhilta sections 1, 2 and 3 are borrowed from the statutory prayers.

30 Yoḥanan b. Reuven ms. Commentary on the Sheiltot, section יתרו.

31 Naḥmanides (לקוטות 2c, cf. S. Bloch {trans.}: {*Toledot*} *Rashi* {by Zunz} f. 43a) reads in Midrash Qohelet 101a (instead of מתורגמנין) חזנין, as does Yuḥasin ed London p. 88.

32 The commentary on the *yoṣer* {for Sabbath} Shuvah (אשחר) cites a passage, allegedly from the Pesiqta, in which דרשנים, פייטנים and קראים are placed side by side.

their way into the European countries where, from about 1040, use was already made of the *piyyuṭim* of Yehudah Ha-Kohen, Yoḥanan Ha-Kohen b.

P. 8

Joshua, David b. Huna, Solomon b. Yehudah, Moses b. Qalonymos, Qalonymos b. Moses, Meshullam b. Qalonymos, Simeon b. Isaac, Joseph b. Isaac, Joseph b. Solomon, Benjamin b. Samuel and many other authors of *seliḥah* poetry. From that period, the formation of the rites of various communities becomes more conspicuous. Scholars and prayer-leaders, who were often from foreign lands and distant cities and not necessarily poets themselves, introduced into a particular place new compositions or provided the *qerovah* with introductions—*reshut*. They also imported other items that were not common, bringing together collections of various authors, or abbreviating them. The cantorial prowess of the prayer-leader, and the popularity of a melody for the *pizmon*, may also have played a part in the choice of items. It is no longer a matter of dispute that the prayer-leader had a major influence on the formation of the rite. Hai Gaon already noted[33] that the higher payment approved for the prayer-leaders was due to their performance with *yoṣerot* and *qerovah*'s at weddings or on festivals, especially if they had delightful voices and cantorial skills.

A mere glance at the standard divine service demonstrates the degree to which national conventions and local conditions influenced liturgical arrangements. Originally, *minḥah* was intended for noontime and the evening service for the dusk hours. When people had to earn their bread by peddling in villages, it became necessary to join *minḥah* with the evening service a few hours before night, and this arrangement survived in Christian countries even after conditions altered.[34] Similarly, the common blessings for the local leaders—the Aramaic יקום פורקן—were still recited in France and Germany long after these authorities had ceased to exist. The more recent prayer for the head of state was differently constructed. Out of the general מי שבירך for the community that was included in Amram's *Siddur* there emerged specific prayers for the charitable, for synagogal benefactors, for women who provided the Torah scrolls with mantles or the

33 Yeruḥam מישרים 29, 3.

34 {Solomon b. Abraham Parḥon on the 'Arukh} entry מנח.

P. 9

house of worship with lighting equipment, for those who were fasting on Mondays and Thursdays, and for the newly wed. There emerged out of the latter prayers poetic blessings for the wedding Sabbaths which enriched the French and old German rites. Connected with this is the custom of the old Gallic church to read out the names of those giving contributions, after which the priest offered a prayer for them.[35] Out of such benefaction, and the zeal to participate in liturgical functions, there also emerged the custom to auction such functions[36] on an annual, monthly or weekly basis, at the Torah Festival in Italy and Germany,[37] on the intermediate Sabbath of Pesaḥ in {North-}Africa, and before the Day of Atonement in Livorno.[38] With regard to the procedure, and the manner in which such sales were made, there was a variety of practices; in Fürth,[39] for example, all the synagogal functions were listed under seven classes. The custom of reading out the names of the deceased during divine worship was already included in the Christian liturgy before the ninth century.[40] This gave rise in the West to an association between the commemoration prayers for the departed and the benefactions, to which were linked prayers for martyrs, as known also in the early Church. The currently common commemorations of the dead arose out of such practices. In different places there certainly were different ways of attaching poetry with parallel topics to the *hafṭarah*. In those places where the reading of the Targum was still practised—and therefore not in Spain—Aramaic ornamentation of the pentateuchal and prophetic readings could be created. In the ritual of the Church Fathers the Sunday before Easter is called 'the Great Sabbath'. This title, which was not yet known in the Pesiqta, was taken over by the Jews, perhaps first in Greece, for the Sabbath that fell on the fourteenth of Nisan, and also for which Yannai

---

35 Oratio post nomina.

36 *Gott. Vortr{äge}* p. 480. Or Zaru'a in Mordechai on Megillah, end. Isaac b. Sheshet 35. Jos{eph} Kolon Responsa 9.

37 Maharil סכה.

38 Azulai לדוד אמת.

39 מנהגים of Fürth § 43.

40 Jac{ques} Goar, *Rituale Graecorum* p. 58: quiet prayer by the priest during Mass, Psalm verses, memorial prayer for the souls of martyrs etc, penitential prayer, *qedushah*, *halleluyah*, silent prayer, hymns; compare p. 143.

P. 10

probably composed his *qerovah* dealing with the firstborn. In due course, anyhow, the last Sabbath before Pesaḥ was called “the great Sabbath” and the poets recited their compositions on that occasion. The origin of the name was forgotten and—apart from more recent attempts[41]—there were in Rashi’s time already three explanations: 1) because of the miracle that occurred during the exodus from Egypt when the tenth of Nisan occurred—according to Seder ‘Olam—on a Sabbath;[42] 2) because of the lengthy lectures about the ritual regulations that applied to the festival;[43] 3) because it was the first Sabbath on which Israel began to fulfil the divine commandments.[44] Now that there was a “great Sabbath” before Pesaḥ, the Romaniote rite gave that title to the Sabbath before the Feast of Weeks, and an old German rite to the Sabbath before the Ten Day of Repentance.

The fates met by communities also created similarly sharp distinctions of rite. The Monday prayer והוא רחום[45] that was unknown in the Orient probably owed its origin to the persecutions by the Franks and Goths in the seventh century. The prayer אב הרחמים on the Sabbath and אנא הבט on the fast-days belong to the twelfth century, while the execration תתנם in France probably dates from the same period. The Jews were locked into their quarter before Easter, so that, if the Pesaḥ festival occurred at the same time, there existed in Avignon and Carpentras a special *nishmat* for “the day of incarceration”.[46]

P. 11

Seliḥah, *zulat* and lament roll out before us special Jewish histories. Originally local, such items gradually became communal property. Form and content varied

---

41 Sol{omon} Luria cited in מטה משה § 542, Eliezer Ashkenazi (מעשה מצרים ch. 15), Joseph de Trani (צפנת פענח 67d), Joseph Steinhart (זכרון יוסף 8a), Azulai (כסא דוד nos. 11 and 15), Luzzatto (אהב גר p. 116), Plessner (*Die kostbare Perle* p. 228). Compare {*Der*} *Orient Lit*{*eraturblatt*} 1841, 220.

42 Ha-Pardes ms. and ed. 60c. Ha-Manhig 73a (cited in Abudarham), שבלי הלקט ms. § 205 (תניא 42 cited in מטה משה loc. cit.), Tosaf{ot} Shabbat 87b (the midrash, which relates the matter but does not employ the name “great Sabbath”, is probably from the Large Pesiqta 17. Compare {on Exodus 12:3} the {Tosafist}commentary מנחת יהודה 35b), pentateuchal Tosafot 33d, Bekhor Shor in פענח רזא {of Isaac b. Judah Ha-Levi} section עקב, Ṭur I 430, Aaron Ha-Kohen 70a (Kol Bo, no. 47), Abr{aham} Klausner in the Maharil 10b. Similar tales in Va-Yosh‘a p. 51, Chronicle of Moses, p. 10.

43 Ha-Pardes, loc. cit., with which compare Ṣedah La-Derekh 4, 3, 3 and Maharil 3a.

44 Maḥzor Vitry, Ḥizzequni on Exod 12:3. Abudarham.

45 *Gott. Vortr*{*äge*} pp. 375, 376.

46 יום ההסגר. Compare החלוץ I p. 26.

according to prevailing ideas; no less did systems and singing accommodate to prevailing taste.

Because there were customs that were not obscured by halakhic rulings but left to their own devices, there were major deviations in the rites of the statutory prayers and the festival services that were already apparent around the year 900. For this reason, and because people were omitting, adding or abbreviating, Sa'adya decided to compose an order of prayer.[47] Some items had completely disappeared from public worship, or were practised only in private devotion, while others had been so altered that it was no longer possible to know their original sense. With regard to some items, he notes that here and there items were introduced by distinguished individuals, while about others he claims that they have no basis in tradition. Items recited in one place were unknown elsewhere, while newer items replaced well-established ones. Sa'adya also criticizes the content of new items, such as those that address angels. The text-books, as well as the communities, differed from each other with regard to the order of the biblical readings, the accompaniment of prayers with *qaddish*, the sequence of individual prayers, the recitative exchange between prayer-leader and community, and in innumerable other ritual arrangements. One could almost believe that one was listening to a contemporary reporter. Thanks to his efforts, individual items are fixed but the freedom of the rite, no less than that of the synagogal poetry, was restricted. Hai Gaon recognized the validity of many types of variation, in matters of prayer and accompanying singing.[48] Opposition to inclusions in the *qerovah* or *piyyuṭ*, especially with regard to הכל יודוך, was removed, but recurred in France in the eleventh century, only to be rejected again by the standing of Benjamin b. Samuel, Elijah Ha-Zaqen and Joseph Tovelem who were legal

P. 12

experts as well as authors of *piyyuṭ*. Poetic recitals were popular and filled the synagogues of Spain and France, Italy and Germany, Slavonia and Greece.[49] Objections from some sides which occurred a century later were of no consequence especially since Rabbenu Tam rejected them out of hand,[50] and the authority of men such as Isaac Ghiyyat and Joseph Migash silenced them totally.

---

47 Communicated by Steinschneider.

48 Compare תמים דעים no. 119.

49 Ha-Pardes 43d, 44a.

50 Maḥzor Vitry (compare *Kerem Chemed* 3 p. 202, 6 p. 30ff), ס' הישר 619ff. Ha-Manhig 17b § 58, שבלי הלקט ms. § 28. האגור {of Jacob b. Judah Landau} § 117.

Minhag stood its ground against distinguished scholarly opinions as well as halakhic prohibitions[51] and the communities insisted on permitting themselves the freedom to listen to whatever *piyyuṭ* they wished. The power of custom was so great that in many parts of the ritual from the Geonim until the thirteenth century there were deviations and fluctuations, and some items that are today accepted unquestioningly were for a long time controversial. Yose b. Yose,[52] and to a degree Amram, did not indeed have the same biblical verses in the *musaf* for New Year as those of Maimonides and ourselves. The insertion זכרנו in the New Year *tefillah* was still not widespread around 840 and was more common at an earlier time in Palestine than in Babylonia. The shofar blowing, which was originally done by each individual, was later performed by an expert and in various places it was not omitted on the Sabbath if a leading scholar was present.[53] Although Amram is against בגלל אבות, it is prevalent in Sa'adya and in our festival *yoṣer*. In the benedictions of the morning service, Pesiqta Rabba (40.4) reads מחיה מתים instead of המחזיר נשמות. The {benediction} מגביה שפלים was accepted in the rites of Seville, Avignon, Rome, and Germany, in spite of the fact that it does not occur in the Gemara, and Amram expresses his opposition to it.[54] On the other hand, Amram, against the view of the Talmud, disapproves of מתיר אסורים[55] and עוטר ישראל, as does Naṭronai of the latter benediction on the grounds that the covering of the head for which it was introduced

P. 13

was different in his day from what it had once been. R. Isaac of Marseilles explains סומך נופלים as an error[56] but it nevertheless remained in the Provençal rite and occurs twice in printed editions of the prayers.[57] The benediction הנותן ליעף כח occurs in none of the early authorities, nor even in Eleazar of Worms, but originated in the German *Siddur*, as well as in the Spanish rite, while פוקח עורים, which was widely accepted, was omitted in Avignon. As late as the fourteenth century it is still mentioned in some Castilian places that part of the *qaddish* had Hebrew, and not Aramaic,

51 Isaac Tyrnau, preface to his מנהגים.
52 Compare Isaac Ghiyyat הלכות MS ר"ה (on the ordering of the verses) and the Book of the Pious 259.
53 Asheri, Rosh Ha-Shanah 4 beginning. Yeruḥam {b. Meshullam} 6.2.
54 שבלי 1.
55 Ṭur I 46.
56 Karo on Ṭur I.1.
57 Compare j. Berakhot 1.6.

wording.[58] Despite Sa'adya and other usages, the Germans retained ואור חדש in the *yoṣer*. R. Samuel b. Meir, however, omitted בא"י at the end of יראו עינינו[59] while Rashi on the Sabbath prayed אתה בחרתנו and not ישמח משה and the latter prayer was restored only by Rabbenu Tam.[60] Against the views of Tractate Soferim—and Pardes[61]—Yehudah Barzilai (about 1130) decided to omit the concluding section כשם שעשית in the thanksgiving prayer for Ḥanukah and his opinion was followed in Lunel.[62] He was also averse to the alphabetical על חטא. Some places had no knowledge of the custom, already known to the Geonim, according to which the community joined in loudly at various points during the recitation of the day's lectionary.[63] The twelve *hafṭarot* of the Pesiqta were flexible in the Spanish rite and only half were included in the Roman rite. Towards the end of the eleventh century, there was discussion in the cities of the Rhine whether והשיאנו was required in the *musaf* of New Year. The custom for the one called to the Torah to repeat after the congregation the phrase ברוך ה' המבורך—as Sa'adya prescribes—was not yet

P. 14

accepted at the beginning of the twelfth century.[64] The prayer formulations used for the silent *teḥinah* that occur in Amram, Sa'adya and Maimonides were not preserved in any rite known to us. Around 1200, the *ne'ilah* prayer was in some places still held at nightfall.[65] Around the same tim—and contrary to the Geonim—the French rabbis decided against שהחיינו on the eve of the second day of New Year[66] and the benediction before *hallel* on Pesaḥ evening,[67] while a hundred years later scholars found it strange that there were so many הרחמן {inserts} towards the end

58 Ṭur I 56.

59 Ha-Manhig 22b § 84, Aaron Ha-Kohen 43b. In Kol Bo 28 the whole passage is lacking.

60 Ha-Manhig f. 26b § 20; it does not fully match Ha-Pardes 56a, where ישמח {משה} does not, however, enjoy the detailed explanation that is offered elsewhere by Nathan b. Makhir (תניא 20b). The mention of ישמח {משה} in לקוטי הפרדס 21d top is not supported by Ha-Pardes 56b middle, where באתה [אחד] is offered instead.

61 43b, 44a.

62 Ha-Manhig 43a. Aaron Ha-Kohen חנוכה § 22. Compare Karo on Ṭur I 112.

63 {Responsa} פאר הדור 90.

64 Compare Amram ms. f. 28b with Pisqey Recanati 71, Yonah Berakhot ch. 7, Abudarham 29a, Ha-Pardes 19d, Aaron Ha-Kohen 22c.

65 {R. }Simḥah cited in Maimoniot תפלה 3.6.

66 מצות זמניות {of Israel b. Joseph} ms. Aaron Ha-Kohen 42a. The opposite view is in Ha-Manhig 52b.

67 Naḥmanides לקוטות 14c. Aaron Ha-Kohen 80c.

of the grace after meals.[68] It is less strange that Meir Rothenburg opposed the recitation of biblical verses during the priestly benediction since differences of option about this had already existed a thousand years earlier.[69]

On the other hand, there were many items that were unknown to earlier authorities but became common in the course of time, having been adopted by individuals and then introduced into the *Siddur*. The ישתבח prayer was once recited immediately after לשם תפארתך. This was what Amram stated and this was the custom in Germany until Shemayah of Soissons introduced אתה הוא and ויושע from France.[70] At the end of ישמח משה in the Sabbath *tefillah*, the phrase למעשה בראשית, which does not exist in Amram or Maimonides, is inserted. The long *musaf tefillah* of New Year was only for the prayer-leader while the individual simply added מלוך and והשיאנו[71] The separation of the fingers during the priestly benediction, based on the Pesiqta, for which Eliezer of Metz knew no reason, was already reported in geonic times and was practised in various ways.[72] The shape of the priests' hands was described by Eleazar of Worms, and by R. Asher and his son Jacob,[73] and the first to change it was Elijah Wilna. The "*yehi raṣon*" after the counting of the Omer, that is first noted by Menaḥem b. Solomon

P. 15

(1139),[74] was prescribed in the rituals from the time of Meir Rothenburg.[75] If the custom for a young bridegroom to read four, seven or nine verses from ואברהם זקן (Gen 24) on his first Sabbath does not date from Sa'adya,[76] then it seems to be from not much later. We encounter the same practice in Spain (Avignon,[77] {North-} Africa, Cochin), Greece, Germany and France where אתניה שבחיה was sung before

68 Ṭur I 189.
69 Aaron Ha-Kohen 109d, Soṭah 40a. מקורי מנהגים {of Abraham Lewysohn} § 39.
70 Hirṣ Trèves {Thiengen 1560} Commentary; compare Roqeaḥ 320.
71 Siddur Amram.
72 'Arukh חלון, Ha-Manhig 20a.
73 Roqeaḥ 323, Asheri Megillah 3. Ṭur I 128. Compare Mordechai Megillah ch. 4 ms. (where Yehudah Ha-Kohen is already mentioned), (נשא) פענח רזא {of Isaac b. Judah Ha-Levi}, Pisqey Tosafot on Soṭah § 44.
74 Cited from שכל טוב in לקוטין ms. § 186.
75 Tashbeṣ 394, שבלי 73, תניא, Abudarham, Abr{aham} Klausner 39a, Maharil, Tyrnau's Minhagim in the notes, {Issachar b. Mordechai} Even Shushan 84b. Also mentioned in Commentary אמרי נועם {of Jacob de Illescas} *parashah* אמור. Compare Lampronti {פחד יצחק} entry חתן f. 61a.
76 Compare Abudarham 85a.
77 My *Ritus* {*der Synagoge*} *von Avignon* 1839 p. 48.

the biblical reading and ירויץ התנא at the end of that same passage. In the preceding *reshut*, which was also practised in Germany, it was generally known as פרשה קטנה, an expression that is also used by Eleazar of Worms.[78]

In the talmudic period, there was neither calendar nor any order of festival prayers. It cannot be said with any certainty whether the benedictions and the various *tefillah*'s listed in Tractate Berakhot were written down; all we can say is that the community did not have anything of the sort to hand. During the divine service they listened to the prayer-leader and whatever was required of the individual was entrusted to memory. The teachers transmitted the order of service orally because they did not tolerate the writing down of benedictions any more than that of aggadah and in controversial cases they left the decision to tradition. From the fifth or sixth century both the Talmud and the liturgical content acquired a written form but with the expansion of talmudic studies the circle grew and divine service found a place at its centre. In this way, two new literary areas were initiated; prayer-books and prayer-orders. Dating from the eighth century, and partly also from the seventh, are lectionaries, Sabbath and festival services. The eighth and ninth centuries see the emergence of halakhic digests, which are partly based on Yelammedenu introductions to the presentations and of which a quarter

P. 16

deal with liturgical questions. Around that time, a Jewish prince of the Khazars seems to have initiated the composition of instructions for prayer-leaders.

Actual rulings by the Geonim on liturgical matters began, if we take no account of some earlier material, towards the end of the eighth century. Jews had spread out to the West, as far as Africa and Spain. In various places the matter of the wording and form of the divine service inevitably gave rise to questions being asked. What is more, the Karaite movement, as well as other sects, increased the zeal of the Geonim, especially when Anan's supporters created their own ways of prayer and festival celebration, so that Naṭronai[79] adds a note to the effect that whoever, in the Haggadah of the Pesaḥ festival, deviates from the customs of the two academies, has not fulfilled his duty. From that period, decisions and dogmas in matters of divine service are transmitted to us by the Geonim[80] Yehudai, Mordechai, Nisi b. Samuel, Joseph b. Abba, Ṣadoq or Isaac, Moses b. Jacob, Palṭoi b. Abaye, Kohen

78 Roqeaḥ 355.

79 Amram ms. f. 53b. Cited by Ha-Manhig 82b, Simeon Duran Responsa part 3 no. 290 [{*Der*} *Orient Lit{eraturblatt}* 1844 no. 42 p. 322].

80 Appendix I {below}.

Ṣedeq, Sar Shalom, Menaḥem, Matathia, Naṭronai, Amram, Naḥshon b. Ṣadoq, Ṣemaḥ b. Ḥayyim, Ṣemaḥ b. Palṭoi, Ṣemaḥ b. Solomon, Hai b. Naḥshon and Sa'adya. In addition to them, there occur the statements of scholars who were resident in other places, such as Eleazar, Ḥefeṣ, Daniel and Nathan.

In the tenth century, knowledge of ritual matters increased while the exclusive authority of the Babylonian academies decreased. Thus, from the time of Sa'adya, citations of geonic decisions become rarer and occur only in the names of Sherira and Hai. In the eleventh century {liturgical} decisions reach Mainz[81] from Jerusalem; from the academy of Hai, last actual Gaon, and from Samuel b. Ḥofni or Samuel Ha-Kohen; from {North-}Africa by Israel Ha-Kohen[82] and Ḥananel. Decisions in Europe

P. 17

are by Ḥanokh,[83] his son Moses[84] and Samuel Ha-Levi[85] in Spain; Meshullam b. Qalonymos from Lucca,[86] Jacob in Rome,[87] Gershom, Joseph Tovelem, Yehuda Ha-Kohen[88] and their followers in France and Germany. The honourable title of "*gaon*" was attached to later scholars, and anonymous instructions flowed into the collections of legal decisions and other collective works in the eleventh and twelfth centuries.

Another influence on the layout of the divine service, even if slower than that of the legal decisions, came by way of the specialized halakhic works, namely the halakhot and the excerpts from them that appeared from Aḥa until Joseph.[89] These text-books did not agree with each other in every individual aspect and their degree of validity varied from country to country. Aggadic items had a more direct impact. In addition to the Pesiqta's, there were special midrashic compositions that were available on the themes of individual festivals, such as, for example, Wa-Yosha' for

81 Maḥzor Vitry 198, Ha-Pardes 42a, אבן העזר 78b.

82 Isaac Ghiyyat הלכות ms. on ר"ה and סכה, cited in שבלי 108.

83 Responsa שערי צדק 22b no. 9. Isaac Ghiyyat cited in Asheri Rosh Ha-Shanah end [Ṭur I 591] Maimonides אגרות {ed.} Ven{ice} 65b [Aaron Ha-Kohen 23b. Abudarham 29d].

84 שבלי 13 beginning, that an unlearned priest takes precedence.

85 Isaac Ghiyyat loc. cit. קדוש, הבדלה, לולב. Aaron Ha-Kohen 19c § 103, 37d § 10, 64a, deriving in part from those halakhot. Compare שיטה מקובצת {Bava} Meṣi'a 170a.

86 Iṭṭur cited in Asheri end of Rosh Ha-Shanah; similarly in שבלי 93, Aaron Ha-Kohen 42a, מצות זמניות {of Israel b. Joseph} ms.

87 {Ḥiddushey} Ha-Aggudah; Benjamin Ze'ev Responsa 234 [read Jacob for Abraham] and notes on Mordechai Shabbat end, מטה משה § 813.

88 Ha-Pardes 60d, 61b. Ṭur I 458.

89 Aaron Ha-Kohen f. 120d.

Pesaḥ, Decalogue midrash for the Feast of Weeks, the Death of Moses for the end of Tabernacles, a Persian midrash for the Ninth of Av;[90] even the content of Josippon was used for this. Wherever such and similar texts were read, there emerged poetic versions, just as poetic targum was created out of a combination of Targum and Aggadah. Already at an earlier time *hafṭarot*

P. 18

were compiled in independent booklets:[91] the Aramaic translation, and later ornamentation, were probably placed next to the *hafṭarah*.[92] At the time of Tractate Soferim the existence of prayer-books cannot be doubted and, once Talmud and Midrash were written down, no prayers, not even *azharot*, *'avodah* and *pizmon*, were left to be memorized. Books of prayers are in any case older than the specific orders of prayer, which reach back no earlier than the eighth century. Meanwhile the first book of this type that we find is that of the Gaon Kohen-Ṣedeq (843), as reported by Isaac Ghiyyat.[93] One generation later, there came the *Siddur* of the Gaon Amram which was widely used in the eleventh century and was the basis of benedictions and the order of the prayers.[94] It is known only in its later revisions that also included *azharot*[95] and *hosha'not*.[96] The version that we have probably dates from no earlier than 1100 and was an abbreviated version of the original which includes daily prayers, the grace after meals, the service for Sabbath and its termination, New Moon days, Fast-days, Ḥanukah, Purim, Pesaḥ, the Feast of Weeks, the Ninth of Av, New Year, Days of Repentance, Day of Atonement and Tabernacles,

90 Codex Rossi 1093 no. 5. The passages communicated by Yosippon from an early commentary (החלוץ 2p. 121) are also to be found in codex Bodleian 255 for Purim and codex H. 17 for Hanukkah, where the topic is eight miracles; I did not notice the expression מדרש.

91 A book of *hafṭarot* from the Persian period mentioning Hai is cited in Isaac Ghiyyat הלכות ms. in Pesaḥim. Around 1080 there is a mention of a biblical manuscript that had come from the Orient in which the *hafṭarah*'s for the whole year were indicated (Ha-Pardes 62a). Ten de Rossi codices (30, 200, 267, 291, 365, 376, 502, 673, 1039, 1084) are dated to the thirteenth and fourteenth centuries.

92 Perhaps the ספר אפטרתא Giṭṭin 60a, compare Rapoport *'Erekh Millin* p. 167 and ff.

93 הלכות f. 19a (according to Dernburg). To this should be related: וכן סדר רב כהן צדק (Ṭur I 481), similarly וכן סדר רב עמרם (Rashi Giṭṭin 59b); compare וסדר ספרים רבים (יסוד עולם {of Isaac b. Joseph Israeli} 4, 18), סדר סדר עולם (appendix to Yuḥasin 164a), שסדר רב נחשון (מעשה גאונים 103), הפרדס אשר סדר רשי (Mordechai Berakhot end), סדר ספר הלקוטים ({*Qunṭres*} *Devarim 'Atiqim* no. 2 p. 8).

94 ס' הישר 74c.

95 Amram ms. f. 62: מתחיל אזהרות ביום ראשון והן כתובות בסדר; Dukes has a quotation from Isaac b. Ṭodros ({*Der*} *Orient Lit*{*eraturblatt*} 1847 26 p. 405).

96 Joseph Ha-Kohen מושעות אל introduction.

and finally the benedictions for circumcisions, weddings and bereavements. The mention of halakhic statements and of individual Geonim often occurs. In respect of both such matters, the *Siddur* of the Gaon Sa‘adya is more economical but,

P. 19

on the other hand, it is more generous with the transmission of *‘avodahs, azharot, hosha‘not, seliḥot* and shorter rhyme-less prayers, not to mention the items that he himself composed. This work, which was frequently mentioned from the twelfth century onwards,[97] and is equally important for the history of both rite and *piyyuṭ*, was rediscovered only several years ago.[98] Just as the decisions stopped with {the death of} Sa‘adya so did the geonic orders of prayer. One century later, the *Siddurim* that were composed by Hai,[99] Nissim[100] and Ibn Gasus were no longer known and seem to have been lost at an early stage. What is then described as a “geonic order”[101] is not an individual work but constitutes what has been derived from rulings and *Siddurim*, so that the expression *“geonim”* must be understood in a broader sense.

Out of the amalgam of prayer-books, prayer orders and halakhic works on ritual, there emerged a more extensive collection that was known as the “*Maḥzor* of prayers”,[102] or abbreviated to *Maḥzor*, borrowing the word מחזור that once described the astronomical or annual cycle. Similarly, a work that deals with Masorah, and was called מחזרתא, was possibly applied only to

---

97 Pisqey Recanati 71, הישר 719, Isaac b. Abba Mari cited in תניא 91, Maimonides Responsa 90, Ha-Manhig 12a, 17b, 50b, 53b, 55a, 69a, 70a, Abudarham in more than forty passages. Moses de Coucy positive commands 48, Israel {b. Joseph} in מצות זמניות MS, שבלי 5. Aaron Ha-Kohen 11a, 25a. {Israel Qimḥi} עבודת ישראל 7b. Isaac Ghiyyat הלכות ms. פסחים, לולב, ר"ה. Hai cited in Ṭur I 481.

98 Communicated by M. Steinschneider in the summer of 1851. It is cited simply as liber liturgicus by Uri (codex 261) and by Wolf *Bibliotheca* (vol. 2, p. 1460); more precisely by Steinschneider in his *Bodleian Catalogue* pp. 2203–16. The publisher of קובץ {J. Rosenberg} Berlin 1856 discusses the *Siddur* of Sa‘adya that is housed in Oxford as if it were a matter known to every printer.

99 Maybe that is the source for the instructions in Alfasi Berakhot 3, and Ha-Pardes 41a.

100 ראבי"ה § 423 cites that *Siddur* but perhaps means the same as that cited from מגלת סתרים by Ha-Manhig (שבת § 20) and that is specifically cited in Ha-Pardes 38d, where [the unnamed] R. Nissim communicates to his father the decisions of the Geonim. One item from that source is included in Aaron Ha-Kohen 63b § 21 כתב הר"ש זל for which Kol Bo 41c has: הרב ר' אשר. האגור {of Jacob b. Judah Landau} (§ 824) also mentions the Seder where Ha-Manhig (81b) makes his citation from מגלת סתרים but what he quotes as from § 53 is actually from § 52.

101 סדר, סדור (Eliezer b. Nathan’s Commentary on the Prayers section I f. 81a, Ha-Manhig 6b, Ṭur I 579, Abudarham ed. Prague 112d, 113a, Ṣedah La-Derekh 4, 5, 2). תקון (Ṭur I 51), מנהגות (שבלי 95).

102 מחזור תפלות in התרומה {Barukh b. Isaac} ms. § 101, which reads במחזור in the printed edition 102; and in § 245 the reference is to מחזור של תפלות.

P. 20

the Pentateuch and then extended to describe the synagogal order[103] that recurred on an annual basis, and was used by the Syrian {Christians} for the breviary.[104] Just as the calendar provided the basis for the festivals and lectionaries, so must the original *Maḥzor* have served as a calendar that was furnished with the prayers and lectionaries for the whole year; but, as the *piyyuṭ* increased, so that calendar moved into the background even if its name, which derived from such a use, remained. In about the year 1100, Simḥah of Vitry compiled a work of this kind, that is known as the *Maḥzor Vitry*. Based on the *Siddur* of Amram—which was similarly called *Maḥzor*[105]—as well as on the work of the Geonim and the teachings of Rashi and his contemporaries, it contains: 1) the order of daily, Sabbath and festival prayer; the grace after meals, the Pesaḥ Haggadah, poetic *ma'ariv*, *hosha'nes*, the Aramaic ornamentation of the Decalogue accompanied by introductions; songs, hymns and prayers for the Sabbath, especially for a wedding Sabbath. 2) Instructions and explanations concerning the divine service and other ritual matters; statutes, regulations, forms of contract and similar items; Masoretic matters, calendrical rules, tables of lectionaries and *hafṭarot*; economic and dietary items. 3) Tractate Avot with commentary, the chapter of R. Meir, Tractates Derekh Ereṣ, Kallah and Soferim, Midrash on the Ten Commandments with an extensive introduction, the work סדר תנאים ואמוראים, explanations of various talmudic and midrashic passages, collectanea.

It is not at all realistic {to imagine} that this work was created with such a rich content but, given the poetic and ritual inclusions, it is completely certain that to a considerable degree the two exemplars known to us represent revisions of the text in the thirteenth century. In any event, it seems that in that *Maḥzor* what was actually free and arbitrary content in the communal divine service for festivals—such as *yoṣer*, *zulat*, *qerovah*, *azharot*, *seliḥah*, *qinah*—were excluded and that these items themselves, or partly together with

P. 21

other Vitry content, later came to be known as the *Maḥzor*. It specifically kept this name until later, while the instructions for ritual grew into independent branches of literature, firstly into *minhagim* and similar works, and the explanations of the prayers into commentaries on the *Maḥzor*.

103 ס' העבור {Abraham b. Ḥiyya} p. 39.
104 Syr{iac} Cod{ex} {in the} Vatic{an} 83.
105 Roqeaḥ 283, כריתות p. 60.

Talmudic and geonic scholars made many references to custom. The customs of larger communities served as guidelines for places nearby, in the same way that teachers and prayer-leaders became authoritative for communities and the activities of forefathers were exemplary for later generations. In fixing readings and rites, one followed the example of prayer-leaders who had become famous,[106] collected what was usually done in important places, and wrote down what had been heard from teachers, or had been witnessed in various communities. This probably accounted for the origin of the "Minhagim" of the prayer-leader Meir b. Isaac[107] in Worms, on the basis of whose statements Rashi himself[108] altered specific items in the ritual. Additional items that he himself introduced, or were guaranteed in his name, may have constituted the content of a work[109] that is perhaps hidden away somewhere. The early sources know of "Minhagim" from France,[110] Lotharingia,[111] Mainz[112] and Speyer,[113] some of which have reached us only in notes made in the writings of Rashi and his followers.[114]

There are only remnants of the מנהגים of Eliezer b. Nathan[115] of Mainz (1150) and the מנהגות of Asher b. Meshullam[116] of Lunel

P. 22

(1170) but what has been preserved for us is the work המנהיג[117] by Abraham b. Nathan of Lunel, who lived in Toledo in 1203, which deals in brief with the ritual

---

106 E.g. Mordechai (Ha-Pardes 45c); Meir (Maimoniot מילה ch. 2, codex H 62 [also in Tyrnau's מנהגים, חול § 9]. Opp. 1073F. and 1606Q [his introduction to a *seliḥah*]); Yehudah Ha-Levi (אסור והתר ms. § 67, for which other mss. have Meir ש"ץ; but that is also what he is called in Minhagim in codex Vienna ms. f. 125).

107 Maharil 27a [ed. 1730 f. 21].

108 Vitry 198. שבלי הלקט ms. § 290.

109 Perhaps the מנהגים לר"ב שליח צבור? See {Luzzatto} הליכות קדם p. 50 at the foot.

110 Roqeaḥ 319.

111 שבלי הלקט ed. 11, ms. § 28.

112 שבלי הלקט ms. 199, 267, 269 [ed. 53, 89], מעשה הגאונים ms. § 144.

113 שבלי הלקט ms. 267, 284, 372 [ed. 93, 121].

114 Compare Ha-Pardes 42a, 45c.

115 Roqeah loc. cit.

116 Citations in Aaron Ha-Kohen, Abudarham, {בעלי} אסופות, {Perushey} Manoaḥ {b. Jacob} 13a, נמוקי יוסף {of Joseph Ḥaviva) (ציצית), תורת האדם {of Naḥmanides} 21d, Isaac Aboab (in Karo on Ṭur I 268); similarly cited in תורת המנהגות (Aaron Ha-Kohen 76c); his הלכות יום טוב in תמים דעים no. 120. In the השגות ms. of Moses Ha-Kohen of Lunel תפלה ch. 10 and elsewhere the name החכם ר' אשר is mentioned.

117 Actually מנהיג עולם, cited by Sol{omon} Adret (Responsa part 1 no. 454), Isaac Abuab (in Candelabrum), Aaron Ha-Kohen, Abudarham, Yeruḥam {b. Meshullam}, Ṭur.

of the divine service. He was a disciple of Isaac b. Samuel and Abraham b. David, had the opportunity of becoming acquainted with the local variations of custom in France, Provence, Spain, as well as perhaps in England and Germany, and made efforts to identify the authority and meaning of customs. Apart from the works of the Geonim, especially that of Amram, he refers to a large number of rabbis in France and Narbonne. In addition to the Minhagim of Abraham[118] of France (perhaps 1230), Meir Rothenburg[119] in Germany and Ḥayyim Palṭiel[120] who probably lived in Bohemia (1280), he also cites other writings with the same title {of Minhagim} from the twelfth and thirteenth centuries, sometimes without any further specification,[121] sometimes with a mention of their homeland—Rhineland,[122] Düren,[123] Vienna,[124] Narbonne,[125] Gerona and Catalonia[126]—which gradually acquired the status of halakhic writings.

Just as the Minhagim emerged out of prayer rites, so did the commentaries out of prayer content. With regard to language and thought, the statutory prayers could be understood. In the time of midrash and developing exegesis, however, one needed an explanation for what lay behind the choice of expression and also for the order itself. There thus emerged for the *Siddur* aggadic and moral explanations, and, later, philosophcial and mystical ones, the beginnings of which belong to the age of Rashi. It was different in the case of *piyyuṭ* which has more obscure expression and content,

P. 23

and where there was a need to explain words and subjects. In the second half of the eleventh century, beginning in France, scholars began to explain more difficult *piyyuṭ* on the basis of the underlying Aggadah, Targum and Talmud, and through the grammatical works of Menaḥem and Dunash. At a later date, glosses of a similar nature, and longer explanations, were attached to the margins of a *Maḥzor* and liturgical glosses to the *Siddur*. Grammarians interwove into their writings

118 Note 2 {below}.
119 Codices Opp. 1283Q, 1284Q, 1569Q.
120 Cited in Klausner and Maharil, signing himself as חפ"ת, that is ח' פ' תולעת.
121 Maimoniot מגלה ch. 2, Mordechai Megillah. Manuscripts: Opp. 727Q and 1284Q, H h 89 in 4.
122 Abr{aham} Klausner 27a. Codex Mich. 457.
123 Tyrnau Minhagim, notes f. 7a, 11b, 14b; מטה משה 700, 770.
124 Tyrnau loc. cit. 7a.
125 Aaron H-Kohen 93b (ובמנהגות), 100d (ובמנהג).
126 Ibid. 95d.

corrections of prayer and *piyyuṭ*. Gradually these commentaries became independent tracts and were sometimes attached to the prayer order of some rites, with text and commentary (as well as order), each constituting a separate work.

Among the earliest interpreters[127] of prayer and *piyyuṭ* are: Yehudah Darshan, Menaḥem b. Ḥelbo, whose explanations of Qalir were perhaps delivered only orally; his nephew Joseph Qara who commented on the *Maḥzor* and especially the *hosha'not*; Meshullam b. Moses of Mainz, Rashi and his disciple Eliezer b. Nathan, whose commentary on the prayer-book and on individual parts of the *Maḥzor* is partially still extant. Among the more significant interpreters who lived between 1140 and 1300 were: Asher b. Meshullam, mentioned earlier; Jacob the Nazir, perhaps the earliest mystical commentator, just as Yehudah b. Yaqar—who dealt only with the prayer-book—was the earliest theological commentator, and his contemporary Jacob Anatoli, was perhaps the first philosophical commentator. In addition: Shemayah of Soissons and Samuel of Falaise (on Tovelem's halakhic order for Shabbat Ha-Gadol), neither of them known other than through citation. More extensive material has been preserved from the writings of Ephraim of Bonn, Eleazar of Worms (on the prayer-book and *Maḥzor*), Meir Rothenburg, the brothers Benjamin and Zedekiah of Rome, and in the commentaries of anonymous collectors that are partially cited in the books of ritual.

P. 24

Already towards the end of the twelfth century, but more clearly in the thirteenth, mysticism gripped the interpreters of the prayer-book. In order to warm up those who were cold, the rational soul was weakened and the imagination was kindled. Secrets were sold to the ignorant that promised future revelations and wealth to their owners. As a result, one then sought deep wisdom in every aggadah and every meaningless practice and the contemporary fashion was to discover secrets everywhere. Counting words and playing with them, exaggeratedly favoured by Eleazar of Worms, outdoing Ibn Ezra in dealing with secret matters, the Sefira's half wisdom and total superstition, and, above all, needy times—all these nourished this tendency. From the time of Isaac the Pious, pure and impure people, with vocation or without, savaged the divine service and prayers, which were no better treated than sacred scripture; they were no longer explained but rather obscured. Even when something was done by better mystics on behalf of spirituality and devotion, and against unthinking sloppiness, the ritual as a whole sustained great loss rather

127 Appendix II {below}.

than any advantage. The prayer attributed to Neḥuniah b. Ha-Qana uses the external structure of the eighteen benedictions for the glorification of the power of the Sefira and calls the divine majesty (כבוד) female. For Moses de Leon, who represents divine service and prayers as a means of godliness leading to higher levels of sanctification, the "Shekhinah" is the female principle of the Primordial Spirit. He and the zoharic Midrash Ruth agitate in the same terms against the recitation of והוא רחום before the evening service of the Sabbath. Abulafia the prophet enters deeply into the mysticism of the way the fingers are divided during the priestly benediction. Joseph Gikatila notes that the omission of even one of the hundred benedictions prescribed for each day damages the Torah, since the balance of mind (נפש) has to give a tithe to the spirit (רוח) and the spirit a tithe to the soul (נשמה), so that it follows that any instance of omission wounds the soul, etc. Azriel before him and Isaac b. Ṭodros after him composed kabbalistic explanation for the *Maḥzor*. Even

P. 25

thicker fog envelopes the liturgical contemplations of the author of the Zohar. Joseph ibn Waqar even attached a commentary to his own Sefira hymn.

Meanwhile, the *Siddur* business, which involved working on identifying the fabric and shape of the divine service, was making progress. Rashi wrote two tracts of this type: Pardes[128] and Siddur.[129] The fate of Pardes was even worse than that of Maḥzor Vitry; it was thrown together with other works of Rashi, mixed with other people's material, and, when it appeared, it was littered with errors. Both the early printed digest, as well as the parts that are in manuscript, belong to different recensions. {Rashi's} *Siddur* that was already used by Ephraim of Bonn appears to be related to Maḥzor Vitry. In these works, the ritual is identified on the one hand, while on the other an attempt is made to explain prayer method in an aggadic way. At the same time, they contain Rashi's discussions of *qaddish* and other prayers. In general, efforts were made to find guiding principles for individual forms of liturgical material. Concerning the wording of the benedictions, whether with ל or with על, and their application, investigations were made by

128 Cited by Eliezer b. Nathan (codex H. 61), Mordechai, Isaiah {Trani} (המכריע 3, 31, 62, 71), Abraham (Bodleian codex 316), Israel Brünn (Responsa 119).

129 Mss. in Parma, Padua, Munich; cited in Roqeaḥ 280 (called מנהגים), Ha-Manhig 61b, 62b, notes on דיני נידה (§ 2 and elsewhere). In Bodleian codex 295 f. 28 it is referred to as: אתחיל סדור ר' שלמה ת"ר מאה ברכות חייב אדם לומר בכל יום שנ'. But this is also the start in: Maḥzor Vitry, the section in Ha-Pardes 57a, שבלי הלקט.

many authors: Eliezer b. Nathan,[130] Joseph ibn Plaṭ,[131] Jacob b. Meir,[132] Maimonides, Abraham b. David,[133] Isaac b. Abbamaris,[134] Eleazar b. Yehudah,[135] Moses of Coucy, Naḥmanides,[136] Aaron Ha-Kohen, Yeruḥam {b. Meshullam}, Finally, Solomon Adret[137] explained that even all those instructions were not satisfactory. The noteworthy books of ritual in

P. 26

the two hundred years after Rashi should include the following:

A book entitled מעשה המכירי was apparently composed before 1100 and the authors were perhaps Menaḥem and his brother Nathan.[138] Yehudah Barceloni wrote a work called העתים which deals with everything relating to the festivals; Joseph ibn Plat, who was also in Rome, two treatises on the benedictions; Abraham b. Isaac's האשכול which is perhaps the work we still have;[139] Isaac b. Abbamari the treatise עשרת הדברות which derived its name from its ten sections, the most important of which deal with the rites of the festivals, in addition to the work Iṭṭur, of which five sections (animal slaughter, circumcision, tefillin, wedding benedictions,[140] fringes and their benedictions) survive only in manuscript. The four just mentioned lived in Lunel, Narbonne and Marseille. Works that belong to North France include that of Elḥanan b. Isaac on the order of prayers[141] and the calendar,[142] and Rabbenu Tam's *Maḥzor* with his corrections and his rules for benedictions,[143] and probably also his order of service for Pesaḥ. Shemayah[144]—perhaps

130 ראב"ן § 35.
131 In Ha-Pardes f. 40 ff and in Abudarham f. 6, compare Asher of Lunel cited in Aaron Ha-Kohen 11c.
132 ס' הישר 27c.
133 תמים דעים 179.
134 Asher {b. Ḥayyim} הפרדס ms. section 9.
135 Roqeaḥ §§ 363 until 366.
136 תמים דעים 186. לקוטות f. 12c ff.
137 Responsa part 3, no. 283, compare part 1 no. 18.
138 Compare אבן העזר f. 84c.
139 This should have been among the manuscripts of Moses Foa; parts of it seem to be in codex Rossi 159 and in the book ברכות, which was called פתרון חלומות, 55b.
140 See תניא 89 and 91.
141 Tos{afot} Berakhot 60b; Mordechai (Halakhot Qeṭanot) calls it תקון תפלין.
142 מנחת יהודה {Tosafist commentary} 10a.
143 Tos{afot} 'Eruvin 40a, Asheri Berakhot 6 § 9, Yeruḥam {Toledot Adam} 16.5 f. 146a.
144 Tos{afot} Pesaḥim 114a. Ha-Manhig פסח § 63, Maimoniot חו"מ 8.

Tam's father-in-law[145]—and Yomtov of Joigny[146] seem also to have written on the same topic. In Germany, the *Maḥzorim* of Shemayah[147] and Ephraim b. Jacob[148] are cited. But the most important work of that period remains the Mishneh Torah of Maimonides in which, for the first time since Sa'adya, a scholarly man sets out for us a prayer text and rituals in an exemplary order. It was not only philosophers and poets who glorified his immortal achievements but also men such as Jonathan

P. 27

Ha-Kohen,[149] Moses of Coucy, Moses b. Naḥman, Estori Parḥi,[150] Isaac Abuab,[151] Solomon Duran,[152] Joseph Colon[153] and Joseph Karo. In the {North-}African countries the rituals were written at that time in Arabic, exactly as they were in Sa'adya's *Siddur*, as indeed were the דיני תפילה ומועד of Maimon,[154] the father of Maimonides. One such work that is provided with a philosophical introduction is the *Siddur* of Solomon of Sijilmasa which has survived (in Oxford) in thirty sections and furnishes us with the tractates Avot and Derekh Ereṣ, as well as attaching rules for the calendar and citations from eleven Geonim. Halakhah's are cited in the name of Joseph ibn Aknin[155] who wrote in Aleppo. Abraham, the son of Maimonides,[156] also has in the second part of his work כתאב אלכפאיה a section on the public divine service.

There followed in Europe, after the period of Tosafot and Maimonides, an epoch in which there was an astonishing degree of activity concerning the structure of the divine service in order to stabilize all its possible aspects. The works that were written at that time (1180–1320) remained the basis of everything in the subsequent centuries. Apart from those works with more general halakhic content, which also had to deal with synagogal customs, the following belong to special circles: the work Roqeaḥ by Eleazar of Worms; the Book of the Pious, in which there

145 ס' הישר 81d top.
146 Klausner 37a.
147 Tos{afot} Niddah 66b.
148 Ms. commentary for the Feast of Weeks.
149 {Responsa} פאר הדור 17.
150 כו"פ {כפתור ופרח of Isaac b. Moses Ashtori Ha-Parḥi} ch. 4 f. 12a: כל כונתו לשמים.
151 Candelabrum ch. 316.
152 Disputation 38b.
153 Responsa 146 (אב הרחמים).
154 Simeon Duran Responsa part 1 no. 2.
155 Solomon Duran Responsa 255, 329.
156 Aaron Ha-Kohen 11c.

are in its 213 paragraphs[157] scattered notes about prayer, prayer method, *Siddur* and *piyyuṭ*; an early treatise that indicates the number of words in all the benedictions and their meaning;[158] the Seder ʻAvodah of Simḥa of Speyer[159] that is probably included in his Seder ʻOlam; a guide to circumcision by Gershom b. Jacob;[160] sections of the ראבי"ה by Eliezer Ha-Levi; redactions

P. 28

of earlier books of ritual by Isaac דורבל;[161] and a *Siddur* by Ḥayyim b. Moses of Evreux.[162] Isaac of Orbeil, a student of Ḥayyim of Blois[163] (1260) composed the book המנהל,[164] the largest part of which was dedicated to liturgical rituals; Nathan b. Yehudah, a descendant of Azriel b. Nathan and a follower of Isaac b. Ṭodros, composed an order of the divine service under the title of המחכים;[165] at the same time Menaḥem Ḥazan b. Joseph of Troyes created an order of prayer that was compiled by his disciple, Yehudah b. Eliezer;[166] both of these items remain unprinted. In Provence, Meshullam b. Meir of Beziers wrote additions to Alfasi; David b. Levi the מכתם; Reuben b. Ḥayyim the book התמיד;[167] Meir, the work המאורות;[168] Gershom b. Solomon the שלמן. Among works whose authorship remains unstated are המועדות משמרת,[169] a treatise על שבע הברכות,[170] סדר חתנים ומילה,[171] הבהיר,[172] and selections

157 §§ 18, 114, 158, 227, 248–59, 553, 601, 748–822, 839–854, 881, 882, 1092, 1148, 1160.

158 Asher, Responsa 4.20.

159 Maimoniot תפלה ch. 3.

160 See *Oṣar Neḥmad* part 2 p. 10.

161 *Kerem Chemed* 3 p. 200. *Zion* I p. 97. Aaron Ha-Kohen 9c where the reading והר בה"ה is wrongly given for וה"ר יצחק בה"ד which is correctly printed in Kol Bo 21 f. 15a.

162 Peres in סמק ms. 149 [ed. 154]. Kol Bo 90 from ארחות חיים part 2, where (see *Meged Yeraḥim* 1, p. 7) Ḥayyim cites his father. In סמק ms. codex Bisliches 59 it states simply סידור ה"ר משה מאיורא.

163 Aaron Ha-Kohen 23c. Kol Bo 20.

164 Cited by Abraham Ha-Kohen (Benjamin Ze'ev Responsa 288).

165 Appendix III {below}.

166 Luzzatto in הליכות קדם p. 50. Cited by Jos{eph} Colon Responsa 9 and undoubtedly identical with what codex Rossi 403 calls the rite of Trèves.

167 Aaron Ha-Kohen 16d, 41a.

168 Kol Bo 108; Aaron Ha-Kohen 4c § 25, 15b § 28, 37d § 12.

169 Abudarham ed Prague 39a 45c [the same as that cited without attribution by Aaron H-Kohen 22a § 3 61b § 11]. 47d, 62d, 63b, 82b.

170 המכריע {of Isaiah di Trani} 61.

171 Codices Rossi 352, 1058. Codex R. 510 consists of only of סדר חתנים.

172 Aaron Ha-Kohen 98c § 13 (lacking in Kol Bo 64 f. 70b).

(ליקוטין),[173] some of which are extant in manuscripts and others known from citations, collectanea (קובץ)[174] and Minhagim.[175]

Halakhah and custom, the art of poetry and Aggadah, mysticism and philosophy had by now left their mark on the formation of

P. 29

ritual. The rites of individual places and countries were enriched by poets, developed by prayer-leaders, supported by the books of authorities, and replicated and fixed in the *Siddur* and *Maḥzor*. Although not all communities in a country set up their divine service in the same manner, each community did know its own and we could have recognized all of these, had the *maḥzorim* survived. Yet, this much is certain: from 1300 onwards the poetic material used for the public divine service was not significantly enriched. It was only those works dating from the end of the thirteenth until the middle of the fourteenth centuries that contributed significantly to the fixing of rites, systems and numerous customs. This particularly applies to the French, German and Italian communities. Some items that had remained flexible until that time became more rigid. For Germany, and, indirectly, for more distant countries, Meir of Rothenburg and his students constitute a point of departure. He himself was the author of סדר ברכות but works attributed to him that are entitled סדר,[176] ליקוטים and מנהגים,[177] whose relationship to each other is not yet clear, are the work of his followers. The book תשבץ written by Samson b. Ṣadoq in 1292[178] is also known as the מנהגי הר"ם and the manuscripts vary greatly with regard to its content, order and scope. As far as liturgical content is concerned, the works of Asheri, Mordechai and Maimoniot (by Meir Cohen), and even that of the Ṭur of Jacob ben Asher, likewise belong to that circle, at the centre of which stood Meir of Rothenburg. Individual items that also belong here are the notes of Pereṣ on the work of Isaac of Corbeil and his other writings, as well as Ḥayyim b. Isaac known as the Or Zaru‘a.

---

173 Kol Bo 4 (לקוטות), Jacob Levi Responsa 10.

174 Klausner 25b, 41b and in codex H h 249. Solomon Luria Responsa 7, 39 and יש"ש Qiddushin 15d. מטה משה §§ 764, 789. Israel Brünn Responsa 15.

175 תרומת הדשן 19. Tyrnau in his introduction and elsewhere, also in his notes. Codices Opp. 455O and 653O. Codices Michael 467, 854. Codex Vatican 45 no. 6. The Minhagim of ms. Vienna codex 75 no. 64, matching my codex 28, is perhaps that of Düren (see above p. 22), where the compiler is a student of a R. Isaac, and I take him to be Isaac of Düren.

176 Codex Michael 465. The סמק ms. from Zürich.

177 Michael 854. Codex Rossi 1131 no. 5 f. 25a-31a. Opp. 1476Q is תשבץ.

178 Aaron Ha-Kohen 5d at the top writes והר"ם כתב which is what we read in תשבץ § 217.

The ritual works of other areas at that time are informative in respect of the excerpts that they offer from older writings and the information they provide about the rites of their own day. In Spain one should take note of: Ḥiyya b.

P. 30

Solomon (around 1300) whose twenty-five "gates" deal with prayers, fasts, lectionaries and similar matters. In addition, Israel b. Joseph of Toledo wrote a work on ritual in Arabic with the title מצות זמניות[179] which was translated into Hebrew by Shemtov Arduṭil. Israel probably also dealt in a separate section with all the eventualities concerning the customary prayers for festivals. At the same time as Israel, Isaac Abuab[180] wrote a work on the ritual, comprehensively covering the whole year. It was in twelve sections under the title שלחן הפנים but, like his halakhic study ארון העדות, is no longer extant. All that has survived is his well-known work "Candelabrum" in which there are individual chapters that offer presentations on liturgical matters. A younger contemporary was Asher b. Ḥayyim of Monzon whose הפרדס dealt with the benedictions in ten sections and appended a digest about the customary usage. David Abudarham, who wrote in Seville in 1340, accompanied his explanation of the prayers with a description and definition of the rites. Meir Aldabi's שבילי אמונה was composed in Toledo in 1360 and most of its seventh section constitutes instruction about prayer, divine service and ethical behaviour. Menaḥem b. Aaron, who likewise lived in Toledo (1374), composed a comprehensive work in 400 chapters entitled "Ṣedah La-Derekh" which gave even more attention to the whole of the divine service. He attempted to justify halakhah and custom on theological and ethical grounds and each of his chapters concluded with a rhymed statement.

We are also in receipt of valuable works in this area from Rome and Provence. In addition to the occasional notes provided in the works of Isaiah of Trani, we should mention here Benjamin. b. Aaron, the well-known *seliḥah*-composer, in whose name a *Siddur*[181] is cited, and who wrote in 1301 סוד העבור that recorded the *hafṭarot* and the annual lectionaries. His brother Zedekiah accomplished even more with both his works, מעשה הגאונים (or ליקוטים)[182] and שבלי הלקט.

---

179 I have not located in the Calabrian ms. the two passages cited from that work by Abudarham 53b, 55a [ed. Prague 75d, 78a].

180 Appendix IV {below}.

181 Codex Sorbonne 102, margin.

182 חיבור in Jos{eph} Colon Responsa 20.

P. 31

The former, which is not actually devoted to the divine service, provides important extracts from Maḥzor Vitry, the writings of Rashi, geonic decisions, and the earlier מעשה הגאונים, and from correspondence with contemporaries, all of which are useful for the history of liturgical ritual. The latter is a work on ritual that deals with the divine service, two abstracts of which have been printed: 1) the so-called שבלי הלקט and 2) what is commonly called, because of how it begins, תניא,[183] but was earlier known as מנהג אבות or ס' המנהג. Both these works belong to the first half of the fourteenth century. We can allocate to that same period the book הנופך[184] which deals with the benedictions, and, from a little later, the book הנייר[185] which lists the norms of the older Italian synagogues. Moses b. Yequtiel of Rome composed his work התדיר in about 1380 and expressed the wish that it should always be available in the synagogues, although only a minimum of the ninety-three sections are by him and only the first third has content about liturgical ritual.

Aaron Ha-Kohen b. Jacob, who was expelled from his homeland of Provence in 1306 or 1320, wrote a book in Mallorca[186] that consists of two parts and is a comprehensive work on ritual called ארחות חיים and, as he himself notes, was for those who had no homeland and no books. The first part covers sixty sections which contain more than two thousand paragraphs on the whole area of divine worship; the second part[187] deals with miscellaneous matters, such as circumcision, mourning customs and other topics of Jewish law books that commonly occur in life. That work, of which Elijah Capsali sent a copy

183 Jos{eph} Colon Responsa 144. The short introduction (יתברך שם to ישעו) is copied with insignificant adjustments into the preface to the Roman *Maḥzor* (ed. 1486, 1521, 1540).
184 Cited in ס' הנייר, in the notes on the benedictions ms. Bisliches 61.
185 Mordechai Finzi in Steinschneider's *Catalogue of the Michael Library* p. 376, Joseph Colon 162, {Gedaliah ibn} Yaḥya 58a, Azulai part 2, p. 91.
186 Luzzatto in *Meged Yeraḥim* p. 6.
187 Citations from there by the author {Aaron Ha-Kohen} in the first part f. 4c § 25 (referring to the halakhah's of נדרים) and 36b [lacking in Kol Bo 24a]: ולמטה בהלכות אבל תמצא כל דין ברכת המזון לאבלים; also in Yeruḥam {Toledot Adam} 135a, Isaac b. Sheshet Responsa 95, 115,{Responsa Ohaley} Tam {of Jacob ibn} Yaḥya 164, Solomon Sedillo (זקן אהרן 209), Benjamin Ze'ev {Responsa} 159 [who calls it ס' האייל but had not himself seen it], Lampronti {פחד יצחק} entry כהן f. 50c.

P. 32

to Padua for printing more than three hundred years ago,[188] remains there, unpublished. The merits of that work lie in its method, richness {of content} and literal citation of sources. It was later abbreviated and altered for German use by Shemariah b. Simḥah, sometimes with a different sequence of sections, and named ספר הליקוטים.[189] Usually, however, it was called ספר כל בו because these two words appear in large print at the beginning of two Psalm verses and were placed in the first edition at the top of {the title-page in} the volume. In the fifteenth century it was still little known.[190] Aaron's book, which was written after the death of R. Asher (1327), was already cited by Yeruḥam[191] and the reputation that it enjoyed is attested by its citations by Isaac b. Sheshet,[192] Simeon Duran,[193] Abraham Zacut and others,[194] especially Joseph Karo. Also belonging to Provence is his contemporary Yeruḥam b. Meshullam, a disciple of Abraham b. Ishmael, who wrote אדם וחוה in Toledo in 1340, in which many sections are devoted to the ritual of the divine service. Perhaps the author of "the Short Manhig"[195] who cited the book המכתם is also to be sought in Provence.

Through that abundance of writings, the thirst for ritual instruction was to some extent quenched. At any rate, in Spain, France and Germany, at that time, spiritual activity was not attractive, and what they already had appears to have been sufficient. The available *Maḥzorim*, in which the prayers were well ordered and accompanied by regulations, but in which the sources were not always specified, achieved a kind of authority[196] and replaced the special

---

188 Compare Meir Padua Responsa 77 f. 86a with Luzzatto loc. cit. p. 73.

189 Responsa אבקת רוכל {of Joseph Karo} 13 f. 10b.

190 The compiler of the Maharil (42a) knows it only from a gloss [the same one that is cited in Benj{amin} Ze'ev Responsa 163]. The booklet שם הגדולים mentions the writer of the Kol Bo. The quotations in Benjamin Ze'ev 176, {Responsa Ohaley} Tam {of Jacob ibn} Yaḥya 35, the Romaniote *Maḥzor*, and in Tishbi (see entry סבר) and elsewhere are from the printed edition. See Note 3 {below}.

191 {Toledot Adam} 169a.

192 Responsa 146 [that is f. 8c, d].

193 Responsa 1, 111.

194 A Mordechai ms. that is 400 years old contains excerpts. Mentioned in {Abraham b. Solomon} ברכת אברהם 11b, Meir Padua loc. cit. [that is f. 9a], Solomon Luria 41c.

195 Solomon Duran 141.

196 Compare the expression מחזור מנהגי הקהלות (cod. Opp. 1484Q).

P. 33

works on ritual. They relied on the *Maḥzorim,*[197] especially the earlier *Maḥzorim*[198] and *Siddurim,*[199] but also at times rejected what was set down there.[200] Just as the content of the *Maḥzor* was formed from individual components, so it was inevitable that, as the material expanded, single parts of the prayers had books dedicated to them. Booklets[201] of *seliḥah*'s already appear in the twelfth century and someone at the time lent forty pfennings for such a collection. This was a large sum since the weekly rental of a horse cost six pfennings and three brothers needed only three pfennings for their daily bread, meat and wine.[202] There were also *Siddurim*[203] or *tefillot*[204] for the daily prayers, for *yoṣerot* and similar items, books of *hosha'not,*[205] and the *Maḥzorim* that specifically contained commentaries on the *qerovah* were also known as קרוב"ץ.[206] The Italian *Maḥzorim* usually contained the services for the whole year. The French[207] appear to have omitted from their *Maḥzor*

197 Commentary on Avot ch. 6 חמשה קנינים במחזורים (also in ms. A. 1441); ms. commentary on Avot ch. 5.3: בבא זו היא כתובה כך במחזורים שבברגויינא. Tos{efot} Pesaḥim 104b explaining the paragraph before נאמן אתה.

198 ס' הישר 144, codex H h 17. Opp. 1073F. Michael 656. Maḥkim MS, ס' קרובה {in} ms. Semaq from Zürich § 148. Aaron Ha-Kohen 64c.

199 קדמונים (המאור {of Zeraḥiah b. Isaac Ha-Levi} Yoma end, Yeruḥam {Toledot Adam} 12, 19, the vocaliser in סמ"ג command 19), ישנים (שבלי 95), זקנות (Aaron Ha-Kohen 100d, 108d); the expression זקן also refers to *Maḥzorim* and other books for the past 600 years or so, compare my *zur Geschichte* p. 203 note 1.

200 ראביה cited in Mordechai Berakhot 5 end, שבלי ms. § 143, Meir Rothenburg ברכות 2a, 9a.

201 קונטריסים, compare the expression קונטרס כעין ספרים שלנו in Responsa {לרמב"ן} המיוחסות no. 199. Isserlein פסקים 94.

202 ראב"ן 149b, 96d, 108d.

203 סדורים Naḥmanides מלחמות Rosh Ha-Shanah end, Isaac b. Abbamari cited by Aaron Ha-Kohen 100c, compare 106d; sometimes refers to the order of prayers, compare Ha-Manhig 12a § 34., 30b § 76; סדורי התפלות Aaron Ha-Kohen 11a, 21b, 100d, 108d, Jonah {b. Abraham} {התשובה} אגרת.

204 Mordechai Yoma, שבלי 16b, Aaron Ha-Kohen 100a § 8, Maharil Responsa 59.

205 Aaron Ha-Kohen 78b § 14.

206 Compare codices Rossi 405, 654, 812. H h 40b postscript; בקרובוץ Ephraim in codex H h 17; מצאתי בקרובץ (notes on Tyrnau 14a § 37); יסד קרובוץ (Maimoniot תפלה ch 6); מחזור של קרובוץ (in חדושי ש"ס ms. Beer in Dresden, section ע"ז).

207 המחזורים בצרפת cited by an Aaron Ha-Kohen in Bodleian codex 255; תפלות צרפתיות (מגן אבות in {Tashbeṣ} 4 f. 46a).

P. 34

the laments[208] and everything that related to fast-days. Incidentally, the Spanish, Italian and French *Maḥzorim* were written in octavo or even smaller formats, often in small script and elegant presentation. Thus, a French *Maḥzor*, which had 775 octavo folios, and which included all the festival services, as well as everything needed for the daily and Sabbath rites, could also contain: explanations of a large number of *piyyuṭim*, pentateuch and hagiogaphy, calendar, scribal rules, the grammatical poem of Rabbenu Tam, formulas, ritual regulations, decrees, a directory of halakhic teachers, and varia. Perhaps it is such volumes that are meant when we hear from France that boys carried home *Maḥzorim* from the synagogue.[209] The fact is that in Germany, with the exception of the *Siddurim* themselves which were available in smaller formats, there were also special collections that were written in quarto, or more usually in folio. When, however, the whole content of the divine service, the prayers and explanations, as well as matters relating to the rite and other inspiring and instructive materials, filled the *Maḥzor*, it was so much that it required a powerful arm to carry it. There are *seliḥah* manuscripts of two or three hundred folio pages and there are *Maḥzors* that have even more folio gatherings. One Vatican manuscript for the Day of Atonement has 264 folios, others that cover the whole year have no less than 347, 366, 375 and 432 folios. A Roman *Maḥzor* has over 500 and the Nürnberg *Maḥzor*, which contains none of the additions of Maḥzor Vitry, has 528 folios.

In contrast to those heavy and precious containers of the communal divine service, there were from that time onwards *Siddurim* of twelve-point or sixteen-point that represented domestic customs and that contained both piety and superstition: prayers for special devotions, counterfeit items, kabbalistic formulas and amulets, the invented names of angels and spirits, along with instructions for the use of Psalms for mundane purposes—all of which items, and similar ones, found refuge in the little *Siddurim*. In the course of time, some of these moved over to the common

P. 35

prayer-books and achieved a valuable status as part of the regular service. The scribes from the first quarter of the fourteenth century, who dealt with what they

208 The expression ספר קנות in תניא 83b seems incorrect; the word קנות on its own occurs in שבלי 89 f. 39 at the foot, ליקוטי הפרדס 17b, Ha-Pardes ms. and ed. 48a, Roqeaḥ 311.

209 Zürich Semaq ms.

called explanations of the prayers, favoured the mystical direction. Among them were Yehudah Romano and, even more so, the Spanish scholars such as Shemtov ibn Gaon, among whose writings there is a treatise on the devotions (כוונות) to be attached to the benedictions and prayers; Pereṣ Ha-Kohen, commentator on the *qaddish*; Samuel Moṭot, who enthused about the Sefira's and was even acquainted with the ten devilish Sefira's that were opposed to the divine versions. He refers the first benediction of the *tefillah* to the Sefira's, the second to the planets, and his interpretation proceeds along those lines. The similar works of Menaḥem of Recanati display the same spirit. For him, the kabbalistic works that were completed in the thirteenth century, especially the Zohar, have an even greater authority. Even those who remained untouched by the Kabbala had an awe of those books, and of their content that is included in the ritual. In 1480, Jacob Landau engages in all seriousness with the zoharic rulings, considering them to be the sayings of a mishnaic teacher. A contemporary, Joseph b. Shraga, drowns the passage אל מל יושב in kabbala.

Because of the persecutions of 1349 in Germany, all mental activity was ruined for a long time. In the second half of that century, some Austrian rabbis collected together Minhagim, which were poor when compared with the Maḥzor Vitry or the works of Aaron Ha-Kohen. Abraham Klausner's Minhagim belong to this genre; the author lived in Vienna in 1380. Dated somewhat later is the minor material of Shalom b. Isaac in Neustadt which was compiled by his grandson, Joseph b. Nehemiah. Also dating from that period are the "little Mordechai" by Samuel Schlettstadt and the supplements to the Semaq by Moses of Zürich,[210] in which individual items belong to this treatment. Another work belonging to that period was the commentary on

P. 36

the daily prayers that takes account of the German and French rites. At that time, Lipman of Mühlhausen wrote an explanation of the Song of Unity and stood up for prayers that were being attacked. A fair number of collections containing Minhagim[211] were the forerunners of two works that were disseminated in the first half of the fifteenth century and gradually became codes for the German and Polish communities, namely, the Minhagim of 1) Isaac Tyrnau and 2) Jacob Mölln Levi. The

210 Appendix V {below}.

211 Codex H h 37 (around 1428), codex H h 249 (from the year 1438), codex R. 1033 no. 1, 1131 no. 1, 392 no. 5.

former provides items of prayer and the synagogal arrangements for all the days of the year. The latter originates in what was known as the "Maharil", a cypher for the name of the Rabbi who died in Worms in 1427. His way of life, his teachings, his essays[212] and his assessments provided his disciples with material for a variety of collections concerning ritual. One of these, edited by his son, is extant in Turin,[213] another is to be found in the Michael Collection,[214] and there are also various other extracts.[215] A work related to these called the "Short Manhig" consists of 143 paragraphs and was composed in 1449. It constitutes the order of prayers according to the German rite, beginning with Nisan and ending with calendrical rules. The actual printed "Maharil"[216] is the redaction done by his pupil, Zalman of St Goar, who collected the material during the lifetime of his teacher, and edited it probably around 1450. Around 1470, Moses Mintz[217] of Bamberg drew up a guide for prayer-leaders, and in Italy ten years later Jacob {b. Judah} Landau wrote the book האגור that transmitted some details about the German, French and Italian rites; he knew of the expert opinions of the Maharil but not

P. 37

the Minhagim.[218] Around 1500, and from then even as late as 1550, the work of Isaac Tyrnau was provided with annotations, called הגהות or ליקוטים, some of which were drawn from manuscript sources.[219]

From the time of Isaac b. Sheshet, the Spanish authors no longer gave much attention to ritual works, and at an even earlier date they were little concerned with commentaries, which their poetry did not require. At best, they dealt with the interpretation of some of the older *piyyuṭim* with halakhic content. Moses Tibbon and

---

212 His {prayer-}order for the special three-day fasts in the year 1420 were in the possession of Jacob Weil (Responsa 157).

213 Codex 102 f. 50. The notations of his son—Maharil had two sons: Simeon and Jäkel—are cited by Benjamin Ha-Levi (for Ḥanukkah) in the so-called מעגלי צדק{*Maḥzor*}.

214 Codices 370 and 371.

215 Codices Uffenbach 102, Rossi 1213 and 1421; probably also codex Uri 283 (compare Wolf {*Bibliotheca*} 3, p. 85, where the reading should be corrected from 1578 to 5187).

216 Called נימוקים (Manhig § 5, 72), קובץ (Benjamin Ha-Levi loc. cit. before Purim), מנהגים של אשכנז (Jacob Levi Responsa 82).

217 Responsa 81.

218 Compare האגור {of Jacob b. Judah Landau} §§ 745 and 746 with Maharil 23b; § 768 with ibid. 11b top.

219 עץ חיים (16a), מהרי"ש (14a), Rulings by Menaḥem (8b, 9b), Israel Brünn (4a, 14b), Jacob of Nordhausen (15b), and a few times in the Semaq from Zürich.

Simeon Duran expounded Gabirol's *Azharot* and later also the *hosha'nas* and some other older pieces, perhaps from [ibn] Abiṭur;[220] David Abudarham [dealt similarly with] an Elijah song and with a *seliḥah*; and Perifot Duran a *silluq* by Ibn Ezra. Ḥayyim Galipapa,[221] as well as Sheshet, the father of Isaac,[222] wrote interpretations of the Spanish *'avodah*'s. The decisions of Simeon Duran[223] here and there touch on the divine service and he is also cited as the author of a book of "Minhagim".[224] There is a similar work by Maimon b. Sa'adya Nagar[225] in Constantine. There are extant copies in manuscript of the ritual work and liturgical commentary of Joseph b. Ṣaddiq in Old Castilian; a digest of the Ṭur by Samuel Even Shoshan; and a work entitled המאסף or אגרת הטעמים by a Spanish author. The last-mentioned, who was also in Saragossa, and was perhaps an elder contemporary of Simeon Duran, provided short expositions of liturgical procedures and the content of prayers for the whole year, primarily in accordance with the guidance in Yeruḥam's work.[226] The volume צרור הכסף by the Lisbon-born Abraham Seba, which was located in Fez, included among other items sections

P. 38

on prayer, festive days, tefillin, circumcision, and mourning rites. Of an earlier date is that part about ritual that was printed in the Maḥzor Roma and in Pesaro (no date) and in later editions with alterations.

220 He is probably the Simeon in codex Rossi 655 where the סדרים of Abitur also occur.
221 What I speculated in 1836 (*Analecta*, no. 1, Yose b. Yose), was confirmed in 1856 (קובץ ed. Berlin p. 118).
222 See עבודת ישראל of Israel Qimḥi.
223 Part 2, no. 248, part 3, nos. 184, 197, 247, 282, 290, 320. Compare Solomon Duran Responsa 606.
224 Abraham Ṭawa Responsa 32.
225 קונטריס המנהגות (Solomon Duran 329).
226 Codex Michael 204 no. 2.

Pp. 38–58

P. 38

The development of the liturgical ritual at the threshold of the modern period requires closer attention. The basic prayers, as transmitted by the Talmud and the Geonim, generally accord with Amram's *Siddur* in all the rites. But sometimes the rite of that *Siddur* matches the Roman one, and sometimes the German or Spanish ones, concerning the place of the Psalms and *barukh she'amar*, and with regard to individual phrases and sentences. Several details of Sa'adya's *Siddur* were preserved in the rites of {North-}Africa, Greece and Crete, as well as in those of Provence and Rome. The most pronounced differences are to be found within the festival prayers, the group of rites in the Islamic world preserving only little of the older *piyyuṭ* and *pizmon*, and only a few individual places preserving the ancient *hosha'na*'s.

That group knows nothing of the poetic *ma'ariv* or *yoṣer*, nor of the *qerovah*, for the three festival days, or for any other special Sabbaths, nor of any Aramaic decorations for Pesaḥ or Pentecost, nor does it know anything about the historical *zulat* and dirges. It does, however, record poetic services for the nights of New Year, for Sabbath eve during the Week of Repentance, and for the Sabbaths between the two fast-days of the Seventeenth of Tammuz and the Ninth of Av. Furthermore, it has an ample supply of *teḥinnah*'s, and of *piyyuṭim* for *nishmat*, *me'ora*, *ahavah* and *ge'ulah*, and an artistic *ma'amad* for the Day of Atonement. The rituals of Rome and Greece also have a *qerovah* for a fast-day.

By way of contrast, the early *piyyuṭim*, with finely fixed structure, and the *seliḥah* in a variety of formats, fill the service of the German-Romaniote group. While in that rite one finds more poetry, here in the Islamic world there is more {midrashic} aggadah. But in the course of time these basic elements fused, with persecution dirges coming to Fez, while metrical lyrics were adopted in Orleans. In certain places, parts of different rites were absorbed into a new ritual format. Some rites, like the communities to which they belonged, disappeared altogether, or formed new branches

P. 39

that subsequently blossomed or withered away. Although names of rites are borrowed from the countries where they originated it should not be assumed that all parts of that country followed the same rite. In the Middle Ages, the borders of states were often casual, liable to change, and unable to exercise any dominant influence, so that regions that were far from each other followed the same rite while those that were closer together may have differed. That is why such pairs as Algiers and Tlemcen, Toledo and Seville, Montpellier and Carpentras, Paris and Maçon, Mainz and Worms, Vienna and Prague have often followed different prayers and customs.

The Spanish, or more correctly the Castilian, rite preserved the purest form of those in the Islamic world. It remained simple and self-consistent within its various parts, and independent of the prolific poets. Questions from Spain were addressed to Naṭronai Gaon, and Amram sent his *Siddur* there, namely, to Meir ben Joseph and Isaac ben Simeon. There are items in the daily prayers that conform, or once conformed, to that *Siddur*, for example, the conclusion of the Torah-benediction,[1] the text of *barukh she'amar*, the reading ריבם לאבות ובנים (in עזרת), the composition of the sections ותן טל ומטר and ולמשומדים in the *tefillah* and the concluding recitations of אין כאלוהינו and פטום הקטרת. Individual elements in the *tefillah* are a combination of Amram, Sa'adya, Maimonides and the German rite. In the case of other sections there are changes that obviously occurred in the course of time, as with prayers that precede *barukh she'amar*,[2] and also the הודו, which is absent from Amram's *Siddur*. The version רצון קונהם (not קונם) in the morning prayer[3] is based on a very old textual variant. Among noteworthy phenomena to be listed are the absence of

p. 40

אדון עולם; the replacement of מה טובו with ואני ברוב (Ps 5:8) on entering the synagogue; the recitation of מוריד הטל in the second *tefillah* benediction. The *qaddish* reads as in Maimonides—without ויפרוק עמיה. On Sabbath eve, והוא רחום is recited exactly as on a weekday[4] and the Mishnah במה מדליקין is inserted before *ma'ariv* proper.[5] אתה הראית[6] occurs when the Torah is brought out, and למשה צוית is recited in *musaf*, as in Maimonides. At *minḥhah* on the Sabbath there is only Ps 111, on the evening of the New Moon Ps 104, and in the *musaf* for the New Moon one passage[7] is identical

1 Ha-Manhig 9b: על דברי תורה as Amram (also in the prayer books). Elsewhere in Spain the benediction concluded with either לעסוק or נותן; compare Aaron Ha-Kohen 5b § 12.
2 The priestly blessing (Aaron Ha-Kohen ad loc.) and a piece of the New Year *tefillah* precede the section from Tamid, the last-mentioned of which is described only by Amram ms., and by Maimoniot as the Spanish order.
3 See {p. 181} note 4 {below}.
4 Ha-Manhig 22b, 23b.
5 Ṣedah La-Derekh 4, 1, 5.
6 Ha-Manhig 27a § 24.
7 Beginning: ויהיה יום החדש.

with that of Sa'adya's *Siddur*. The simple character of this rite is demonstrated in the intensive use of the Psalms on the Day of Atonement and the Ninth of Av, in the removal of the Targum, and of יקום פורקן on the Sabbath, and in the use of some identical phrases for weekday and Sabbath. Only two Sabbaths are distinguished by the recitation of some pieces of Yehudah Halevi's poetry: his *mikhamokha* on the Sabbath before Purim and his *azharot* on the Great Sabbath. For other Sabbaths there is no *piyyuṭ*, nor is there any *qerovah* for New Year or the three Pilgrim Festivals. Poetic pieces, as for example for the evening of New Year, and for the prayer for Ṭal {dew} etc., are never too long. The cantor has his place on the almemar. It is also reported that during the *qedushah* in Spain one has to look downwards while in France and Germany upwards.[8] It is specially reported of Toledo that Psalms were recited at the end of every morning service, and רצה only at the *minḥah tefillah* on a fast day.[9] In Seville, as in Toledo, one completed *ma'ariv* for the Sabbath as on a weekday, said במה מדליקין after *ma'ariv*, and הודו only on the Sabbath and at a circumcision, while the prayer רבון העולמים לא אל is wholly absent.[10] In both places איזהו מקומן is omitted when prayers are recited in a house of mourning.[11] At a later date[12] it is reported that in Seville meat was not consumed during the mourning period. In the sixteenth century there was a congregation from

p. 41

Cordova in Constantinople,[13] and one from Lorca in Magnesia.[14]

The first information conveyed about the rite of Aragon is that the children sat on low stone benches in the synagogue.[15] In Saragossa and Fraga, the *musaf tefillah* on New Year was not recited first by the congregation alone but loudly together with the cantor. The ignorance of most of the congregation is given as the reason for this omission. *Avinu malkenu* was recited also on the Sabbath and *'alenu* was prayed aloud.[16] In addition, it was reported from Saragossa that אל מלך נאמן was

---

8 Ha-Manhig 16b [Aaron Ha-Kohen 18b], Ṭur I 125.
9 Ha-Manhig 20b, 17b.
10 Ṭur I 267, Abudarham 31d, 33c, 14b.
11 Ibid. 85c.
12 See Lampronti {פחד יצחק} entry מנהג f. 136b.
13 El{ijah} Mizraḥi, Responsa 13.
14 אבקת רוכל {of Joseph Karo} 206.
15 Sol{omon} Adret Responsa, section 2, no. 52.
16 Isaac b. Sheshet Responsa 37, 512.

never recited[17] and that משיב הרוח was included only after the 24 November:[18] from about 1350 the book of Esther was recited in Spanish for the women on Purim.[19] Qalir's *piyyuṭ* must have been used there, at least on the Four Sabbaths.[20] When there were two Torah readings, *qaddish* was recited after each;[21] the same applied in Morocco. In some places in Aragon there was a communal hut {=*sukkah*} on Tabernacles.[22]

Catalonia was once closely connected with the south of France. Consequently there could later be a discussion as to whether Gershom's decrees for Germany and France also applied to Catalonia.[23] The essential Spanish rite had much in common with that of Provence, and occasionally matched that of France, as, for instance, with the recitation of pieces of Qalir's poetry.[24] On Friday afternoon, *qaddish* was inserted between the silent and publicly recited *tefillah* at *minḥah*.[25] When the Torah Scroll was taken out on the Sabbath אשרי was also sung before גדלו, and the Torah scroll was displayed after the words הכל תנו עז.[26] On the intermediate Sabbath of a festival the *hafṭarah* benediction concluded with השבת,

p. 42

while in Toledo and elsewhere ישראל והזמנים was added.[27] In Barcelona, as also in Mallorca, only one *qaddish* was intoned after the Torah reading; a concluding *barekhu* was recited for latecomers only at the evening prayers for Sabbath and festivals.[28] On the evening of Purim and at the morning service on the Ninth of Av ובא לציון was customary,[29] but neither of these occurs in the Spanish rite. On Tabernacles the final הודו is repeated;[30] the *hafṭarah* of the Torah Festival is the same

17 Aaron Ha-Kohen 27d.
18 Simeon Duran, Responsa, section 3, no. 123.
19 *Gott{esdienstlichen} Vortr{äge}*, p. 413.
20 Ḥasdai (אור ה' 2, 6, 2) is aware of one item for Shabbat Parah.
21 Isaac b. Sheshet, Responsa 321.
22 Aaron Ha-Kohen 111d, Kol Bo 80a, compare Ha-Manhig 64a.
23 David b. Zimra, Responsa, ed. Livorno no. 95 {actually 94}.
24 Ibn Shuaib {דרשות} 45c.
25 Kol Bo 35, beginning.
26 Aaron Ha-Kohen 22b.
27 מצות זמניות {of Israel b. Joseph} ms.
28 Isaac b. Sheshet Responsa 321, 334.
29 Aaron Ha-Kohen, 120c, 96a.
30 Simeon Duran, Responsa section 2, no. 205.

as that of Spain.[31] At a circumcision, the circumciser used to say all the benedictions, which was not the case in Toledo.[32] In Barcelona, *avinu malkenu* was never said on Sabbath, nor on the Day of Atonement. The only exception to this was in Gerona[33] where there was also a custom on the closing eve of the Day of Atonement for everyone to take a light when leaving the synagogue.[34] There, on the Sabbath, no more than seven people were ever called to the Torah.[35] We learn incidentally that seats in the synagogue were sold.[36]

The Catalonian rite for New Year is as follows: On the preceding Sabbath two poetic pieces by Pinḥas Ha-Levi—*azharot* concerning the shofar and a *pizmon*—were recited together with the accompanying verses. The evening service of the festrival is identical to that of the later Spanish rite. On the morning of the first day the following items occur: 1) *Reshut* יעלה by Yehudah, 2) *Moḥarakh* רעה by Moses ben Ezra; 3) *Nishmat* ידידי עליון, 4) *Qaddish* יה שמך, 5) *Ofan* ידי רשים, 6) *Zulat* אלהי מעשיו, 7) *Qerovah* אתה כוננתנו, all by Yehudah Ha-Levi, the last one interrupted by 8) *Pizmon* ירצה צור Yehudah, 9) *Mostejab* מלך שדי by Gabirol, 10) *Seliḥah* מלאך שמך by Yehudah, 11) *Mostejab* חסדי ה' by Ibn Ezra. After ואתה קדוש יושב there follow: 12) יוצר רום Isaac, 13) שני ימים Solomon [for the Sabbath], 14) *Mostejab* לאדיר נורא Solomon, 15) *Tokheḥah* אם חסדך שכחנו Moses ben Ezra, 16) *Pizmon*

p. 43

יעלו לאלף Yehudah Ha-Levi, 17) Hymn אדירי ישורון Isaac ben Yehudah, 18) *Silluq* יראי ה' הללוהו Yehudah Ha-Levi, which completes the *qerovah*. With the exceptions of numbers 2, 12, 13, 15, the same sections are in the rite of Aragon, which recites numbers 3 and 4 on the second day. The relationship between the rite of Avignon and those of Algiers, Tunis and Tlemcen is shown in the following table:

Avignon	*2.3.4.*5.6.7.8.13.17.18	[The asterisked items are recited on the second day.]
Algiers	1.2.3.*4.5.6.7.8.13.16.17.18	
Tunis	1.2.3.5.7.8.16.*17.18	
Tlemcen	1.2.3.4.5.6.7.8.16.17.18	

31 Aaron Ha-Kohen 26c.

32 Asher {b. Ḥayyim} Pardes ms.

33 Isaac b. Sheshet Responsa 512. Aaron Ha-Kohen 107a.

34 Abudarham.

35 Simeon Duran Responsa, section 2, no. 70.

36 Sol{omon} Aderet Responsa section 4 no. 319.

On the second day of New Year, the *Maḥzor* contains the following pieces: 1) *Baqashah* אלהי אל תדינני, 2) *Reshut* שואף Gabirol, 3) *Moḥarakh* מי יתנני Yehudah Ha-Levi, 4) *Nishmat* ישורון יום זה Isaac Ha-Levi, 5) *Ofan* חרדו רעיוני Ibn Ezra, 6) *Zulat* שב מן הפסילים Solomon Gerondi, 7) *Qerovah* אדר היקר Joseph; these are interrupted by 8) *Pizmon* יום לריב Levi, 9) המלך ה' רום, 10) מחסי לשחר Moses ben Ezra, 11) עת שערי רצון Maimonides, 12) *Mostejab* אמיץ גוזר, 13) *Pizmon* ה' אלהיכם לכל Isaac, 14) *Mostejab* תקע בשופר, 15) *Tokheḥah* יגדל נא חסדך, 16) Hymn מלאכי צבא Moses, 17) *Silluq* לך יאתה Isaac. The Aragon rite, which has numbers 1 and 4 on the first day, also omits here {on the second day} four numbers (3, 5, 9, 15), as well as the *moḥarakh* and the *tokheḥah* on both days. The relationship to the four previously mentioned rites is obvious from the following table:

Avignon	*1.*2.*3.*5	[The asterisked items are recited on the second day.]
Algiers	*1.2.3.6.8.11.13.16.17	
Tunis	*1.2.3.8.*10.*11.*12.13.*14.15.*16.17	
Tlemcen	*1.2.3.6.*8.*9.*11.13.16.17	

The Catalonian *qerovah* is replaced in these rites with other pieces, as may also be said about the *zulat* and other items in the rite of Avignon. Some {Catalonian} items have been completely eliminated as, for example, the *zulat* in Tunis, and the *tokheḥah* in Tlemcen and Algiers. The Catalonian rite does not have any poetic pieces for *musaf* of the {New Year} festival, and this also applies to the other four rites, with the exception of Avignon. The *pizmon* texts for the [shofar] blowing are: 1) קול שופר הדרור, 2) ה' בקול שופר, and this order is reversed in the Aragon and

p. 44

other rites. Both of these texts are replaced by others, the first in Avignon, and the second in Tunis.

The Castilian communities, which in early times celebrated both evenings of New Year with many poetic texts, have only the two pieces by Yehudah Ha-Levi (nos. 4 and 5 {listed above} for the first day) for the daytime worship. Some individual communities also add no. 2 of the first day{'s list} and nos. 1 and 2 of the second day, as well as שופט כל. Poems recited on the second day were שפל רוח, the *baqashah* ה' יום לך, and, in later editions, also the *pizmon* למענך אלהי by David and יענה כבר. In the Spanish rite—except in some later materials—one finds among the poetry only המלך ה' רום (no. 9).

The Jewish community on the island of Mallorca, which was linked with Provence and Catalonia,[37] represented a midway point for Jews fleeing from those communities to North Africa, and their rite must therefore have been Catalonian-{North-}African. In the capital city, where they were permitted only one synagogue, there were more than a thousand families who had originated in Catalonia, Provence and France, and owned more than sixty Torah scrolls.[38] One later community converted to Christianity;[39] one established itself in Tenes, west of Algiers.[40] With regard to the basic prayers, we learn that, after הודו, they also added ה' מלך (Spanish), and that the ending of the benediction ישתבח—as well as that of *barukh she'amar*—read מלך מהולל,[41] which occurs in R. Azriel and matches only the rite of Rome.[42] There too, following the ruling of Shemtov Falcon (ca. 1350), no more than seven people were called on the Sabbath to the Torah reading.[43] The text ארור המן, which is prescribed in tractate Soferim, was omitted on Purim eve and ויהי נועם and ויתן לך were also not recited when Purim occurred on Saturday evening.[44] On the seventh day of Pesaḥ ישמחו השמים was skipped.[45]

p. 45

At the conclusion of the Day of Atonement, when it fell on the Sabbath,[46] they did not recite ויהי נועם (Spanish) and the *qedushah* in ובא לציון. Similarly, they also omitted on the eve of such a Sabbath במה מדליקין[47] and during the day the first verse of Ps 92.[48] {In this rite} the last הודו of *hallel* was not repeated and בגלל אבות was not usually said on the Torah Festival.[49] The other observations transmitted by Aaron Ha-Kohen[50] are more a reflection of the statements made by the books of

37 Compare the document in החלוץ 1, pp. 33, 34, and my *Geschichte {und Literatur}*, p. 523f.
38 Simeon Duran Responsa section 1, 51, sections 3, 5 and 30.
39 Ibid. section 3, no. 227, compare section 2, no. 225.
40 Ibid. section 3, no. 46.
41 Aaron Ha-Kohen 6a § 19, § 38.
42 Other textual readings are: מלך גדול (Amram, Sa'adya), אל מלך גדול (French, German), האל המלך גדול (Romaniote), מלך גדול ומהולל (Spain, Aragon, Avignon, compare Abudarham).
43 Solomon Duran Responsa 429; Notes on Simeon Duran Responsa, section 2, no. 70.
44 Aaron Ha-Kohen 120c § 31.
45 Simeon Duran section 2 no. 246.
46 Aaron Ha-Kohen 108ab.
47 Ibid. 106c.
48 Simeon Duran section 2 no. 248.
49 Ibid., section 2 no. 205. Aaron Ha-Kohen 26c § 58.
50 80cd (Pesaḥ evening), 77d (*hallel*), 99c § 3 (New Year evening), 26 a d, 27 a b ({Torah} readings).

ritual rather than based on any special usage of Mallorca. On the other hand, one may consider, as common usage there, other prayers mentioned by him, such as the verses said by the priests, a short grace after meals, and the insertions made in that prayer on special occasions, the communal prayer מצלאין, and a few others.

The rite of Provence, which in some individual respects[51] matches that of Spain, is in its whole poetic structure identical to that of Catalonia. There is, however, an influence by French elements in parts of the basic prayers[52] as well as in the custom of reciting חזק at the conclusion of each of the pentateuchal books[53] and the order of the צדקתך verses at *minḥah* on the Sabbath. When Purim falls on Sunday, in most places {in Provence} the Fast of Esther is observed on Friday,[54] while elsewhere and in Catalonia this occurs on the preceding Thursday. In the Haggadah of Passover evening it was common to add אמרו כשירד, which apparently originated in Sa'adya's *Siddur* but was omitted in other places. Qohelet was still recited in the leaf-covered hut {=*sukkah*} on the Eighth Day of Tabernacles.[55] The daily prayer for rain began there in the month of Ḥeshwan. In Narbonne or Lunel the order of Tovelem appears to have been common.[56] In Narbonne all seven people called to the Torah remained on the *bimah*

p. 46

and, following the {Torah} reading, the one most honoured was given the task of rolling the scroll.[57] Other common customs of that place are found in {the works of} Abraham of Lunel and Aaron Ha-Kohen. In a British Museum manuscript (14761), which can be ascribed to the rite of Provence, there is a *ṭal-qerovah* for Pesaḥ which seems older than that of Gabirol and the *hafṭarot* have the Targum for each verse. The *mikhamokhah* is by Yehudah Halevi, the *nishmat* by Joseph ben Isaac and Isaac, a *yoṣer* by Menaḥem, and the *ofan* מידך יה by Naḥmanides. The well-known poem פסח מצרים אסירי יצאו follows the Haggadah in accordance with the rites of France and Avignon. The cycle of prayers in other manuscripts preserves a Provençal rite that appears to have belonged to Montpellier. Just as in Avignon and Algiers, the Sabbath and festival in Montpellier were adorned with *reshut*, *nishmat*, *qaddish*, as well as

51 Ha-Manhig חול §§ 15, 19, 21, 56, 66; שבת 21; ר"ה 9, 23 [the second occurrence of the word בצרפת f. 55b line 9 should be corrected to בספרד]; י"כ 57; סכות 53; פסח 89.
52 Ibid. חול §§ 54, שבת 2, 4, 8, 42, 60, 62, ר"ה 5, 7.
53 Ibid. שבת 57.
54 Aaron Ha-Kohen 94b, 120b. In Kol Bo 45 f. 45d: בארצות הללו.
55 Ha-Manhig סכה 57.
56 Ibid. פסח 12, compare §§ 58, 67, 78, 83.
57 אבן העזר 80a.

yoṣer and *ofan* up to *mikhamokhah.* There is a *qerovah* for the Four Sabbaths and, according to one manuscript, also for the Sabbath before the Ninth of Av, as well as for the dew and rain prayers, and for New Year. The Great Sabbath and the Sabbaths before and after New Year have *azharot.* In addition to including the ancient payyeṭanim and the Spanish poets, the compositions of Provence and Catalonia made a special contribution to the festival prayers of this rite.

As is obvious from the following compilations on the Feast of Weeks, which are documented in two manuscripts belonging to Provence and in a printed edition of the *Maḥzor* of Algiers, the relationship—or if you like—the identical nature of Provence and Catalonia concerning the festival rite was replanted in Africa.

Ms. A

(First day)

1.	*Reshut*	יום מעמד סיני
2.	——	ישן ולבו ער
3.	——	צור לבבי ומעריצי
4.	*Moḥarakh*	דת אלהים
5.	*Nishmat*	יונה השוחרת
6.	*Qaddish*	שחק כדק
7.	——	מי יוכל בסוד
8.	*Barekhu*	שם אלהי צבאות
9.	*Yoser*	ישוב לאחור צל
10.	——	יומם ולילה
11.	*Ofan*	אבות קדושים
12.	*Me'orah*	השכל והדת
13.	——	ים סוף וסיני
14.	*Ahavah*	נודע בכל המון
15.	——	אל יגלה לעיני
16.	——	ירשו למצער
17.	*Zulat*	ודעי יגוני

p. 47

(Second day)

18.	*Reshut*	יעירוני בשמך
19.	*Nishmat*	יחידים זרע
20.	——	ישורון מטיף
21.	*Qaddish*	אודה לאל לבש
22.	*Ofan*	אדון בעזו
23.	——	יה אנה אמצאך
24.	——	יקר אדון
25.	*Me'orah*	צורי עון מריי
26.	*Ahavah*	אם תאהב
27.	——	יונה מה תהני
28.	——	זהב זהב זהב
29.	*Ge'ulah*	אמון יום זה
30.	*Introduction of Azharot*	שולמית שחרחורת
31.	—— *Prohibitions*	ארחות תושיה
32.	*Pizmon*	יום יצאה כלת
33.	*Pizmon*	שוכן עד גאלנו
34.	*Fetching the Torah*	שובה אלהי שבות
35.	*Shalom*	יחיד שוכן בזבולך

Ms. B	Algiers
1.	1.
4.	4.
19.	12.
6.	19.
11.	[39]
12.	26.

14.		*Barekhu*	[41] נעים שמך
Ahavah	[36] אל בדתך	*Zulat*	[42] אומר לצפון
15.		[40]	
17.		*Pizmon*	[43] בצור מנוסי
30.		30.	
32.		32.	
Reshut	[37] ידידי השכחת	18.	
	[38] ישיבוני סעיפי	*Moḥarakh*	[44] אל אלהים נצחי
20.		20.	
Qaddish	[39] קול מהלל	*Me'ora*	[45] כימי הנעורים
22.		*Barekhu*	[46] עם בחרתם
25.		[36]	
9.		*Ge'ulah*	[47] ישעך אקו
26.		*Pizmon*	[48] אלה מתימן by Simeon Duran
28.		6.	
16.			
29.			
Azharot-Introd.	[40] אמת עלי		
33.			

The two manuscripts share Gabirol's *Azharot*, as well as twenty items. Manuscript A has *reshut* 37 for the first day of the Festival of Pesaḥ. The edition of the Algerian *Maḥzor*, in which there are evidently omissions, have no more than twenty-one items, with ten of them from the first manuscript and three from the second one. With the exception

p. 48

of some idiosyncrasies, the rite of Avignon, where the community was established in the twelfth century[58] and had six synagogues[59] 300 years ago, belongs to the family of the Provence rite. Since the daily worship of the Spanish rite is not significantly different, the similarity of the grace after the meals to that of the Romaniote *Maḥzor* is noteworthy. Perhaps it derives from Saadya's *Siddur*, in a similar way to כמו שנכון etc. in the New Moon *tefillah* and the נהודך in *barukh she'amar*, which Maimonides also has. Amram's *Siddur* matches מושך etc. in אמת ויציב and the well-known additions after the final benediction of the evening prayer—these and various other items are characteristic of the French rite. These include: אהבת עולם in the morning prayer, the version of *barukh she'amar*, עושה שלום at the end of the

58 Ṣedah La-Derekh 1, 1, 36. *Archives Isr{aélites}* 1840 p. 533, compare Ha-Manhig 31b, 73b.
59 Bartol{occi} *Biblioth{eca}* vol. 3, p. 757.

grace after meals, יקום פורקן—actually only one—on the Sabbath, תכנת in the *tefillah*, fifteen Psalms before נשמת (fourteen in the German rite, sixteen in the French rite). Idiosyncrasies include the benediction סומך נופלים, the regular use of שלום רב instead of שים שלום in the *tefillah*, the expression הגבור והנורא instead of הקדוש in the New Moon *tefillah* (אתה יצרת), the benediction שנתן ריח טוב בפירות in the *havdalah*, the addition ועל ירושלם עירך after ופרוס עלינו at the end {sc. on the eve}of the Sabbath, and the text of the רצה benediction of the *tefillah*[60] that is cited in Wa-Yiqra Rabba {7.2}[61]

Special Sabbaths are celebrated on Friday evenings with poetic stanzas, which either precede the prayers or are part of their liturgical function. On festival days, sections of the prayers on the one hand and synagogue rituals on the other are framed by short poems, which derive from larger pieces or have been compiled from them. Although the character of the festival liturgy is that of the Provence, the content of that rite has been influenced by that of Spain, as well as Provence, because at least forty poets, whose names are known to us, have embellished the Avignon rite.

p. 49

This is the only rite in the Spanish group that has poetic *teqiata*'s for New Year. On the Feast of Weeks the text ארעא רקדא, also known in the French rite, precedes the recitation of the Jerusalem Targum. In the morning Gabirol's *Azharot* are read and in the afternoon those of Isaac Qimḥi. With the exception of *silluq*, the other pieces of *qerovah* poetry are placed after the *tefillah*. A comparison with the Provence rite provides the following table of poems for the last two days of the Pesaḥ festival.

	Ms. B		Algiers		
1.	*Reshut*	יקרה תהלתך	1.		
2.		למתי זרוע	17.		
3.	*Moḥarakh*	אומן פלאך	4.		
4.	*Nishmat*	ישראל עמך להללך	אתה נורא אתה		[28]
5.	Before ואילו פינו	משל בגאות הים	שבעה שחקים		[29]
6.	*Qaddish*	שעה ניב דל	7.		
7.	*Ofan*	יחיד בגאונו	*Barekhu*	השתחוו וברכי	[30]
8.	*Me'orah*	נאוה בעז	12.		

60 173b.
61 In more detail in my *Ritus {der Synagoge} von Avignon*.

9.	———		*Reshut*	שרש בנו	[31]
10.	*Ahavah*	יפה נוף	*Mokh.*	נגדך אשים	[32]
11.	*Zulat*	אז ישיר ינון	*Ofan*	יה שכינתך	[33]
12.	*Ge'ulah*	יום ליבשה	*Nishmat*	שזופת שמש	[34]
13.	*Mikhamokhah*	מי אשש	*Qaddish*	אל תשמח גילי	[35]
14.	*Shalom*	קוראים בלבב	*Me'orah*	כל פה צח	[36]
15.	*Reshut*	בצר פקדנוך	*Barekhu*	זמירות אפצחה	[37]
16.	———	גלילי זבול	*Ahavah*	אהבה נוססה	[38]
17.	*Moḥarakh*	כל הנשמה	*Ge'ulah*	אם יום פדותי	[39]
18.	*Nishmat*	יפת עלמות	———	כל ימי צבאי	[40]
19.	*Qaddish*	אודה לאל לבש	*Zulat*	תביאמו ותטעמו	[41]
20.	*Ofan*	שמים מספרים			
21.	*Me'orah*	אשפיל לך			
22.	———	הסתיו ארח			
23.	*Ahavah*	הידעתם ידידי			
24.	———	מה תספרו			
25.	*Zulat*	אחד עשר			
26.	*Ge'ulah*	צור המקורא			
27.	———	ידעתי חי			

p. 50

Avignon

16.			[31]		
Reshut	שחר לך אשפוך	[42]	*Reshut*	יריעות שלמה	[59]
——	ייטב להודות	[43]	——	נשמה שנתת	[60]
17.			*Moḥ.*	רוח ששוני	[61]
Moḥ.	נוצר ונבצר	[44]	——	יעלז כבודי	[62]
——	אשכר יקר	[45]	——	הלל תהלל	[63]
Nishmat	ישורן ישורר	[46]	——	תנו שיר	[64]
6.			*Nishmat*	שארית עדת	[65]
Qaddish	ייטב לאלהים	[47]	*Qaddish*	רחמי ידיד	[66]
——	שתה גבול	[48]	——	קול מהלל	[67]
Barekhu	יפי שירי	[49]	——	חסדי אל	[68]
——	החריב אל	[50]	*Barekhu*	יענו תהלות	[69]
Ofan	בארצות האל	[51]	*Ofan*	חיה עצומה	[70]
Me'orah	מיום גלות	[52]	——	ישעך יזכירו	[71]
——	אור אמונה	[53]	*Me'orah*	אסירת צרים	[72]
Ahavah	ספרו לי	[54]	——	הקץ לשבי	[73]
——	מועד פדות	[55]	*Ahavah*	יביא לחדרו	[74]
Ge'ulah	ארבעה עמדו	[56]	——	בעלת אוב	[75]
Shalom	רחש תנין	[57]	——	יעלת צבי	[76]
——	רצה שיחי	[58]	*Shalom*	יה בשיר	[77]
			——	מבשר עיר	[78]

In the aforementioned manuscript A we find eight numbers for Pesaḥ (4, 6, 10, 12, 15, 16, 17, 25), no. 19 for the Feast of Weeks, four (31, 33, 34, 35) that occur in the *Maḥzor* of Algiers, and only no. 71 from the Avignon *Maḥzor*. The London manuscript, which has some different items from manuscript A, has only nos. 9, 10, 12, 16, 31, 33.

The rite of Carpentras, where a synagogue was permitted in 1372, is originally the same as that of Avignon, but differs here and there in the wording, in the order of pieces and even has poetic items that are more abbreviated and others that are omitted. For Shabbat Zakhor it has its own *zulat* as well as some local festal memories. It should be noted that there are large differences in the worship of fast-days, and of the day before the Day of Atonement. The communities of l'Isle and Cavaillon shared the Avignon rite; in the latter place Ps 142 was recited before *ma'ariv*. In recent times, when the population of these cities has changed, a unification of the rites of Avignon and Carpentras appears to have been made.

p. 51

Various rites undoubtedly had their place in Sicily: we soon hear about a relationship with Rome and also about old Spanish poems that were customary there. In the year 1300 someone seems to have suggested some innovations there, namely, the reading of the Decalogue in the morning and the repetition of the *tefillah* in the evening service.[62] Later we note a connection between Sicily and Mallorca. It is reported in 1480 that those Jews, like the Spanish and the {North-} African, recited the evening prayer shortly before dark.[63] When in the sixteenth century older and younger Sicilian communities and some from Messina settled in centers of the Ottoman Empire[64] such as Constantinople, Saloniki, Lepanto, Patras, Arta, Damascus, they recorded the custom of reading on the Sabbath the whole of Holy Scripture in the course of a year.[65] In more recent times they also preserved their various customs on particular festivals.

It is already obvious from what was earlier reported about the festivals of Pesaḥ, Weeks and New Year that the order of worship in Algiers, most of whose communities originated in Catalonia and Mallorca,[66] was that of Provence. In fact,

62 {Zunz,} *Zur Geschichte* p. 524 note b.

63 האגור {of Jacob b. Judah Landau} § 327. Cf. Isaiah de Trani on Berakhot (בית נתן 41a).

64 *Zur Geschichte* p. 530. Elijah Mizraḥi Responsa 7.

65 באר מים חיים {Ḥayyim b. Jacob Obadiah} Preface.

66 Responsa of Isaac ben Sheshet (107), Solomon Duran (413) and Abraham Tawah (f. 89a); they were called "those who wore the Spanish hat (קפרון)".

the structure of the basic and festival prayers on the Four Sabbaths is almost indistinguishable from the Avignon rite. Slowly they introduced into the Algiers rite other poems by later poets, especially for domestic devotions and for the penitential period, and some of these also appear in the *Maḥzor* for the New Year days. The order of the poetic content on the first day of Tabernacles is: 1) *Reshut* יצב גבול שמש, 2) *Mokh.* שם אל אשר, 3) *Ofan* מחנות עליונים, 4) *Nishmat* ישרון החוגג שבעת, 5) *Qaddish* יחד קרבי, 6) *Me'orah* שאלו ידידי, 7) *Barekhu* השתחוי וברכי, 8) *Ahavah* חופף עלינו and 9) *Ge'ulah* יהמה לבבי. Of those texts a total of five occur in manuscript B, but only one (1) for that day, two (4, 8) for the next day, one (9) for the Torah Festival, one (3) for Shabbat Ha-Ḥodesh. Avignon preserved only

p. 52

two (3, 5) but actually for use on the other days of that festival. When days of public mourning fell on festivals and the Sabbath—with the exception of *Shabbat Zakhor*—the whole *qerovah* up to *magen* was omitted.[67]

The rites of Constantine, Oran, Tlemcen and Tunis all belong to the Provence group and their basic texts and poetic contents are therefore largely in agreement with those of Algiers. In Constantine they said והוא רחום before all three daily *tefillah*'s (and not only before the evening one), but they omitted the ending of השכיבנו.[68] In all these places, and certainly also in other {North-}African communities, the *Azharot* of Isaac ben Reuben and Sa'adya's Arabic exposition of the Decalogue are read on the Feast of Weeks, but the Blessings of Jacob, the Song of Moses and the Ten Commandments are recited in Aramaic and Arabic. The order of the New Year festival in Constantine is similar to that of Algiers; the same applies in the case of the Four Sabbaths and the Great Sabbath. In one *Maḥzor*, which originates in Oran, thirty-eight poets are mentioned[69] among whom, apart from those well-known from Spain, there are six later ones and twelve authors known from the Maḥzor Avignon. In Tlemcen and Algiers they introduced newer introductory material for the New Year festival.

Tripoli seems more closely related to the old Spanish rite. The five Sabbaths before the Day of Atonement are distinguished by their early morning devotions. The evenings before both days of New Year were celebrated by *seliḥah* and *baqashah* in Algiers, while the structure of the rites of Tripoli, Oran and Tlemcen are reminiscent of those that apply to the days of repentance in Avignon: *pizmon* and

67 מנהגים of Algiers, at the end of the Responsa בית יהודה (Livorno 1746) f. 107c § 6.
68 Solomon Duran Responsa 20, 329.
69 Compare Luzzatto in *Kerem Chemed*, vol. 4, pp. 27–33.

mostejab follow each other in dealing with the themes of the three groups of New Year verses. The worship begins at night and finishes towards morning. There are thirty-nine poetic prayers, a large number of which occur partly in the Castilian *Maḥzor* and partly

p. 53

in the *seliḥah* of Oran and other {North-}African locations.

Fez, to which Sherira and Hai Gaon sent their decisions,[70] had even closer connections with the Spanish order of prayer, even if the wording and overall order of Maḥzor Avignon dominates in the basic prayers and in the four *yehi raṣon* pleas after the Torah reading. *Barukh she'amar* follows the Spanish version, as does the *tefillah* and the silent supplication, which adds only a few penitential verses. In *nishmat* the section from מי ידמה until וקדוש שמו is missing. There is a short introduction before והוא רחום in the evening prayer. The prayer או"א החל at the termination of the Sabbath has a different conclusion[71] and there is an addition before ותמלוך in the New Year *tefillah*. Neither the three pilgrim festivals nor the New Year days have *qerovah's*. On the first day of Pesaḥ a section of the Aramaic translation of the Pentateuch is read, as well as the *azharot*, and on the seventh day there is an Aramaic *reshut* before the *hafṭarah* Targum. No *piyyuṭim* are read on the Feast of Weeks other than Gabirol's *Azharot*, or on Tabernacles other than *hosha'na*'s and the prayer for rain. Among the festival prayers of the early morning liturgy on New Year's Day one meets some of the Castilian rite and that of {North-}Africa mentioned above. There are idiosyncratic variations with regard to the three Psalms 121, 122, 123. In another manuscript originating in Fez, this service more closely matches the old Spanish rite, with twenty-one of its thirty-eight poems occurring in the Castilian *Maḥzor*.

There are also no *piyyuṭim* in the current rite of Morocco for the three pilgrim festivals, and the *Azharot* of Isaac ben Reuben are read on the afternoon of the Feast of Weeks. Those who are called [to the Torah] on festivals, including a "bar-mitzvah" boy, are greeted with poetry.[72] On the Torah Festival the *mafṭir* is accompanied by a Palestinian Targum. The Sayings of the Fathers or Mishnah Avot are translated into Arabic. This also applies to the section Gen 24:1–10, which is read for a young bridegroom. In

70 Mordechai comments on Ketubot. Cf. Appendix I {below}.
71 Beginning ברוך מפיר עצות, ending ברוך מחדש מעשה בראשית וחונן הדעת.
72 *{Allgemeine}Zeit{ung} d{es} Judenth{ums}* 1839 p. 278.

p. 54

Morocco and in Tetuan everybody brings salt into the synagogue on the second evening of Pesaḥ and then takes a little bit of it home.[73]

Traces of the influence of Sa'adya's *Siddur* appear in the rites of Sicily, Tripoli and Fez and they must have already rooted themselves in {North-}Africa at an earlier time, because the *Siddur* of Solomon composed in Sijilmasa already includes from Saadya's *Siddur* the *ma'ariv* service for the Sabbath, the section of אתה גאלת in the Haggadah of Pesaḥ, another version of the *havdalah*, as well as *hosha'na*'s, *seliḥot* and *azharot*. The Geonim Naṭronai,[74] Ṣemah ben Ḥayyim,[75] Sherira[76] and Hai are connected with Qairouan. In the year 930, 'Uqba, who came from Baghdad and was leader of that community of Qairouan,[77] and Nissim who wrote his *Siddur* there a hundred years later, could have informed us about the rite of that centre. But what we know is only that the leader just mentioned had a special seat of honour next to the holy ark and that the Torah scroll was brought to him there after the Kohen and Levi had read their pieces, while everyone else had to present himself where the Torah was located. Even earlier, the people of Qairouan were criticised for the way that they ended the blessing over wine (*qiddush*)[78] on Passover eve with the phrase בחר בנו לרוממנו. Some of them there read Psalms on the eve of the Day of Atonement or indeed on Sabbath eve.[79] We are also informed that Hai Gaon was asked why the Jews of the Maghreb did not drink water[80] at each quarter of the year; that a certain Itiel from there brought geonic responsa to France;[81] and that they deleted certain passages of Sa'adya's work in Qairouan. As indicated by questions to Naṭronai about the version of the *ma'ariv* on Sabbath eve,[82] and by other data, Sa'adya's *Siddur* was already commonly known in {North-}African locations at an earlier time.

73 משא בערב {Samuel Romanelli} p. 47.
74 Samuel in אגור ms. (Dukes in {*Der*} *Orient Lit*{*eraturblatt*} 1851 p. 358).
75 Eldad, end. Ha-Pardes 21b.
76 Responsa of the Geonim no. 91. Arukh אבי״.
77 Compare Ha-Manhig 32a § 58 with Yuḥasin 120b.
78 Amram ms. 59a, compare Ha-Manhig 88a.
79 Responsa of the Geonim ed. 1802 no. 52.
80 Abudarham 73a.
81 Perhaps those that are mentioned in ליקוטי פרדס 20a.
82 Amram ms. f. 29, Ha-Manhig 23b § 2.

p. 55

If Sa'adya wrote his *Siddur* in Fayyum, we can perhaps identify in that volume the basic features of the old Egyptian prayer book, especially his version of the *tefillah*, which was then the common practice there, but which was no longer such a normal feature in the time of Maimonides. It should also be noted that in Fustat in particular there were two synagogues representing Babylonian and Palestinian worship with regard to the lectionary cycles, one reading in one year and the other in three years, as still practised in 1170, and that on the Feast of Weeks and the Torah Festival they had joint divine services. Both these synagogues were still standing in 1550 although the Jewish residents had already moved to Cairo.[83] From 1200, the Maimonidean order of prayer dominated in Egypt, Palestine and Maghreb,[84] and widely among the Mostarab communities, consisting of the natives of Egypt, Tripoli and Syria, who were later also known as Moriscos,[85] and who were distinct from those who had emigrated from Europe. These Moriscos were distinguished in various communal institutions[86] by language and by the pronunciation of the letter *shin*, which the Spanish and French could not distinguish from *sin*.[87] Such Mostarab communities are especially mentioned in Cairo,[88] Aleppo[89] and Damascus—where they had their own cemetery and had once to demolish their synagogue[90] because of the proximity of a mosque in the neighbourhood—and nearby Jubar, Sidon, Safed—where they shared a synagogue with the Fez Jews—and 'Ain el Saitun, Shechem and other places in Palestine.[91] In 1559 the community in Cairo still followed the practice that Maimonides established with regard to the cantorial repetition of the *tefillah*. In those communities the benediction להכניסו is recited before the {circumcision}operation as laid down by Alfasi and the son of Maimonides,[92] The

---

83 {Issachar} Even Shoshan 33b.
84 אבקת רוכל {of Joseph Karo} no. 32.
85 Barukh *Reisebericht* 21a.
86 David ben Zimra, Responsa, ed. Liv{orno} no. 69, Yomtov Ṣahalon, Responsa no. 173.
87 Azulai ברכי יוסף on Ṭur I 50. David Qimḥi on Judges 13:6 {correct to 12:6}.
88 Levi ben Ḥabib, Responsa 26.
89 אבקת רוכל {of Joseph Karo} no. 52.
90 Ibid. nos 113, 122. Barukh, ad loc. 22a.
91 Barukh, ad loc. אבקת רוכל {of Joseph Karo} no. 190. {Issachar} Even Shoshan 59b, 61a.
92 Moses Alashkar, Responsa 18.

p. 56

purchase of synagogue honours is often an inherited right.[93] Some communities read the Torah without using the cantillation.[94] In the order of *hafṭarot* they follow Maimonides and they have no *hafṭarah* on the afternoon of the Ninth of Av, in accordance with Amram and Maimonides.[95] *Kol nidrey* is not customary, nor are the laments on the three Sabbaths[96] before the Ninth of Av. במה מדליקין is recited after *ma'ariv* as among the German Jews.[97]

It is customary in Egypt and the Orient to call more than seven people to the Torah reading on a Sabbath which involves celebrations, and to repeat the text.[98] Meanwhile, there is no clear and obvious message about general matters with regard to worship conducted in the scattered communities of Asian countries. Although the Spanish *Maḥzor* is introduced there in most cases, there are numerous examples of rites based on old traditions, as well as other instances where more recent material is added, as for example many poems by Najara. In Smyrna on the Feast of Weeks there is a special procession with the Torah scrolls, at which several poems from recent times are recited. Tyre reads the book of Esther on the 14th and 15th of Adar.[99] Aleppo is mentioned in a number of old festival prayers; of twenty-four items that were common on the Sabbath of Repentance, and of which only 13 have survived, some are also customary in Tripoli. The names of the authors of seven of these poems are: Mazhir, Joab the Greek, Abbasia, Sasson Ha-Levi, Solomon Ḥaver and Israel ben Aaron Ha-Kohen. Della Valle too speaks about that synagogue. In the neighbouring Ḥamat there existed some ritual variations from the code of Maimonides[100] and in Damascus and Cairo there was a genuflection ceremony[101] during the evening prayer at the recitation of 1 Kings 18:39. In the first-mentioned place there were, in the first half of the sixteenth century, a Spanish, a Mostarab and a

93 Jacob Berab, Responsa no. 49.
94 מצרף לחכמה {Joseph Delmedigo} 10a.
95 {Issachar} Even Shoshan 90a, 63b.
96 David ben Zimra, Responsa ed. Liv{orno}, no. 33, section 3, no. 645.
97 Jos{eph} Karo on Ṭur I 270.
98 {Issachar} Even Shoshan 55b, 56a.
99 {Responsa} פאר הדור 105.
100 אבקת רוכל {of Joseph Karo} 54.
101 {Responsa} פאר הדור 104.

p. 57

Sicilian[102] community. In the thirteenth century it is reported that there was no suspension of the shofar blowing on the Sabbath.[103] In Baghdad, Benjamin counted twenty-eight synagogues and Petaḥiah {of Regensburg} 31. The recitation of the prayers was divided among a number of cantors. The Psalms were sung and during the intermediate days of the festivals this was done to the accompaniment of instruments. ישתבח preceded the Song of Moses. As is well known, Amram's *Siddur* has in the morning service neither the recitation of this song nor the passage of Neh 9:6–11, both of which were introduced at a later period.[104] Currently there are seven synagogues there.[105] In Mosul, Ḥarizi found a lovely synagogue, but he was not pleased with the long and inferior *piyyuṭim* that the cantor recited without ever mastering the language. The synagogues in Persia, Kabul and Bokhara are still awaiting professional reports by travellers.

Ibn Wahab (ninth century), Benjamin and Maimonides mention the Jews in India. We have a more recent but incomplete report about the rite of the communities of Cochin[106] on the west coast that were built by Syrian and Egyptian Jews, and about Sengili. It is basically Spanish with traces of the geonic orders {of prayers} and is enriched by the poetry of the sixteenth and seventeenth centuries. The marriage ceremony is of the oriental type. Several of the common prayers are also recorded in the Romaniote *Maḥzor*. The conclusion of the wedding benediction and the Pesaḥ prayer אתה גאלת are from Sa'adya. The Azharot of Elijah Adeni ben Moses, a student of David Vega, have the same poetic structure as that of Gabirol ending in רים. A variety of poetic material has been borrowed from the old Spanish rite, namely, the prayers on the Torah Festival and the prayer לך חנות. From the German rite they borrowed the hymn אשריך הר העברים and the songs חדש ששוני and אחד הוא יודע. The poem שיר חדש written by Yehudah Ha-Levi for the birth celebration of Isaac ben Barukh

102 Barukh, *Reisebericht* 32a, Jacob Berab, Responsa 33. {Issachar} Even Shoshan 7b.
103 פירושי מנוח {Manoaḥ b. Jacob} 31a.
104 Compare Ha-Manhig 10b § 24, Roqeaḥ 320.
105 Petaḥiah {of Regensburg} ed. London p. 82.
106 W. Schultz (1658) quoted in{ J. J. }Schudt {*Jüdische Merckwurdigkeiten*} 1, p. 41; Buchanan quoted in Ritter, *Geogr{aphisch-statistisches Lexikon}*, section 5, p. 595, where it is reported only on the basis of Hebrew correspondence. On the literature, compare Steinschneider, *Bodleian Catalogue*, p. 2722ff.

p. 58

belongs to the circumcision poetry while his ישרו בעיני, which is also to be found in the Maḥzor Vitry, belongs to the week of wedding feasts. The end of the *qaddish*, the Aramaic דכירין, has survived in the prayer book of Kaffa. The grace after meals differs from all other versions, including those of Amram, Sa'adya and Maimonides, although some parts are reminiscent of those three authorities. Solomon b. Mazaltov and Israel Najara are the authors of some items.

Other poets mentioned are Aaron Ha-Kohen, Obadiah b. Aaron Ha-Kohen, Benjamin, David b. Samuel, Eleazar, Ephraim b. Ṣalaḥ, Isaac Ḥazan, Jacob b. Benaya, Yehudah Kohen, Joseph b. David, Levi b. Moses, Maali, Manṣur, Moses b. Yehudah, Nehemiah b. Abraham, Nissim, Solomon b. Nissim, Solomon Kohen, Shemariah, ... b. Sa'adya. At least six of these belong to the Middle Ages.

About the liturgy of Jews in China, one witness reports that it is, with few exceptions, Spanish, although there are a few German elements.[107] The Sabbath morning service begins with a hymn by Eleazar, in which each stanza ends with ברוך שאמר והיה העולם. This is apparently an introductory poem to the *barukh she'amar* which seems to have been alphabetically arranged, as in the Greek rite. There is also mention of a poetic *nishmat* by Eleazar, perhaps referring to אשחרה לעזרה. The Torah reading is prefaced by a blessing for those who are devoted to the study of the religious law. The Aramaic announcement of the New Moon begins אציתו שמעו כהניא but we are not informed about the beginnings of any other prayers. There are among the *havdalah* lyrics a song for Elijah in Aramaic and a Hebrew hymn with stanzas ending in יה—, both of which occur in Maḥzor Vitry. The alphabetical thanksgiving for the conclusion of the Haggadah is probably אתה גאלת. Also for the Pesaḥ festival there is a hymn by Eleazar. The *musaf* for New Year, which is wholly similar to that of the German rite, is adorned with a hymn by Eviatar about God's throne, but the service for the Ninth of Av does not differ from the Sefardi rite.

107 *Jewish Chronicle* 1853 nos. 356, 358.

Pp. 59–85

Now we must turn back to Europe in the pre-modern period in order to look carefully at the German-Roman group of rites. The first of those that calls for the researcher's attention is the French rite, if only for the reason that, although it was eventually lost, it was totally rooted in the Middle Ages. The morning service began with Ps 5:8 and other verses, similar, but not totally identical, to those of Maḥzor Roma. What follows the benedictions אשר יצר and the others are: the prayer שתתן חלקי בתורתך which is partially the same as the Roman recension—which is at the beginning of Amram's *Siddur* but not in the Gemara—four additional *yehi rașon* texts,[1] the Torah benediction ending with כנגד כלם, the section about the daily offering (Tamid), איזהו מקומן, ר' ישמעאל, לעולם יהא, as far as לעיניכם אמר ה', and some verses. The communal service began[2] with "*barukh she'amar*", which on the whole matches the German rite but in a few expressions borders on that of Sa'adya. In *hodu*, ופדנו למען חסדך (end of Ps 44) is followed by five verses that appear in no other rite and אשרי is preceded by nine other verses that include the word אשרי. "Wa-Yosh'a" or the Song of Moses was recited daily.[3] In the *yoșer*, the paragraphs תתברך ה' אלהינו בשמים and והאופנים וחיות הקדש are also for weekdays. While the expression קונהם and the omission of אור חדש match the Spanish and Roman rites, the alternative ולעלמי עולמים משך חסד ליודעיו (in אמת ויציב) is as in Amram's *Siddur*. In the *tefillah*, מוריד הטל is said in some places[4] in the second benediction [Maimonides]; the ending of the thirteenth benediction is ובחסדך נשענו, virtually as in the Roman rite. Those called to the Torah also leave their heads uncovered.[5] In ובא לציון

P. 60

the position of למען יזמרך is almost the same as in the Spanish version but it is enriched by a large addition. There then follow *qaddish*, Ps 83 as well as some other verses (Ps 5: 11–12; 40:17), the prayer יהי ה' אלהינו עמנו, as in the Roman rite, except for the verse כי כל העמים, which is at the beginning in the Spanish rite, and is here placed at the end. *Qaddish* by a youth and *'alenu* end the divine service. For

---

1 a. שתשכן בפורנו (Berakhot 16b), b. שתתן לנו (ibid.), c. שתצילנו היום, d. שלא אחטא (ibid. 17a).
2 תשבץ 217. Asher Responsa 4.20. Aaron Ha-Kohen 5c.
3 Ha-Pardes 57c.
4 Tos{afot} Ta'anit 3b.
5 Or Zaru'a cited in דרכי משה Ṭur I 282. Comp{are} Ha-Manhig 15b § 45, who praises the Spanish for covering their heads (at prayer). In the fifteenth century Israel Brünn (Responsa 34) still permits sitting with uncovered heads.

domestic devotion: the older Seder Eliyahu is set out, similar to the familiar מעמדות, in which there are also eleven verses that begin and end with the letter *nun*; the two poetic pieces אתן תהלה לאל and אתה מבין תעלומות that belong to the order of service for the Day of Atonement; the passage אביי מסדר; and the section about the Manna (Exod 16:4). In the evening service, the community responds to the verse והוא רחום יכפר of the prayer-leader with the verse Deut 4:31, a custom that Aaron Ha-Kohen also mentioned.[6] In the Roman rite there are similar alternatives. In אמת ואמונה the place at which מלכותך ה' אלהינו is read is as in the Spanish *Maḥzor.* After the *tefillah* one said פטום הקטרת, which was also common elsewhere.

On the Sabbath, they say אדיר אדירנו and, before גדלו, also Ps 19:8–9,[7] but neither ויהי בנסע nor ובנחה. The two יקום פורקן prayers are merged into one. The *qedushah* for *shaḥarit* is נקדישך ונעריצך and for *musaf* כתר.[8] The *hafṭarah*'s do not vary from those of the Germans.[9] For the translator, there is an introduction and a conclusion, both in Aramaic. The divine service for the afternoon ends with צדקתך. In several places Ps 67 was common at the beginning of the evening service; it is absent in other rites, in German manuscripts, and in various Greek communities. Following אמר רבי יוחנן there is the passage אמר ריב"ל from Tr{actate} ‘Avodah {Zarah} 19b. At either the commencement of the Sabbath, or at its conclusion, various hymns and songs were customary.

When a festival fell on a Sabbath, Joseph Qimḥi's יום שבת זכור was intoned before מגן אבות בדברו in the evening, Benjamin's *qedushah* וחיות בוערות at *shaḥarit,*

P. 61

and a special אלהיכם at *musaf.* On festive Sabbaths, poetry was attached to specific sections of the *yoṣer*, to שים שלום, and sometimes to אל ההודאות (end of ישתבח), תהלות לאל (end of עזרת), and *mikhamokhah.*[10] Newly-wed men and their wedding attendants received special greetings when they went up to the Torah, and blessings in Hebrew and Aramaic when they came down again.

The Sabbath of בראשית had a *yoṣer* by Samuel b. Yehudah and the second Sabbath of Ḥanukah one by Isaac b. Samuel. The Four Sabbaths have *yoṣer* poems by Qalir but not in their entirety, other *zulat* poems, and some by Isaac Ghiyyat. Yehudah Halevi's *mikhamokhah* is used on the Sabbath before Purim, while Purim

6 F. 43a § 1 (cited in Kol Bo 28 f. 25b).
7 Tos{afot} Megillah 32a, Compare Soferim 14.14.
8 Compare Ḥizzequni {on *parashat*} האזינו.
9 De Rossi *Annal{es}* p. 88.
10 Tos{afot} Rosh Ha-Shanah 34b. Compare *syn. Poesie* pp. 61, 63, 65.

has a special *ma'ariv* and a *qerovah* by Qalir. The Great Sabbath also has a {poetic} *ma'ariv* and a hymn by Isaac Ghiyyat as well as Tovelem's *yoṣer* and *qerovah*. When the New Moon fell on a Sabbath, a *qerovah* by Qalir was recited. No announcement of the New Moon for Av on the preceding Sabbath took place;[11] perhaps in earlier times only the "*yehi raṣon*" was omitted. The end of the New Moon benediction read ברוך מקדשך ברוך מחדשך; the former ברוך occurs in Zedekiah,[12] the latter in Eleazar of Worms.[13]

The character of the divine service for festivals {in France} is as the German rite, although there are some differences in the content of the *Maḥzor*. On festivals and on special Sabbaths, such as the one before the Feast of Weeks, the one on which *naḥamu* was read, and the one during the Days of Repentance, short poems were sung when the Torah was taken out. There was a poetic *ma'ariv* on the festival evening, including that of New Year. On the three major {pilgrim} festivals, the מפטיר reads the first three verses of the *hafṭarah* and the translator recites a poetic introduction and then the Targum on those three verses. After that, each single verse is accompanied by a translation, followed by a concluding hymn in Aramaic and the usual *hafṭarah* benedictions. On the final two days of Pesaḥ and on the Feast of Weeks, poetic ornamentations

P. 62

accompanied the Targum. On the Feast of Weeks, an Aramaic introduction precedes the Targum of the pentateuchal sections and there is a poetical "*dibra*" for each individual commandment. An *ahavah* was inserted on both of the first days of Pesaḥ and on the second day *azharot* on the subject of the ritual rules for the intermediate days. The *yoṣer*, *qerovah* and poetic ornamenations for the seven days are by Joseph Tovelem and for the eighth day by Benjamin b. Azriel. On the seventh day there is the *zulat* אז בהיות by Amitai, on the eighth אזכיר בתחן by the aforementioned Benjamin. The Haggadah of the first evenings concludes with the hymn יצלצלו which follows ישתבח and Ps 134.

On the Feast of Weeks, the poetry of Simeon and the even more artistic poems of Tovelem were in common use. On the first day in *musaf* (at שלש פעמים) they recited both אזהרת ראשית and תחלת כל מעש, while on the second day they read the Azharot of Elijah Ha-Zaqen. The *piyyuṭ* of the Festival of Tabernacles resembled

11 Codex Opp. 1484Q.
12 שבלי. 46
13 Roqeaḥ 229.

that of the German rite; the Intermediate Sabbath had the *yoṣer* אמנם מפי מונה while that of the Eighth Day had Qalir's *qerovah* אחות. The reading was עשר תעשר which was, as an opening, used elsewhere, and at later times, only on a Sabbath.[14] On the first day of the New Year festival the introduction to the *qerovah* was by Moses b. Samuel, on the second day by Tovelem. As well as the *piyyuṭ* of Qalir and Simeon, there are, for the first day, items by Tovelem, Joseph b. Qalonymos, Benjamin b. Samuel, and for the second day by Benjamin b. Samuel and Yehudah. The shofar benediction has the reading על תקיעת שופר.[15]

The rite of the English communities was to a large degree probably similar to that of France, if not totally identical with it; the Jewish authors of that area wrote and spoke French. Indeed, Meir Rothenburg[16] regarded France and England as one country. No more details are actually known. What we have are manuscript *Maḥzorim* with explanations from England in the twelfth century. Jacob of London

P. 63

translated the Haggadah for the Pesaḥ festival for women and children.[17]

A branch of the French rite is that of Burgundy.[18] The scholars who hail from there—Eliezer b. Aaron, Meir, Tobias b. Elijah—were disciples of French rabbis, whose customs they followed. Not only in Champagne but also in Burgundy they obeyed, for example, the regulations of Rabbenu Tam with regard to the blowing of the shofar on the Trumpet Festival.[19] Since Arles was once a part of the Burgundian kingdom, and is already mentioned as such by Meshullam b. Qalonymos, it may be that some {rulings} found their way from Provence to Dijon and Maçon via Arles. They departed from the general French custom only in some individual usages relating to the festival prayers, as partly in the poetic *ma'ariv* where they made some additions, otherwise known as *bikkur*; the deviation was more pronounced in the *hosha'na*'s. In the case of Jose's *teki'ata* אהללה, they also had the additional biblical verses, as in the German rite, and on the Feast of Weeks they

14 Compare Ha-Manhig 71a § 52. Maḥzor Vitry, לקוטי פרדס 13b; differently in ספר האורה (Ha-Pardes 62b).
15 Ha-Manhig f. 53 § 9, Abr{aham} Klausner 5a.
16 Responsa in 4 no. 117.
17 דרכי משה Ṭur I 473.
18 בורגוניא (Gershom cited in ראביה 900 and in Responsa Yehudah b. Asher 51b). In a decision in בית האוצר {Luzzatto} 57b. Benjamin of Tudela. R. Isaac cited in Mordechai: מזוזה. Ha-Manhig 54b, 83b. Tos{afot Bava} Qama 58a. Maḥkim ms. ms. commentary (above, p. 33).
19 Ha-Manhig 54b.

had, in addition to Elijah Ha-Zaqen's *Azharot*, the *azharot* אתה הנחלת. On the two final days of Pesaḥ, the *ge'ulah* is customary and on the eighth day there is also a *qerovah* by Isaac b. Joseph. The Feast of Weeks has a poetic *nishmat* and on the first day a *qerovah* and a poetic ornamentation of the Decalogue by Benjamin b. Samuel. In the *tefillah* of the penitential festivals the third ובכן is replaced by ואז, which is also the text of Maimonides and the Maḥzor Roma. The text והחיות ישוררו in the *yoṣer* was not customary on those days.[20] On New Year's Day some places also added האוחז to the *rahiṭ* התכן (from the *shaḥarit* of the Day of Atonement).[21] The אחר קדוש by Benjamin had an addition about the martyrs who were burnt to death. The *yoṣer* of Meir b. Isaac was used on the eighth day of Pesaḥ, the second day of the Feast of Weeks, and the Intermediate

P. 64

Sabbath of Tabernacles. The prayer for rain on the Eighth Day of Tabernacles does not have זכור אב at the end. The poem ישבחונך by Isaac b. Abraham was recited on the Sabbath following Tabernacles. On festivals and Sabbaths, the *qedushah* follows immediately after ובכן ולך תעלה and the poetic *silluq* is lost. There is, however, a *silluq* for the seventh day of Pesaḥ and poetically enhanced *qedushah* for *musaf* on festive Sabbaths. The *havdalah* for the termination of the Sabbath matches the German rite but has, after the word ויקר, a large addition that begins בשמחה נועדנו.

Beginning in the final years of the fourteenth century, many French Jews emigrated to Italy, especially to the cities of Piedmont,[22] where they then established communities that followed the French rite. In one of those, we find, around the year 1510, some deviations from its prayer-order: on the New Year festival they skipped the poem ואתה אזון כל by Qallir; they had on *musaf* the *reshut* איככה [by Joseph Tovelem] and אסתופף; for the eighth day of Pesaḥ the *yoṣer* ויושע שושני by Simeon; for the first day of the Feast of Weeks his *qerovah*; and for the Intermediate Sabbath of Tabernacles the *yoṣer* אמנם מפי. The *ma'ariv* also does not match that of Burgundy. The communities of Asti, Fossano and Moncalvo in Piedmont probably also belong to this branch, which makes use of the German *Maḥzor*, but for the penitential festivals they did retain much of the French order of prayer.[23] In Asti, they marked the eighteenth of Iyyar with celebrations, at which poems by Joseph Conzio

20 Against ר"י (Tos{afot} 'Arakhin 10b) but in agreement with Moses b. Ḥasdai (Ms commentary on the *piyyuṭ*).
21 Approved in the pentateuchal Tosafot (דעת זקנים 74d).
22 Jos{eph} Colon, Responsa 81. {Gedaliah ibn} Yaḥya שלשלת 62a.
23 Luzzatto אבני זכרון p. 167, בית האוצר 50a, הליכות קדם p. 51, מבוא p. 7.

were recited, and for that same community Elijah Levita wrote a special *Seder* for the Pesaḥ festival. The custom was reported of Piedmont[24] that every day after the morning divine service the *tefillah* was repeated at the almemar for those who had arrived late, and this also originated in France.

Lotharingia,[25] which once extended over a large part of what is today

P. 65

Germany, Belgium and France, was, still even around 1300, when its borders were reduced,[26] known as the kingdom of Lotharingia, also by Jewish authors of that time,[27] and was still distinguished from France and Germany.[28] The teachers of Rashi and his son-in-law, Meir, were called the rabbis of Lotharingia,[29] regardless of the fact that Mainz,[30] which is listed next to Lotheringia, and Worms, were undoubtedly German places. One formal certificate from France[31] in around 1150 includes: Troyes, Auxerre, Rheims,[32] Paris and the surrounds, Lyon, Carpentras, Lombardy, the coastline, Anjou, Poitou, and "the major figures of Lotharingia".[33] One early scribe—even if not be taken too literally—includes R. Gershom and his contemporaries among such figures. What is certain is that Rashi, especially, as

24 Judah Mintz Responsa 15.

25 לותיר, לותייר (incorrectly להויר in מעשה הגאונים ms. § 180). In a ms. commentary on the Pentateuch, section ראה: לותרניא.

26 The Duke of "Lothir" occurs in Azriel b. Joseph (Haggahot Mordechai, Qiddushin § 1008; the name of the country is not given in Jos{eph} Colon Responsa 2 and שלטי הגבורים {Joshua Boaz on Mordechai Bava} Batra 2).

27 Joseph ibn Plat (Ha-Pardes 39d, 41c), Roman rabbis (בית האוצר {Luzzatto} 57a), Abraham b. David (מקובצת on Bava Meṣi'a 161d), Ephraim b. Jacob (ס' זכירה p. 2), Eleazar in the Haggahot Asheri end of Tr{actate} 'Avodah {Zarah}. Compare the next footnotes.

28 במלכות לותיר ולא בצרפת (Roqeaḥ 382), באשכנז ולותיר (Moses de Coucy, Prohibitions 65 f. 19a).

29 Ha-Pardes 35a. Samuel b. Meir {Bava} Batra 150b, 158b, which has רבותי שבלותיר (Mainz?). Tam in 720 הישר and cited in שבלי 11 [compare 95]. R. 'Samson is mentioned together with the nobles of the kingdom of Lotharingia (אסור והתר ms. § 27).

30 Ṭuvia {b. Eliezer} on Song of Songs (בקהלות אשכנז). Isaac of Marseilles calls R. Isaac b. Yehudah who studied there הצרפתי, see אוצר נחמד 1 p. 25, compare שבלי 93 and Kol Bo 99a.

31 Kol Bo 117, Meir Rothenb{urg} Responsa ed. Prague towards the end, ed. Cremona no. 72.

32 In the editions רייש or ריאשו.

33 גדולי לותיר (Kol Bo 117. Sol{omon} Luria Responsa 29), for which there is also גאוני לותיר (Ha-Pardes 35a, Maimoniot in סדרי תפלה, שבלי 11 and 95), הגאונים שבלותיר (Ha-Pardes 48c, ליקוטי פרדס on the Ninth of Av, Mordechai Pesaḥim ch. 2 end), זקני לותיר (Tos{afot Bava} Batra 74a), חכמי לותיר ('Iṭṭur {of Isaac b. Abba Mari} 90a).

well as his progeny, were in touch with these figures.[34] We hear not only about Lotharingian teachers, manuscripts,[35] commentaries[36] and Tosafot[37] but also about its rite.[38] In any event,

P. 66

it is in such areas that we should seek the connecting routes between the French and German *Maḥzorim*. As in Burgundy, it was also customary in Lotharingia to add to the Babylonian *azharot* those of Elijah Ha-Zaqen, so that the Castilian Menaḥem b. Aaron[39] could write that those *azharot* were genuinely French and German. Joḥanan Ha-Kohen's poetic ornamentations for the Feast of Weeks were recited in Lotharingia as well as in Mainz. With regard to the details of that rite, we learn that in the morning service the Torah benediction read לעסוק בדברי תורה; the benediction להכניסו was uttered before the act of circumcision; and they fasted a week before the New Year.[40] On the New Year festival in Lotharingia and Mainz, most said והשיאנו, which was not the case in Germany and France.[41] On Purim, the two *qerovah*'s of Qalir had not yet been inserted. It also seems that R. Tam's *ma'ariv* (אדיר ונאור) for the Eighth Day of Tabernacles was also part of the Lotharingian rite.

From the fourteenth century one no longer hears about Lotharingia but about France and Germany[42] which are cited with each other and to which are added the third rite of Spain,[43] Provence[44] and Slavonia.[45] Just as Spain constituted the centre-point of the Babylonian group, so Germany, earlier as Germania and later

34 Maḥzor Vitry § 198 (the same in ס' הישר 699, Ha-Manhig 33a, Tosafot, Asheri and Mordechai on Pesahim 10 [105a]), ס' הישר 81a, 85d. 'Iṭṭur loc. cit, Tos{afot} Berakhot 18a and {Bava} Batra loc. cit. Compare above, n. 29.

35 בספר לותיר (ס' הישר 81a).

36 חדושי נדרים ms.

37 ס' הישר 85d.

38 שבלי ms. § 28 [ed. 11].

39 Ṣedah La-Derekh 4.4.6.

40 Ha-Pardes 39d, 41c. ראביה § 532. Compare above p. 55.

41 הפרדס 42a. Asheri Rosh Ha-Shanah towards the end.

42 Asheri Berakhot 1, Rosh Ha-Shanah 4; an early ruling cited by Meir Rothenb{urg} Responsa 112d. Often in Asher's Responsa.

43 Maimoniot שחיטה ch. 11.

44 Ha-Manhig 69b § 38 followed by Aaron Ha-Kohen 78b § 16.

45 Meir Rothenburg Responsa ed. Cremona no. 117.

as Ashkenaz,[46] also known by foreigners as Alemannia,[47] was the centre-point of an extensive circle of rites. Before the year 1000 there was barely any identifiable difference between the early French and the early German synagogal worship,

P. 67

both of them matching Amram. This changed when ritual regulations from Rome reached the circles on the Rhine, and when scholars of Jewish law and synagogue poets arose in France. Additionally, numerous persecutions had effects on the German rite. Within such German circles, however, various customs evolved and deviations became visible, so that 500 years ago, in matters of ritual, there was already a noticeable difference between western, central and eastern Germany, out of which there emerged the rites of the Rhine,[48] Saxony and Austria. In addition to these, there were individual places that greatly differed from each other in the matter of the festival prayers.

According to the German custom, the first benedictions of the morning service were prayed in the synagogue, so that communal worship started off with them. When the prayer-leader reached the biblical verses, he paused so that the congregation could join in and say these loudly at the same time with him, as also specifically with the verses מי כמכה and ה' ימלך.[49] The prayer מלכנו, which occurs in Amram and was recited by Rashi every day at the end of the *tefillah*, had an addition in honour of the martyrs.[50] There was a similar addition to the second paragraph of the grace after meals that was customary in both western and eastern Germany.[51] The passage ויהי בנסע as well as ובנחה came later, initially only on the Sabbath. In

46 Josippon 6.9. Hasdai's letters. Amram MS. Rashi (Deut. 3:9, Sukkah 17a, Ḥullin 93a and elsewhere), Samuel b. Meir (Maimoniot in סדר תפלה), Eliezer b. Nathan (גזירת תתנו beginning), Ha-Pardes 40d, Sa'adya on Dan 7:8.

47 Josippon 1.1, פרקי משיח p. 72, Ha-Pardes 43d, Ibn Ezra on Obadiah end, Benjamin of Tudela, an early ruling cited by Meir Rothenb{urg} loc. cit. Ha-Manhig 35b, 69b, 83b, 116b. Jonah {b. Abraham} אגרת התשובה. Solomon Verga {*Sheveṭ Yehudah*} (32a) mentions Alemannia next to Ashkenaz, presumably defining the latter as referring rather to the eastern countries.

48 רינוס the Rhineland (אבן העזר § 299; Meir Rothenb{urg} Responsa 284 and 112d, in no. 117 in quarto ed.; Responsa {on Maimonides} אישות nos. 13 and 25. Pisqey Recanati 93; often in Maharil, Israel Brünn and {Israel} Isserlein). {Cited as} סדר ריינוס in codices Michael 465, Opp. 1283Q and elsewhere: compare above, p. 22. It is also sometimes found in codex Michael where the Austrian and Rhineland rites follow the same path.

49 שלטי הגבורים {Joshua Boaz} Megillah 4.

50 Codex Michael 533. Compare Roqeaḥ 323.

51 Or Zaru'a ms. Eleazar b. Yehudah's liturgical commentary ms. codex H h 37.

Rhineland the method of chanting the pentateuchal readings on the penitential festivals was called *"Stuben-Trop"*.[52] The custom of using a spice-box at the *havdalah* ceremony was introduced following the precedent of Ephraim of Bonn;[53] Eliezer of Metz used a bag for this purpose.[54] The benediction

P. 68

for the new moon had the addition כשם שאני רוקד.[55] On the New Year festival, חי וקים was omitted from the *qerovah*;[56] this practice is old, as is the recitation of the *qaddish* by an orphan.[57]

The German rite rarely has a poetic *nishmat*, a *reshut* at best on the Day of Atonement, hardly ever *mikhamokhah*, but it often has a *yoṣer* and an *ofan*. The summer Sabbaths are furnished with a *zulat*; the *musaf* of festive Sabbaths with אלהיכם; the Sabbaths between the four פרשיות with a *yoṣer*; the poetic *ma'ariv* with *bikkur*;[58] the grace after meals on the day of a circumcision with poems; and the sabbath meals with table hymns. The *reshut* and *yoṣer* for the Sabbath of newly-weds were composed by eighteen poets, half of them from Germany. The early payyeṭanim form the basis of the divine service for festivals and they also belong to the French *Maḥzor*; added to them are Meir b. Isaac, Yoḥanan Ha-Kohen, David b. Gedaliah and others. Broadly stated, the German rite contains a great deal from the French rite, much from that of Spain, and individual items from that of Provence, while a significant proportion is idiosyncratic, or related to the Romaniote. The early manuscripts provide major differentiations, depending on time and area. With regard to the situation in earlier centuries, one can report with certainty only about a few places.

The most important city, with regard to the order of the western rite, is Mainz, which regarded itself as even more noble than Köln.[59] Unmarried men there did not put on a prayer shawl.[60] Additional details of the rite in the eleventh and twelfth centuries are provided by Maḥzor Vitry, Ha-Pardes, and Zedekiah

52 Codex Michael 469 § 59. Manhig ms. §§ 55, 62, 73. Maharil 64a.
53 Or Zaru'a ms. Tashbeṣ 86. Mordechai Berakhot 8. Ṭur I 297.
54 לקוטין ms. § 223, where, however (instead of Ephraim), mention is made of Jacob b. Yaqar and Jacob of Hornbach; the latter is known from Meir Rothenb{urg} 112c.
55 Roqeaḥ 229.
56 Roqeaḥ 200. Abr{aham} Klausner cited in Maharil 50a.
57 קדיש יתום or קדיש לנער [in mss]. Compare Roqeaḥ 50, 53.
58 *Syn. Poesie* p. 70.
59 Maharil 84a.
60 Ibid. 83b.

Ha-Rofeh while those of the fourteenth and fifteenth centuries by the Maharil and manuscript Minhagim. On the Sabbath, the verses of הודו were shared between the prayer-leader and the congregation, each reciting half. On the Sabbath after Tabernacles

P. 69

it was customary to include poetic chants in the *nishmat.*[61] On the first day of Ḥanukah, Qalir's *qerovah* was recited. On Purim it was announced that the banging should be limited to the reading of the names of Haman's sons. The first day of Pesaḥ had a special *qerovah* and the Feast of Weeks the *silluq* אז טרם[62] by Joḥanan Ha-Kohen. The memorial prayer for departed souls was not recited on any festival.[63] Worms, which is often mentioned together with Mainz, retained, even in later times, much of the earlier character of the rite. Even today its order of worship does not include אדון עולם (except on the eve of the Day of Atonement), לכה דודי, אקדמות, and Ps 67 and 144 at the termination of the Sabbath. They do not omit the silent meditation (תחנון) on the fifteenth of Av or the eighteenth of Iyyar, nor do they do so in Regensburg.[64] On the last day of the Pesaḥ festival, those who perished in Prague in 1389 were remembered. Apart from its own *zulat*, it had the following customs: embellishments of the *nishmat* on Shabbat Bereshit; Qalir's *qerovah* on the eighth day of Tabernacles and his *qedushah* on Tabernacles; and a poetic *ma'ariv* on the New Year festival that is similar to the one preserved in the Greek rite. The priestly benediction was also performed at *shaḥarit.*

With regard to ritual matters in Speyer, there is already information before 1100 that deals with mourning rites, the New Year festival, and the Ninth of Av.[65] On that fast-day, the prayer shawl was put on, while later in the remainder of Germany they refrained from doing so. On the eighth day of Tabernacles the prayer-leader announced loudly: משיב הרוח.[66] They did not wait for anyone who might have left during the divine service of the synagogue.[67] In the fourteenth century, the order in Rheims was identical to that of Rothenburg. As is well known,

---

61 Codex H h 61.
62 Maharil 24b, 27b. Codex H h 37.
63 Codex H h 249.
64 Abr{aham} Klausner 41a.
65 Ha-Pardes 42a, 44c, 48a, 49a b. לקוטי 13a, 17b c, 18b. שבלי 88, 89, 93. Parallel passages in Roqeaḥ and מעשה הגאונים.
66 Ha-Pardes 45c, שבלי 53a.
67 Ha-Pardes 47d.

Meir b. Barukh hailed from Worms. In Rothenburg on the Sabbaths of Zakhor and Parah, and perhaps also in Speyer, they seem not to have recited the *shiv'ata* of Qalir but—as was customary in Köln—that of Meir b. Isaac. On the Great Sabbath they said the *zulat* אשכולות and on the Feast of Weeks

P. 70

they recited the *yoṣer* of David b. Gedaliah. In Köln, where the synagogue had stained glass windows in the twelfth century, they observed the old {German} and French custom of sounding the trumpet four times at the conclusion of the Day of Atonement.[68] On the intermediate days of Tabernacles, the custom was to read those biblical texts prescribed in Rashi's order, but not those in Amram, or the practice followed in Mainz.[69] A *Maḥzor* that was written in Ulm in 1450 is in Parma (R. 653). The synagogue in Regensburg—that followed the Austrian rite[70] in the order of prayer for the Day of Atonement and in some mundane matters—had two square slabs of marble on which the Tetragrammaton was inscribed.[71] The singing of the *barukh she'amar* on the Sabbath lasted an hour.[72] A father did not follow the corpse of his eldest child who predeceased him,[73] a custom that is otherwise unknown. In Regensburg, as in Erfurt, it was customary at the ceremony for the redemption of a first born to recite שהשמחה במעונו.[74]

The rite of Saxony, in which Erfurt and Magdeburg were the most prestigious communities, seems to be related to that of Nürnberg. There, boys who still had a month before they reached the age of thirteen sometimes conducted the service.[75] More than is the case elsewhere, the *yoṣer* and the *zulat* for the Sabbath borrowed items from older pieces of *piyyuṭ* on certain festivals. There, for the Sabbath of בשלח, they had *yoṣer* and *zulat* texts by Simeon and an *ofan* by Moses b. Isaac; a *yoṣer* etc by Ḥayyim b. Barukh for the Sabbath when the Decalogue was read; a *ge'ulah* by him and by Meir b. Yeḥiel. In addition, their poetic *ma'ariv* was different from that of the others.

68 Ha-Pardes 44d, לקוטי פרדס 13b, compare Ha-Manhig 62a § 69.
69 אבן העזר 82b. Compare Vitry ms. and Ha-Manhig 70b.
70 Jacob Weil Responsa 66. Maharil.
71 Moses Mintz Responsa 76. {A.} Margaritha {*Der gantz Jüdisch Glaub*} p. 295.
72 Ibid. p. 177.
73 Isr{ael} Brünn Responsa 98.
74 Jac{ob} Weil Responsa 189. Israel Brünn Responsa 121.
75 Maharil 79b.

The festival rite of Vienna, and of Austria, and also that of Hungary, was generally that of central Germany, the same as the later Polish *Maḥzor*.[76] It was reported in the thirteenth century that, despite the view of R. Tam,

P. 71

there was no longer any objection to the inclusion of אות מבראשית in the grace after meals at the celebration of a circumcision, nor to the additions at *ma'ariv*.[77] The thanksgiving benediction after drinks followed the text of the Jerusalem Gemara.[78] The custom in Austria[79] was to say the passages הא לחמא or עבדים היינו from the Haggadah at the afternoon service on the Great Sabbath and was only a short time ago abolished in Poland.[80] It is noteworthy that when the Song of Moses or the Decalogue is part of the lectionary on a Sabbath or festival, it is intoned only by the reader, and then read by the assembly.[81] In Austria[82]—as well as in Erfurt[83]—they abstained from consuming the fat of an animal's belly, while in the Rhineland they considered it permissible. The latter, on the other hand, would eat no duck while they did so in Styria.[84] The Jews of Austria also ate lappish goose,[85] put on their prayer straps differently,[86] kindled the lights of Ḥanukah from the right to the left,[87] let the mourning beard grow for twelve months[88]—in Rhineland only for three—and recited Ps 91 on returning from a funeral. In the latter circumstance in Alsace, it was customary to say Vidduy.[89] Abraham Klausner[90] relates individual ritual observances of his time, as, for example, the omission of במה מדליקין when a festival occurs on a Saturday.

76 See Klausner 8a, 13a, 19a, 20a, 21b, 40a b, 41a, 42a b.
77 Or Zaru'a ms. [Haggahot Asheri Berakhot 1].
78 Likewise in Sa'adya, ibn Plat, Meir Rothenburg and {Rabbenu} Asher.
79 Klausner 40b and Tyrnau. In a Minhagim ms. of the fourteenth century the custom is limited to 14 Nisan that falls on a Sabbath, citing Amram.
80 מעשה רב {Elijah of Vilna} 177.
81 תרומת הדשן no. 24.
82 Tyrnau Introduction.
83 חדושי אגודה {of Alexander Süsslin Ha-Kohen} 80b.
84 Isr{ael} Brünn Responsa 146.
85 Maharil Responsa 100.
86 Ibid. 30.
87 Isserlein תה"ד 106.
88 Maharil 108b and Responsa 22.
89 Ibid. 23.
90 5a, 7a, 8a b, 25a b, 40b, 41a.

The differences between the various German communities that resided in Italy are mostly insignificant; their order of prayer is originally that of Swabia. The same applies to Switzerland, to where most of the Jewish residents had emigrated from southern Germany or from neighbouring French localities. In Bern they followed the practices of Swabia;[91] they also chose the same *seliḥah*'s. We are informed of a special case in Bern, in which

P. 72

Moses Kohen (about 1410) once omitted from the Pesaḥ Haggadah the מה נשתנה because when he had lifted the dish his little daughter had already asked questions and thus made its recitation superfluous.[92] Such behaviour is rare because the German Jews are otherwise considered pious[93] and punctilious observers of their traditions. The French rabbis[94] attempted to make everything more difficult in the places where they were welcomed. For instance, they did not put salt on the matzot[95] even if great authorities declared it permitted,[96] and even if the Jews of Poiton also did so,[97] following the example of pious Jews in France. We are grateful to them for having retained, because of their specific characteristic, early *piyyuṭ*.

The Jewish population of Slavonia, which in earlier times included Bohemia, partly originated in Byzantine countries and also had some similar rituals and poetry. Canaan—as the Slavic countries were called[98]—and France held on to *piyyuṭ*[99] and both countries agreed in the matter of the lectionary for the festival of Pesaḥ.[100] Eliezer b. Nathan[101] speaks of the teachers of earlier times in Canaan which he visited and where he observed various customs. Around 1100,[102] there

91 Maharil Responsa 35.
92 Maharil.
93 *Zur Geschichte* p. 179.
94 Compare שבל דרכם להחמיר (המכריע {of Isaiah di Trani} 10 f. 6c).
95 Semaq 219. Asheri Pesaḥim 2 § 23.
96 Ha-Manhig 78b. Maimoniot חו"מ 5.20.
97 The Zürich Semaq ms.
98 My comments on Benjamin of Tudela (vol. 2 pp. 226–229) and in Frankel's *Zeitschrift* (1846 p. 382 and following); S{elig} Cassel *Historische Versuche* p. 8 and ff., article Juden [in the {Ersch & Gruber}*Encyklopädie*] pp. 130, 145; Rapoport *Kerem Chemed* part 6 p. 165.
99 Ha-Pardes 43d.
100 Maimoniot תפלה ch. 13.
101 אבן העזר § 8 and f. 70a; *tefillah* commentary ms.
102 כשבאתי מרוסיאה לשם in a ruling (in מעשה הגאונים ms. § 291) which is related to Ha-Pardes 18b top and 33c.

was an expert in religious law in Russia,[103] or Galicia, and at a later date Eliezer of Prague[104] is probably that scholar who notes in Maḥzor Vitry that questions had been addressed to him from Russia. In the thirteenth century, writings came to Regensburg[105] from Russia and Isaac of Russia lived there.[106]

P. 73

But there were also in the twelfth century scholars in Bohemia who communicated with their German and French brethren:[107] Isaac Ha-Lavan b. Jacob,[108] Eliezer b. Isaac[109] and Isaac b. Mordechai[110] also lived in Germany. Prague is already mentioned in the works of Yehudah Ha-Kohen[111] and later by Eliezer b. Nathan[112] and the explanations of words in the languages of Canaan or Bohemia, which we encounter in the works of Qara and other French and German rabbis of the twelfth century, testify to the connections between Germany and Slavonia. From the thirteenth century there is mention of Poland[113] but only rarely. The Germans who immigrated there soon became the majority and displaced the local language of the earlier population.[114] As the German elements grew, the Polish rite of Bohemia and the neighbouring countries became a branch of the German rite and this, together with some remnants of the older period and of the French rite, had more in common with that of Saxony than that of the Rhineland. Thus the traces of early Byzantine origins became blurred. When Israel Brünn (about 1460) describes a

103 רוסיא is mentioned next to Canaan by Benjamin {of Tudela}, next to Bohemia by Asher Responsa 52.3; it also occurs in אבן העזר § 5.291 and f. 74b, Jos{eph} Colon Responsa 185, Israel Brünn Responsa 25, 73. Vat{ican} Codex 300.
104 Or Zaru‘a cited by Elijah Mizraḥi Responsa 53.
105 *Isr{aelitische} Annalen* 1839 p. 222 and *Gesch{ichte} des Judenthums* part 2 p. 427.
106 Luzzatto in *Kerem Chemed* 7 p. 69.
107 Or Zaru‘a ms. Haggahot Asheri Ḥullin 4b], compare אבן העזר 70a.
108 In my *zur Geschichte* pp. 33, 93, ראביה 917, *Kerem Chemed* 3 p. 201 [from {Maḥzor} Vitry].
109 *Zur Geschichte* p. 49.
110 Ibid. p. 33. Or Zaru‘a ms. [Haggahot Asheri Mo‘ed Qaṭan 3].
111 ראביה 900.
112 אבן העזר 84c. תתנ"ו p. 12.
113 Isa{ac} of Chernigov who offers explanations by way of רושיאה by which he means Russian (ס' השהם of Moses b. Isaac}), Jacob of Cracow (Meir Rothenb{urg} Responsa 864). Does פולום (ibid. 85) mean Poland? פולוניא is mentioned by Naḥmanides on Gittin 7b but there it is Bohemia that is meant; פולין in a manuscript held by Luzzatto (*Kerem Chemed* 7 p. 69).
114 שאינם בני תורה is how Israel Brünn (Responsa 55) describes those from Cracow, as {R.} Antoli {Ha-Dayyan}had once done regarding Syracuse.

matter of ritual,[115] he places together Poland, Silesia, Austria and Moravia, or Austria, Poland, and Saxony. Incidentally, the ritual information that is occasionally provided after 1400 about Prague, Egger, Brünn and Breslau is not of great consequence for history.

What is noteworthy in the Polish rite is the omission of the phrase אפילו שעה אחת in {the benediction} אשר יצר, the placing of the Torah benediction before אלהי נשמה, the use of the plural in the

P. 74

expressions used in the first *"yehi rașon"* of the morning service, and the groups of verses inserted in the ויתן לך prayer at the termination of the Sabbath. Of the two versions of אל ארך אפים, which are also in the French and Spanish rites, only one was customary in Greater Poland. The short אמת ויציב that precedes the poetic *zulat* and is missing in many *Siddurim*, and also not customarily inserted in the whole of Germany, was noted in an early book of ritual.[116] The אין כמוך that was usual on the Sabbath is an abbreviation of the prayers that were recited at that place on the high holidays according to the Roman rite. The regular recitation of אב הרחמים on the Sabbath is German and the inclusion of והחיות when a poetic *ofan* is said is of French origin. The prayer-leader always began the solemn recitation in the *nishmat* with the words האל בתעצומות while the German rite varied the opening in the case of each individual festival.

Everything in this rite that concerns *piyyuț*, and that deviates from the current modes of the German *Maḥzor*, originates in the older French and German rites. Examples are: the variety of *yoșer* content (Tabernacles, New Moon, the second הפסקה {between the Four Sabbaths}, *naḥamu*, {the Sabbath of} Repentance, circumcision) and the *ofan* ({the Sabbath of} בראשית and New Moon); *zulat* for the first day of Tabernacles and its intermediate Sabbath, the Great Sabbath and the {Pesaḥ} seder; in the prayer for rain זכור instead of איום; the grace after meals at the celebration of a circumcision; the *reshut* for חתן בראשית; and the יה אלי before אשרי on the three major festivals. Items that belong particularly to the central German and Austrian rites are: five {poetic} *ma'ariv* prayers (for the seventh and eighth days of Pesaḥ, the second day of the Feast of Weeks, and for Tabernacles and its Eighth day), *ofan* and *ahavah* on the Sabbaths between Pesaḥ and the Feast of Weeks, the recitation of the *ofan* on the four festival days (seventh and eighth days of Pesaḥ, Eighth Day of Tabernacles and the Torah Festival) and the nine Sabbaths

115 Responsa 121, 102 f. 44a.
116 Shorter Manhig § 131.

(the intermediate Sabbath of Tabernacles, Ḥanukah, the four Sabbaths and the two הפסקות in between, and the Great Sabbath), *zulat* for the Sabbath of Repentance, the circumcision Sabbath, the הפסקות Sabbaths between the Four Sabbaths, *ge'ulah* on the seventh day of Pesaḥ, *nishmat* on the Torah Festival, *me'orah* on Purim. The poems שור אשר (for the second day of Pesaḥ) and אז היתה (for the first day of Tabernacles) come from the early *Maḥzor*. Variations for New Year's day come from the French rite, especially the introduction to the *qerovah*, a different conclusion of *mehayyeh*;

P. 75

the items אתה הוא, אם אשר, וחיות, and אתה קדוש; in the *musaf* both stanzas of מלך עליון and the omission of verses from Jose's אהללה; and some items from the Roman rite.[117] Five *piyyuṭ* pieces[118] and Qalir's *qerovah* for the Ninth of Av are absent, while a *yoṣer*,[119] though not composed for these days, was inserted on the four Sabbaths before the Feast of Weeks.

Broadly stated, the rite of the German Jews was everywhere at one in its connections with the French rite. A German author[120] could therefore state 330 years ago that the Jews in Germany, Bohemia, Moravia, Silesia, Poland, Prussia and Hungary had one order of service which virtually matched the one that had come from France. Indeed, individual {German} items, that are cited by Tyrnau, such as the *zulat* אין זולתך on the Sabbath after the Feast of Weeks (central German), or the *ofan* שש כנפים on Sabbath Bereshit, have since then also disappeared. Some have survived only in individual places. In Posen and the surrounding area,[121] the *ofan* עזוז by Ezra, the *ofan* במרומים, the *ma'ariv* אקחה and the addition סכת שלום—they were all already common in Germany around 1300; the *yoṣer* for a circumcision recited there was the German one. The *ofan*'s יחיד and ויושע אל and the *zulat* אור ישראל (Pesaḥ festival), that were customary in Brünn and elsewhere, were from the French rite. The *ofan* שאלו שחקים that was earlier customary only in Brünn has since then been incorporated into the Polish *Maḥzor*.

---

117 חמול על in *musaf.*

118 אזכרה (Pesaḥ evening), עד לא (first day of Tabernacles), both texts of אשריך (Torah festival), זאת הוקשה ({*parashat*} Parah).

119 אגורה, אשיחה, אומץ, ארנן.

120 Margaritha {*Der gantz Jüdisch Glaub*} p. 230.

121 ואגפיה so expressly in Maḥzor Prague 1585, in Mordechai Jaffe's Levush and in the printed קונטרס.

The Lombardian rite forms a bridge between the German and the Romaniote rites. Although this country is mentioned in Jewish writings as early as the tenth century,[122] and note is taken of the populations of Venice,

P. 76

Verona, Milan, Mantua, Pavia, Genoa, Pisa and Lucca, the history of the synagogal life of these communities is almost entirely unknown. A tradition about two early payyeṭanim was linked with Lucca and mystical ideas may have passed by way of the prayers from Asia to Germany via Lucca. In Lombardian places there was probably an order of prayer that one might call either early-German or early-Roman because at an early date it was not very meaningful to distinguish between these two designations. In about 1150, Joseph ibn Plat speaks about the Torah benediction that is common in the morning service of Lombardy and shortly afterwards we learn from others that the one called to the Torah himself reads {the portion} and that the *qerovah* of Yannai that was customarily read in Germany on the Great Sabbath is not recited there. Since the fourteenth century, the communities have been divided between the Roman or Italian on the one hand, and the French (German) on the other.[123] It was for one of these German communities resident in Italy that the Short Manhig was composed and the Maharil speaks of them.[124] From a *Maḥzor* that was written in 1491 we are informed, among other things, that at that time the Roman rite also dominated in northern Italy (codex Rossi 1146).

Rome, one of Israel's earliest settlements in the diaspora, was already linked with Palestine in the time of the Soferim. The דור ודור that occurs in Amram in the daily *tefillah* originated there. Items {from Rome} that also occur in Sa'adya's siddur include: בגלל אבות at the end of the evening prayers {before the *'amidah*}; the first benediction before the שמע, the version of the אמת ואמונה, and the ומאהבתך (instead of אתה קדשת) in the *tefillah*, on the Sabbath eve; the recension of אתה אחד at *minḥah* on the Sabbath; ראשי חדשים until ולמחילת עון {on Rosh Ḥodesh}. The following agree with Amram: the Torah benediction, the *ahavah* in the morning

122 לונגוברדיאה or לומברדיא: Josippon, Rashi (Beṣah 33a), Eliezer b. Nathan (ראב"ן 63c), Joseph ibn Plat (Ha-Pardes 41c), פרקי משיח p. 72, Kol Bo {§}117, Abraham b. David הקבלה 46b, Benjamin de Tudela, Ephraim b. Isaac (ראביה 551 and Mordechai ms.), Ephraim b. Jacob (MS commentary), Eleazar of Worms (Ms commentary), Yehudah Kohen (מדרש החכמה ms.), Moses of Coucy (סמ"ג 39c) and many later sources.
123 Note 5 {below}.
124 לולב f. 71b.

prayers (beginning אהבת עולם), the beginning and end of ותן טל in the *tefillah*, the text תקנת in the *musaf* for the Sabbath,[125] the end of *nishmat*, the *qedushah* כתר, that part of the evening prayer

P. 77

after ברוך ה' ביום and the אתה הבדלת at the termination of the Sabbath; in addition, the daily אין כאלהינו that was also customary in Spain, Styria, Hungary and other places; the *mafṭir* on the second day of Tabernacles; the version of the צדוק הדין added to the grace after meals for mourners. The first "*yehi raṣon*" in the morning prayers has a lengthy insertion. הודו, which also includes Ps 19 and Ps 99, occurs, as in the Spanish rite, before "*barukh she'amar*". יראו עינינו and יקום פורקן are lacking; the announcement of the New Moon begins כך גזרו. *Minḥah* on the Sabbath has a set of verses before אשרי; at the termination of the Sabbath in ויתן לך there are insertions and transpositions, that partially contain the verses of the Polish prayer-books. Items that match the rites of France and Germany are several *ma'ariv* versions and *yoṣer*'s for Pesaḥ, the early Aramaic ornamentations of the Decalogue, for example חנניה until the letter *lamed*, the Babylonian Azharot, the *yoṣer*'s for New Year, Tabernacles, Ḥanukah and the Four Sabbaths, the *silluq* ונתנה תוקף and many pieces by Qalir. There are also items from later authors, for example, Benjamin, Joab, Matathia, and Moses, introductions for *nishmat* and poetry for עושה השלום, these last two as in the French rite, but there are no *ma'ariv* additons, no *yoṣer*'s for weddings and circumcisions and no poetic *nishmat*'s. The daily morning service has Solomon {ibn Gabirol}'s hymn שלשים ושתים נתיבות (refrain יעירון)[126] which is also in the Avignon rite but is laid out in the Spanish *Maḥzor* as a *reshut* before {the '*amidah*} and in the Romaniote as a conclusion, and appears as an *ahavah* in German manuscripts of the thirteenth century. Special characteristics are the *qerovah*'s for fast-days, the poetic announcements of the festivals, and the triumphal song תאיר נגה on the Pesaḥ

125 Also Ha-Pardes 57a, Ha-Manhig שבת § 42, Romaniote *Maḥzor* and other rites cited in Tishbi under תקן; these others do not include Avignon, Carpentras, Germany, France, and contemporary Rome, which have the text תכנת, as do Sa'adya, Abudarham, Aaron Ha-Kohen 65c, דעת זקנים (פנחס), תניא 21b.

126 The addition כל ברואי מעלה—from the *Royal Crown* {of Gabirol}—first occurs in the Spanish *Maḥzor* (editions 1519, 1524, 1544, and in the בקשות without date and in quarto format), from where it invaded the Romaniote (ed. Venice) and later the Roman *Maḥzor*; a ms. of the Avignon *Maḥzor* from the year 1541 does not yet have it. Compare Luzzatto מבוא pp. 17, 18.

festival. They borrowed from Spain Gabirol's Azharot, Yehudah He-Levi's Esther-poem and the *pizmon*

P. 78

of various authors. Gradually, the poetic stock melted away; already in the fifteenth century they stopped reading the *qerovah*'s for New Year, the three festivals, and Purim, as well as for "*Ṭal*" and "*Geshem*". Qalir's *teki'ata*'s, which were recited in Ibn Ezra's time, disappeared. Even the seventh day of Pesaḥ, the Eighth day of Tabernacles and the Four Sabbaths have only one *yoṣer*. Between Pesaḥ and the Feast of Weeks, only the final Sabbath before the latter has any items of *piyyuṭ*; *zulat* poems are also often lacking.

There is no doubt that the Roman rite spread itself broadly on various fronts. Already in the eleventh century, the Roman teachers of religious law were sent questions from Germany and France requesting information about customs. Many cities in central Italy followed the Roman rite, as for instance, Arezzo,[127] Bologna,[128] which, together with its surrounds, had eleven synagogues,[129] Florence,[130] Gubbio,[131] Imola,[132] Recanate,[133] San Severino;[134] most probably also the Marca area, which counted thirty-four synagogues in 1563, Ancona, Ascoli, Cingolo, Fano,[135] Ferrara, Perugia, Pesaro, Ravenna—Romagna had thirteen synagogues—Riete, Sinigaglia, and Urbino. Manuscripts have various deviations, such as other *yoṣer*s for the Great Sabbath and Pesaḥ, and their own poetry for Purim, "*Ṭal*" and "*Geshem*". These should be regarded as the customs of different communities within the same ritual area.

Southern Italian places, such as Capua, Naples,[136] Amalfi, Salerno, Benevent, Brindisi, Sulmona, and in Puglia, for example Trani, Bari, Otranto, Lecce,[137] Tarent, Siponto and Melfi, generally followed the Roman usage, although their own poets enriched the liturgy and their own teachers set down the order. It may also be the case that the relationship

127 אריין codex Harl. 5686.
128 Ibid. in the appendix of added תחנונים.
129 Bartolocci *Bibl{iotheca}* vol. 3 p. 757.
130 Where a Roman *Maḥzor* was written in the year 1441 and was sold in 1461.
131 Codex Rossi 1007.
132 Codex Rossi 325, codex Sorb{onne} 98.
133 Codex Rossi 420
134 *Maḥzor* from the year 1424.
135 ראביה, as also in the Responsa of Yehudah b. Asher 52a.
136 Compare codex Rossi 965.
137 Codex Rossi 89.

P. 79

between such places and the prayer order of the Greek Jews was stronger in those places than it was in Rome. Isaiah of Trani has the Torah benediction that follows Maḥzor Roma, the Gemara and Amram, and not as in Germany and Lombardy. He knows of the *qerovah*'s for fast-days and one for the Hosha'na Day.[138] A *Maḥzor* with unknown items by Qalir and introductory poems by Elijah b. Shemayah perhaps belong to those areas.[139] At the beginning of the sixteenth century, refugees and expelees created Apulian and Calabrian communities in Arta, Valona, Saloniki, Constantinople and in other places in the Ottoman counries, but no reliable information is known about their liturgical peculiarities.

With regard to the prayer order of the Greek or Romaniote communities[140] which existed,[141] or still exist, in Constantinople, Saloniki, Adrianople, Gallipoli, Chios, Sofia, Kastoria and other places, the first reliable data that we receive is from the Romaniote Maḥzor (from 1520). It includes, together with the {benediction} על נטילת ידים at the start of the morning service, the beginning of the Tractate Berakhot, with the first part of the Mishnah and the first passage of the Gemara, several Psalms, *'alenu*, and אוחילה. Matching the Roman prayer order are: יהי כבוד following directly after "*barukh she'amar*"; the texts of the *yoṣer*, the ויתן לך, and the grace after meals. As in the French rite, אין כאלהינו is said daily. One called to the Torah repeats the words of the reader,[142] while at an earlier time, like the usage of the communities of Lombardy, he himself read.[143] איזהו מקומן and אלהי נצור are lacking. The Sabbath has its own text of "*barukh she'amar*" which is alphabetic, but not rhymed, and which is preceded by many Psalms. The section במה מדליקין is read before *ma'ariv*.[144] The יקום פורקן is not customary. At the end of the morning service on the Sabbath

138 המכריע {of Isaiah di Trani} 61; on תענית 13a.

139 Mich{ael} 446.

140 רומניאה Sa'adya on Dan. 7:6. 'Iṭṭur {of Isaac b. Abba Mari} f. 15a. Vat{ican} codex 364.

141 Mentioned in the Responsa of Elijah Mizraḥi [Collection 2, no. 24], Elijah Ha-Levi, David b. Zimra, Samuel de Medina, Solomon Kohen (Part 2 nos. 95, 145) and others; compare Jost *Geschichte* {*der Israeliten*} part 8 p. 473f.

142 Elijah Ha-Levi Responsa 60.

143 ראביה 551.

144 Compare Aaron Ha-Kohen 62a § 15.

P. 80

יגדל and אדון עולם are sung. The last-mentioned has two additional stanzas which match a cantorial insertion about the Sefira's, of which Lipman of Muhlhausen may be the author.[145] The announcement of the New Moon is in Aramaic. In the twelfth century, the benediction before the *hallel* was recited only by the prayer-leader.[146] At *minḥah* on the Sabbath, they read Pss 111 and 112, and in other places also Ps 75, and at the termination of the Sabbath they read twenty-two Psalms—but not Ps 144. The *tefillah* for the Three Festivals has, before והשיאנו, a long addition that begins with אתה חי לבדך and is not everywhere customary. On festivals and special Sabbaths the presentation was beautified by poetic introductions, followed by *yoṣer*, *ofan*, *zulat* and *mikhamokhah* poems. On the eves of the Four Sabbaths, which were called ערכים, they have Qalir's *shiv'ata*,[147] but at the morning services no items by Qalir are offered, only other *piyyuṭim*. Purim and fast-days have *qerovah*'s but not the Three Festivals or, in some places, also not New Year. All festivals, however, even the Day of Atonement, have poetic *ma'ariv*'s but, as in the Italian rite, no additions. In addition, on festivals and special Sabbaths they use poetic versions of *qaddish* and *barekhu* and on the Sabbaths before Pesaḥ, Feast of Weeks and New Year, they have announcements that they call poetic. It is the custom to recite the *yoṣer* of Solomon b. Yehudah on the first day of Pesaḥ and that of David b. Huna on the second day; on the second day of the Feast of Weeks that of Benjamin b. Samuel; on the second day of Tabernacles the *yoṣer* and *zulat* of Benjamin [probably {Benjamin b.} Samuel], and on the Feast of Weeks the Babylonian *Azharot* and those of Gabirol. Instead of the last mentioned, some say the *Azharot* of Elijah Chelebi. Together with the early *piyyuṭ*, there are also poetic pieces by Spanish, French, Italian and Greek authors. While the Romaniote *Maḥzor* includes Targum with the *hafṭarah*'s for all the days of the Pesaḥ festival, here this is the case only on the final day. The *hafṭarah* itself is not from Isaiah ch. 10 which, following

145 בכושרות {Ephraim b. Joseph Jawrowower} f. 18. {הנאמן} שומר ציון {*Der Treue Zions Wächter*} (1852) no. 125.
146 Ha-Pardes 40d.
147 הכרזה.

P. 81

the Gemara,[148] is used in all the ritual works and rites, but the Song of Deborah; that is also the case in Meliana.[149] The *hafṭarah* for the Torah Festival is 1 Kings 8:22–34, which is at variance with that of Rome, which has 1 Kings 8:54–9:1, and that of other prayer-orders which read Joshua 1, but does match that of the Halakhot Gedolot. This rite also lacks poetic *teki'ata*'s but does have Qalir's poems for *Ṭal* and *Geshem*. At the end of the Pesaḥ Haggadah עושה פלא is sung together with אז רוב נסים. The book of Qohelet is divided up among the four festive days of Tabernacles and read at the afternoon service. The recitation of האזינו (instead of אז ישיר) on the Ninth of Av is Spanish usage. We have a report from about 1500 that the Greek communities pray *shaḥarit* before sunrise.[150]

One early manuscript that probably does not belong to Constantinople but does contain the Greek rite, has both יקום פורקן prayers, *piyyuṭ* for the festivals partially other than those in the printed *Maḥzor*, Aramaic introductions to the *hafṭarah* Targums on the festival of Pesaḥ, the additions to the *ma'ariv* as in the French rite, the *qerovah*'s of the German rite for the final day of Pesaḥ, the *Azharot* of Benjamin b. Samuel, together with those of Gabirol and Elijah Ha-Zaqen, and a special *reshut* for Qalir's *Ṭal*. It also differs from the order of the Romaniote Maḥzor on the Four Sabbaths and on the Sabbaths of a circumcision and a wedding. The *qerovah* for the Ninth of Av continues through the final four benedictions of the *tefillah*. A manuscript apparently in the possession of Luzzatto reflects the same rite, although from a later date. A third manuscript has, for Purim, after אמל ורבך, four additional items that continue the story, also a *qerovah* for *Ṭal* with four items that we do not have, which complete the introductory verse of Proverbs 3:20 and {the acrostic giving} the name {of the poet} [עזר--].[151] The intermediate Sabbath of Pesaḥ has a *yoṣer* by Benjamin b. Samuel, the eighth day of Pesaḥ one by Menaḥem b. Mordechai Ha-Parnes, and the second day of the Feast of Weeks

P. 82

the *qerovah* of Joḥanan Ha-Kohen b. Joshua, of which only individual parts are to be found in the French and older German rites.

148 Megillah 31a and Rashi.
149 Simeon Duran part 3 no. 121.
150 נחלת אבות {Abarbanel} ed. 1566 f. 27d.
151 Correctly supposed by {E.} Landshuth *Onomasticon* {*Auctorum*} part 1 p. 34.

The rites of Corfu and Kaffa belong to the Greek family. The Corfu rite's stock of poetry[152] for the three festivals has some common factors with the Romaniote and others with the manuscripts mentioned above. On the evenings of festivals, special Psalms are read: on the first day of Pesaḥ, Pss 105, 136 and 150; on the seventh day Ps 18; on the Feast of Weeks Ps 68; on Tabernacles Ps 76; and on the Eighth Day Ps 6. This order of prayer follows Amram's instruction and begins the recitation of אשר בגלל אבות on the Torah Festival with a benediction. Among the poets {whose work is used} in the festival prayers are to be counted: Mazaltov, Isaac b. Abraham Ha-Parnes, Abraham b. Gabriel b. Mordechai, and Moses Ha-Kohen[153] whose poetry is read on Shabbat Zakhor. At the beginning of the sixteenth century, the Corfu Jews had a synagogue in Arta,[154] and Joseph b. Abraham, who belonged to the Romaniote community and expounded the *Maḥzor*, was living in Corfu in 1554. The city of Kaffa in the Crimea, where both the Rabbanite and Karaite communities appear to have been in communication with Constantinople around 1500 and earlier,[155] may initially have adhered completely to its Romaniote rite. Gradually, variations became customary: some penetrated the morning prayers from the Spanish prayer-book; one passage in the *yoṣer* before והוליכנו קוממיות; the presence of איזהו מקומן and אלהי נצור; and the absence of הודו .ר' ישמעאל is customary only on the Sabbath; the alphabetical *barukh she'amar* used on the Sabbath is rhymed; the section כלם אהובים in the *yoṣer* continues in the alphabetical mode.[156] דכירין is commonly used instead of יקום פורקן which is also lacking here. On the Sabbaths between Pesaḥ and the Feast of Weeks, an alphabetical litany beginning 'אין קדוש כה is recited after the *qaddish*. The poetic

P. 83

introductions used on the Sabbaths when the Decalogue is reached in the lectionary seem to be of more recent origin whereas the reading of the little Book of Antiochus at *minḥah* on the Sabbath of Ḥanukah is earlier. The community in Korassow follows the same rite.

Since we have nothing to report about Georgia and Armenia, we may immediately turn to the original site of Jewish divine service, namely, Palestine and

152 Luzzatto in {*Der*] *Orient Lit*{*eraturblatt*} 1848 p. 483 and in a list that he shared with me.

153 In ישיר משה {Moses Ha-Kohen of Corfu} Mantua 1612, Saloniki 1614.

154 David Ha-Kohen Responsa no. 13.

155 Elijah Levi Responsa 28.{Responsa Ohaley} Tam {of Jacob ibn} Yaḥya 110. Codex Leid{en} 52 no. 9.

156 כלם ותיקים זכים חפצים טהורים ישרים כבירים לובשים עז ותפארה.

Jerusalem. From the time that it became dominated by the Romans and the Arabs, Palestine was no longer the homeland of a nation,[157] nor was Jerusalem the seat of permanent communities.[158] The Jewish population of Jerusalem, alternately vassals, prisoners and foreigners, often changed after the period of the Crusades. While there were around 1167 two hundred Jews there, there were only two a hundred years later. Two hundred years ago there was no German Jewish community there. Currently, one finds there remnants of prayer-orders that were customary among European Jews but there is no local and organic creativity. Very little has been transmitted from early times about the Palestinian custom,[159] only that, for example, the *tefillah* is recited aloud,[160] contrary to the Palestinian Talmud, that the benediction צמח דוד was attached to the previous benediction, which was still the case in Qalir's age, and that when it came to that point in the benediction of the *hafṭarah*, the community stood up and joined in with נאמן.[161] When seven people had recited their prayers and not heard *qaddish* and *qedushah*, one of them could, after *qaddish* and *barekhu*, immediately pray the *yoṣer*, the *shema'* and the *tefillah*.[162] For putting on tefillin they had their own benediction.[163] As early as the ninth century, the usage was to say at *ma'ariv* only the beginning and end of the paragraph about the fringes.[164] Because of the celebration of Nicanor's Day

P. 84

(13 Adar), the Fast of Esther could be held on three different days of Adar.[165] The *qedushah* beginning אתה קדוש is said only on Sabbaths, Festivals and minor festivals.[166] Around 1000 they prayed the *tefillah* of the evening service while still

157 Baḥya Deuteron. end and {his} כד הקמח (מילה end), which, since the Exile לא נתישבה שם שום אומה ולא תתישב. Compare תשבץ 562.
158 Compare my note in {the London 1840–41 edition of *The Itinerary of*} *Benjamin of Tudela* 2, p. 89.
159 Ha-Manhig 18b § 64. Compare, concerning hallel on New Moon, Parḥi ch. 14, end.
160 See שאילת שלום {on the Sheiltot} 4b § 138.
161 Soferim 13.10
162 Ibid. 10.7.
163 See Ṭur I 29.
164 Halakhot Gedolot 1d, compare Berakhot 14b.
165 Soferim 17.4, 21.1.
166 Soferim 20.7. Tos{afot} Sanhedrin 37b and Asher Tos{afot} Sanhedrin ms. Aaron Ha-Kohen 65c [Kol Bo 37f. 40c]. In חדושי אגודה of {Alexander Süsslin Ha-Kohen} 78a the words אלא בשבת are lacking. Compare Landshuth *Siddur* {*Hegyon Lev*} p. 55.

daylight but the *shema‘* and its attached sections only when night had fallen.[167] On the Torah Festival, some read the passage Deut. 30:11.[168] Rashi saw the practice of a Palestinian Torah reader who accompanied his musical modulations with hand-signs. New Year's Day—on which והשיאנו was not omitted there[169]—consisted of one day, until in about 1140 the second day was introduced by Provençal [immigrants].[170] In about 1325[171] Shemtov speaks about the somewhat different method of blowing the shofar employed by one of the Spanish Jews. אל מלך נאמן was not customary.[172] On the eve of the Ninth of Av it was announced aloud how many years had passed since the destruction of Jerusalem[173] and on the day itself the Song of Moses was not recited.[174] According to those reporting in the first half of the sixteenth century, the divine service in the Jerusalem synagogues is similar to the Spanish, with a daily priestly benediction. *Yoṣerot*, by which we should understand *piyyuṭ* as a whole, seem not to have been common. Both in the morning and in the afternoon, the *Middot* are recited before "*taḥanun*", three times on Monday and Thursday. On weekdays, someone preceded the Torah scroll with a burning torch; on the Sabbath no more than seven persons were called to the reading. *Seliḥah*'s were said after and not during the *tefillah*.[175] The lectionaries for Tabernacles deviated from what was then common; a Levite always read the section about the Golden Calf and did so in a

P. 85

mournful tune.[176] At that time the German custom of rereading the *tefillah* out loud at *minḥah* was introduced in Safed.[177] Currently in Palestine there are only communities that follow the Spanish or German rites; the latter have three synagogues in Jerusalem, the former four.[178]

---

167 תמים דעים 172. Aaron Ha-Kohen 12a § 2.
168 Aron Ha-Kohen 26c.
169 Ha-Pardes 42a.
170 Zeraḥiah Ha-Levi on Beṣah ch. 1. Compare there Alfasi, Maimonides, יום טוב 1.21, Parḥi ch. 14 f. 79a. Elijah Ha-Levi Responsa 163.
171 מגדל עז {of Shemtov ibn Gaon}in {the laws of} שופר ch. 3.
172 Aaron Ha-Kohen 11d.
173 Parḥi ch. 51 f. 426b. {Issachar} Even Shoshan 69a.
174 Ha-Manhig ch. 51a § 28. Compare above p. 81.
175 Barukh אלה מסעי *{Reisebericht}* ed. Livorno f. 25b, 26a.
176 {Issachar} Even Shushan 69a, 76a.
177 Karo on Ṭur I 234.
178 *Israel{itische} Annalen* 1839 p. 218. חבת ירושלם {of Ḥayyim Horowitz} f. 39ff.

Pp. 85–106

The relationship of the various rites to each other in individual parts of the divine service is clear, primarily in those parts that had little or no basis in early times but nevertheless succeeded in developing fixed formats. Counted among such parts are, among others, the reading of Avot on the Sabbath, poems about Moses on the Torah Festival, the laments of the Ninth of Av, and the *hosha'na*'s.[1]

Avot, usually called the Sayings of the Fathers, was, according to a report by Sar Shalom,[2] read together with the section "Pereq R. Meir" in Baghdad or Sura on the Sabbath at the end of the *minḥah* service. It appears that this usage, which was initially only in the academies, spread to communities near and far and had already become part of the synagogal service by the eleventh century. To that development we owe the fact that we have commentaries by Meshullam b. Qalonymos, Rashi, Samuel b. Meir, Ephraim, Jacob b. Samson and many later authors, even if not yet on Avot R. Nathan. The season in which this reading took place and the number of extracts that were read—and here and there expounded—on each Sabbath were matters that varied from place to place. In Germany it was done in summer and winter,[3] but later only in the summer, as was the arrangement in most places in France.[4] They began on the first Sabbath after Pesaḥ and read one chapter on each Sabbath. When the six chapters were finished, which happened soon after the Feast of Weeks, they started again from the beginning and read two chapters on each Sabbath,[5] as was the usage in, among others, Mainz and Frankfurt,[6]

P. 86

completing the reading on the Sabbath before the Seventeenth of Tammuz. In other places, such as Morocco for example, they read three chapters each Sabbath until that point. Some read from the Feast of Weeks until {the weekly portion} ואתחנן, others from {the weekly portion} יתרו until ואתחנן. The Jews of Austria read one chapter each Sabbath from Weeks until Tabernacles so that the three cycles began,

1 *Syn. Poesie* pp. 71–74.

2 Amram. Ha-Pardes 56c.

3 Aaron Ha-Kohen 66b § 6, Kol Bo 40 f. 41b.

4 Ha-Manhig שבת § 65. Maḥkim ms.

5 Maharil 26a.

6 מנהגים ms. Codex Opp. 1489A, Q. נוהג כצאן {of Joseph b. Moses Kosman} 61b. מטה משה ed. Amst{erdam}.

respectively, on {the weekly portions of} נשא, פנחס and שופטים.[7] The reading of Avot was done in Spain only between Pesaḥ and the Feast of Weeks[8] while in Burgundy it was done only in the winter.[9] In Provence, they began in the month of Iyyar, read two chapters each Sabbath from יתרו until מסעי, except on the New Moon, or when a festival occurred in the subsequent week.[10] In other places, as for example in Worms, they did not suspend the reading even on a festival.[11] In Würzburg, in the case of such suspensions, they read two chapters on the Sabbath after such a festival.[12] In Spain they read Avot in the divine service of the morning.[13] The usage of the Mustarab community of Safed was that when seven Sabbaths preceded the Feast of Weeks they read on the seventh Sabbath the chapter דרכן from Derekh Ereṣ Zuṭa.[14] It seems that this is an old custom that originated in{North-}Africa, where the Siddur of Solomon of Sijilmasa adds to Avot and the "Chapter of R. Meir" {the chapter} דרכן together with other chapters of Derekh Ereṣ Zuṭa. Apart from its ethical content, Avot was also connected, because of the way it starts with the Torah and Moses, with the Sabbath lectionary and the festival marking the reception of the religious law.[15] It was also connected explicitly with the statement about the death of Moses which is said to have taken place on Sabbath afternoon.

The celebration of the Torah and the memory of Moses's death are the themes of the Torah Festival, or the last day of Tabernacles. Probably of Babylonian origin,[16]

P. 87

the celebration of this festival expresses itself in two ways: joy at the religious law and lament about Moses; the liturgical elements of that day express both of these. That joy was the source of the early usage to call to the Torah many or all of those present on that day,[17] as was the case in the fourteenth century in {North-}Africa,[18]

---

7 Aaron Ha-Kohen loc. cit. § 7. Maharil loc.cit.
8 Abudarham 53b, Aboab נהר פישון no. 63.
9 Maḥkim ms.
10 Ha-Manhig and Aaron Ha-Kohen.
11 מנהגים MS. Maharil. יוסף אומץ {of Joseph b. Moses Hahn} § 857.
12 Codex H. 182a
13 Ṭur I 292.
14 {Issachar} Even Shushan 32a, 87a.
15 Compare R. Israel {b. Israel} in Abudarham, loc. cit.
16 y. 'Avodah {Zarah} 1.1, end, has no trace of it, but the Zohar (פנחס column 344) has R. Eleazar preaching about the eighth day of the festival and his חדוותא דאורייתא.
17 Ha-Manhig 71b, Aaron Ha-Kohen 26c.
18 Isaac b. Sheshet Responsa 84.

in the sixteenth century in Palestine,[19] and until recently in most German places. The name שמחת תורה, which is unknown to the Talmud, the Pesiqta and even to Amram, is used by Hai,[20] Menaḥem b. Makhir,[21] and in the earlier poetry;[22] in a sense it encouraged the joyful half of divine worship. What is perhaps related to it is the custom, perhaps of French origin,[23] for the one who finishes (מסיים) the Torah as חתן תורה and the one who begins it again (מתחיל) as חתן בראשית to be awarded a ceremonial *reshut* and other marks of honour. Although the custom is earlier than Meir b. Isaac, it did not reach Spain, where the designations of חתן are not in use and where it is probably the same person who finishes and restarts the Torah. In Rome we find only half of that custom: there is only a חתן תורה and the reading of the final part of the Torah is followed by a recitation by heart of the first five verses of Genesis added by the congregation. On the other hand, the custom was absorbed in the German—and Romaniote—communities and the Festival even has a poetic *nishmat*. Since such a poem was also read on the Sabbath of a bridegroom, the festival is here entitled the celebration of the "Torah groom".

A sadness at the passing of Moses[24] was already to be seen in the synagogue around 1000; they removed from the scroll of the law its vestments, probably during the delivery of an appropriate sermon. If such a sermon did not consist of the

P. 88

well-known midrash about the death of Moses itself, then it was at least the poetic reproduction that was common in the Greek rite. The Moses poems that are related to the pentateuchal readings—whose content was also mostly used in the *yoṣer* and the *zulat* of the Festival—are partially early. Amram mentions אשר בגלל אבות, Ibn Ezra {refers to} the earlier צעקה יוכבד, a poem that was common in Algiers and formerly in Amsterdam. Provence, Avignon and Algiers have יצורי כצל; Spain, Fez and Cochin have וזאת הברכה; Abraham's אשריך הר העברים is encountered in the prayers-books of France, Provence, Germany, Spain and Cochin. The most frugal with this

19 {Issachar} Even Shoshan 56a, 70a.

20 Compare Ha-Manhig 72a with Aaron Ha-Kohen 26c, Isaac Ghiyyat cited in Jos{eph} Colon Responsa 9.

21 *Reshut* מרשות מרומם, perhaps the same as is mentioned in Ha-Pardes 46b, 61d.

22 מרשות האל, שמחו בשמחת, שישי ושמחו, אשבח שם.

23 Ha-Manhig 71b.

24 The expression פטירת משה (*syn. Poesie* p. 73, {L.} Dukes, {*Zur Kenntniss der*} *Rel{igiösen} Poesie* p. 60, 146) also occurs in Ha-Pardes 61d, לקוטי 20a, and also as a heading for the poetry in the *Maḥzor* (Calabrian ms. H h 129, codex Copenhagen, and in the Romaniote and Algerian *Maḥzorim*).

literary type are the rites of the French and German communities, in which the joy of the festival overwhelmed the grief, while the rites of Rome and Cochin are richer than those of Spain and Provence. In Provence,[25] the one who was called to the Torah himself read the final eight verses of the Pentateuch, which relate the death of the lawgiver, without the accompaniment of the Torah reader. Everywhere, the *pizmon* followed the *hafṭarah* and אשרי and was recited, before the Torah was taken back, by those knowledgable in religious law "who began the lament about Moses our teacher with the Torah on their arm."[26] In the *Maḥzor* of Rome and Avignon some of these poetic items are in fact called "songs of lament".

On the Ninth of Av, however, the date on which the destruction of the Temple was recalled, the melancholy over the glory that had disappeared would perhaps have been sufficiently expressed by the biblical laments, if new pains had not inspired fresh laments. So the lament became the permanent thing of which Israel remained conscious, the one freedom that they had under oppression. The three Sabbaths that preceded the fast were already marked in the early Spanish rite by elegiac chants. All the *yoṣer* sections, from the opening (*reshut*) until the *ge'ulah* were mostly treated poetically by the masters on those Sabbaths. One unique manuscript contains more than 160 such items, of which some were transferred into the standard laments of the *Maḥzor*.

P. 89

With regard to the genre just mentioned, their number is considerable and most of them are composed by Spanish, {North-}African and Provençal poets. They rarely describe the misery other than in general terms, only elaborating poetically on the themes of early times. Also, few of these relate to the period of the payyeṭanim. The earliest printed Spanish *Maḥzor* has thirteen items for the evening and twenty-six for the morning of the Ninth of Av; in the afternoon they have poems of consolation. Fez has nineteen items for the evening and forty-eight for the divine service in the morning, including one lamentation for the persecutions suffered in Toledo, Seville, Mallorca, Aragon, Oran and other places. Another manuscript originating in Fez has for the whole mourning period forty-nine poems, and a Castilian *Maḥzor* has seventy-three, including one in Aramaic by Yehudah Ha-Levi. A manuscript from Algiers has eighty poems of lament, most of them composed by locally born poets, the series begun by Isaac b. Sheshet and Simeon Duran. The Avignon *Maḥzor* has

25 Ibn Shuaib דרשות end.

26 Mahkim MS; then cited by Aaron Ha-Kohen 26c (Kol Bo 12c).

thirty items, of which only eight belong in other Spanish rites, while the Carpentras *Maḥzor* does not have quite the same number and at times has different items. That whole collection of rites has the Zionide of Yehudah Ha-Levi and—with the exception of Avignon—the *seliḥah* אלה אזכרה about the Ten Martyrs. One Provençal ritual has a *qerovah* by Yehudah Ha-Levi for the Sabbath before the fast, and for the fast-day itself poems by Abraham Ha-Levi, Solomon Bonfed and Isaac Zabara. In Jerusalem they recite one Arabic elegy and in Persia items written in Judeo-Persian.[27]

The songs of lament in the German-Romaniote rite have a different character since they all rest on Qalir's elegiac basis. It is possible that Qalir himself called individual sketches קינות in his large tableau {of poetic compositions}[28] but this designation was not yet employed by Amram or Sa'adya when dealing with what was recited on the Ninth of Av. But certainly in the eleventh century,

P. 90

if not already earlier, individual pieces by Qalir were designated by that name.[29] The later poets had in mind not only the events relating to the destruction of the Jewish state but also the sad fates of their own time and these elegies were presented on that special day of sadness.[30] The earlier Roman rite preserves a most faithful version of Qalir's mourning ceremony; his treatment makes the long journey from melancholy to freedom by way of pain, consolation and hope, beginning with the *tefillah* and ending with prayers of consolation. The Greek rite included alternative components but preserves *qerovah*'s and consolatory items. The German order omitted consolation and the Rhineland rite replaced the Roman *qerovah* and chose another item by Qalir, of less sombre colour, and some individual elegies. To these latter were later added poetic laments that were composed in the period between the twelfth and fifteenth centuries, with the whole selection ending with Zionides. Poland has no *qerovah*'s. The custom varied greatly from place to place. A *Maḥzor* from the first third of the fourteenth century has, for the divine service of the morning, twenty-two items by Qalir, two Spanish, eighteen others, five Zionides; one *Maḥzor* from that same century has twenty-one items by Qalir, three Spanish, twenty-eight others, five Zionides. A ritual from Rhineland, written in about 1428, has forty-nine songs of lament. Qalir's poetry always forms the beginning; one manuscript from 1290 contains eighteen of those, while the Short Manhig and the

27 Munk *Notice sur {Rabbi} Saadia {Gaon}* p. 68.

28 אוי כי מחלוקת end: רשום קנות.

29 לומר קנות {in the} *seliḥah* אתאנו לך יוצר for 17 Tammuz. Compare Josippon p. 882.

30 Commentary on II Chronicles 35:25.

later German order of prayer have seventeen. Perhaps some of these are intended for presentation at the end of the *tefillah*. The German *Maḥzor* that seems to be from Saloniki in 1554 contains seventy-one: three for the evening, sixteen by Qalir, thirty-nine others, and thirteen Zionides. In the edition of Lublin 1617 one counts fifty-nine: four for the evening; sixteen by Qalir, twenty-one by others, eighteen Zionides, including laments about the horrors of the fourteenth and fifteenth centuries. A manuscript of the Romaniote rite has for the evening twelve poems, among others by David and Yehudah; for the day there are several otherwise

P. 91

unknown items, one of which has pictures of the zodiac together with 449 stars crying with the Israelite tribes. In the Romaniote *Maḥzor* there are poems only for the divine service of the morning, namely, thirty-three elegies including about eighteen by Qalir, and only two Zion poems, of which one is also common in Algiers. It concludes with poems of consolation. It cannot be doubted that Qalir's poetry was part of the usage among the French communities; we are not informed of any other lamentations in their *Maḥzor*.

The Day of Hosha'na, commemorating a Temple ceremony by way of seven processions, just like the prayer devoted to rain, has generated a whole series of prayers, some of which have already accompanied the processions on the previous days of Tabernacles. Those items that seem to belong to the earliest are למענך, למען אלהינו אלהי and למען אמתך; they were soon followed by items from the layout of Qalir and Sa'adya; and finally poetic pieces by Joseph Abitur, the old French {rite}, Isaac, Moses b. Ezra, Isaac Seniri, and later authors. As in the case of the lamentations, the rites of Rome, Greece and Germany prefer, in the case of the *hosha'na*'s, to adhere to Qalir. The most faithful to Qalir is the Roman *Maḥzor* with seventeen items, of which we find that the German has twelve, the Romaniote twelve and the French thirteen in their *Maḥzor*s. Of the fourteen items that are in the Romaniote *Maḥzor*, there is only one, אנא רחום, that is missing in the German rite. All twenty items of the German rite are also in the French order, in both of which there are alternative enrichments that deviate from the above-mentioned rites and from each other. One *Maḥzor* from 1278 contains twenty-nine *hosha'na*'s, of which sixteen also occur in the German rite; among them are one by Abitur and two by Joseph Tovelem. On the other hand, we find in one prayer-book from 1290 thirteen poetic items for the first six days of the festival, besides seven by Qalir, one by Abitur, and one by Isaac. Among the twenty for the Day of Hosha'na are to be noted eight German, one Spanish, one Roman, and three by Isaac; and three French items that are lacking in the *Maḥzor* already mentioned. Among the twenty-three items in a manuscript of Luzzatto's from 1301

P. 92

there is only one that is not to be found in that earlier *Maḥzor* {of 1278} but it lacks אדמה מארר which is also absent from the Roman and some German rites. A French community in Italy around the year 1510 has twenty-four items among which there are seventeen German and one by Abitur; eight items that are in the 1278 *Maḥzor* are here lacking. The rite of Burgundy, especially that of Maçon, differs more drastically. There, one finds, apart from the introductory למען אלהינו, six items together with three others that begin כהושעת, of which two are in the German ritual. There are, for the Hosha'na Day, fifteen items, of which five are by Isaac and six in Maḥzor Roma. Therefore, there are in the French rite only half, and in that of Burgundy only a third, that are from Germany or Qalir. When Amram speaks of an "alphabet" that was recited at *musaf* on the festival, and when Sa'adya[31] refers to other items that were common in Palestine and Iraq but not included by him, it then seems that Palestine and Persia had different *hosha'na*'s and that Palestine had those of Qalir.

In Saadya{'s *Siddur*} we find three groups {of *hosha'not*}: 1) For the first six days (excluding the Sabbath), there are two items for each day, of which the second begins תענה and concludes with a short אנא אל נא and with תבנה ציון; 2) These ten are repeated on the Hosha'na Day but are concluded with אמרו לנמהרי ,תענה אמונים and קול מבשר; 3) On the Sabbath there are seven numbered poems beginning אנא which, in the Spanish rite, are distributed among all seven days. The second group, with אמרו, is not customary today but was perhaps introduced in Egypt and Qairouan. Out of the first group, the first item is transferred into the rites of Spain, Constantine, and Fez; the second and third into the rites of Fez; and the fifth (מארוד) into that of Sicily; one that is similar to the fifth (מארם) is common in Fez. Only {the poem} תענה is characteristic of all the German-Romaniote orders. Accordingly, in the latter rites Qalir dominates while the Spanish follow Sa'adya.

The *hosha'na*'s

P. 93

that were limited to two in the orders of Qalir and Saadya were extended in the Spanish rite. Abitur added another three to those with the result that the order there on weekdays is constituted as follows:

1) Introduction למענך אלהינו and 2) למענך אדיר daily; 3) אנא according to number, 4) one with two lines that conclude with biblical verses, 5) אנא with four lines in

31 Steinschneider *Bodleian Catalogue* p. 2209.

which the rhyme is decided by the numbered order (ראשון, שני and so on) of the days. 6) The hymn כהושעת, in which the same numbered order forms the rhyme in the stanzas.[32] The conclusion consists of the short כהושעת מאז and some biblical verses, between which a short *pizmon* was interposed but only at a later date. In the rites of Algiers, Avignon and Carpentras, nos. 2 and 4 are lacking; both these latter, however, have in their place a new poem between 1 and 3: Avignon has a poem by Abitur with a continuous rhyme, Carpentras one by Moses b. Ezra with each verse of the stanzas with the same beginning. Avignon omits the short כהושעת and inserts on each festival day a *pizmon* between the biblical verses. In Fez, nos 1 and 2 occur only on the first day and another *hosha'na* precedes these; on the subsequent days an item is recited before no. 3 so that no. 4 is also lacking here. The daily recitation concludes with כהושעת מאז, with *hosha'na* אנא אל אחד, and with two prose prayers, one of which is analogous to the תבנה of Sa'adya. On the Sabbath, Spain has three items, Algiers a *hosha'na* by Abitur, Avignon and Carpentras another *hosha'ana* by Abitur, plus, between nos. 5 and 6, an אנא poem, the stanzas of which all have that same beginning and are reminiscent of Sa'adya's Sabbath order.

In the rite of Sicily, the order is as follows:

1) Introduction למען אמיתך, 2) a short *hosha'na*, sometimes one of Qalir's, 3) either a two-line rhyme or a continuous one, 4) אנא אחוז כס, 5) אני אמרתי אל, 6) a numbered אנא ending with תתפרקון.[33] On only the first festival day is the introduction followed by a *hosha'na* למען and is אל נא inserted as a conclusion.

P. 94

The Hosha'na Day was also regarded as the precise time when those heavenly decisions that had been made on the Day of Atonement took effect, which is why that night was called "the concluding night".[34] Traces of this notion go back to the twelfth century; they believed that they could recognize, in the shadow of the moon, whether someone could survive the year, and the superstition of that time also had its prophylactic. Some fasted on that day;[35] in France they lit lights, as before the Day of Atonement. In some places they said אבינו מלכנו and similar prayers. The evening before, they read an abbreviated Pentateuch,[36] and in the

32 *Syn. Poesie* p. 74.
33 Compare Aaron Ha-Kohen 78b at the top.
34 Roqeaḥ 221, Ha-Manhig 69b, Naḥmanides שבלי שלח, 121, Zohar צו, Baḥya כד הקמח entry ערבה, Abuab Candelabrum 152, Ibn Shuaib דרשות f. 90b, Aaron Ha-Kohen 78b.
35 Simeon Duran Responsa part 3, no. 160.
36 Romaniote *Maḥzor*.

Spanish rite parts of the divine service took on the character of a day of repentance. The seven processions around the almemar are accompanied by prayers and pieces of *seliḥah* ritual. The merit of seven biblical heroes is mentioned and the prayer at each circuit consists of a section of the *pizmon* יה איום and two other stanzas,[37] the second of which makes a link between the name of the hero and one of the Sefirot. In this form these prayers are at most six hundred years old; the earlier rites of Avignon and Carpentras, although they use the *seliḥah* ritual, know nothing of them. The same may be said about the order in Fez where twelve *hosha'na*'s together with יה איום in its entirety precede the processions. The Sicilian rite has three למען *hosha'na*'s and the *hosha'na* מארוד before the circuits; Carpentras and Spain partially, and Fez wholly, follow the same customs and the conclusion matches Sa'adya's Siddur. The Spanish rite on that day uses the אנא that is built on numbers; that of Carpentras uses Seniri's poetic cycle of numbers; that of Avignon uses sixteen items, among them Qalir's אביעד and תתננו. Perhaps אל למושעות was also customary in some places in Provence. One Provencal *Maḥzor* contains nine *hosha'na*'s that

P. 95

do not occur elsewhere, among them three by Abitur and one by Isaac. In the Spanish *Maḥzor* the conclusion consists of nine items, of which seven are by Abitur. The preference in France and Germany was to celebrate each day in the synagogue as a festival: they said נשמת, על הכל before bringing out the scroll, היום תאמצנו at the end of the *tefillah*, and then אין כאלהינו. In particular in Worms the *qedushah* of the Sabbath was customary, and the Psalms that were said on a Sabbath were sung.[38] All in all, the festive day overwhelmed the penitential day, and outside the synagogue no more was to be seen of the Day of Atonement.

But the Day of Atonement did not always have the sombre look lent to it by the Middle Ages. In the period of the Soferim, dancing was still done in the vineyards on the atonement day. It seems that at the beginning of the fourth century it was still not the case that everyone spent the whole day in the synagogue, otherwise it could not have happened that in a time of prohibition, and with a risk of discovery, they were able to postpone the fast-day to the next Sabbath.[39] The structure of the *tefillah* was not yet fixed in the third century; here and there it was concluded

37 *Syn. Poesie* p. 306, no. 6. {M.} Sachs {*Die*} *rel*{*igiöse*} *Poesie* p. 52.
38 ליקוטין ms. Roqeaḥ 223.
39 {b.} Ḥullin 101b.

with *ne'ilah* (without the evening service). "In the morning", it states in Amram's Siddur,[40] "... the prayer leader at *shaḥarit* recites atonement prayers in the first three benedictions of the *tefillah* . . .in our assembly only a little is added: *seliḥah*'s and penitential items are obligatory. After לפני ה' תטהרו (Levit. 16:30) there are seven *seliḥah*'s. In the first three benedictions of *musaf*, he can insert much or little, depending on the wish of the community; the *qerovah* is optional, but an *'avodah* is obligatory. At *minḥah* it is not customary for us to include items of penitence and *qerovah*. *Seliḥah*'s are optional. At *ne'ilah* אבן מעמסה and three *seliḥahs* are recited." At that time, on the Day of Atonement, *piyyuṭ* such as the *seliḥah* was still a fluid component of the divine service: the status of *qerovah*'s was in accordance with the wish of the assembly

P. 96

and it had no importance in the academy; *'avodah* and *seliḥah* were considered as main items but even in later times their composition was by no means unchangeable. In the prayer order of the evening, there was no poetic addition after אבינו מלכנו and the penitential ritual, the "*Kol Nidrey*", was not mentioned at all in the *Siddur* {of Amram}[41] but it was described in a later redaction as a Spanish custom and recited only by the prayer-leader. The prayers without rhyme that Sa'adya mentions, and both אתה מבין passages, were perhaps composed for the evening service. In the Roman rite, "*Kol Nidrey*" is read, as in Amram and Aaron Ha-Kohen, but—as in Sa'adya[42]—the first lines are also in Hebrew [not Aramaic]; instead of the penitential rituals, there are only later compositions and a large group of verses that begin with סלח נא. The Romaniote rite has the penitential ritual but it is interlaced with later poetic *seliḥah*'s, among them one item by Joḥanan Ha-Kohen. Psalms precede "*Kol Nedarim*" and the *ma'ariv* is poetic. In the French and German orders, they begin with a large group of verses, the first of which start with בית יעקב (Is. 2:5) and the last of which begin שמע תפלה (Ps 65:3). The French rite goes on uninterruptedly until על עירך ועל עמך (Dan 9:19); this is followed by *seliḥah*'s, זכור, the confession, either with אמנם אשמנו or אתה מבין תעלומות and the conclusion of the penitential ritual.[43] The German rite also has אבינו מלכנו, as in Amram's *Siddur*, and,

40 Ff. 77b, 78b, 79a, compare Abudarham 62d.

41 Compare Aaron Ha-Kohen 105d with אבן העזר 75d, where the words דרב עמרם have apparently been lost; immediately afterwards the text reads ומצאתי גם בסדרו; compare a similar expression on 77a.

42 מצות זמניות {of Israel b. Joseph} ms.

43 רחמנא שזיב וכו' ובזמן קריב אמן.

from the thirteenth century, the Song of Unity. The Roman rite has in common with these two rites only the יעלה תחנונינו and uses כי אנו עמך in the morning prayer.

There is another custom that is attached to *Kol Nidrey* and goes back to Meir Rothenburg. It spread from Germany in the thirteenth century[44] into other countries, that it to say, Avignon, Aragon

P. 97

and Greece, and perhaps also France, and became general at a later date. Before the beginning of that release formula, a public request was made to allow those who had transgressed,[45] and were under the threat of excommunication, to join the prayers, or—according to a different version—to permit the assembly to pray together with such individuals.[46] Since anyone who was under such a ban was forbidden to take any part in public divine service,[47] as had already been imposed on the followers of Anan,[48] so it was inevitable that, when there was oppression from outside and internal impotence, and such a threat was the only means of making an impression, such a response was required, since it was often the case that no attention whatsoever was paid to an announcement.[49] The appeal to aggadic statements[50] that permitted association with sinners is the justification and not the motivation for such a custom.

The influence of *piyyuṭ* pushed into the background the statement of the Gaon about the divine worship of that day. *Qerovot* and hymns were counted as *seliḥah* poems, without objection. The poets clothed the *seliḥah* with the robes of their poetic material and, armed with the divine word from their national history, demanded from God mercy (רחמים) and forgiveness (סליחה) for one doing penance (מתודה). Every prayer underwent a poetic expansion by way of *qerovah*, hymn,

---

44 Ṭur I 619. Ṣedah La-Derekh 4, 5, 7 includes France but—for the earlier period—Vitry, Maḥkim and the mss. do not support him. There is another example of his inaccurate characterisation of צרפת on p. 66 above. Menaḥem Meiri of Perpignan also refers to Meir of Rothenburg as "the head of the yeshivah of צרפת" (introduction to Avot).

45 עברייינים. The word עבריין occurs in b. Shabbat 40a, לקח טוב (מטות, beginning), Rashi (אוצר נחמד Part 2 p. 176), Ha-Manhig 21a, Kol Bo 116 and 130, Haggahot Asheri Shevu'ot 4 beginning. Menaḥem of Merseburg {at the end of Jacob Weil's Responsa} 73c has עברייינות.

46 The various formulations read: i) להתפלל עם ה- (Tashbeṣ 131), ii) להתפלל ל- (Aaron Ha-Kohen 106b, Kol Bo 68, end), iii) מתירין חרם ל- (Maimoniot and Mordechai), iv) מתירין ל- (Ṭur, loc. cit.).

47 Palṭoi Gaon in Responsa שערי צדק 75a.

48 Amram ms. f. 54.

49 חידושי אגודה {of Alexander Süsslin Ha-Kohen} on Sanhedrin.

50 b. Keritot 6b [Yalquṭ Exod 107b], Wa-Yiqra Rabbah 30 f. 201a, Rashi on Exod 30:34.

rahiṭ, and confession. Here too the Palestinian rites went in a similar direction; on one side the German, and on the other the Romaniote.

P. 98

All four orders of prayer have common *yoṣer* and *ofan* poems; only the Romaniote rite has its own *zulat* built on Ps 103:1–13. In the *qerovah* for *shaḥarit* the two branch-rites separate: the German one has the *qerovah* of Meshullam while the Romaniote has that of Qalir. Testimony to this, apart from that of Ibn Ezra, who wrote his attack on Qalir's *qerovah* in Rome, is to be found in an early *shaḥarit*-introduction contained in a Roman *Maḥzor* which is perhaps earlier than the common one of Moses b. Benjamin; it actually concludes with the same words (והוד שושן) with which that *qerovah* begins. The Roman and the German rites have the *tokheḥah* אנוש מה יזכה. Up to the *qedushah* both Romaniote rites are similar, partially even identical; but the Greek lacks the atonement prayer אשפכה while the Roman lacks וקרא אופן. On the other hand, the Romaniote וזה אל זה אומרים was also included earlier in a Roman *Maḥzor*. Instead of the Roman אשר אימתך, the Romaniote *Maḥzor* has a shorter אשר אימתו, and, instead of אמיצי, אמרתך and אך אומרים, the latter rite has only אלה סליחות, אבירי לב and only the beginning of באנף. The אמרו אלהים differs in each of the two rites and the *silluq* for *shaḥarit* and *musaf* are interchanged. After the *silluq*—which has much in the Romaniote that is lacking in the Roman—all affinities cease: the Roman *Maḥzor* moves closer to the German; the Romaniote concludes the *piyyuṭ* of *shaḥarit* after the three early items אופל אלמנה, אתה מבין סרעפי and אעשה למען שמי. The passage which Ḥadasi cites from Qalir perhaps belongs among the lost parts of that *piyyuṭ*. Only Rome has the large confession prayers [Nissim, Baḥya].

The French *shaḥarit* is by and large the German, and this is even truer of the Polish. Both רוממו prayers are lacking and, instead of the אל ברוב *qedushah* associated with *musaf*, they say immediately after מקום כבודו the *qedushah* אחד קדוש. The *rahiṭ*[51] based on the verse Jerem. 10:7 (מי לא) was distributed among the first three *tefillah*'s of the day, and, in one of those, the prayers תתנם and תאפדם are recited, as a curse and a blessing. As in the German

---

51 *Syn. Poesie* p. 99.

P. 99

Maḥzor, this section of the service concludes with האזורים באהב. One should note that after the *seliḥah*'s there is אתה מבין תעלומות and—different from the German version—{the *piyyuṭ*} יום. The {*piyyuṭ*} אהללך בקול is lacking.

The earlier German rite had the complete version of מעשה אלהינו, each stanza of which is followed by {the text} מעשה אנוש which is included in the Polish *Maḥzor* only in the first stanza. Also occurring there after ככתוב שובה ישראל are the items יום אמיץ זה and אמרתי לפושעים which, in the Roman *Maḥzor*, precede that same ככתוב. In the German rite, only the first four and the final two stanzas have remained of that אמרתי, which is absent from the Polish *Maḥzor*. Before ואתה רחום מקבל it was customary to say אתה מבין סרעפי which is currently retained only in the Greek rite.

Before *musaf*, the Greek and Italian rites have the *qerovah* of Joḥanan Ha-Kohen, beginning אשען, that is already known in our recension of Amram's *Siddur*. An early *Maḥzor* of the Roman rite preserves an introduction to that {*qerovah*} by Elijah b. Shemayah that ends with the word אשען. The structure of that *qerovah*, which alternates with a hymn and an atonement prayer, is similar to that of Qalir but at the end of the three benedictions of the *tefillah* the word כפר is said and not סלח or רחום as in Qalir's. The *piyyuṭ* אמרו לאלהים, which has only one section in the Roman *Maḥzor*, is complete in the Romaniote rite (*shaḥarit*). The *silluq* concludes with ונתנה תקף. There must have been a Greek rite that formerly had another *musaf qerovah*, from which the text אתה קדוש אדון כל נשמה[52] among others was preserved in the third benediction of the *tefillah* and was borrowed by the Karaites for the Sabbath morning. In that same benediction the Romaniote *Maḥzor* has another three stanzas by Joḥanan, to which there also apparently belongs a fourth one which contained the name of his father (Joshua). In several items, the Romaniote *Maḥzor* is more frugal than that of Rome. The ending ויקראו זה in the *silluq* is absent from the Greek, early German and Italian-German rites. In Corfu,

P. 100

a *mikhamokhah* by Moses Ha-Kohen, who lived in the sixteenth century, is common.

The French *musaf*, which begins with the introductory ארעד, is by and large similar to that of the Polish *Maḥzor*. Instead of the items אל תזכר לנו, אך אין לנו אלה or אך אומרים, one finds the early penitential prayers אתאנו עדיך לחלות and אדם אם יבא.[53]

52 Cited in *syn. Poesie* p. 484.
53 Compare *syn. Poesie* p. 157, no. 4.

There, instead of אילי מרום there is אור נגה and later the *silluq* מי ימלל but without ונתנה תקף. The *qedushah* is the one that occurs in the Roman and German *shaḥarit*. Following האוחז it has: 1) האחד בעולמו (German), 2) האומן במעשה אצבעותיו, 3) האראלים אומרים, 4) האומרים אחד אלהינו (used in the Roman rite at *shaḥarit*, somewhat divergent in the German rite). In the *Maḥzor* of Burgundy, אהלת מתוחים follows לפני ה' תטהרו and is used at shaḥarit in the Roman rite; it is not mentioned by R. Nathan in the Maḥkim. After the *seliḥah*'s no *piyyuṭ* is recited.

The earlier German rite, unlike the contemporary one, was more closely related to that of Rome. Between אין ערוך and the *silluq* it had, instead of the five of the German *Maḥzor* and the seven of the Polish one, twenty-six items most of them with a *rahiṭ* that began with ובכן, among them four[54] that are in the Roman rite and one[55] in the Romaniote rite [*shaḥarit*]; the item אין כמוך אלה סליחות has its parallel in the Romaniote *minḥah*,[56] and בקצף אם אשמינו is analogous to what is found in all three other rites. Three items[57] are parallel to the prayers of curses and blessings in the French rite. Out of the seven items that follow האוחז—of which there are four in the German *Maḥzor* but none in the Polish—the first two[58] were both already included in the Roman *Maḥzor* four hundred years ago. An analogous item to the *rahiṭ* רוממו of *shaḥarit* is one that also occurs in the *musaf*;[59] the early rite of Rome knows of two similar *rahiṭ* poems for *minḥah*.[60] Now only the Polish *Maḥzor* still has אז מלפני בראשית and it also has half of the אמרו לאלהים that the Roman rite has in *shaḥarit*; some more of it is included in the *musaf* of Posen where, however, three stanzas read differently and five

P. 101

are lacking. As with the *qerovah*, the German rite has exchanged the verses of יום as compared with the Roman rite; what the latter has for *shaḥarit*, the former has for *musaf*, and vice versa.

The *'avodah* constituted a significant part of the *musaf* and in the earliest times probably used only the relevant section of the Mishnah Yoma, or perhaps the whole tractate, as was still the usage here and there in the time of Amram.

---

54 המכירים את המון, אל אמונה אתה, אלהים אין בלעדיך, אל עורך דין באמת.
55 אלה סליחות.
56 אין כמוך אדיר.
57 תתן אמת ליעקב, תתן תהלה לעמך ישראל, ה' מלך אבדו גוים.
58 האל המהודר, יאדירוך יאמירוך.
59 רוממו אדיר במעוניו.
60 רוממו תומך תמימים, רוממו אדוני האדונים.

Naṭronai Gaon[61] mentions an *'avodah* אתה כוננתה, most probably the early one that was common in Spain;[62] Amram's *Siddur* mentions two, namely, אצלצל and אשנן; and one Gaon mentions the *'avodah* אספרה גדולות which is perhaps the same one that is later Yose's *'avodah*[63] and that begins in Sa'adya{'s *Siddur*} with אזכיר גבורות . It is remarkable that the four rites have *'avodah*'s other than those just mentioned, each one in fact with its own: Rome has אזכר סלה with no introduction; just as the Romaniote *Maḥzor* has the *'avodah* אדרת by Solomon Ha-Bavli. In the French rite, אתה כוננת עולם is introduced by אתן תהלה and in the German rite there is אמיץ כח by Meshullam, which is preceded in manuscripts by the *reshut* אטיף ארש. Some places at an earlier time had an *'avodah* at each *tefillah*: for example, אתה כוננת for *shaḥarit*, אזכר סלה for *musaf*, אספר גדולות for *minḥah*. The Geonim already expressed opposition to this, although they themselves permitted it in Baghdad.[64] The *'avodah* אדרת appears to have been common somewhere in Arelat or Lotharingia, just as some Italian places had the *'avodah* of Ibn Ezra. In a variety of places in eastern and central Germany, probably in Saxony or Bohemia, they recited the *'avodah* אשוחח, which is in rhyme and perhaps by Qalir, so that only its conclusion would belong to Meshullam b. Qalonymos. The early French אתה כוננת is still customary in the three Piedmontese communities mentioned above (p. 64).

The transfer of the presentation of the high priest's service into prayer represents a period, already reached in Sa'adya's day, in which a contrast is

P. 102

drawn between the glorious past and the miserable present, and in which penitence is encouraged. This theme was already expressed poetically before Sa'adya and by the four rites in the following ways: 1) The prayer of the high priest, which occurs in the German, Roman and Romaniote *Maḥzorim*, following the completion of the service, is the alphabetic שנת אוצר הטוב which has four or five less letters of the alphabet in the Roman rite.[65] The latter rite also has a triple alphabetic *yehi raṣon* (שתאמץ) and the French rite has one that is more similar to that of Spain

61 Roman *Maḥzor* ms. Harley 16577 after *minḥah*, just as in Isaac Ghiyyat (Geiger, *Zeitschr{ift}*, part 5, p. 399). Compare Ha-Manhig 61b.

62 Compare Steinschneider *Jew{ish} Literature* p. 159.

63 ראביה ms. § 529.

64 ראביה as also in Is{aac} Ghiyyat (loc. cit., p. 398). Ha-Manhig loc. cit.

65 The letters ג ד ו ש are lacking; and the letter ט has also become a ג in the early German *Maḥzor*. When חיים טובים counts for ח and ט, these two letters are wholly lacking; compare Luzzatto מבוא p. 35.

(שנת אורה). 2) The beauty of the high priest, or מה נהדר, is poetically described in the German rite (כאהל הנמתח) and in the Romaniote *Maḥzor* (דומה לארז גדול). 3) The glorification of the Temple or בהיות ההיכל was expressed in the [earlier] German rite by בהיות ארון קדש בבית and in the Romaniote by בהיות ארון הבית על כנו. 4) אשרי עין in the German *Maḥzor*. 5) What has now gone is described by three poems beginning אין לנו לא, of which one (לא אישים) is in Sa'adya's *Siddur*, and in the Polish and Spanish *Maḥzorim*, while the two others (לא אורים and לא ארמון) are common in the early German rite. The beginning and end of the last-mentioned poem are still to be found in some editions of the German.[66] With the exception of the {high priest's} prayer, neither the Roman nor the French rite has the additional poetic descriptions. In Sa'adya, no. 5 (אין לנו) continues at its end with a passage אתה טוב לנו מכל to which are joined three biblical verses, each beginning with טוב, while in the German *Maḥzor* there is a whole series of plaintive prayers that flow into the *seliḥah*'s.

At *minḥah*, the rites diverge more substantially from each other than in the earlier *tefillah*'s, especially if one takes into account the smaller size of that service. The Roman rite has a *qerovah* by Qalir, the Romaniote has one by an unknown poet, the French and the German have one by Elijah b. Mordechai. This applies, then,

P. 103

to the five *qerovah* items before ואתה קדוש אל נא.[67] What follows thereafter is represented in this table:

Roman:		**Romaniote:**	
1.	אדר בתואר	12.	אתן תהלות
2.	אנא חון		two short
3.	אתה אל רחום		preludes
4.	תכון ארשת ms.	13.	המכירים את המון
5.	אל אדיר רב	14.	אראלי איום
6.	ובבא אחרן *Silluq*	15.	כי רכובו *Silluq*
7.	וחיות ארבע נושאות *Qedushah*		
8.	אפננת	16.	אין כמוך אדיר
9.	אצתי in responses		אצתי
10.	אשפך תחנה	17.	יום אתא לכפר
11.	מי אל כמוך with refrain אומן אמונים		

66 כל בו קטן, Homburg 1749, p. 253, the stanzas with א' ב' ג' ד' and ק' ר' ש' ת'.
67 *Syn. Poesie* p. 66.

French:		Early German:	
18.	אתה הוא אלהינו	26.	יחלנו לך, with the refrain אנא הצליחה
19.	אליך אורי וישעי		אפאר למלכי, here and there also
		27.	תגלה מלכות
20.	אפאר למלכי		אתה אל רחום
	אתה אל רחום		אדר בתואר
	אל אדיר רב	28.	אראלי הוד
	כי רכובו		כי רכובו
21.	קדשוך בנפש *Qedushah*	29.	כבודו אמוניו *Qedushah*
22.	האוחז		
23–25.	the final three *Rehiṭim*		
	of the verses מי לא יראך,	30.	יום אשר הוחק
	of which the last is	31.	אדון אביר with refrain
	מאין כמוך.		מי אל כמוך

Items 1, 2, 4, 5, 6, 8, and probably also 7, are by Qalir, 12 is by Yehudah Ha-Kohen, 19 by Benjamin, 23, 24 and 25 by Qalonymos, 26 by Yehudah; item 18 occurs in *shaḥarit* in the Polish *Maḥzor*. The hymns that precede the *silluq* (5, 14, 28) everywhere have the same refrain (מיכאל מימין), which is perhaps earlier than Qalir. The early German *qedushah* is incomplete in the *shaḥarit* of the Romaniote *Maḥzor* and is not re-introduced into the *Maḥzor* until Heidenheim.

P. 104

Items 20, 3 (without the final two stanzas) and 1 are still common in Posen.[68] The Polish *Maḥzor* has retained only the refrain of the first and last of these while 26 and 27 have disappeared completely, and in the Polish rite only some stanzas have remained of item 31 (Roman rite for *musaf*). There is no doubt whatsoever that the earlier Romaniote rite also had a *qedushah* with מי אל כמוך at the end.

The four rites have the same qerovah for *ne'ilah* but מערב עד ערב is lacking in the Polish *Maḥzor* and the *silluq* שערי ארמון is lacking in the printed Roman rite. In the manuscripts, the latter item is enclosed by two other pieces: איום אלהינו and מלאכים מרופפים. In the early German rite, and still in the Italian-German one, יעלה ויבא is followed by the prayer אז לפנות ערב of which the Posen rite has retained the first two and the last two stanzas, while the German and Polish *Maḥzorim* have only the three refrains. At the end of the *pizmon*, the Polish *Maḥzor* also has some stanzas that must have belonged to a larger piece. In all the rites, there existed, before או"א מחל and after היה עם פיפיות, a prayer of sixty-six or sixty-nine lines

68 לבוש on Ṭur I 623 § 3.

beginning אבן מעמסה,[69] that currently occurs only in the Asti rite and in the Romaniote *Maḥzor* but is already mentioned in the later recension of Amram's *Siddur*. Rome concludes with אל בפלשך and אשמינו תבלע. The French manuscripts have yet another *qerovah* for *ne'ilah*, אהבתי מעון by Joseph b. Jacob. The poetic stanzas of the piece אתא בקר that precedes the *qedushah* include the word "evening" or "night". The *qedushah* (וחיות בוערות) itself, however, is borrowed from somewhere else. The poem אילי מרום from the Roman *shaḥarit* also occurs in the French rite but with deviations.

In the order of prayer of the Spanish rite for the Day of Atonement it is rare to find anything that can be dated from before the eleventh century other than the basic prayers, the penance ritual, אוחילה and the conclusions of מי אל כמוך. With regard to the essential Spanish rite, the *Maḥzorim* of Spain and Tripoli have the *'avodah*

P. 105

and the *yehi raṣon* that follows it, while those of Avignon and Burgundy have the stanzas with which the *yoṣer* begins.[70] One manuscript includes after the *qedushah* of *shaḥarit* a non-rhyming alphabetical piece, the lines of which commence with the form האומר, הבונה—a kind of development of the pieces האוחז and האדיר—and on the basis on which Moses b. Ezra[71] probably constructed his *silluq*. The Spanish *ma'amad*[72] was artistically constructed on a payyeṭanic base and some of its parts allude to others and are appropriate only for specific places in the liturgical presentation. The *qerovah*'s for *shaḥarit* and *musaf* by Gabirol, Ghiyyat, Moses b. Ezra and Ibn Ezra mention at the end of the [first] three benedictions of the *tefillah* the first verse of the {Pentateuchal} reading or specify the relevant prayer;[73] anyhow—as is already the case with the payyeṭanim of the *minḥah* and *ne'ilah* prayers—their character is illuminated by the content of the topic. No rite honoured that integrity, and every *ma'amad* was shortened and blended with extraneous material. A Spanish *Maḥzor* from about 1400 has *qerovah*'s by Gabirol (*shaḥarit*), Ibn Ezra (*minḥah*) and Abitur (*ne'ilah*); in *musaf* by Ghiyyat and Gabirol. The *qedushah*'s are by Abitur (*shaḥarit*) Yehudah Ha-Levi (*shaḥarit* and *musaf*), Ḥiyya, Moses b. Ezra

69 The words טרם יבוא שמש, cited in Maimoniot תפלה ch. 3, are from this *piyyuṭ*.

70 אור עולם (*syn. Poesie* p. 61) and ויהי הכל.

71 *Syn. Poesie* p. 99.

72 Ibid. p. 79 and following.

73 תפלת יוצר (Joseph איומה), מוסף (אב ידעך ms; Gabirol, Ghiyyat), שנית (Gabirol, Ghiyyat), זה פעמים (Moses b. Ezra).

and Ibn Ezra; the *vidduy* by Nissim, Yehudah Ha-Levi and Shemtov Ardutil; the thirty-three *pizmons* have eight known and several unknown authors. Avignon and Carpentras stay mainly with Moses b. Ezra but the *'avodah* is by Ibn Ezra. Constantine and Algiers also have the *'avodah* by Moses b. Ezra. Tlemcen has *qerovah*'s by Gabirol (*shaḥarit*), Ghiyyat (*musaf*) and Abitur; Tunis mostly agrees with Algiers but in *musaf* with Tlemcen. Tripoli mainly follows Isaac Ghiyyat with only individual items by Abitur and others. One Fez rite has Ibn Ezra's "*magen*" for *ne'ilah*, in addition to the early Spanish *qerovah*'s, Nissim's *vidduy* for

P. 106

the evening, a different one for *minḥah*, with a total of only twelve items in common with Avignon, none of them in *musaf*. One different and earlier Fez rite—which up to that point is similar to {Shemtov} Arduṭil's *vidduy* in the Spanish rite—actually has in *musaf* a strong affinity with Avignon although it totally lacks *qerovah*'s. One order of prayer from Provence (or Catalonia) has *qerovah*'s by Moses b. Ezra (*musaf* and *ne'ilah*) and Ibn Ezra (*shaḥarit* and *minḥah*), *silluq* by Moses b. Ezra (*shaḥarit*), Yehudah Ha-Levi (*musaf*) and Ibn Ezra (*minḥah*), Abitur's *'avodah* and, in addition, a variety of items by other poets. The order in that manuscript lacks "*Kol Nidrey*" which was not common in Catalonia, and therefore also not in the main synagogues of Algiers,[74] but {was recited} in Toledo, Saragossa, Pamplona[75] and elsewhere. Catalonia has *qerovah*'s by Ghiyyat (*shaḥarit* and *musaf*) and Moses b. Ezra (*minḥah*, apart from "*magen*" which is by Ibn Ezra, and *ne'ilah*), *silluq*'s by Yehudah Ha-Levi, Ghiyyat and Moses b. Ezra. These latter two are the main representatives of the Day {of Atonement in Catalonia} although in a manuscript of a closely related rite such a role is taken by Abitur and Moses b. Ezra. The "short *'avodah*"[76] of *shaḥarit* is common to all these orders of prayer. The Aragon *Maḥzor* has specific *pizmonim* by Yehudah Ha-Levi for the evening, two by Ibn Ezra for *shaḥarit*; the third *qerovah* poem in *musaf* is by Isaac Ghiyyat. Everything else is shared between the two earliest *ma'amad* poets, Abitur and Gabirol.

74 {ספר דיני} מנהגי ארג{י}ל{ed. R. Y. S. Tseror} f. 107b § 7.
75 Isaac b. Sheshet Responsa 394.
76 *Syn. Poesie* p. 80.

Pp. 106–116

Therefore, we must search through the prayer-orders of individual countries for those parts of the *ma'amad* that are not yet totally lost. The result, which could be equally significant for the history of both poetry and ritual, is provided by way of the following overviews.

1. Joseph b. Isaac ibn Abitur

A)	*Shaharit*:	1. Introduction to "*barukh she'amar*" ברוך אשר אשש[1] (Aragon, Catalonia, Provence,

P. 107

			Montpellier; the {North-}African rites excluding Tripoli),
		2. Introduction	to "*nishmat*" אשכימה שחר (Aragon; Tripọli [stanzas 7, 8 and 13 are lacking]),
		3. *Nishmat*	ישראל כולם (Aragon),
		4. *Qedushah*	ליושב תהלות. . .אפודי שש[2] (Castile, generally Spanish, only א until ל)
		5. היום יכתב	(Provençal and French rites; Polish *Maḥzor*),
		איומה בחר	
		6. היום תישע שוחריך	(Fez, Tlemcen).
B)	*Musaf*:	[perhaps]	7. *Qerovah*-fragment[3] (unknown Greek rite),
		[probably]	8. מלאכי צבאות חילות, only א until נ,
			9. ובכן תתאדר ותתחסן,
			10. ובכן תאבד זדים (corresponding to ה' מלך אבדו p. 100 above),
		11.	המאדירים המאמירים,
		12.	Introduction to תמלוך אלהי כיום מועד:ותמלוך אתה (items 8 until 12 in *Maḥzor* Harl. 5530),
		13.	Introduction to the *'avodah* אבואה ברשיון (Aragon, Catalonia, Montpellier),
		14.	*'Avodah* אל אלהים בך

1 Attributed to Isaac ibn Ghiyyat in a *Maḥzor* ms. and then in {M.} Sachs {*Die*} *rel*{*igiöse*} *Poesie* p. 264 and in חופש מטמונים {ed. Berl Goldberg, Berlin, 1845} p. 85; corrected by me in {E.} Landshuth *Onomasticon* {*Auctorum*} p. 93.

2 Assigned to Yehudah Ha-Levi in ed. 1519 f. 331b, where on f. 350b, and in manuscripts, במרומי ארץ is attributed to ibn Abitur; hence the error in Sachs op. cit., p. 251.

3 See above p. 99.

		15.	A מה נהדר beginning כאחלמה (Spanish rite) [perhaps] 16. Prayer תאיר אורנו (Spanish; with variants in *Maḥzor* Harl. 5530).
C)	*Minḥah*:	17.	*Magen* שלישית שוקדת שלישיה,
		18.	*Keruj*[4] יבואו ותבשרם,
		19.	*Meḥayyeh* יונה מצפצפת,
		20.	*Keruj* ישע ועוז,
		21.	*Meshalesh* צפרתי משחר,
		22.	For the Sabbath: יום זה נפגשו,
		23.	ישרים שלשה,
		24.	היום יודע אל רם,
	[perhaps]	25.	ישראל עמך שמך, א until ט,

P. 108

		26.	ישראל למטה מחילה שואל, א until ע,
		27.	ישראל למטה מקדישים,
		28.	אדר אלהותך,
		29.	*Silluq* את אומץ אמנותך,
	[probably]	30.	*Ḥaṭanu* את שם ה' אברך, א until יו"ד.
			[Tlemcen and cod. Bodl. 602 have items 17 until 20 and 29; *Maḥzor* Aragon has 19, 20, 21, 29; Harl. 5530 has items 22, 23, 26, 27, 28. Item 23 is also in the French *Maḥzor* and 26 in a *Maḥzor* from Fez (Bodl. 611). The prayer היום (24) is in the rites of Aragon, Catalonia, Montpellier, Tunis, Algiers, Fez, and also cod. H h 205. Item 25 is among the pieces in an early rite of Aleppo; the חטאנו (30) is in a *Maḥzor* from Tripoli].
D)	*Ne'ilah*:	31.	Introduction וארץ אשא (Tripoli),
		32.	*Magen* ברביעית עורכת (32 until 37 are in the rites of Aragon, Castile, Tlemcen, Tripoli),
		33.	*Keruj* ויושיעם,
		34.	*Meḥayyeh* במקהל מצער,
		35.	*Keruj* ישעך ועזך,
		36.	*Meshalesh* יחידים קדמו,
		37.	*Silluq* ארשת שפתי,
		38.	אראלי זבולים (Continuation of the *Silluq* in *Maḥzor* Aragon),
	[perhaps]	39.	*Qedushah* אראלים, א until נ and יו"ד (Spanish),
	[perhaps]	40.	סלח נא לעון (Spanish, ed. 1519), is in any case earlier than the *seliḥah* with a similar beginning (in Maḥzor Tripoli) by Joseph b. Meir.

4 *Syn. Poesie* pp. 66, 80.

2. Solomon Gabirol b. Yehudah

A)	Evening:	1.	גדל יגוני (Tripoli),
		2.	*Tokheḥah* שטר עלי (in all the Spanish orders, in most of the evening prayers).
		3.	שלח מלאך (Fez).
B)	*Shaḥarit*:	4.	Introduction to "*nishmat*" אלהים אלי (Fez, Spanish *Maḥzor*, in which nine stanzas are lacking before the final one),

P. 109

		5.	Introduction to "*magen*" וארץ אשפיל (5 until 10 in Tlemcen, Fez, Aragon, and Castile [where 7 and 9 are lacking]),
		6.	*Magen* אבן בוחן,
		7.	*Keruj* שמע לחש,
		8.	*Meḥayyeh* אזי בהר המור,
		9.	*Keruj* שלום לרוב,
		10.	*Meshalesh* איש תם,
		11.	*Silluq* ה' אל אדיר (Aragon),
		12.	Short *'avodah* שעה זכרון (Catalonia, Fez),
		13.	אנושים וענושים (Montpellier and Fez),
		14.	*Tokheḥah* שוממתי (Aragon),
		15.	שכחי יגונך (Spanish).
C)	*Musaf*:	16.	*Magen* שולמית יספה (16 until 20 in Aragon, only 16 in Spain and Fez),
		17.	*Keruj* שמך להלל,
		18.	*Meḥayyeh* ציצת חבצלת,
		19.	*Keruj* שתחפץ לקבץ,
		20.	*Silluq* אאמיר אאדיר,
		21.	*Tokheḥah* שוכני בתי (Spain and Catalonia; in the other orders for *minḥah* or *shaḥarit*),
		22.	ה' מה אדם[5] (Spain, Montpellier; Catalonia for *shaḥarit*)
		23.	Introduction to the *'avodah* ארוממך (Spain, Fez and Tunis),
		24.	מה נהדר beginning באפוד חשן (Aragon),
		25.	אשרי עין (Spain, Fez and Aragon),
		26.	ובכן היה לאין (Aragon).
D)	*Minḥah*:	27.	*Magen* שלישית שוקדת משלשת (Aragon),
		28.	*Keruj* שחותי לפניך (Aragon).

5 In a ms. this follows immediately after the *mostajab* אנושים, as a *pizmon* after a *rahiṭ*; compare *syn. Poesie* p. 99 and following.

3. Isaac Ghiyyat b. Yehudah

A)	Evening:	1.	יעשה תבואה (Montpellier and Catalonia. Used for the tenth night of *seliḥot* in Tlemcen, Oran, and Tripoli),

P. 110

		2.	יום נועדו,
		3.	יום דרוש,
		4.	יה לשועת (Avignon; in cod. Paris suppl. 13 for the daytime prayers),
		5.	ירצה עם אביון (Spain, Aragon, Avignon, Fez. In Tripoli at the evening prayer for New Year).
B)	*Shaḥarit*:	6.	Before "*barukh she'amar*" יה צור אור,
		7.	Introduction to "*nishmat*" אעירה שחר אשוני לב,
	8.	*Yoṣer* אלהי אחפש,	
	9.	until 40 is a *ma'amad* beginning with the Introduction to "*magen*" (וארץ אבך), ending with *pizmon* יד תתיר. Included are:	
		13.	יום צדו (Spain, Aragon, Avignon, Fez),
		16.	יום צעקו (apart from those four rites, also in Montpellier, cod. Paris, Harl. 5530),
		19.	יום עירום (Montpellier, Aleppo ms.).
	41.	*Silluq* אתה אל מסתתר (cod. Paris; an Algiers synagogue Al-Hara, perhaps Guadalaxara,[6] in Ms. Sachs),	
	42.	Short *'avodah* אחלי בזכרי (Harl. 5530),	
	43.	ירצה לפניך (Avignon).	
C)	*Musaf*:	44 until 66, *ma'amad* before the *'avodah*, beginning with "*magen*" יונה שוכבת, ending with *pizmon* יתרת כל גביר. Included are:	
		45.	יוספים שנית (all Spanish and Provençal rites),
		47.	*Meḥayyeh* אבני קדש (Spain and Fez),
		48.	אלהים מה טובו (Castile),
		50.	*Meshalesh* תמימי ארח (Castile, Aragon, Fez).
	63.	Introduction to the *'avodah* אכון לחלות; 64. *'Avodah* אל אל אשא; 65. מה נהדר beginning בצאתו מן הדביר; 66. אשרי עין ראתה ישראל.	
	67.	*Tokheḥah* משמך רהו (Fez).	

6 Compare {M.} Sachs {*Die*} *rel{igiöse} Poesie* p. 327.

P. 111

D)	*Minḥah*:	68.	(*Magen* יספה שלישית) until 75 (יום זה הואל); including 73. *Tokheḥah* מה יתרון in Aragon for *musaf*, with item 75 also in Fez.
	[Probably]	76.	*Qedushah* אומץ אדיריך (in Ms. Sachs).

All unspecified numbers are included in the *Maḥzor* from Tripoli and a large proportion of them in the above-mentioned Paris codex.

4. Moses b. Jacob ibn Ezra

The most complete version of Moses b. Ezra's *ma'amad* is in the *Maḥzor* of Avignon[7] while the next best is in that of Carpentras. There are parts of it in the rites of Provence, Algiers, Fez and Tunis, and individual items in the rites of Castile and Catalonia. Avignon has seventy-two items, namely, three for the evening, thirty-four for *shaḥarit*, fourteen for *musaf*, ten for *minḥah* and eleven for *ne'ilah*, but of the twenty-four *rahiṭ* and *pizmon* poems on the verse in Ps 35:10,[8] which follow directly after the *tokheḥah* התבוננו, it has only seven items; one item (כל אשר עלה) is in the *Maḥzor* of Carpentras, another (אם רב עוני) in the rites of Oran and Tlemcen, and the remainder are preserved in cod. Harl. 5530. His *'avodah*[9] is in the rites of Algiers and Constantine, and its Introduction in those of Spain, Algiers, Tunis and Tlemcen. In addition, there are in other rites the following poetic pieces, which were not customary in Avignon.

A)	Evening:	מנום אנחה (Constantine, Algiers ms., and Tripoli),
		שירי ילדי (Montpellier, Catalonia. In Tripoli for the Sabbath),
B)	*Shaḥarit*:	אליכם אקרא (Montpellier and Catalonia),
		מלך מכל על (Fez and Tunis),
		מפלאי מרומות (cod. Harl. 5530),
		A מי כמכה (Ad loc., the beginning is lacking).
C)	*Musaf*:	אתה אדון לכל (Harl. Cod. Paris suppl. 13 and Fez),
		הן לא (Fez),
		ידענו אלהים (Harl. H h 205),
		חלו נא (Harl. Aleppo ms. In Tripoli for the Sabbath of Repentance),

7 Compare my *Ritus {der Synagoge} von Avignon*, especially nos. 75, 83 and 90 (p. 481) in the *{Allgemeine} Zeitung des Judenthums* 1839.
8 *Syn. Poesie* pp. 99, 100.
9 .אל אלהי אבותיכם

P. 112

D)	*Minḥah*:	יה אשר אשפך (Catalonia, Aragon, Montpellier, Tunis and Algiers),
		מחטאתי אדאג (?) (Montpellier),
		דות נפש (Harl.),
		משכי על (Castile, Montpellier, Tunis, Algiers and Fez).
E)	*Ne'ilah*:	אל נורא (Spain and Aragon; incomplete in the *Maḥzor* of Avignon).

5. Yehudah b. Samuel Ha-Levi

A)	Evening:	1.	ברכי אצולה (Avignon and Algiers. In Catalonia and in cod. Paris for *shaḥarit*; in Spain for the Sabbath before the Day of Atonement; in Tripoli for the second night of *seliḥot*),
		2.	אלהים שחרתיך (Avignon, Maḥzor Oran),
		3.	משתחוים (Spain, Aragon, Catalonia, Provence, Avignon, Fez, Algiers, Tunis and Tripoli),
		4.	*Vidduy* beginning רבש"ע צופה כל נעלם טרם (Fez; Castile has this same item for *minḥah*).[10]
B)	*Shaḥarit*:	5.	ה' נגדך כל (Aragon, Catalonia, Provence and Algiers. In Fez in the evening; in Avignon for the termination of the Sabbath),
		6.	*Silluq* אלהים אל (Spain. In Provence and Catalonia[11] for *musaf*),
		7.	מי כמוך יחיד (Fez),
		8.	למתודה (Fez).
C)	*Musaf*:	9.	*Qedushah* במרומי ערץ (Spain and Fez),
		10.	*Silluq* ארץ התמוטטה (Spain and Fez),
		11.	אשרי עין ראתה (Spain),[12]
		12.	ידי דלים (Avignon, Fez),

P. 113

		13.	ישן אל תרדם (Catalonia, Provence, Algiers, Tunis and Aleppo. In Avignon and Tripoli for the week of repentance
		14.	יצו האל (Spain. In Aragon and Fez for Shaharit; Fez II and cod. Paris for *minḥah*),
		15.	יה למתי (Fez; cod. Paris for *minḥah*),

10 The {poem} טרם אענה which occurs in the Avignon *Maḥzor* ({my} *Ritus* op. cit. {n. 7 above} p. 380) and in {L.} Dukes *Moses b. Esra* {*aus Granada*} p. 93 belongs to the last-named poet and {E.} Landshuth (*Onomasticon* {*Auctorum*} p. 76 no. 112) needs to be corrected accordingly.

11 Compare Isaac b. Sheshet Responsa 157, where this *silluq* is cited as customary in Barcelona.

12 Lacking in ms. Calabria.

		16.	ימינך נושא (Castile, and cod. H h 205; in Fez for *shaḥarit*).
D)	*Minḥah:*	17.	יה שמע (Spain, Fez and Tlemcen),
		18.	יצרי ראשית (Spain and Fez; Avignon for the week of repentance),
		19.	אבל אשמים (cod. Paris),
		20.	יום אעטך (cod. Paris; Tlemcen ms. N. 51 for the nights of repentance).
E)	*Ne'ilah:*	21.	ידידיך מאמש (Spain, Fez, Tlemcen and Tripoli; cod. Paris),
		22.	ידעו הבנים (Catalonia. Tlemcen and Tripoli for the week of repentance).

It is not known whether Yehudah Ha-Levi actually composed a *ma'amad*, including *qerovah*'s and an *'avodah*.[13] We also have only a few *mostajab* items by him.

6. Abraham b. Meir ibn Ezra

A)	Evening:	1.	אשרו דרכיכם (?) (Spain in ed. Isaac Gershon),
		2.	אשתחוה אפים (Spain; Aragon, Avignon and Tlemcen for *shaḥarit*).
B)	*Shaḥarit*:	3.	*Zulat* אחלה פניך (items 3 to 16 in Montpellier, 3 to 15 in Catalonia, and 3 and 4 in Tunis and Algiers),
		4.	אמרים עמכם,
		5.	Introduction to "*magen*" וארץ אקוד,
		6.	אהבת קדמונים,
		7.	*Magen* אמונת השרש,
		8.	יענה כבר אבות (Aragon, Spain, Avignon, Fez and Tripoli),
		9.	*Keruj* אמץ בן,

P. 114

		10.	*Meḥayyeh* אלמד ארחות,
		11.	*Keruj* אל ביתך,
		12.	*Meshalesh* אמון יוכח,
		13.	אפס גאון עזי,
		14.	אפיל תחנתי לפניך (Fez. The first three stanzas in Avignon for the preparatory day {before Atonement}),
		15.	*Mostajab* קרבת אלהים. . .אחרי שובי,
		16.	אמונתך רבה,
		17.	ארחותיך למדני (Fez and cod. H h 205),
		18.	אלהי הרוחות לכל *qaddish* (Tunis).

13 {M.} Sachs {*Die*} *rel*{*igiöse*} *Poesie* p. 301.

C)	*Musaf*:	19.	Introduction to the *'avodah* אזכיר סדר (Avignon and Carpentras),	
		20.	*'avodah* אמוני לבב (Avignon and Carpentras),	
		21.	אשרי עין (Spain),	
		22.	אל מעמדי (Montpellier, Carpentras, Avignon, Fez),	
		23.	נאור מקור (Montpellier, Carpentras, Avignon, Fez, Algiers),	
		24.	כל תהלותיך (Montpellier),	
		25.	טובך אל תצפין (cod. H h 205),	
		26.	אמנם כי דבריך (that same codex, and Fez).	
D)	*Minḥah:*	27.	*Magen* אשלש תפלות	Items 27 to 32 in Montpellier and Catalonia; 27, 29 and 31 in Castile; 27 and 31 in Fez (cod. Luzzatto); only item 27 in cod. Paris suppl. 13.
		28.	*Keruj* אדני נאמי	
		29.	*Meḥayyeh* בקר יערב	
		30.	*Keruj* ארנן בקול	
		31.	*Meshalesh* השכם והערב	
		32.	*Silluq* אחד לבדו.[14]	
		33.	מעלות השחר (Castile and Montpellier),	
		34.	אשם וזע (Spain, Algiers ms.),	
		35.	אל בית המלך (Spain. Avignon for the Fast of Gedaliah, Tripoli for New Year),	
		36.	את חפצי (Harl. Oran for the termination of the Sabbath),	
		37.	בן אדמה (?) (Spain),	
		38.	אלהי קדם (Spain).	
E)	*Ne'ilah*:	39.	*Magen* אשל צדק (Fez),	
		40.	*Silluq* אמת בספרך (Castile, Fez cod. Leid.).	
F)	*Tokheḥah*'s for the Day of Atonement:			
		41.	אבי עבור על (Manuscript in *Ginzey* {Oxford, ed. Dukes} p. 33),	

P. 115

	42.	אימות עלי נפלו (Castile, Fez in both codd.),
	43.	אין מלה בלשוני (Spain, Montpellier, Catalonia, Fez. Avignon for the week of repentance),
	44.	אם לא תדעי (Fez, Manuscript in *Ginzey* {Oxford, ed. Dukes} p. 33),
	45.	ימי האדם צבא (Catalonia, Montpellier, Avignon, Algiers and Tunis),
	46.	ישני לב מה (Catalonia, Montpellier and Tlemcen. Avignon for the termination of the Sabbath),
	47.	נפשי אל צור (Catalonia, Montpellier, and Fez in *Ginzey* {Oxford, ed. Dukes} p. 35).

14 This was customary in Barcelona according to codex Rossi 835 (Dukes {נחלת יעקב} נחל קדומים p. 41, טעם זקנים {of Eliezer Ashkenazi of Tunis, 1854} p. 78).

It turns out then that the older synagogues have preserved for us a total of 181 items by Isaac Ghiyyat and Moses b. Ezra; Avignon provides for the latter while Tripoli mainly for the former: only its *ne'ilah* has been lost. On the other hand, only sixty-eight items of the work of both earlier poets, and sixty-nine of that of the two later ones, have remained in the order of the divine service. Lacking from Abitur's poetry are everything for the evening, almost everything for *shaḥarit*, *rehiṭim*, the short *'avodah*, the *qerovah* for *musaf* and probably an אשרי עין; from Gabirol's poetry everything after *nishmat*, the third item (*meshalesh*) in *musaf*, probably an *'avodah*,[15] *minḥah* (except for "*magen*") and the whole of *ne'ilah*. Missing from Yehudah Ha-Levi's poetry are the introduction, the *yoṣer* and the *qedushah* for *shaḥarit*, and from Ibn Ezra's everything from the *reshut* to the *zulat* in *shaḥarit*, the entire *qerovah* in *musaf*, and at least three items in the *qerovah* for *ne'ilah*; altogether we may be missing almost half of all the poems. There is no doubt whatsoever that one section of the *pizmon* of those poets belonged to compositions for the Day of Atonement; there were certainly also several *seliḥah*'s that are scattered among the Spanish and non-Spanish[16] *Maḥzor*'s and that were originally *rahiṭ* and parts of the *ma'amad*.

P. 116

The abbreviation of the *ma'amad* and a degree of confusion about the works of the masters were caused in specific communities by the preservation of some older items, as well as by the work of other poets, some of them later, who replaced the earlier ones. To such belong:

Castile:	1. אנא בקראנו David, 2. אריד בשיחי Joseph ibn Suli, 3. למענך אלהי David Beqoda 4. יה איום, 5. לכו נפיל Ḥiyya, 6. Qedushah בני עליון, 7. צופיה עינינו לך Solomon Ghiyyat, 8. שעה שועת דלים Solomon, 9. המבדיל Isaac.
Catalonia:	10. אנשי לבב Isaac, 11. אעזבה מחשבות, 12. מבורך זה היום Moses, 13. זועק בקראו Zeraḥiah Ha-Levi, 14. אסיר מעל, 15. מראש מקדמי עולמים Naḥmanides, 16. אדני האדנים, 17. אזמרה למפיק, 18. אצלצלה ברכותיך, 19. בטרם אמון; introduction to the *'avodah* אנא אל נאור, מה נהדר beginning כאור בקוע, an אשרי עין beginning ארון הקדש; יעזב רשע נתיבו; אמללנו בנפש, אזמר לאל, מחטאתי אדאג and מיחד כל יום all by Moses, אנא ה' חתמנו Jacob, and items 1, 4 and 9.
Tunis:	29. לך ה' הצדקה Zeraḥiah, 30. שעה שועי, 31. מי אשר יכול, 32. אמצה ממנו, the two *'aqedah*'s in the Spanish *Maḥzor* and items 1, 4, 9, 15 and 19.

15 The one disliked by Arama (see S. Sachs התחיה p. 58) is the shorter one for *shaḥarit*, see above pp. 106 and 109.
16 E.g. כל שנאן, ה' שם, מעון אדיר, ה' מעון, ה' אלפת among others.

Algiers:	35. אוילים מדרך, עין אשא, סלח רשעתי, מלכי אהודה, אלה מהימן (Aramaic), שמו לעד Samuel, 41. אדני חזקי Simeon Duran, 42. דלנו יה; items 4, 9, 12, 15, 19, 29, 30 and 32.
Fez:	43. הלילה דלתיך, אבינו אל ארך, אלהי אל תדינני, 46. יה להלל Isaac; יערב לפניך כמו, *Mostajab* והוא הדין, ברחמיך אלהי and בחסדך יה by Benveniste, 51. את הוא אלהא, אלהי אמן יחיד Isaac, רצה רינת, אסיר בכלוא Jacob, יערב שיח Joseph, יום אקרא בקול, סלח בוראי; items 1, 2, 3, 4 and 7.

In addition another manuscript contains: 58. *pizmon* יה שכיר by Yequtiel b. Ḥazan, 59. *Mostajab* יום תקומם by Yehudah Ḥarizi.

Pp. 117–39

Apparently it was not only the *qerovah* and *'avodah* texts that were subject to change but also *seliḥah* and *baqashah* poems. Because it was unlimited in use, closely associated with the whole divine services, and always newly designed, the *seliḥah* indicated more powerfully than the other poetic compositions the differences between the rites. *Seliḥah*'s came and went, mustered together in their own collections for choice as favourites, occupying different places within the rituals and later acquiring different names. In the Spanish *ma'amad*, the *seliḥah* was, together with the *pizmon* and the *mostajab*, a complementary part of the {penitential} ritual while in the Palestinian rites the *seliḥah*'s—perhaps with the exception of *ḥaṭanu*—were inserted as desired between poetry and penitential ritual. They therefore found their place not in the *Maḥzor* but in *seliḥah* collections, unless, as in the case of the Roman rite, the *Maḥzor* included the *seliḥah*'s in its content. In Spain they preferred to call both the ritual and the collected verses *seliḥah*'s[1] while the poetic items had their own special names.[2] Although the penitential ritual itself had the same elements in all the synagogues, it underwent important and diverse adjustments. It was substantially and variously reshaped, but it failed to maintain the complete form that it had in Amram's *Siddur* even if here and there it was expanded. The alphabetical compositions אל ארך אפים and לך ה' הצדקה, as well as the many רחמנא passages that are included in Sa'adya's *Siddur*, remained alien in the established rites and only some individual parts are to be found in the ritual of Tripoli.

Amram commences with לך ה' הצדקה; שומע תפלה appears in the fourth set of verses. An "*avinu malkenu*" is recited towards the end, as it is Germany, France, and Rumania. Germany does indeed start off like Amram but שומע תפלה follows immediately while in the Roman and French rites that prayer is used at the beginning.

P. 118

The Roman rite includes thirteen Psalms and has four *avinu malkenu* texts; the French rite concludes a lengthy set of verses with לך ה' הצדקה and then brings in תנות צרות. In both these rites, the verse from Num 14:19 (סלח) is recited before the first poetic *petiḥah*, as on the evening of the Day of Atonement. In the Romaniote *Maḥzor*, the set of verses begins with אתאנו and is followed at intervals by six other

1 *Syn. Poesie* p. 77. Abudarham explains that אל תעש עמנו כלה belongs to the סליחות that is, to the penitential ritual.

2 *Syn. Poesie*, pp. 88, 89, 98, 135 and 147; also רהוטה (*Ritus {der Synagoge} von Avignon* p. 290. Comp Tanḥum on 1 Sam 16:23 p. 28 with *syn. Poesie* p. 60 note a), and השתחויה (see below p. 134).

sets. Spain, Fez and Avignon commence in the same manner as Amram's *Siddur*. In these three rites, חטאנו צורינו and "*shema*" follow on closely, as they do in the old German rite for the morning of the Day of Atonement. Avignon has both of these before the *vidduy* and has the poem אלהי ישראל constructed in the manner of "*avinu malkenu*" but not the Aramaic prayers מחי and מרן. Kaffa mostly matches the Spanish order, with five Psalms leading the way and towards the end there are some litanies that are reminiscent of Amram and the rite of Tlemcen. There are also items that are from the rites of Fez and the newer Italian communities. Tripoli, which commences with כי על רחמיך, has לך ה' הצדקה in the fourth set of verses and accompanies the *Middot* with their Aramaic translation. The prayer orders of Spain, Tlemcen, Rumania and Kaffa conclude with Ps 130, which appears in Amram before *barukh she'amar* on the Day of Atonement.

The manner in which items from the ancient rites gradually developed into independent prayers most clearly demonstrates that אבינו מלכנו was not yet to hand in the period of the Mishnah. Appeals beginning in this way are said to have been used by Akiva on a public fast in two formulations[3]—or, according to other sources, in three[4] or five[5]—formulations. Later they entered the penitential ritual, were multiplied, and reached the number of twenty-one or more in the geonic period. Samuel the Pious, who ascribes the whole of "*avinu malkenu*" to Akiva, found that the numerical value of his name corresponded either to its first formulation[6] or to its total number

P. 119

of words.[7] That said, the wording and the number of these formulations do differ in the various rites. The French order in a manuscript from the year 1290 has three otherwise unknown formulations.[8] Out of the geonic order, the Roman rite omits two and the Spanish rite four. Jacob b. Asher[9] asserts that the formulations were arranged alphabetically as in Amram and that they were prayed in this way

3 b. Ta'anit f. 25b

4 Alfasi. שבלי 94.

5 עין יעקב.

6 אבינו מלכנו חטנו לפניך [without an *alef* in חטנו, as is noted] amounts to the same total [478] as the phrase רבי עקיבא יסדו, if the three words are counted together (MS commentary).

7 עקיבא יסדה [262] indicates the numerical value [in the Fürth *Maḥzor* the count is 256 words] (ראבי"ה cited in Hirș Trèves {Thiengen 1560} and מטה משה § 802).

8 כתבנו in the books of מזונות, רפואות and שלום.

9 Ṭur I 602.

in the German synagogues; only manuscripts know nothing of it. His claim would be more appropriate for אלהינו שבשמים the fifth stanza of which, in the Roman rite, matches the third stanza of "*avinu malkenu*". In the *Maḥzor* of Spain, Aragon, Kaffa and others, the former is indeed laid out alphabetically. In Spain in the earlier period "*avinu malkenu*" was not customary in the Ten days of Repentance.[10] Later, nineteen items were chosen and were matched to the nineteen benedictions of the *tefillah*. Seven of these nineteen are, however, missing in the geonic siddur. The ruling of Aaron Ha-Kohen,[11] according to whom the correct order should be 1) מחוק, 2) מחול, 3) מחה, was observed only in Aragon, Avignon, Rome and Rumania. Amram has only מחוק; the German, French, Spanish and Algerian rites place מחול before מחוק; the Catalonian rite has מחול and the later German (and the Polish) rites have מחוק at the end. The expansion of the formulations took place gradually and not always to the same degree. Tlemcen expanded them only for the Day of Atonement and, while the Germans increased the number, the Spanish reduced it. The number of formulations of "*avinu malkenu*" are 22 (Amram), 23 (Spain), 25 (Tlemcen for the New Year), 26 (Montpellier[12]), 27 (Spain, around the year 1600 and the Algiers *Maḥzor*, ed. 1598), 28 (Aragon, Algiers ms., Constantine ms.), 29 (Catalonia, Spanish *Maḥzor* ed. 1519, Rumania, Kaffa), 30 (Rome[13]), 31 (Tlemcen, Asti), 34 (Avignon, Greek ms.),

P. 120

35–38 (Worms, Swabia, mss. of the German rite), 38, 40 and 41 (France), 42 (Poland), 43 (central Germany around 1330), 44 (Germany, Posen, Lithuania). For the past five hundred years there have been no significant variations to report in those liturgical numbers, after Germany had previously doubled the number in Amram. Only the pious of Saloniki have brought the number up to 53.

The groupings of penitential verses to which the poetic *seliḥah*'s were attached were no less varied.[14] According to midrashic procedure[15] and the verse types contained in the *tefillah* for the New Year festival, several verses of the same kind were combined, with the very same word sometimes standing at the top and at

10 Ha-Manhig 53a § 7.
11 106d.
12 It has both texts of הרם קרן and concludes with אל תשיבנו ריקם מלפניך.
13 Nine items appearing in the Fürth order are missing there.
14 *Syn. Poesie* p. 76 and ff.
15 Sifre נשא (the verses dealing with חננו, שלום, and שמר), Tanḥuma 66c (עד אנה), often in Pesiqta. Cmp. *gott. Vortr.* p. 326.

other times occurring within the text. The words of this type are primarily the following:

אודה and אודך,[16] או,[17] אל,[18] אלהים,[19] אליך,[20] אם,[21] אני,[22] אתה,[23] בוא,[24] בוש,[25] בטח,[26] גדול,[27] הושע,[28] היינו,[29] זכור,[30] חטא,[31] חיים,[32] חננו,[33] חסד,[34] טוב,[35] ה',[36] ירושלים,[37] כי,[38] לך,[39] למה,[40] למען,[41] מלך,[42] נפש,[43] סלח,[44] עד אנה,[45]

16 Festival of Atonement (Catalonian).
17 Before the *seliḥah* אין כמדת, in mss.
18 Roman group 6, French and Worms group 3, in the Italian *seliḥah* before אדון בשפטך and איתן למד, in the German before אל ימעט.
19 Prague *seliḥah* [Alt{neu}Schule] 42, Lithuania 30, Avignon f. 20 a,b.
20 German 101, Italian 147, Worms group 30.
21 French group 4, beginning.
22 After לפני המלך in the Tlemcen rite for New Year.
23 In שומע תפלה in Amram, Rome, Avignon 11b; in the German rite before *ḥaṭanu*.
24 In שומע תפלה.
25 Roman group 6.
26 Amram, Roman group 5, in the Italian rite before מפלטי.
27 Avignon at night 2 and 6.
28 Amram, French group 6, Worms group 22, Prague 122, Italy 117, Avignon 71a.
29 Amram, Worms and codex H h 15 before אלה אזכרה.
30 Amram, Worms group 17, 13, Roman group 3, French 8, Tlemcen for the New Year.
31 Prague 109.
32 Lithuania and Prague before the *seliḥah* חיים ארוכים.
33 Worms group 8. Italian rite for *musaf.*
34 French group 7.
35 In the German rite before any *pizmon*.
36 Worms group 26 and 44, Tripoli 5b, in the German rite before אומץ יוסיף; in the Spanish rite on the evening of the Festival of Atonement.
37 In the Lithuanian rite before ירושלים.
38 In שומע תפלה, in the German rite on the fifth day and on ער"ה {eve of New Year}, in the Italian rite for *shaḥarit*, Avignon 12b, Worms group 2 and 31.
39 שומע תפלה.
40 Roman group 2, French group 4, Worms group 12, in the Italian rite for *musaf,* in the Avignon rite in the days of penitence.
41 Worms group 9, in the Italian rite for *musaf,* according to a ms. in נוהג כצאן {of Joseph b. Moses Kosman} 76c.
42 Avignon f. 48, in Tlemcen for the New Year, in Lithuania and Prague before the *seliḥah* מלך אחד.
43 Prague 78 and 87.
44 Worms group 14.
45 Italy 49.

P. 121

עון,[46] פדה,[47] צדק ומשפט,[48] קוה,[49] קול,[50] קומה,[51] קרוב,[52] שוב,[53] שלום,[54] השתחוה,[55] שם,[56]
שמע,[57] שפט,[58] תבא,[59] תפלה.[60]

The use [of the verses] and their combination was a matter of preference. In Italian, French and German manuscripts one sometimes finds that the sets of verses have been put together before the *seliḥah*'s and it is rare for two manuscripts to match each other in the number of sets or in their content. Cod. Uri 269 has 9 sets, Opp. 1601Q has 13; one French *Maḥzor* of the thirteenth century has 13 after שומע תפלה and a later one has 8, which, however, differ from the 8 of the Roman *Maḥzor*. Opp. 1104F has 17 sets, a Berlin manuscript has 18, Cod. Opp. 1105F has 21, and Cod. Opp. 1106F has 22. While the Worms order {of prayer} has 41 sets in manuscripts, it has 45 in printed edition. In the manuscripts, the verses are not in a smaller hand than the *seliḥah*'s but sometimes in a larger one. Here and there they also immediately attached to the set of verses a *seliḥah*, especially in the penitential ritual. This usage was still maintained in the first Soncino editions. In the case of the verses themselves it was often permitted to make a change from the singular to the plural,[61] and

---

46 Worms group 21. In the German rite for *musaf*.
47 In the German rite before ארכו, Avignon 78a.
48 In Montpellier in the evening. Worms group 25.
49 In the German rite before מקוה and in the Lithuanian before אויתיך קויתיך and before אך בך מקוה.
50 In the German rite 142, in the Italian before אני הוא השואל.
51 Roman group 4, for *shaḥarit* (in a German ms.), Avignon 20a.
52 In the German rite for *musaf*, and in the Lithuanian for ער"ה {eve of New Year}.
53 Amram. Worms group 6.
54 In the Lithuanian rite before the *seliḥah* שלום תשפות.
55 Seder Troyes ms. and Avigdor Qara (cited in מטה משה § 29), where a list is given of thirteen השתחויות in accordance with Mishnah Sheqalim 6. They occur in the rites of France, Spain and partly of Rome in שומע תפלה.
56 In the Italian rite for *minḥah*, Lithuania 79.
57 Amram, French group 5, Worms group 18, 32, 44, and in the Spanish rite for the evening of the Day of Atonement.
58 Worms group 25, Italy 55, Lithuania 29.
59 In the German rite for *shaḥarit*, Worms group 9, Avignon 7b.
60 Roman group 1, Worms 19. In the Castilian rite for the festival of Atonement, Tripoli 3b.
61 Abudarham 22b, Responsa אבקת רוכל {of Joseph Karo} 24 a,c.

this was later regarded as obligatory.[62] Placing the refrain דרכך אלהינו at the top of the sets of verses may be traced back to the Day of Atonement liturgy.[63] In some rare

P. 122

instances one finds that a *seliḥah* has been placed before a set of verses with which it does not correspond.[64] One prayer-leader, R. Simeon,[65] even stated that, as long as it was not noted as unusual, one should recite before the performance of the *seliḥah* the verses which are used in the *seliḥot* of the Pesiqta.[66]

Penitence is expressed through prayer and fasting; the penitential ritual together with the *seliḥah*'s were therefore an inseparable element of fasting, and no fast day could be without a *seliḥah*; for its part the recitation of a *seliḥah* without fasting was regarded as inappropriate. The earliest expansion of the *seliḥah* was done during the penitential week that preceded the Feast of Atonement and that was already known in ancient times as the "Ten Days of Repentance" and was designated as such by the poets.[67] The prayers often began at midnight,[68] or at least before daybreak,[69] two hours before dawn,[70] so that these days were also called אשמורות, especially in the Spanish rite. The New Year festival, already as a sacred day of judgement, belonged to this penitential cycle, and one had to prepare oneself for this by way of *seliḥah*. Such days of preparation, usually known as days of *seliḥah*, began in Germany on the Sunday before New Year and, if that festival occurred on a Tuesday, one week earlier.[71] In Barcelona they began on 25 Elul, while in Lucena, {North-}Africa and some Persian

62 Marginal notes on the Rom{an} *Maḥzor* ed. 1587 section 2 f. 2a.
63 *Syn. Poesie* p. 163.
64 Job 17:9 (ויאחז) which precedes the *seliḥah* את פני מבין, which used that verse according to the precedent in the Pesiqta (Yalquṭ Numbers 224b).
65 Opp. 1073F.
66 Yalquṭ Numbers 224b.
67 עשרת ימי תשובה (Qalir, New Year, *seliḥah* סלח נא), עשרת ימי פגיעה (*seliḥah* אשם בעלי), 'עשרת ימי תחנוני (Yehudah Ha-Levi מגדל עז), עשרת ימים ידועים (Abitur, *hosha'na* אחלה), עשרת הימים (מי גוי, משאת כפי), לילות עשרה (ידיו, אמנת), ימים עשרה (אתאנו עדיך), ימים עשרת (אתה אל נורא, ארבעה פרקים, אם עונינו ענו, יה לשועת, מעונה אלהי), בין כסא לעשור (הורית, בין כסא).
68 חצות לילה (*seliḥah*'s חצות לילה, אקום חצות, יה על מי, בזכרי על, חרדתי etc), בלילות or לילה very often (אתה אלהי, במוצאי, אדון כתקח).
69 קודם עמוד השחר (אליך האל), אשמור (אקרא בשמך, אילותינו), ראש אשמורות (יונת אלים, יחידה לתנות, תורה החמודה), בשלישית אשמורת (חוקר), באשמורת לילה often.
70 {A.} Margaritha {*Der gantz Jüdisch Glaub*} p. 51.
71 Roqeaḥ 207, Maharil Responsa 172.

places they began on 1 Ellul,[72] so that the Day of Atonement came out as the fortieth day,[73]

P. 123

on which, according to Seder 'Olam (ch. 6), Moses had delivered to the people from Sinai the {divine} forgiveness. There were some who fasted until nightfall[74] during each of those forty days and in Lotharingia they did so during the week before the New Year festival.[75] Originally they did so in Germany mostly from the first day of *seliḥah* and they prayed the *tefillah* that was usual on fast-days, but later, already four hundred years ago, this was no longer customary.[76] Not counting the Sabbaths, there were twenty-five such early devotions, for which *seliḥah*'s and prayers were composed, especially on the first night,[77] and for the preparatory day of the New Year festival. In the ancient world, individuals,[78] and in the early Middle Ages, distinguished men, observed that day as a fast.[79]

The two weekdays on which biblical readings took place—to which reference was perhaps made in Luke 18:12–13—were marked in the ancient world by synagogal visits which the working class did not have the leisure to undertake on other weekdays. In the early Middle Ages these two days were observed by the pious as fasts and thus as days of penitence.[80] In Amram's *Siddur*, the silent penitential prayers are preceded on those two days by: 1) two sets of verses, 2) אל מלך יושב, the *Middot* and the confession of sins; then followed by: 3) זכור ברית, 4) חטאנו צורנו, 5) a prayer אדון הרחמים, 6) the alphabetical אבינו אב; concluded with Ps 20, "*avinu malkenu*", ואנחנו לא נדע and *qaddish*. The first set of verses, also interwoven with liturgical phrases, occurs only in the Romaniote rite, the second only in the Roman *Maḥzor*, which also has numbers 3 and 6 as well as an alphabetical אב הרחמן. Thus, missing from these two mentioned

72 Nissim, Alfasi and המאור {of Zeraḥiah b. Isaac Ha-Levi} on Rosh Hashanah 1. Ha-Manhig 55b. Hai {cited} by Isaac Ghiyyat (Candelabrum 290).

73 ויתקדמו ארבעים (Abitur אחלה).

74 *Syn. Poesie* p. 82.

75 ראביה 532.

76 Isserlein פסקים 35.

77 For example, בתחלת תחנוני by Joseph, יום לאל by Isaac Ghiyyat, מדי ימי by Moses b. Ezra, and some others.

78 Y. Ta'anit 2.12, y. Nedarim 8.1.

79 Pesiqta ולקחתם, Va-Yiqra Rabbah ch. 30.

80 Bereshit Rabbah, ch. 76 f. 85c. Table of Fasts at the end, Yelamedenu ['Arukh שני], Tanḥuma [הישר 537, Roqeaḥ 209, שבלי 92], Midrash ויכלו [Roqeaḥ ad loc.]; Midrash [Ha-Manhig 19b].

rites are והוא רחום, which is customary everywhere else, as well as both instances of אל ארך אפים. As far as the recitation of the *Middot* is concerned,

P. 124

Aaron Ha-Kohen already noted[81] that some [Spanish] rites have them with the confession and והוא רחום, that others [Avignon] have them [preceded by אל ארך אפים] after רחום והוא, and that there are also those who do not recite them at all. This latter policy is that of the French and German rites, in which there are no examples of what is the second item in Amram's *Siddur*. No. 4 חטאנו occurs only in Avignon and the prayer in no. 5 in none of the rites; but two parts of it[82] were transferred to the Spanish ritual on a fast-day. Most of the rites use Ps 25 for the silent penitential prayer but the German rite has Ps 6. The rites of Avignon, Spain, France and Germany follow that prayer with the intoning of ה' אלהי (beginning with Ezra 9:15 and ending with Exod 32:12); the first two rites offer a poetic *teḥinnah* beginning ה' while the latter two follow it with a version of הבט with four stanzas—or five according to the French rite. The formulations of "*avinu malkenu*" are customarily only four [Spanish], three [Romaniote] or one [German]. The liturgical order of Fez, which is generally the same as that of Spain, inserts between the *seliḥah* אנשי אמונה אבדו and the confession of sins the Roman passage ועתה ה' אלהינו, two verses that begin שוב, *shema'* and אחד הוא אלהינו.

On these weekdays, they originally located the Purim fast and the scholars' fast in the month of Nisan[83] and later the fasts commonly held after the Pesaḥ and Tabernacles festivals and less commonly after the Feast of Weeks.[84] The observance of these three fast-days, which is first mentioned by Gabirol and Amitai,[85] was already given the higher status of public fasting in France and Germany at an early date. In Provence, they were considered more like private fasts while in Italy they were not even universally observed.[86] Individuals who were pious fasted on Mondays and Thursdays from the first of Iyar until the Feast of Weeks and from the first of Ḥeshvan until Ḥanukah, and some even from the first of Sivan until the Day of

81 21d. 22a.
82 חיים שאלנו and רחמים בקשנו.
83 Soferim 21. 3, 4.
84 Roqeaḥ 212.
85 שני חמישי ושני (אפפוני מים, נחר בקראי).
86 Asheri Ta'anit, Ṭur I 429, 492, Jos{eph} Kolon Responsa 9. Maḥzor Bologna 1540 section 1, end of תמים דעים. פסח 177.

Atonement, amounting to about 35 fast-days.[87] The 6, 8 or 11 fast-days of a leap-year were located only on Thursdays

P. 125

but this is first known only in the fifteenth century and its origins are to be sought in Moravia or Poland.[88] *Seliḥah*'s, sometimes specially composed for the purpose, were recited on all those fast-days.

The *seliḥah* was also introduced into the fast-days that marked historical events since the purpose of the fast-day was to provide repentance for those guilty of sins. Thus in ancient times the divine service on the morning of the Ninth of Av was devoted to *seliḥah*[89] so that the prayers for that day are called *seliḥah* in Sa'adya's *Siddur*, even if the content and structure may be set side by side with the laments composed by Qalir. Nevertheless, the elegiac character of that day gradually displaced the *seliḥah*, as already in Germany, Poland and Italy from the thirteenth century;[90] vestiges of it did, however, survive in the rites of Provence, Avignon and Spain (in the afternoon service). On the other hand, the *seliḥah* remained an essential component of the other public fast-days that gradually became the norm, among them the Seventeenth of Tammuz that was already marked as special in the Mishnah, and the Day of Gedaliah that was part of the Week of Repentance. There is no doubt that they all became universally customary in the eighth century because R. Aḥa prescribed them, and special items were already compiled for their divine services before the time of Sa'adya. Naḥmanides[91] therefore explains them as having equal status to the Ninth of Av.

---

87 Aaron Ha-Kohen 93a,b, Ḥizzequni {on *parashat*} עקב.

88 מנהגים {Tyrnau} Purim note 10. מטה משה § 1024

89 Amram ms., as well as in Ha-Manhig 50b, ראביה 890, Ṭur I 559, Ha-Pardes 48c, אבן העזר 83b, Aaron Ha-Kohen 95d § 19 [omitted in the Kol Bo].

90 Or Zaru'a ms. and in Asheri Ta'anit ch. 4.

91 Aaron Ha-Kohen 94b.

There is a table of fasts[92] that dates from the first centuries of the geonic period and that lists, apart from the four public fasts, a number of other fast-days amounting, depending on which recension is followed, to 21,[93] 22,[94] 23,[95] 24,[96]

P. 126

or 25, and in some manuscripts to more than 36. They include 19 days marking death or unfortunate events that were detected in the biblical books, such as the death of Moses on 7 Adar, the death of Ezra[97] on 9 or 10 Ṭevet, and the civil war with the tribe of Benjamin on 23 Shevaṭ. Eight days were devoted to the sad occurrences of later times, such as the execution of distinguished people, {the martyrs} Pappus and Julianus (Hebrew: Shemayah and Aḥiyah),[98] the detention of Akiva, the Greek translation of the Pentateuch, and the disputes between the schools of Shammai and Hillel. It is reported that on 24 or 27 Adar the Alexandrians attached the name of God to a precious stone—perhaps to a crucifix. 17 Tishri marks the murder of the son of R. Jonathan, as reported in the Kol Bo. There are other such days that are noted but their [historical] bases are unknown. The reason for the 9 Ṭevet is even to be kept secret, and the fact is that Abraham b. David (1161) did not know it. The basis of the secret, as indicated by Hadasi and heard by later individuals,[99] was perhaps that the chronologists[100] calculated that the birth of Jesus was on that day, and between the years 500 and 816, the 25 December fell on 9 Ṭevet twelve times.[101] The fasts, however, remained to a large degree only paper fasts and were unknown

92 In Latin: {A.} Reland, *Antiq{uitates}* 4.13.5 p. 260, together with the Fasts Chronicle edited by Selden in his {*Tractatus*} *de Synedriis* vol. 3 ch. 13 [from here, {J.} Basnage {*Histoire de la Religion des Juifs*} vol. 6 ch. 29 p. 681ff], the calendar edited by {G.} Bartolecci, *Bibliotheca* vol. 2 p. 554ff, and the festive days listed by {A. G.} Waehner, *Antiq{uitates}* vol. 2 p. 110ff. In German from the text לבוש cited in {J. C.} Bodenschatz, *Kirchliche Verfassung*, part 2 p. 89, {K.} Anton, *Jüd{ische} Gebräuche*, part 2 p. 218.

93 Ṭur I 580.

94 Halakhot Gedolot, Amram, Aaron Ha-Kohen.

95 Kol Bo.

96 Kohen Ṣedeq and the Romaniote *Maḥzor*.

97 Mentioned in the *seliḥah*'s אזכרה מצוק, ישב בשמים and שעה עליון.

98 An early translation of Sa'adya's theological work, section 4. 'Arukh s.v. הרג and compare the *seliḥah* אז בגורי with the lament אהלי איכה.

99 Commentary on the Chronicle of Fasts ed. Dyhernfurth {1810}.

100 ס' העבור {Abraham b. Ḥiyya} p. 109.

101 In the years 503, 522, 587, 598, 606, 636, 682, 701, 720, 739, 777, 815.

to the people. The Gaon Kohen Ṣedeq himself had nothing to tell questioners about their origin.[102]

The situation is different with regard to local fast-days which were established in various places and were liturgically celebrated to commemorate suffering and rescue, dangers and sacrifices, as well probably as unfortunate experiences, and form part of the *Siddur* according to individual rites. The best-known are:

P. 127

1 Nisan. In Erfurt they fasted until noon and recited *seliḥah*'s.[103]
9 Nisan. In Carpentras a Jew was murdered in 1682. Because of the pending trial, the people attacked the Jewish quarter but the attack was thwarted.
23 Nisan. To commemorate the slaughters of the year 1147 which took place on the seventh day of the{Pesaḥ} festival, they instituted, in Köln[104] and in other places, fasting and *selihah*'s for the day after the festival. In Prague they fasted on that same day because of the murders in the year 1389.[105]
23 Iyyar. Fasting, six *seliḥah*'s and memorial prayers for departed souls in Worms, because of the First Crusade.
25 Iyyar. In the year 1631 Cavaillon was cleared of the Black Death on that day.
1 Sivan. A half-day fast in Worms because of the First Crusade.[106]
13 Sivan. A ceremony in Frankfurt am Main, concerning the year 1241, immortalized in a *zulat* and two laments.
20 Sivan. In the Middle Ages an annual fast was held in France, England and Rhineland for the martyrs of Blois (in 1171) to whom were dedicated two laments[107] and six *seliḥah*'s.[108] A fast was held from 1649 on the same date in Poland in commemoration of the Chmielnicki massacres.
25 Sivan. Erfurt[109] commemorated the slaughters of the time of Eleazar, who lost his family there, and his *zulat* זולתך אין אל was included in the prayers on the Sabbath after that date.

102 מעשה הגאונים 216, שבלי 92, תניא 62.
103 Jacob Weil דינין 41.
104 Munich codex 4.
105 *Syn. Poesie* p. 45. {A.} Würfel, *{Historische Nachrichten von der} Juden{-Gemeinde, welche ehehin} in {der Reichsstadt} Nürnberg {angericht gewesen}* p. 102.
106 Roqeaḥ 212. Maḥzor Cremona 128b. חות יאיר 1{by Yair Ḥayyim Bacharach} 126. Worms מנהגים.
107 למי אוי and אללי לי.
108 ה' אליך, יה תשפוך, אשיחה במר, אש אכלה, אמוני שלומי, איש לבוש.
109 Compare *syn. Poesie* p. 26.

P. 128

29 Sivan. The community in Cavaillon celebrates the release from a blood libel (1713).
5 Tammuz. On the evening of 4 Tammuz (27 June) 1096, there were terrible events in Xanten and the surrounding area. If, as in the original year, that date fell on a Sabbath, a *zulat* (אהבתיך by Amitai, or אלהים באזנינו by Eliezer b. Nathan) was recited. If it fell on a weekday, there was a fast.[110]
6 [or 9] Tammuz.[111] Fasting in Rome because of the burning of the Pentateuch in Paris (1246). It is included in the list of fasts given in a manuscript version of Tanya. The fast was held on the Friday of the week of *parashah* חקת.
10 and 11 Tammuz. Fasting and joyous celebration in Algiers because of the rescue from the Spaniards who attacked the city in 1775.
18 Tammuz. A Purim in Candia.[112]
20 Tammuz. An attack on the Jews in Pforzheim in the year 1271.
29 Tammuz. Fasting in Nürnberg, probably in commemoration of the year 1096 in which the terrible events concluded {at the end of} Tammuz. On the next day, the New Moon {of Av}, Regensburg was subjected to no more than looting.
5 Av. An outbreak of fire in Posen.
6 Av. Celebration in Oran to mark the occupation of the state by the French in the year 1830.
8 Elul. On this day, a Sunday, the Jews in Mainz were killed in the year 1349. The recitation of a *zulat* on the Sabbath of {*parashat*} שופטים—originally 7 Elul—is still practised in Worms.
17 Elul. On this day in the year 1268, twenty-one scrolls of the law were burned in a synagogue in Rome. In some manuscripts the Tuesday of *parashah* נצבים is noted as a fast-day but in that year that day came out as 24 Elul.

P. 129

27 Elul. This was once a fast-day in Frankfurt am Main because of the expulsion in the year 1614.[113]

110 Codices H h 206, Mich. 537, Opp. 1483Q
111 Compare *syn. Poesie* p. 30. The date of the sixth of Tammuz is given in the lament שמש וירח.
112 Lampronti {פחד יצחק letter} ד f. 81a.
113 יוסף אומץ {of Joseph b. Moses Hahn} 953, compare { J. J. }Schudt {*Jüdische Merckwurdigkeiten*} part 2 p. 55.

4 Ḥeshvan. A Purim in Algiers because of the defeat of the Spanish army in the year 1541.
12 Ḥeshvan. Fasting in Regensburg for those who were lost in Munich (1285).
14 Ḥeshvan. Celebration in commemoration of the capture of Prague in the year 1620, 10 November.
5 Kislev. In Posen. On this day, (on 10 November) in the year 1687, a struggle began against masses of the populace, which lasted three days.
15 Kislev. Celebration in Carpentras, marking the {rescue from an} attack on the street of the Jews in the year 1512.
24 Kislev. During the night of 29 November 1687 a fire broke out in Ferrara in a baker's house that was next to the Ghetto.[114]
20 and 21 Ṭevet. Fasting and a minor Purim in Ancona, marking the earthquake in the year 1691.[115]
24 Ṭevet. Conflagration in Frankurt am Main on 14 January 1711.
29 Ṭevet. Fasting in Worms, even if it falls on a Friday; five *seliḥah*'s are recited.
13 Shevaṭ. This appears as a local festive day in a *Maḥzor* from Provence.
18 Shevaṭ. A Purim in Sicily that was still being celebrated by Sicilian communities at the end of the sixteenth century.[116]
28 Shevaṭ. The community in Avignon was spared an impending danger in the year 1757 by the saving of a Christian life. It was prescribed as a festive day and a special על הנסים was composed for it.
2 Adar. In Prague to commemorate a stressful event in 1611; it was celebrated from 1613 with *seliḥah*'s that were composed for that day.
10 Adar. In Worms, in commemoration of 1349.
19 and 20 Adar. Fasting and a Purim in Frankfurt am Main, because of the rich milk persecution.[117]

P. 130

27 Adar. A Purim of the Mostarab community in Cairo, with the reading of their own "Megillah"; marking the removal of a tyrannical Pasha.
29 Adar. A *seliḥah* worship in Nürnberg and Fürth; that day is mourned in the lament אל אבל by Yehudah b. Qalonymos.

---

114 Lampronti פחד יצחק}letter} 'ח f. 44a.
115 אור בקר {of Joseph b. Solomon Fiametta} f. 48.
116 Lampronti {פחד יצחק letter} 'מ f. 137c.
117 יוסף אומץ {of Joseph b. Moses Hahn} 1109. {A. R. G. C.} Matthäi {*Beschreibung des*} *Purim* {*Festes*} p. 2.

In the year 1742 an annual fast-day was instituted in Livorno because of the earthquake.[118]

Such local fast-days were in essence not different from those exceptional fast-days that were customary in the ancient times and for which the Mishnah already provides a prescribed liturgy.[119] This was somewhat expanded in the geonic period,[120] given its own *qerovah* in the Roman rite, and various *pizmonim* in the Spanish rite. Countrywide plagues, persistent droughts and dangers were the inspiration for such fasts, which, unlike the local commemorations, were certainly not given the higher status of annually recurrent events. The *seliḥah* character is the same in both cases and sometimes the trouble[121] that inspired the prescription of the fast-day[122] is explicitly noted. The fasts that were proclaimed in Rome in 1321, in Spain in 1348, and in Worms in 1420 were of such a sort. There are therefore *seliḥah*'s that plead for food,[123] rain,[124] the cessation of rain-storms,[125] the avoidance of disease[126] and the tribulations of war.[127] An early Roman poet wrote a *seliḥah*[128] on the occasion of a solar eclipse warning, like the prophets earlier, about superstitions concerning natural phenomena. Most of the *seliḥah*'s were dedicated to dangers and oppressions[129] and

118 Azulai, חיים שאל part 2 no. 11.

119 *Syn. Poesie* p. 83.

120 Sherira (Naḥmanides לקוטות 5a), Maimonides תעניות 4, Ṭur I 579; almost identical text in a ms. of מצות זמניות, {of Israel b. Joseph} codex Leiden 94, in Abudarham and Ṣedah La-Derekh. Abbreviated in the Spanish *Maḥzor* ed. 1519 f. 404 ff.

121 (אנא האל) ביום צרה; בצרתה *seliḥah*, (אנא השם) לעת צרה, (אנשי אמנה אבדו) בעת צרותנו, (תחרות) בעת צרה.

122 (אקרא אל) בתענית, (אילותי) בתעניתי, (תעינו) ותענית קבעה; תענית צבור קבעה.

123 תמור, תענית.

124 בניך, אשימה, אשפוך, אפוסי, אחזוני, אבלה, אל באפך.

125 אז בשפוט.

126 על זאת, אם בניך, אליך ה' נשאנו, אליך ה' נפשי, אל רופא, אבלה נבלה.

127 *Syn. Poesie* p. 363.

128 אתה גלית.

129 אל קנוא, עמך אלהים, שמך הגדול, אני בעת, ממצר, תחרות, אויבים חיבים, אילותי, ידך הרם, אקרא יומם.

P. 131

described religious persecutions, blackmail,[130] desecration of graves,[131] confiscation of books,[132] clothes marking,[133] anti-talmudic agitation,[134] and informers.[135] Some of them[136] that were dedicated to dangers that had been overcome sound like psalms of salvation. Fast-days, like *seliḥah*'s, were the offspring of events and, because of their unchanging themes, they could, in fresh circumstances, again be used in the divine service.

Even more clearly than in the case of *piyyuṭ*, the liturgical orders of various countries differed from each other in the matter of *seliḥah*'s. The *qerovah*'s were not much written after the twelfth century, but the *seliḥah* poetry persisted. While the festival prayers remained unchanged, the *pizmons* that were inserted {in the *seliḥah*'s} underwent alteration. Like the paintings of the ancient world, the midrashic poems could meet the needs of various times but each of those sought the expression of their own sorrows. The daily silent prayer itself even had a different form in Amram and Maimonides and in the prayer-books and, to no less a degree, the prayers for Monday and Thursday, as well as the composition of the penitential rituals, had to put up with alterations; indeed, in the exceptional case of whether to omit the silent *taḥanun*, Tractate Soferim and the rites of Mainz and Worms, Catalonia and Mallorca, each goes its own way. While the Spanish recite their poetic *teḥinnah*'s every Monday and Thursday, the German *teḥinnah* is reserved only for the *seliḥah* days, and the *seliḥah* that begins ה' ה' only for the three-day Monday and Thursday fasts. Conversely, the Germans here and there pray שומר ישראל in three stanzas on a daily basis, while the Spanish recite it in four stanzas, and the Romans in five, only on a fast-day.

The fragmentation of an early *seliḥah* order is already demonstrated in the ritual for the four fast-days. Sa'adya's eleven items are complete only in the prayer-book of Kaffa, while only five reached the Roman *Maḥzor*,

130 אויבים קמו.
131 אויה.
132 ישני, אוחילה.
133 אותותינו.
134 אל מי, אנא מהרה, אריוך, אראלים, אבות.
135 אגיד נפלאותיך.
136 Roqeaḥ 245. Maharil beginning. Aaron Ha-Kohen 69a § 33.

P. 132

one of them the Spanish and the German rites, and none the Avignon rite. Of the four *seliḥah*'s for the Fast of Esther in the Romaniote *Maḥzor*, only one occurs in any of the other four rites. As for the other early items for the Fast-Day of 17 Tammuz, there are two in the Kaffa and Romaniote rites, two that occur only in the Romaniote rite, two in an early Greek rite, one in Germany and Italy, and one in Spain. Similarly, the five items for 10 Ṭevet are scattered among the various countries. As for the *seliḥah*'s that are included only in the German orders for that fast-day, both freedom of application and diversity of usage can be demonstrated. The manuscripts contain some sixteen *seliḥah*'s for that day, namely: 1) אזכרה מצוק, 2) אבן הראשה, 3) אבותי כי בטחו, 4) אדברה, 5) שמע עליון, 6) אום קרואה, 7) אודה עלי, 8) אריד בשיחי, 9) תעינו כצאן, 10) אפפו עלינו, 11) אפפו עלי, 12) אבותי כרבת, 13) איך מכל, 14) כנסת ישראל, 15) ישראל כניתו, 16) איומה נדגלה. Among these, items 7, 8 and 12 (of the *ḥaṭanu* type) are used at will, while 15 and 16, though written for that fast-day, do not occur in any of the rites. With regard to the remaining items, this is how they are used for the divine service: a) 1 and 2 (Abraham Klausner), b) 1, 2, 3 and 4 (same source, different rite), c) 1, 2 and 3 (Tyrnau's book of ritual, Polish *seliḥah*), d) 1, 2 and 4 (a manuscript with a *seliḥah* list), e) 1, 4 and 5 (rite of Saxony), f) 2, 3, 4, 6, and 7 or 8 (Maharil and the German order), g) 2, 3, 4, 6 and 9 (codex Leiden), h) 2, 3, 4, 6 and 10 (H h 15), i) 2, 3, 4, 11 and 12 (Worms), k) the five items in Maharil [f] and 12, 13 and 14 (Mainz), l) the same five and 1 and 5 (a fifteenth-century codex), thus amounting to eleven different combinations in the German synagogues for just one fast-day alone.

As the vigils of the penitential period were filled with poetic *seliḥah*'s, the presentations for each individual night only gradually moved away from their spontaneous nature. The similar character of all the individual *seliḥah* days is dominant only in the Castilian rite which, besides its somewhat enriched ritual, includes the recitation of a few *pizmon* texts. Most of the other countries make daily use of a number of different items that they have chosen from the collections {of *seliḥah*'s}.

P. 133

In the Romaniote *Maḥzor* there are 118 items for the penitential period, including 7 *petiḥah*'s, 13 *ḥaṭanu*'s and 14 *tokheḥah*'s; one Roman manuscript from the year 1426 includes, besides 15 {*seliḥah*'s} to accompany the penitential ritual and a total of 30 for all the public fast-days, 28 items for the Ten Days of Pepentance. In addition, there are 95 *selihah*'s of all types—certainly not counting those for the four fast-days, the Day of Atonement and various special occasions—that were certainly also in good use. Later that number was reduced to about 40, out of which the prayer-leader chose his favourites, as is specifically indicated in the year 1760.[137]

Tripoli has some eleven specific items for each morning *seliḥah*, but also other items for each day: beginning with a *petiḥah* and ending with a *ḥaṭanu* that follows a *tokheḥah*. Initial and concluding items always belong essentially to the old style, while the poetry that is added in between those is the work of the Spanish poets. For the 23 days that precede the New Year festival, they have a special item for conclusion, mostly by Isaac Ghiyyat. A *seliḥah* divine service for early morning is also held on the Sabbaths of that period, such as was once the case in Spain where on such a Sabbath the *Middot* were recited.[138] The rites of Oran and Tlemcen commonly have for the 25 *seliḥah* nights six items for each, mostly the compositions of well-know poets: Isaac Ghiyyat usually begins these and also mostly concludes them. For the 26 evenings before New Year and the 6 evenings afterwards, another {North-}African manuscript (Bodl. 613) contains a total of 391 items, with between 9 and 19 for each evening. The poetic לך ה' צדקה, of which there is a similar version in the rites of Tlemcen and Tunis, is followed by a *tokheḥah*, a "prostration"[139] that is similar to one of the German *petiḥah*'s or the *rehuṭah*'s of Avignon, a *pizmon*, with a set of verses that concludes with a *mostajab*, two *teḥinnah*'s and one metrical *baqashah*.

P. 134

The Avignon rite[140] has 132 poetic *seliḥah*'s for the penitential service. Directly attached to each of the three essential *seliḥah*'s, without any biblical verses interposing, are a *tokheḥah* and a *rehuṭah*, and then the *Middot* and a set of verses. Here too a *baqashah* provides the conclusion. Such early devotions are provided for six days with—as in the North African rite—a special order for the night when the Sabbath has terminated. On the day of the New Year, 14 items are recited (a *seliḥah* and a *tokheḥah* after the first station, and two *seliḥah*'s after the second); on the Ten Days of Repentance two *mostajab*'s are inserted after the first two stations. On the day before the Day of Atonement, however, there are four stations, each one of them beginning with a *mostajab*; the conclusion consists of a *mostajab* and a

137 תחנונים ed. Venice.
138 תקון שבת בנתים in a ms. of Maḥzor Calabria. Isaac b. Sheshet, Responsa 512. Ṭur I 602.
139 השתחויה, originally part of a non-metrical בקשה, see {my} *Ritus {der Synagoge} von Avignon* p. 455, in numbers 6 and 9.
140 Compare *Ritus {der Synagoge} von Avignon* (loc. cit. numbers 72 and 75).

teḥinnah. On the day, Carpentras even has six such stations, with several items that are different from those of Avignon.

From as early as the thirteenth century, the French orders limited themselves to a certain sphere of *seliḥah*'s and *tokheḥah*'s but the application remained flexible. In a *Maḥzor* from the year 1278, there are 177 *seliḥah*'s, half of them also customary in Germany, but with a larger number of *pizmon* and *tokheḥah* items from the Spanish rite. A later *Maḥzor*, the prayer-order of which is partly that of Burgundy, contains 240 *seliḥah*'s, half of which are identical with those of the older *Maḥzor*. Neither in those two nor in other old manuscripts is anything prescribed for individual days. The 95 items that Menaḥem of Troyes lists to a large extent match those of the two above-mentioned *Maḥzor*'s; he does not prescribe but merely makes a recommendation for the penitential period and the eve of the Day of Atonement, adding: "Whoever recites many *pizmons* is praiseworthy because the language of the Castilian [Yehudah Ha-Levi], or Ibn Ezra, or the *seliḥah*-composer (סלחן) Moses [ibn Ezra] is superb, the last-mentioned best in *seliḥah* and *pizmon*; so Ibn Gabirol in rhyme, as the Castilian in an *ahavah* and Ibn Ezra in an *ofan*."

In Germany at the same time (1280),

P. 135

it was primarily for the days before the two festivals that *seliḥah* items or certain *petiḥah*'s and *'aqedah*'s were prescribed.[141] A *petiḥah* was said only on the first day {of *selihah*'s}. On the day before the New Year festival, 20, 21 or 22 *seliḥah*'s were recited, as well as the *yehi raṣon* from Sa'adya's *Siddur* that includes the confession of sins and is therefore called "*vidduy*". A *Maḥzor* from the year 1331 contains some 140 items for the penitential period. Incidentally, almost no collection of *seliḥah*'s from that time classifies the *seliḥah* by days, only rather by types. Of the 112 items in the Leiden manuscript, it is noted only of one, that is of no. 82, that it is intended for the day before the Feast of Atonement. In the Semaq edition from Zürich, the choice of items for the public fasts (תענית צבור) is at the discretion of the prayer-leader and Abr{aham} Klausner (around 1380) says that on the day before the New Year Feast {the text} תפלה תקח (Meir b. Isaac) "together with other *taḥanun*'s" should be recited. A codex from around 1420–1430 regards as notable only the *seliḥah*'s for the first day and for the days before the two festivals, with 14 specified for the day before the New Year Festival. Only a note on the Maharil[142] prescribes the number

141 Maimoniot תפלה end. Codex H h 30.
142 Ed. Sabbio{neta} 54a.

and type of items for the Ten Days of Repentance, and {only} in Oppen. 1601Q are the *seliḥah*'s ordered according to days.

According to that provision {for each day of the *selihah*'s}, ten items were recited and these were: a *petiḥah*, three *seliḥah*'s, one שלישיה,[143] one שלמונית,[144] an *'aqedah*, a *pizmon*, a *ḥaṭanu* and a *taḥanun*. The *'aqedah* for the days of repentance and for the Feast of Atonement appears to be French in origin; it occurs only in the French and German rites. In the rites of Poland, Posen and Prague, the *pizmon* precedes the *'aqedah*. In those orders almost all the *ḥaṭanu* items are omitted, including the one that memorializes the Ten Martyrs, which is preserved only in Posen. Also only there and in Lithuania did *seliḥah*'s survive that were based on the שמע. These, as well as חטאנו צורנו, originated in the penitential ritual but they did not remain universally customary. The genuinely German communities of our time recite 5 *seliḥah*'s, the Polish 3, the Alt{neu}schule of Prague 4.

P. 136

The Polish rite also has one item less in the days of penitence. The day before the new Year festival has 33 *seliḥah*'s in the rite of Köln, 23 in those of Alsace and Lithuania, 20 in the earlier rite of Swabia and 22 in its contemporary form, 20 in the German rite, 19 in that of the German communities of Italy and in the Alt[neu]schule of Prague, 18 in Polish places, 16 in one community that was probably in central Germany,[145] and 14 in Worms. The distinction between the German and Polish rites is most pronounced on the day before the Atonement festival. While the former mark the day in almost the same way as the day before New Year, the latter recite only three items, one in two lines, one in three lines, and one *pizmon*.

The more that the stock of *seliḥah*'s increased and that of the poets decreased, the more one had to be careful about the selection, especially for the Day of Atonement, given that the time available for prayer was shortening. That is why in Germany and France there are virtually simultaneous instructions about this. There and then the supply of poetry had almost withered while in southern Europe it was flowering afresh. For the Spanish and Provençal rites, where a fully constructed *ma'amad* was inserted and there were no standard *seliḥah*'s, there was no need to make such a selection; on the contrary, the *ma'amad* was abbreviated

---

143 *Synag. Poesie* pp. 91, 135.

144 Ibid. p. 167.

145 A handwritten marginal gloss in an edition of סליחות Prague 1529.

by the omission of some *pizmonim* and *mostajab*'s. There were, however, certain prayers that were common to almost all those rites; such as the poetic confession of sins by Gabirol and Yehudah Ha-Levi, and individual *tokheḥah*'s, like Gabirol's שטר or Moses Ibn Ezra's מצעק, that were even adopted in the French rite. The early Spanish, Catalonian and Fez rites have more *tokheḥah*'s by {Abraham} Ibn Ezra; that of Tripoli some by Isaac Ghiyyat; and Avignon, the later Spanish, Algiers, and Tunis, those of Moses Ibn Ezra. An early rite of Aleppo contains for the Day of Sin 24 items, 10 of which are in the Tripoli *Maḥzor*. In the Roman rite the *Maḥzor*'s of the fourteenth century already have certain items for that day, including many by Benjamin b. Abraham, but the *musaf tefillah* of that rite has neither *seliḥah* nor *vidduy*. The Romaniote *Maḥzor*

P. 137

includes for the five *tefillah*'s 91 *seliḥah*'s which were different from those usually used on the penitential days; the choice was left to the prayer-leader.

The number of *seliḥah*'s that were incorporated was also dependent on another element, that is, on the recitation of the *Middot*. About this there were different stipulations: Naṭronai and Amram have for the five *tefillah*'s 3, 7, 5, 3 and 3 recitations respectively. In Narbonne they had 5 and (not 3) for *ne'ilah*. Sa'adya[146] had 13 *seliḥah*'s for *shaḥarit*, 7 for *musaf*, 3 for *ne'ilah* and the number of *Middot* was probably the same. Some Geonim had 7, 7, 6 and 3 while others had a total of 10 with actually only one for *ne'ilah*.[147] In some places[148] it was common to have 7, 8, 3 and 3, sometimes with only 4 or 5 instead of 8 for *musaf*. The Spanish rite had 3 for each *tefillah* during the day, with 6 for the {previous} evening. The early Catalonian rite had 3 for each *tefillah* during the day but later had 5, 6, 2, 1 and 4 for the five *tefillah*'s. Tripoli appears to have had a total of 17 recitations; the Tunis rite had 5 for each of four *tefillah*'s and 3 for *ne'ilah*; and Tlemcen had 5, 5, 7, 6 and 3. The numbers used in other places[149] were 3, 6, 4, 3 and 4, or 5. In those 16 different ways that have just been mentioned the total number of *Middot* that were usually recited amounted to one of the following numbers: 10, 17, 18, 20, 21, 22, 23 and 26. Among the orders of prayer, only the French and the German communities had Sa'adya serving as their guideline, and then later several others, including Eliezer

146 Steinschneider, *Bodleian Catalogue* p. 2210.
147 Responsa of the Geonim 1802 no. 194.
148 Aaron Ha-Kohen 106d, 107c, d.
149 Ibid. f. 108a § 44.

Ha-Levi, who recommended for *shaḥarit* 13 recitations.[150] The expansion of those numbers in each of the five *tefillah*'s matched the strictness of the French rabbis of that century, as was the case with Nathan b. Yehudah[151] and Menaḥem of Troyes. Although the Germans did not adopt that expansion for the evening and the *ne'ilah* services, they still significantly increased from then on the number of *seliḥah*'s in the three other *tefillah*'s. There are therefore only a few remaining manuscripts of the German *Maḥzor* which have less than 13 recitations in *shaḥarit* and less than 30 *seliḥah*'s in total for the three *tefillah*'s already mentioned. The

P. 138

Maimoniot, which is later than the Menaḥem to which reference was just made, already have 16 for shaḥarit, two *Maḥzor*'s of the fourteenth century have 17, and a *Maḥzor* from Breslau actually has 21 items.

In his *Siddur*, Sa'adya already sets out some *seliḥah*'s for the Day of Atonement, with the exception of the evening and *minḥah* services. Menaḥem, however, specified for the French rite *seliḥah*'s and *pizmon* only for the evening service. For the other *tefillah*'s, he is satisfied with providing a list from which a choice might be made. In order to leave space for other items, no *seliḥah* should have a permanent place unless it was composed specifically for that *tefillah*. That said, there is a manuscript from the year 1301—in the possession of Luzzatto—that refers individually to 11, 15, 13, 12 and 12 *seliḥah*'s, making a total of 63. A French order of prayer preserved in an Italian community and dating from the beginning of the sixteenth century has: 12 *seliḥah*'s and two *'aqedah*'s for the evening, 18 for *shaḥarit*, 15 for *musaf*, 11 for *minḥah* and 9 for *ne'ilah*. In each *tefillah*, the concluding section consists of a *tokheḥah*, an *'aqedah*, a poetic ה' שמעה—which is still customary in Asti—and a *ḥaṭanu* of choice.

In Germany there is a manuscript from the year 1258 belonging to the west, as well as another from the year 1331 belonging to the east, that have some *seliḥah*'s for the Day of Atonement that differ sharply from each other. Manuscripts as well as editions with fixed rites, as well as showing that individual places—Köln, Nürnberg, Neustadt in the Palatinate, Prague, Posen and Worms—followed their own orders of prayers, also testify to the diversity of their origins and in the choices they made. For the first three *tefillah*'s, Worms had 26 *seliḥah*'s; most manuscripts between 32 and 36; Swabia 33; Alsace 37;

150 Ha-Manhig 61b § 63. Mordechai on Yoma. Asheri on Yoma ch. 8.
151 Maḥkim ms.

one *seliḥah* edition from the year 1536 had 39; Lithuania 41; the German rite 42; the orders of Cracow, Posen and Neustadt each had 45; a manuscript in Breslau, the Austrian rite in the Prague edition of 1609, and the Alt{neu}schule of Prague each had 49. The Nürnberg *Maḥzor*—which is closest to the Polish rite and most distant from that of Worms—contains, for the three *tefillah*'s mentioned, 56 *seliḥah*'s, actually offering twice as much for *musaf* and three times as many for *minḥah* than the number in the Maimoniot.

P. 139

The French and the early German rites for *ne'ilah* had *seliḥah*'s as well as *pizmonim*. One *Maḥzor* from the beginning of the fourteenth century noted that one said more or less *seliḥah*'s depending on the time available. On the other hand, the Maimoniot[152] knows only of the *pizmon* and H h 30 has only the first two stanzas {of each piece}. From as early as the thirteenth century, only the first stanzas of certain *pizmonim* were sung. Mich. 444 actually contains the *pizmonim* in their entirety but has only the first stanzas in larger script and with vocalization. The Nürnberg *Maḥzor* has complete versions of two *seliḥah*'s and four *pizmonim*. In the middle of the fifteenth century the Short Manhig reported that if time was lacking for *seliḥah*'s one should recite [Gershom's] זכור[153] in full but only the first stanzas of the remaining *pizmonim*. In the printed editions the זכור also remains abbreviated, while of the *seliḥah*'s for *nei'lah*, Frankfurt, Alsace and the southern Germans have one, Poland the halves of two,[154] and Germany none.

152 On תפלה (f. 136) and שביתת עשור.
153 See *Synag. Poesie* pp. 95, 172.
154 ומי יעמד (in תעלת צרי) and מרבים צרכי (in אדון כתקח).

Pp. 139–56

In the course of the centuries, the compositions of the synagogal poets suffered not only the errors of the copyists and distortions, that were the fault of the commentators, but also losses and alterations. Even arbitrary, though not always appropriate, use amounted to an injustice to the author. Attachments to the *seliḥah*'s, with their recitation of the {Thirteen} *Middot*, included pieces of *qerovah's*, a short *'avodah* by Moses b. Ezra, Ezovi's *zulat*, Seniri's *qaddish*, as well as *ofan*'s, *ge'ulah*'s and *baqashah*'s. *Rahiṭ* compositions by the Spanish poets occur as *seliḥah*'s and the very same piece appears in a different guise in the various rites. An example is Yehudah Ha-Levi's ירושלים למוגיך which is a *zulat* in one manuscript, a *seliḥah* in the *Maḥzor* of Tripoli, and is called a pretty song by the Karaites. In addition, what was regarded as too long for standard use was abbreviated; some parts of the *yoṣer*'s, the *qerovah's* and the festival songs were

P. 140

skipped, with the result that when they were copied they were not pointed, or they were completely abandoned. Already six hundred years ago, the verses that accompanied the term ככתוב[1] in the *qerovah*'s, and in *Tal* and in *Geshem*, were hurried through, or they were skipped. Individual verses introduced by ונאמר remained in the Maḥzor's without points or simply disappeared. The *rehiṭim* from the *shaḥarit* service on the Day of Atonement were distributed among the various *tefillah*'s of that day; individual items from among the prayers between אופל and תקפו recited after the *'avodah* were omitted. Once the Maharil did not recite the rhymes אחת ושתים כנחת in the *'avodah* beginning אשוחח or אמיץ, they were not printed. The *qerovah*'s of Qalir for Purim, *Tal* and *Geshem* lost their concluding sections; as for his *shiv'atah*'s for the Sabbaths of Zakhor and Parah, only the first two sections were being recited in western Germany around 1400, the remainder being left in the *Maḥzor* without points. Castile eliminated from the festive *qerovah*'s the *keruj* or concluding stanzas while the Spanish rite ultimately did the same to the *yoṣer*'s and *qerovah*'s. Rome retains only the actual *yoṣer*. Omissions include the *silluq* in Burgundy, the poetic *barekhu* in Provence, most of the *zulat* in Avignon, and everything that follows the poetic *nishmat* in Carpentras. The French (and Polish) rites omit the biblical verses in Yose's אהללה while the Germans eliminate the *qedushah* אז מלפני בראשית and the *qerovah* of the final day of Tabernacles. Inattention

1 Book of the Pious 256. Tashbeṣ 102.

on the part of the community and lengthy singing on the part of the prayer-leader may also have been the occasion for similar changes while other distortions of such texts as Gabirol's אלהים אלי and Johanan's ידידים bordered on sloppiness.

Some abbreviations appear to be better founded. In various places in France and Germany, as early as the thirteenth century, they made omissions in the New Year hymn מלך עליון. They later did the same with the hymn passages of מעשה אלהינו which has verses that contrast God with the earthly king, or at least with mortals. Because of such content, the poems of Benjamin b. Samuel, Joseph b. Qalonymos and one

P. 141

anonymous poet were not preserved in their entirety. In the rites of Avignon[2] and Tripoli מלך עליון remains intact. Four hundred years ago any indecent references concerning Adam, Noah and the Patriarchs were omitted from the poems of Qalir and Joḥanan for the Feast of Weeks; such passages by Qalir were, however, retained in the German translation until the year 1600.

Omissions in the synagogal poetry are innumerable: they extend over *pizmon*'s, hymns, *hosha'nah*'s, and include the alphabetical litanies, among which it was often only the first parts, or sometimes only the beginnings and ends, that were recited. In the Tripoli rite the sections כ to ש are lacking in the poem לך ה' הצדקה באטום (Sa'adya's *Siddur*), while in Aragon the sections ו, ח, נ, ע, צ are lacking in the רחמנא (Spain). In the poem מה נאמר לפניך אדון הסליחות which is inserted into the *tefillah* for the Day of Atonement according to the Catalonian rite, all sections after the letter ט are lacking. The hymns with the refrains ה' מלך, ה' מלך and ה' ימלוך are mostly incomplete. Specifically, the rites of Avignon and Carpentras decorated their divine service with complete or half stanzas from the greatest variety of poems which are for us the ruined remnants of lost poems. Tashbeṣ and the rabbis of the first half of the fifteenth century[3] already prescribe abbreviations in all parts of the German divine service. In the *musaf* of the Festival of Atonement, with the sole exception of אופל אלמנה, only the beginnings and ends of other such laments are recited; similarly, in the case of אבן מעמסה, at best only the stanzas from א to ל or the first stanzas are recited. The *reshut* on a wedding Sabbath was reduced from four to two sections, and of the other chants {for the bridegroom} only the beginnings were offered. With regard to היום תאמצנו, which was originally composed for the

2 Op. cit. {*Ritus der Synagoge von Avignon*} p. 302.
3 Tashbeṣ ms. § 411. Cod H h 37, Maharil and a ms. of the abbreviated Manhig.

penitential festivals, Avignon and the Spanish rites—also in Abudarham 58a—have the letters א to כ while the French, German and Polish rites have א to ד and ת along with some additions for the Festival of Atonement. It is complete only in the Roman *musaf* and in some Spanish

P. 142

Maḥzors. As far as the אנא ה' הושיעה of the Torah Festival is concerned, the German rite has until ג and the Roman rite (for the last day of Pesaḥ) until ט; it is complete in the early German and Polish *Maḥzors*. Of the poem אשריכם ישראל the German rite has the introductory part, the Roman rite until ח, Carpentras until יוד; it is complete in the French *Maḥzor* and among the Karaites. Cochin has אשר בגלל אבות until פ. Only א until ד have been preserved of אראלי מעלה. The Spanish lament אך זה היום has nine stanzas in the editions, ten in Maḥzor Avignon, eleven in the Castilian *Maḥzor*, but actually in both these latter cases only until ט. A third of the Roman version of אמרו לאלהים is represented in the German rite, and the Romaniote rite's version is reduced to a half in the Roman rite. Seniri's האל העירה, consisting of six stanzas, has only three in the German *Maḥzor* from Saloniki.

The abbreviation of individual *seliḥah*'s goes back almost as far as the twelfth century. Eleazar b. Yehudah already observed[4] that it once happened on New Year's Day, when a circumcision was being celebrated, that the first stanza of [Gershom's] *seliḥah* זכור הברית that precedes the *Zikhronot* verses was recited and the remainder left for later. Separation led to abbreviation. In fact, that *seliḥah* was already abbreviated in manuscripts and only a remnant was transmitted to the editions. Several *seliḥah*'s are to be found, also in manuscripts, in incomplete alphabetical sequence; the theme that precedes the *mostajab*, as well as the stanza that precedes the alphabet, were also omitted. Some items were divided up on the Day of Atonement at the discretion of the prayer-leader and the {Thirteen} *Middot* were recited at the end of each one of them, as was specifically done in the French rite with אמנם אשמינו and in the German with אותך אדרוש and תעלת צרי. Sometimes only one of the parts was then used and that is why only that part occurs in the *Maḥzor*, *seliḥah*'s are interrupted in the middle, and parts[5] are mistaken for the whole. In this way, or through other accidents, some poems lost half their content.[6] A particular

4 Roqeaḥ 112.

5 E.g. קולי למלך, פניך האר, מרבים צרכי, מעשה ידינו, מלכנו באנו, כסא כונן, טובך יאבה, אילותי.

6 Examples: אחלה פני, אויבי ועויני, אודה עלי פשעי, אודה עלי חטאתי, אדום מזה, אדם אפר, אגגי אשר חשב בשמך, אתהלך קודר, אנוש איך יצדק, אנא זכור נא, אמון פתחי, אלהים אתה כוננת, איך הסתיר, איום ונורא צום לחום.

P. 143

case that deserves to be cited is that of Gabirol's *me'orah* שני זיתים of which only half was recited in Worms because nothing else was available.[7] Two stanzas from the middle of Tovelem's *seliḥah* איחד צורי were omitted and the author of that poem was identified as Joel. The prayer of Sa'adya, usually known as *vidduy*, did not fare any better; the second half, with additions[8] and insertions,[9] was recited on the day before the New Year festival according to the French and German rites. An abbreviated version was used by the Roman and the German-Italian communities in the event of epidemic and danger; most of it was retained in the Lithuanian rite; but barely half of the whole prayer in the printed editions of the German, Polish and Italian rites; only the Romaniote *Maḥzor* has it all. Most of the *pizmonim* for *ne'ilah*, already abbreviated in the *seliḥah* booklet of Augsburg 1536, thus remained unknown.

Though rare in *piyyuṭ*, there is a complex *qerovah* that contains individual items by various authors. We find such a situation with regard to the *seliḥah* אבד הוד, which seems to have been constructed from two parts, of which the first is reminiscent of Elijah b. Shemayah and the second of Benjamin. Sometimes in the course of synagogal use, two different items are placed closely together and they are then merged together as one in the editions. This is what occurred in the case of the above-mentioned ומי יעמד at *ne'ilah*[10] as well as the first four stanzas of אליך צורי that were joined up with most of אלה אזכרה, and with אות ברית, or one part of אשמתינו כי, that were joined up with parts of Gershom's זכור. Additions and expansions were suffered by virtually all the statutory prayers, as is demonstrated in the *yoṣer*, the *tefillah*,[11] *barukh she'amar*, which grew from ten[12] to forty sentences in the rite of Kaffa, the *avinu malkenu*,[13] the על חטא,

7 Ḥayyim Yair Responsa 238. נהג כצאן 48b. Worms מנהגים and {M.} Mannheimer, *Die Juden in Worms* p. 23.

8 אנא הבט as well as תתברך.

9 As with: ולמען הקדושים, השנה הזאת הבאה עלינו, and the item והנה כל גוים etc.

10 Above, p. 139.

11 *Gott. Vorträge* pp. 367–71.

12 Ṣedah La-Derekh 1, 1, 23.

13 Above, p. 119.

P. 144

and the הרחמן verses of the grace after meals. The same applies to היה עם פיפיות,[14] the *silluq* for *musaf* according to the Roman *Maḥzor*,[15] and many other prayers. The liturgical poetry met the same fate. The poem יום יום ידרשון for the eve of the Day of Atonement attracted seven new stanzas in a French *Maḥzor*. The early German rite of the New Year festival concludes the *teki'ata* of the *Zikhronot* with some stanzas[16] in remembrance of the martyrs. Three interpolations were made in the *zulat* אלהים באזנינו of Eliezer b. Nathan but only one of them, by Eliezer Ha-Levi, later survived. In the fourteenth century, Ibn Ezra's *ge'ulah* אל ישראל was expanded with a stanza by Solomon of Perugia, and barely fifty years later the manuscripts included the extension as part of the original text. Menaḥem's lament אללי is three stanzas shorter in the printed editions, and shortly afterwards five stanzas longer, than in manuscript. The *'aqedah* איתן למד had one extra stanza in the Worms rite; איתן לומד was refashioned in the Tripoli *Maḥzor*. In the *seliḥah* תאבתה two stanzas were inserted before the final one and appear to have been borrowed from two different items. The poem מלכי מקדם by Mordechai has another stanza after the fourth, perhaps by a certain Isaac b. Jacob. As one early commentator suggested, there was a Jacob who martyred himself for the sake of his co-religionists; be that as it may, what is sure is that the extra stanza is responsible for the fact that the author of the *seliḥah* is called Mordechai b. Jacob and not Mordechai b. Shabbethai. Both of the final stanzas of Abitur's יערכו were cut out,[17] with the first stanza being altered and a new stanza placed at the beginning, with the resultant creation of an anonymous אנא סלח נא. An obvious falsehood was perpetrated when, at the beginning of the seventeenth century, the final stanza of Yehudah Ha-Levi's ברכי אצולה was omitted[18] and over it was printed the name of Naḥmanides. It is equally striking when two otherwise different *seliḥah*'s share a common stanza.[19] Two other *seliḥah*'s have an epilogue at the end;

---

14 Compare Rapoport on קליר {*Bikkure Ha-'Ittim* 10} p. 116.

15 Above, p. 99.

16 Note 6 {below}.

17 *Syn. Poesie* p. 228.

18 With regard to the supporting documentation, which I presented to the scholars of Berlin (on 29 May 1834), compare Plessner *die kostbare Perle* pp. 241ff, {M.} Sachs {*Die*} *rel{igiöse}* *Poesie* p. 306.

19 אחז בשרי and ארבעה מלכיות.

P. 145

similarly,[20] Meir's *'aqedah* אל הר המר has three additional stanzas by Eleazar b. Yehudah, which were composed at the time of an impending danger, but then later, either wholly or partly, remained attached to that *'aqedah*. There is also the remarkable case in which four additions, under the name of Joseph, were made to the six early fast-day *seliḥah*'s.[21]

Intentional changes to the texts are less common. From the early period one should note the changes made in the computation of the calendar years, as, for instance, in the *seliḥah*'s אוחילה מעי, גרוני נחר, תהיינה עיניך.[22] Some three hundred years ago, in the *seliḥah* שלש עשרה, the imperative form was changed to the future tense,[23] to avoid the impression that one was addressing one's prayers to the {Thirteen} *Middot*. At a later date, some emendations were made in Mordechai's משאת כפי for use on the minor Day of Atonement, an activity that was called "cleaning up the highway".[24] In the course of a later publisher's reworking of a text containing a *silluq* for *minḥah* by Abitur an incorrect line was inserted.

Generally, there were, however, many instances of change towards the end of the Middle Ages that were occasioned by situations and events, without the conscious involvement of the worshippers. Gutenberg and Luther had no less influence on the synagogal rites than Kabbala and the Inquisition. From as early as the first decade of the fifteenth century, the detailed rules and instructions in the ritual manuals left almost nothing in the control of the prayer-leader whose stature had already been reduced from its sometime greatness and who was no longer the poet nor the legal expert: no prayer-leader in Germany or Poland had ever functioned as both. Once the art of book-printing had made manuals and prayer-books accessible to everyone, the publisher took the place of the concerned prayer-leader. Printing set the borders, rich manuscript collections became a sterile possession; the items that were included

---

20 אלה אזכרה and אם יתקע.

21 יהמו was added to three *seliḥah*'s (אבלה נפשי, אגגי בהעמיקו, אז בבוא), ירח to אזכרה מצוק, יודע to אמנם אלהי, שגיא to אגגי אז.

22 Luzzatto מבוא p. 20.

23 חלי, בקשי changed to אחלה, אבקש etc.

24 נוהג כצאן {of Joseph b. Moses Kosman} 36d.

P. 146

became the decisive ones, the standard nature of the texts that everyone possessed produced uniformity: *minhag* was based on the printed editions. Within forty to fifty years, those countries that had Jews and printers, printed Hebrew prayer-books. The German rite started things off (Grace after Meals 1480, *Seliḥah* booklet, n. d. and 1496, Prayer-book 1508, *Maḥzor* c.1521), together with the Roman rite (Prayer-book and *Maḥzor* 1486, *Seliḥah* booklet 1487, *Hosha'na* booklet 1503), followed by the Polish rite (Prayer-book 1512, *Maḥzor* 1522, *Yoṣerot* 1526, *Seliḥah* booklet 1529, all of them in Prague), the Spanish rite (n. d. and 1519), the Greek rite (1520), the Catalonian rite (1527), Aragon (n. d.), and the Karaite prayer-book (1528).

From 1492, expulsions drove Spanish Jews to Italy and Turkey, Italian and Sicilian Jews to the east, and Austrian Jews to the west; the Spanish rite found a place in numerous cultured communities, together with the German, French and Greek, as well as the Mostarab and Palestinian rites, and the printing presses made them familiar with the Spanish *Maḥzor*. Not only in the first years of those resettlements, when the newcomers were often unable to have their own synagogues,[25] but also later, even in flourishing Saloniki, members of the different communities sometimes prayed in the same synagogue, that is to say in a Spanish one. In that city, there were, in around 1540, at least fourteen different communities[26] with more than twenty synagogues; between eighteen and twenty-eight alone were burned down in the conflagration of the year 1545. With the exception of the German rite, almost all the others had adopted the Spanish order of prayer; it is indeed reported that the Sicilian prayer-leaders

---

25 Jacob Ḥabib cited by Karo on Ṭur 1 154.

26 German, Castilian, נוה שלום, Gracia or לוית חן (compare Amatus {Lusitanus} {*Curationum Medicinalium*} *Centuria{e Septem}* 7 p. 181), Aragon, Catalonian, Portugal or Lisbon, Evora, Italian, Calabrian, Apulian, Sicilian (compare my *zur Geschichte* p. 530), Greek, Provençal (Responsa דברי שלמה, אמרי נועם {of Joseph Shalom Gallego} Amsterdam f. 141a), which are mentioned in Almosnino's Sermons, the Responsa of Elijah Mizraḥi (47, 57, 79), {Responsa Ohaley} Tam {of Jacob ibn} Yaḥya (33), Samuel de Medina and others.

P. 147

had forgotten their own rite.[27] The attractions of Spanish poetry, which were already effective in the Middle Ages,[28] also played a part in that development, especially since close proximity made borrowing that much easier. Gabirol's Kingly Crown became popular even in Poland;[29] compositions from abroad, such as אדון עולם and יגדל, became constituent parts of the daily prayers[30] in German synagogues. Similarly, the different versions of halakhic instructions by Maimonides, Asher and Karo could gradually be condensed into one uniform code (שלחן ערוך) and also disappeared when the individual currents of the various rites, compositions and prayer-orders dried up into one solid mass. They deleted and added to the old and to the new, to *piyyuṭim* and *seliḥah*'s, and transmitted to the new generation the hymns and psalms of the Middle Ages in the form of a torso, or even only a relic, so that the concern for their {synagogal} usage blurred the notion of their artistic nature and the memory of the spiritual achievement of the author.

The informer also had a share in the changes made to the *Maḥzor.* The accusations against the Talmud had already extended to the Jewish prayers in the Middle Ages. It was therefore often the case that, out of fear, the owners of prayer-books scored through and erased, or cut out complete pages, as well as changing words here and there. R. Yeḥiel of Paris already had to defend "*Kol Nidrey*" against an informer. In about 1370, they attempted a demonstration against *'alenu* in Spain[31] and, although that effort came to nothing, the sword of Damocles continued to hang over the worshippers. Every device was used at public disputations to invoke fear. This explains the policy of Lipman of Mühlhausen (about 1410) in his book Niṣaḥon. The persecutions that were encouraged by the preachers[32] increased in the second half of the fifteenth century.

P. 148

This is the reason why an anonymous writer responded in the year 1488 to the baptised Jew Vicenza that the *seliḥah* and *zulat* poems were for private prayer and had no wider status, so that the community should not be answerable for them. At that

27 Samuel de Medina Responsa part 1 nos 34, 35.
28 כסאות לבית דוד, ch. 9. Compare above, p. 134.
29 חג פסח f. 12b.
30 מטה משה § 31. יוסף אומץ {of Joseph b. Moses Hahn} § 60.
31 Ṣedah La-Derekh 1, 1, 36.
32 Jos{eph} Colon Responsa 192 הדורשים מכתי הכומרים {the preachers from the priestly orders}.

time the Inquisition became controllers of Jewish curses and sighs. As linguistic expertise and printed books facilitated insights into the synagogal prayers, and as, at the same time, the clerical regime saw itself threatened by the Reformation, so did the supervision of books become more intense, and increasingly hateful censorship placed shackles on the Jewish prayer-books. Sometimes only the vowel-points remained of the words that were missing and in most cases the blank spaces were not filled.[33] While some individual units of prayer disappeared completely, others remained in mutilated state, or were altered. After the expulsion from Naples and the rise of the Jesuits, the persecution appears to have increased, as clearly occurred in Bohemia. It was these circumstances that may have led Rabbi Meir Katzenellenbogen of Padua, around the year 1542, to make changes in the *seliḥah* -booklet of the German community: some expressions in the text were altered and six items were deleted and replaced by others.[34] Such an arrangement was also followed in the *seliḥah*-booklet published in Hedernheim in 1546 from which "all offensive and dangerous matter has been removed". From that time onwards it was not only the *Siddur* and the *Maḥzor*, but all Jewish printed works, that suffered the yoke of the converted Jews who were hired by the Dominicans. Since censorship was soon no longer enough, they confiscated whole works, arranged public burnings of the Talmud, and R. Meir of Padua had to complain to a friend[35] that he could not offer sufficient rulings because physical punishments were given for the possession and study of the Talmud. In the year 1559 the prayer-books of the Prague community

P. 149

were taken to Vienna for an inspection to be carried out. The blank passages that could still be seen in the Venice *Maḥzor* of 1568 gradually disappeared; they were clandestinely removed from existence. From that time onwards the mutilation of words, lines and paragraphs in the Italian, German and Polish editions of the prayer-books, later aggravated by overseers and accommodating editors, maltreated poetry and veracity.[36]

Although printed books and ecclesiastical pressure now impoverished the public divine worship, this did not happen to the liturgical literature which actually increased. Printing duplicated both the old and the new items that had originally

33 Compare Margaritha {*Der gantz*} *Jüd{isch} Glaub* pp. 226, 286.

34 אליך אקרא, את הקול קול, אלהים אל דומי לדמי, ה' אלהי רבת, אני יום אירא, ישראל עמך [communicated by Luzzatto in 1852]; the first three are actually included in Maḥzor Cremona 1560.

35 Responsa שארית יוסף {of Joseph b, Mordechai Gershon}, no. 1, f. 3a.

36 Appendix VI {below}.

been composed for domestic devotion or for private fasts; examples are prayers in prose, *yehi raṣon*, the expanded eighteen benedictions of the days of penitence, versions of אלהי נשמה, expanded "*'alenu*", the glorifications of the Sefira wrapped up in the *tefillah*'s with liturgical contemplations of mystical content. By around 1500 the Kabbala had struck deep roots and ritual questions were addressed by way of Zoharic texts.[37] The books by Meir Gabbai, Solomon Alqabeṣ and Moses Cordovero, and, even more so, the activities of their disciples, spread super-piety and exaggerated worship, so that there was everywhere a sense of the esoteric, even in the vowel points.[38] At the beginning of the seventeenth century, Ḥayyim Vital, Isaiah Horowitz and Hirṣ b. Jacob, with their Lurianic involvement, made their appearance with new prayers, outrageous verbalizations and incomprehensible meditations (כוונות), so that they could, by way of such systems, dominate devotional books, Sabbath orders of prayer (from 1614), grace after meals and the night prayer, and finally also the public prayer-books. Thus, for example, they had at one point in Spain recited Ps 67 on the days of the Omer Counting because it consists of seven verses and forty-nine words.[39] At a later time, they found that the fifth verse had forty-nine letters. Now it was said that Psalm 67 was engraved on David's shield in the shape of a candelabrum; in fact an Italian siddur

P. 150

of the fifteenth century had that Psalm in the shape of a candelabrum, followed by *yehi raṣon* and some biblical verses. That is how it was printed in Prague in 1581, and from about 1635[40] it appeared on the title-page of the Siddur and the design was even pinned to the inside of the holy ark.[41]

Most of the Jewish prayer-books were covered, and the most beautiful poems defaced, by such mystical items which were largely incomprehensible, if not meaningless. No rite was spared as is demonstrated by every *Siddur* and *Maḥzor* from Tlemcen to Kaffa. Superstition and the worship of spirits were perpetuated by innumerable *yehi raṣon* prayers, angelic names and sefirotic bombast so that the meaning of the public worship of God was forced into the background, and a whole shebang of amulets was introduced into the prayer-book and among the people.

---

37 Elijah Mizraḥi Responsa 1 and 2.

38 Compare Meir Lublin Responsa 83.

39 Abudarham 27c.

40 Steinschneider *Bodleian Catalogue* 2133A.

41 Responsa צמח צדק {of Menaḥem Mendel Krochmal} no. 50.

What is owed to that same kabbalistic and ascetic trend, which established itself from Palestine to Italy and Poland, from Poland to Germany and Holland, and from Jerusalem and Livorno to the Barbary coast, is the introduction of new fast-days such as that of the minor Day of Atonement, early morning devotions, special groups on Mondays and Thursdays, sorrowful night vigils and other special groups. Texts chosen from the German, Roman and Spanish collections of prayers, as well as new items, were composed largely with kabbalistic content, and the new form of worship was explained as more important and salutary than the statutory prayers.

Such liturgical institutions were not entirely new. R. Jonah already recommends that at least one day a month should be reserved for fasting and prayer; hence the custom of some to fast on the day before the New Moon.[42] In the book Raziel[43] fasting on the day before the New Moon of Sivan is recommended as a means of improving one's spiritual capacity. Around the year 1500, there were some who used to engage in fasting on the day before New Moon;[44] only towards the end of that century, and

P. 151

actually first in Palestine, was such fasting regarded as the regular custom of communities or groups. Israel Najara composed a specific prayer for such an occasion;[45] Menaḥem Azariah de Fano[46] recommends such a fast-day and calls it the minor Day of Atonement of the pious, suggesting that it should be practised on the Monday or Thursday that precedes the New Moon. Mordechai Jaffe[47] is not yet familiar with a minor Day of Atonement and calls the day of the New Moon itself—as within the *tefillah*—a day of atonement; meanwhile in 1614 Yehudah of Modena wrote his *pizmon* for that festive day, Abraham Griani prepared a special order of prayer for it in 1626, and Luria's *Siddur* disseminated it among the rites.

Around 1530 there were groups that fasted and prayed on Mondays and Thursdays; these groups are said to have spread from Jerusalem to Saloniki and perhaps

---

42 Zürich Semaq § 4, gloss.

43 F. 45a.

44 Margaritha op. cit. p. 38. מנות הלוי {of Solomon Alqabeṣ} 9a. מטה משה 758. סדר היום {of Moses Ibn Makhir} 80b.

45 עולת חדש no. 40.

46 Responsa 79. תקוני תשובה Venice 1600.

47 לבוש Part 1, no. 422.

as far as Kaffa.[48] In Safed,[49] from the year 1559, ten men held a fast on which they spent the whole day in the synagogue as on the Day of Atonement. Just as the Day of Atonement was transplanted into every month, so it seemed appropriate to extend the devotions of the *seliḥah* days into the whole year. This was the origin of the groups for early devotions[50] first found in the German community of Venice in 1596.[51] In the Italian community of that city, the above-mentioned Fano similarly adopted the practice.[52] The custom, which was still cited as a new one in 1622,[53] was disseminated from there to the whole of Italy. These devotions began in Mantua in 1616; in Modena in 1623 four brothers set up furniture in their house for that purpose.[54] In the year 1647, the first Polish edition of a "*Tiqqun*" for such prayers appeared.

The midnight laments over the exile, like the individuals' devotion, is old;[55] but the special order of vigils came from Palestine about 280 years ago, from where the

P. 152

reconstituted rabbinic schools of Jerusalem, Safed and Tiberias had, through their students, spread the custom among the Turkish lands. Other communities, such as Mantua in 1610, received it from there[56] especially since special prayer-books were published for the purpose. In Verona in the year 1655 such a group for laments was established,[57] a practice then followed in Venice, Prague[58] and other places. The laments and the prayers were largely composed by Palestinian Jews of the sixteenth century.

Most of the groups were spared the kabbala and retained practical functions. Thus, for example, the group responsible for burials, which surrounded itself with special aura, specifically composed their regulations together with prayers. A group of this kind was founded in Prague in 1564. In accordance with a custom that emanated from Italy, these groups had an annual fast-day, as for instance, in

48 See Hirș Trèves {Thiengen 1560} on the silent *teḥinnah*.
49 {Issachar} Even Shushan 64b.
50 {Entitled} שומרים לבקר.
51 סליחות Venice 1600 f. 126.
52 Responsa loc. cit. מעירי שחר {of Aaron Berekhiah b. Moses} 264b.
53 Steinschneider *Bodleian Catalogue* 3003.
54 כנף רננים {of Joseph Yedidiah b. Benjamin Yequtiel} preface f. 3.
55 Asheri Berakhot 3a, Meir Aldabi {שבילי אמונה} 99c.
56 Moses Zacut in codex Bisliches 55 f. 12a. שערי ציון {Amsterdam 1735} introduction.
57 Menaḥem Novera preface to תקון חצות Mantua 1746.
58 שערי ציון Amst{erdam} f. 71a.

Posen and Frankfurt on the Monday before the reading of *parashah* שמות and in Lemberg on the Thursday beforehand; in Hamburg on the day before the New Moon of Adar; in Dresden on 7 Adar; in Berlin on the day before the New Moon of Nisan; in Halberstadt on 15 Kislev. The evening assembly for the Feast of Weeks and the Hosha'na Festival that originated in Safed bore a kabbalistic stamp that was particularly strong; the holy Zohar played the central role in this. Around 1600 these assemblies were common in the Orient and from 1650 printed instructions became numerous.

Through the dissemination of various forms of printed *Siddurim*, grace after meals booklets and *Tiqqun* texts, prayer texts, both customary and novel, made their way from other rites and from the works of the kabbalists into the rites of the communities where they established themselves and in no small degree modified public worship. The following examples are from the prayer-books of the German rite:

1) אדון עולם, 2) יגדל, 3) the song of unity. These three items were originally common only in the evening service for the Day of Atonement,

P. 153

the last mentioned particularly for those who remained in the synagogue all night. In the year 1549 it was still being noted that it was being recited daily "in some places".[59] 4) The recitation of the verse from Num 10:35 when fetching the Torah scroll, though recommended in Maḥkim, was not previously common in Germany, and occurs only in some manuscripts for Sabbath. It is lacking in Margaritha[60] and in the edition of תפלה published in Prague in 1541. 5) The Zoharic בריך שמיה, which first appears in Italian private prayers of the year 1540, was included in *minhag* books from 1599[61] but only later in the *Siddur*. 6) The Sabbath song לכה דודי by Solomon Alqabeṣ originated in the *Tiqqun* for the Sabbath. 7) The Zohar (64a) refers to the use of the verse in Ps 65:5 at a circumcision and this is recommended by Meir Gabbai;[62] in the sixteenth century it was not yet in any prayer-book. There were other items, borrowed from the Spanish rite, that were recommended for private devotions and penetrated the *Siddur* in this guise, such as, for example,

---

59 Octavo סדור Venice 1549, at the end.

60 Op. cit. p. 277.

61 סדר היום {Moses ibn Makhir} ed. 1599 f. 22a, תחנות Basle 1609, יש שכר Prague 1609, תחנות ובקשות Prague 1615.

62 תולעת יעקב {of Meir ibn Gabbai} 49a.

the hymn of Joseph ibn Waqar, the prayer חשתי,[63] the Kingly Crown,[64] the prayer for the deceased, especially many *yehi raṣon* texts, some of them old[65] and others newer versions from Laṭif,[66] Luria and his followers; similar prayers were those recited silently by the prayer-leader on the high holy days, by the congregation before the sounding of the shofar, and by the individual before performing a religious requirement. In addition, some prayer texts were newly introduced into the oriental, {North-}African and Portuguese rites and into the Italian, German and Polish communal customs.

After the prayer text was printed it was then the turn of the commentaries. Apart from the work of Abudarham which appeared in Lisbon in 1489, there were from among the earlier scholars who expounded the daily prayers only one commentary from the fourteenth century[67] and excerpts from Azriel and Eleazar[68] that were printed. With regard to festival prayers there is

P. 154

precious little to show before the middle of the sixteenth century; most of them were only scattered marginal glosses, such as are found in the Catalonian *Maḥzor*, the Venice *seliḥah* of 1548, the Prague *Maḥzor* of 1549, as well in the Roman *Maḥzo*r of 1587 and the זולתות of Tannhausen in 1594. Expositions attached to the text are to be found in the *Siddur* of 1525 for the *hosha'na*'s, the German *Maḥzor* (Saloniki 1554, Sabionetta 1557, Venice 1568), the Polish *Maḥzor* (Lublin 1567), in which Abraham's glosses [1549] were multiplied by Mordechai b. Yehuda and Naftali b. Joel Schwarz.[69] Detailed comments occur in the Romaniote *Maḥzor* on four *piyyuṭim*,[70] in the Roman *Maḥzor* of Bologna 1540 (Joḥanan Trèves) and in individual editions of the rites of Spain and Greece, in the works of Simeon Duran, or among later scholars such as Joseph Ha-Kohen (1554), Moses Nigrin, and Moses Pisante (1569)[71] who sometimes deal with the daily prayer but more commonly with the *'avodah*,

63 In תפלה Venice 1599. Hanau 1611 (Steinschneider {*Bodleian Catalogue*} 2109, 2117).
64 About 1623, see Steinschneider {*Bodleian Catalogue*} 2126.
65 יום א' שמזלו אריה (Raziel {Ha-Malakh} 34b, Spanish *Maḥzor* ed. 1519 f. 64); שתהא שעה זו (ms. Calabria, Roman *Maḥzor* 5b).
66 תפלה Venice 1606 part 8 cited by {Abraham} Portaleone {שלטי הגיבורים} {Joshua Boaz} 109d.
67 Trino 1525.
68 Cited by Hirṣ Trèves, Thiengen 1560.
69 Steinschneider {*Bodleian Catalogue*} 2454.
70 Yoṣer, אור ישע, Qalir's *Ṭal* and *Geshem*, *'Avodah* אדרת; and one passage is expounded from Benjamin's כך גזרו.
71 Compare the preface to נר מצוה {of Moses b. Ḥayyim Pizanti}{and his} ישע אלהים pp. 29, 47.

hosha'not and *azharot*. Solomon Ha-Levi's commentary on the *musaf* prayer for the New Year[72] has remained unknown.

Actual commentators are to be found in the German and Polish *Maḥzor* of the final third of the sixteenth century and include Mordechai b. Yehuda, Ṣevi b. Ḥanokh (*Seliḥah* 1570, 1584), Mordechai Kohen [and Ṣevi] (*Maḥzor* 1584), Asher b. Joseph (Lamentations 1585, *Yoṣerot* 1589), Isaac Levi (German *Maḥzor* 1600), Abraham Levi (*Seliḥah* Posen 1608). The order of שומרים לבקר was expounded in 1647 by Isaiah b. Ḥayyim. These commentaries, which were largely based on their medieval predecessors, are to a considerable extent free of the mystical obfuscation that haunted the daily prayers more than the *Maḥzor*. From 1568 there are in particular places in the *Maḥzor* headlines that provide the "meditations of the poet".[73] This procedure has now been standard for about a hundred years.

Translations of the prayers into the vernacular[74]

P. 155

existed earlier than is generally thought, since there exists a French translation of a poetic *ma'ariv* dating from the fourteenth or fifteenth century. The song "Almighty God" was already printed in 1526; the Hymn of Unity in German translation in 1540. Judeo-German translations appeared in the following order: 1562 the *tefillah* together with *hosha'not* and *ma'arivim*,[75] 1571 *Maḥzor* for both penitential festivals by Avigdor b. Moses, 1574 the Polish *ma'arivim*, 1594 individual *seliḥah*'s, 1600 Benschbuch (the chants in rhyme), *Maḥzor* for the three pilgrim festivals by Anschel of Posen, 1602 the Polish *seliḥah*'s by Jacob Levi of Teplitz, 1605 *Yoṣerot*, 1609 the Hymn of Unity by Avigdor Eisenstadt. Anschel freely weaves into the translation of the *azharot* some gratuitous moral admonitions, such as "and do not shout aloud in the streets about your good deeds since they should not be known by anyone else but God."[76]

After a long interval, German translations appeared in Amsterdam: 1674 Gabirol's Kingly Crown, 1688 a German *seliḥah* by Eliakim, 1698 the lamentations [in Dessau], 1704 the order of שומרים לבקר by Mrs Ellusch. The תפלה published in

72 לחם שלמה {of Solomon b. Isaac Ha-Levi} 24a.

73 כוונת הפייטן.

74 Ms. evidence in cod. Vat. 316, 332, Munich 88, Oppenh. 1489A, Q. De Rossi cod. Ital. 6 and 7. Compare *gott. Vorträge* p. 442.

75 {M.} Saraval's *Catalogue {de la Bibliotheque}* no. 1368. Steinschneider {*Bodleian Catalogue*} 2086.

76 Section 8 Letter 'ה.

Amsterdam in 1766 provides in German headings the "meditations of the poets" as well as the *ma'arivim* and the *hosha'not*. Incidentally, the texts of those commentaries and translations, namely, on the *piyyuṭim* and the *seliḥah*'s, remained stable and virtually as in their original form. The *seliḥah* expositions of Mordechai were still printed in Prague in 1782, and Anschel's *Maḥzor* version still in Fürth in 1792; even corrupted items remained stable: the worshipping rabbi did not dare to change anything even if it was recognized as wrong.[77] Only *teḥinnah*'s for women were sometimes newly produced (first editions in Prague in 1590, and Amsterdam 1648).[78]

The appearance of liturgical regulations (דינים, מנהגים) kept pace with the publication of the liturgical text and translation; selections from earlier works, as well as new editions, in Hebrew and in translation (Judeo-German, with a few

P. 156

in Italian and Spanish), were attached to the *tefillah* and the *Maḥzor*; the *Maḥzor* printed in Saloniki 300 years ago included the running commentary מעגל צדק; in later editions (firstly in Venice in 1599) these compilations were entitled הדרת קדש. With such content laid down to the smallest detail and divided into innumerable requirements, the only task left to the public was to ascertain what to say and what not to say: biblical verses, Psalms, passages from the Gemara and the Zohar, *piyyuṭ*, penitential prayers, hymn of unity and kabbalistic formulas—all were recited and were recommended—already by Abraham Portaleone in the year 1612—for recitation. Menaḥem b. Zeraḥ divided up the Psalter for recitation in the course of a month, but in Ferrara the חתן תורה on the Torah festival recited the whole Pentateuch.[79] Samuel Aboab[80] was against the multiple recitations of the mourner's *qaddish*: but the multiplication increased as a result of ignorance. Similarly, the last remnant of freedom with regard to determining the divine worship was lost, and all that remained for choice were the cantorial melodies, the casuistry of the visiting rabbi, and the entertainment of the wedding guests by the buffoon.

---

77 Lampronti {פחד יצחק} entry מנהג f. 137a
78 Steinschneider {*Bodleian*} *Catalogue* p. 477.
79 Lampronti {פחד יצחק} letter ח end.
80 Responsa 183.

Pp. 156–62

Before we pursue further the fate of *piyyuṭ*, it is necessary to take a look at the rites of the followers of Anan who tackled life under the banner of literalism and therefore called themselves Karaites. The Ananites were primarily concerned to replace the Geonim; retreating into the Pentateuch, they wrote a new code of law and the results of their exegesis had to be the opposite of everything that was customary in Israel. So they found that the word ממזר did not mean a bastard or the issue of a forbidden relationship but a person with damaged testicles, and that the firstborn animal meant only the oldest member of the herd.[1] Anan offers proof that the Pesaḥ cakes are to be made from barley flour and that a fowl is not to be slaughtered but

P. 157

has to have its neck pinched;[2] the circumcision has to be performed with scissors[3] and it is wrong to light torches in that connection.[4] Everywhere one encounters the opposite of what had been sanctioned for hundreds of years; the permitted became forbidden and vice versa. Accordingly, entering into a marriage with one's niece[5]—a worthy act for Jews—was forbidden; similarly, warming up food and cohabiting on the Sabbath,[6] as well as moving out of the house and circumcision.[7] It was not permitted to cook meals on New Year, the Feast of Weeks, or the Feast of Booths.[8] Not only was it not permitted to kindle lights on the Sabbath but Anan wished to have all burning lights extinguished.[9] The provisions of this new law-book consistently bear the character of an organized opposition;[10] later it was taught that a marriage had to be enacted not by one of the three methods stated by the Mishnah but by all three;[11] legal slaughter requires the cutting of four

1 לקח טוב f. 80b.
2 Compare Dunash, entry מלק, Eliyahu in {אליהו} אדרת 39d, 63a.
3 Hadassi {Eshkol} section 301.
4 Caleb, appendix to אדרת.
5 See Niṣaḥon section 66. Parḥi, section 5, end.
6 Responsa of the Geonim, ed. 1802 no. 34. Hadassi {Eshkol} section 147. Eliyahu, op. cit. section 8 f. 28b. Compare Ibn Ezra on Exod 34:21.
7 Semag, prohibition 66. Hadassi {Eshkol} sections 147, 301.
8 Hadassi {Eshkol} section 147.
9 Book of the Pious 1153, *gott. Vortr.* p. 236, Eliyahu op. cit. section 17.
10 Compare לקח טוב on *parashah*'s צו and אמור.
11 Eliyahu loc. cit.

vessels (instead of two);[12] leaven should not be sold on Pesaḥ.[13] Contracts had to be in Hebrew (not Aramaic), and the scrolls of the Law should have pointing and cantillation;[14] Pesaḥ should be celebrated only on Monday, Wednesday or Friday[15] (days that were ruled out in the Jewish calendar) and the Feast of Weeks should fall on a Sunday, as taught previously by the Boethusians.[16] Fringes should have seven threads (instead of eight) on the corner of every garment and so on. As against the thirteen *Middot* they taught their own twelve[17] or fourteen[18]—of which numbers ten and eleven are the same as those of the Rabbanites[19]—and while Maimonides later laid down thirteen articles of faith, they found that there were—as in Islam—

P. 158

ten.[20] In the interpretation of the Prophets they were motivated by the same hatred: they identified the two women in Zech 5:9 as the seats of learning of the Geonim in Sura and Nehardea,[21] or the academies of Babylonia and Jerusalem.[22] Nevertheless, they accorded themselves the geonic titles and even called themselves Gaon and Rabbi.[23] Since the composers of the Mishnah originated in the Hillelite family, they went along with Shammai, and since the Masoretes opted for the text of Ben Asher, they adopted the text of Ben Naftali. Their arrangements for divine worship are of a similar hue. The name of the New Year festival as well as the sounding of the shofar were abolished and the festival was given the biblical name of יום תרועה. The Fast of Gedaliah was transferred from the third to the twenty-third of Tishri, that of the Seventeenth of Tammuz to the ninth of that month, that of the Ninth of Av to the seventh and tenth of Av. Ḥanukah, the Hosha'na festival, the second day of festivals, *qaddish* and the statutory *tefillot* were cancelled.

12 Karaite דיני שחיטה {ms.}.
13 Trigland, {*Diatribe*} *de* {*Secta*} *Karaeorum* p. 264.
14 Hadassi {Eshkol} section 8.163.
15 Hadassi {Eshkol} section 185.
16 See Ibn Ezra on Lev 23:11.
17 כתר תורה MS כי תשא.
18 Hadassi {Eshkol} sections 174, 175.
19 Midrash Psalms 93.
20 Hadassi{Eshkol}. Karaite Siddur part 2. Trigland {*Diatribe*} p. 283.
21 ס' העשר {in מבחר ישרים (Koslov 1835)} ad loc.
22 Hadassi {Eshkol} section 122.
23 גאון יעקב; see Cod. Leid{en} 52 no. 13, end; גאונים cited by Aaron in {the Karaite} Siddur section 2 p. 174. The note in {Jost} *Geschichte des Judenthums* part 2, p. 381 is not valid.

As to their earliest order of prayer, we have no information; they cited as the founder some fictitious contemporary of Ezra. Collections of biblical verses, as well as prose and some poetic items, seem already to have existed before Sa'adya; there is mention of a *Siddur*[24] of Suleiman David b. Hassan, of opponents of *piyyuṭ* and of Jeshua who appeased them,[25] and of Karaites who permitted prayer in any chosen language. A composition by Solomon Yeruḥam occurs in the [Karaite] prayer-book.[26] Other items seem to be early, although they may have been borrowed.[27] In the year 1161, however, Abraham b. David maintained that there were neither songs nor poems of consolation among the

P. 159

Karaites, while the finest poetry was to be heard in the synagogues of the Rabbanites.

The current order of Karaite prayer, furnished with poetry, was created towards the end of the thirteenth century and the rite is in existence from the subsequent century. The history of that divine worship is insufficiently well known for us to be able to specify what the earliest composers found, omitted or added; thus it does not follow that, if an item is missing in the Karaite order, it must necessarily be late.[28] What is, however, undisputed is that the Rabbanite Jews, because of their animosity towards the supporters of Anan,[29] never adopted anything from the Karaite ritual.[30] The Karaites, on the other hand, who also later abandoned, to a large degree, their halakhic opposition, borrowed seriously from the Rabbanite *Siddur* and *Maḥzor* and introduced the items themselves, or adaptations of them. Such items include: the benedictions of the morning prayer; many benedictions relating to enjoyment, especially שהחיינו; the bedtime prayer;[31] an expanded יעלה ויבוא,[32] reminiscences of the *qaddish*;[33] items from the *tefillah*,[34] אין כאלהינו, as well as the

24 ס' המצות by Levi (cod. Reggio 5), compare Steinschneider *J{ewish} Literature* pp. 117, 168.
25 גן עדן in cod. Warner. 21 f. 92b {*Der*} [*Orient Lit{eraturblatt}* 45 1843 p. 718].
26 Part 3 f. 65b [p. 119], compare תקון in Wolf {*Bibliotheca*} part 4 1071.
27 אפס ארון ({in the Karaite Siddur} Part 3 f. 32 or p. 54), in which each stanza finishes with the word כהן and which is reminiscent of לא אורים in cod. Leipzig. 6 and cod. Harl. 7618. Compare above p. 102.
28 Contrary to Jost *Geschichte d{es} Judenthums* part 2 p. 263.
29 Appendix VII {below}.
30 Contrary to J. Reifmann זרחיה {...תולדות} p. 69.
31 *Siddur* part 4 p. 81.
32 Op. cit. part 2 p. 164, part 3 f. 87 [p. 156].
33 Op. cit. part 1 f. 17a [p. 30], part 2 f. 104a [p. 211].
34 ברכנו בברכה part 1 p. 83, part 2 p. 112.

prayer for rain on Shemini ʻAṣeret and the prayer for dew on the Pesaḥ festival, for which an haggadah is made and entitled "the little *hallel*"; the marking of the "great Sabbath" and the reading of the book of Ruth on the Feast of Weeks. For each of the Sabbaths before that feast-day—instead of Mishnah Avot—one seventh of Ps 119 is read;[35] in the month of Ṭevet special prayers are recited on Monday and Thursday nights. The removal of the Torah scroll is marked with the verse ויהי בנסוע; the reading of the Pentateuch, which is earlier started in spring, is annually completed on Shemini ʻAṣeret; with regard to the *hafṭarah*'s, on twenty Sabbaths they are the same as those of the Rabbanites, and half of them match the list in the Pesiqta.[36] Their prayer-book also contains:

P. 160

או"א החל עלינו (abbreviated), רחם על ציון (from the Ninth of Av), אחד אלהינו גדול after the *qedushah*'s, או"א מלך רחמן (from *musaf*),[37] the prayer חטאנו צורינו,[38] the bridegroom's song חתן נאה,[39] a variety of citations from the Romaniote *Maḥzor*, for example ויבנהו בנין משוכלל,[40] and the benediction after the reading of the book of Esther. The seven wedding benedictions and the מי שברך are imitations; so also the *qiddush*, *havdalah* and the grace after meals, although they occupy as many as sixty-one quarto leaves. The blessing תרבינה שמחות[41] which is based on the greeting as formulated in the midrash[42] is not only adopted but is reformulated for the formal naming of girls.[43]

The same situation appears in the matter of *piyyuṭ*. One encounters the items אתה קדוש אדון (from a *musaf qerovah*), the alphabetical אנא רחם ציון, אנו עבדיך, יגדל אלהים, שמחו ידידים and אשריכם ישראל or their imitations:[44] the form and content of the synagogal poetry were used as models by the Karaite authors, especially by Aaron b. Joseph who, for example, composed a *seliḥah*[45] the strophic endings of

35 Cod. Leid{en} 52 no. 10. Differently in *Siddur* part 1 pp. 103 and 320.
36 There is a list in אדרת 59d; in the *Siddur* different *hafṭarot* are prescribed for זאת, תהיה ,שמות, מסעי, נשא, sometimes as the Rabbanite custom, and דרשו is prescribed for וילך.
37 *Siddur* part 4 f. 55 [208].
38 Yefet in cod. Leid{en} f. 452.
39 *Siddur* part 4 f. 43b [72].
40 Op. cit. part 1 p. 30, part 2 f. 126a [173] etc. Compare *syn. Poesie* p. 436.
41 *Siddur* part 1 f. 117 [171], part 4 f. 73 [61].
42 יהא אח לשבעה, compare לקח טוב (נשא), תניא 94, 95, *gott. Vort.* p. 268 note d.
43 תהא אחות לשבעה ואם לשמונה בנים זכרים (*Siddur* part 4 p. 63).
44 Op. cit. part 2 ff. 141, 158 [235ff.].
45 אנא ה' part 1 f. 89 [p. 127]. Compare *syn. Poesie* p. 100.

which were constructed from Ps 51. His Pesaḥ poem,[46] which is reminiscent of a *silluq*, is constructed from Pesiqta and Tanḥuma, with verses interleaved from Song of Songs; in a *seliḥah*[47] and a *baqashah*[48] he uses phrases from the *tefillah*[49] and concludes a *vidduy* with a statement from the Mishnah;[50] in his *piyyuṭ* Moses even dies from a divine kiss. An imitation of the Song of Unity is composed for Shemini ʻAṣeret; the *haṭanu* and the *vidduy* are patterned after their equivalents in the Spanish and Romaniote rites; one also encounters examples of the penitential prayer and of *rehiṭim*. Yehuda Marli weaves into his large hymn a

P. 161

talmudic passage[51] and Yehudah Tishbi incorporates into his *seliḥah* היום יהי רצון an expression from the atonement prayer;[52] Aaron includes in one *piyyuṭ* a part of Ibn Ezra's introduction to the Pentateuch,[53] and Yehudah Ha-Gibbor displays in his *Azharot* his admiration of Maimonides.[54] The whole poetic content of the divine service is shaped in such a way, sometimes in imitation and sometimes by borrowing. Not only were Yehudah Ha-Levi, Gabirol and Mordechai b. Shabbethai imitated but the poetry of many synagogal poets was also transferred into the Karaite prayer-book. While the glory of Anan as the Nasi and the "Head of the Nation" and the truth of his teaching were proclaimed on every Sabbath and festival,[55] and the Rabbanites were cursed on the Day of Atonement,[56] their devotion was performed through the prayers of forty anti-Karaite poets, that is to say, of Aaron Hammon,[57] Avishai,[58] Ibn Ezra,[59] Abraham b. Isaac, Abraham Ha-Sefardi[60] (probably the rabbi who lived

46 *Siddur* part 2 f. 94ff. [12, 106ff.].
47 אמנם הקלנו part 3 f. 57 [98].
48 אנא אלהינו loc. cit. p. 31.
49 הלא לפניך גלוים, וקרע שטר, על חטא שאנו חייבים.
50 ואם אין אני לי מי לי part 3 f. 11b [20].
51 אין לך עשב מלמטה etc. Part 3 f. 47b [82].
52 Part 3 f. 99 [172] על חטא שאנו חיבים.
53 For *parashah* דברים: בלקח טוב ואור עינים.
54 For *parashah* משפטים.
55 Part 1 f. 151a [303], part 2 f. 126b, 131b, 144a [141, 174, 240].
56 Responsa זקן אהרן no. 29.
57 Part 4 no. 135.
58 Part 4 no. 91.
59 כי אשמרה, אלהי קדם.
60 Part 2 ff. 86, 105 [pp. 130, 146, 161, 162].

in Arta in the year 1521[61]), Antoli,[62] Ḥayyim, Ḥarizi, David, Eliakim,[63] Ephraim,[64] several Isaacs,[65] Israel Najara, Yehudah Abbas, Yehudah Balaam,[66] Yehudah Ha-Kohen, Yehudah Ha-Levi, Yehudah b. Shemariah,[67] Joseph,[68] Joseph b. Israel, Joseph Qalai, Joshua, Mevorakh, Mordechai Comtino, Mordechai b. Shabbethai, Moses, Moses b. Ḥiyya, Nehemiah, Shabbethai Rofeh,[69] Solomon Gabirol, Solomon b. Mazal-tov, Solomon,[70] Samuel,[71] Shemayah, and several anonymous others.[72]

P. 162

The ritual for the atonement period is profoundly marked by Rabbanite influence. New Year's day is the first day of penitence; the days of prayer begin on 2 Tishri. Weighty sets of verses, with the concluding חטאנו צורנו, are accompanied by Aaron's five poetic items: 1) a חטאנו of four lines, 2) a four-lined *tokheḥah* with longer lines, 3) a three-lined *vidduy* in which every third line is a biblical verse, 4) a rhythmical *taḥanun* in the style of a *pizmon*, 5) a *seliḥah* in which the concluding stanza is from the Bible. These are followed by a prose prayer, the passage ויחל together with the *Middot*, Aaron's poetic פסוקי תשובה, and Ps 32. After the repeated recitation of the five poems, following the same order as in the first instance, the ויחל passage is recited a second time together with the *Middot*. On the morning of the Day of Atonement, long sets of verses are followed by the alphabetical *vidduy* אשמנו, borrowings from *musaf*,[73] a litany in which each line begins with יום, similar to items in all the rites. There are then fifteen litanies, almost all of which belong to the *seliḥah* ritual or are imitations of it, and once again biblical verses etc., with the whole thing

---

61 משפטי שמואל {of Samuel b. Moses Qal'ai } 79d, compare {Responsa of} Benjamin Ze'ev 12, 14, 422, David b. Zimra on אה"ע 58a.
62 Part 4 f. 56a [209].
63 מחה חטאי כמו ענן (in אלהי עז) reminiscent of Ibn Ezra's אמר ענן ימחה שמו כענן (Exod 34:21).
64 Part 1 f. 174a [p. 207].
65 E.g. ישני חברון and Part 4 nos. 19, 24, 48.
66 Steinschneider *Hebr{äische}. Bibliogr{aphie}*. p. 70.
67 *Siddur* part 3 ff. 115, 116, 156 [198, 199, 269].
68 Part 4 no. 53.
69 פאר חתני, in the course of transposition of the stanzas שבתי has become תשבי in part 4 f. 39a [p. 65].
70 שלח צירי part 4 no. 93, probably by Solomon החבר the author of שמע קולי in cod. Uri 290 no. 22.
71 ישמח חתן part 4 no. 56, touching on the question to R. Yose (Bereshit Rabbah ch. 68, Wa-Yiqra Rabbah ch. 8).
72 אליכם אישים, אדני האדונים in the rite of Tripoli, influencing נהרו אל part 2 p. 73, part 3, p. 128, אנא רחם ציון, על ארמון אשר נטש, צור משלו אכלנו, אדון עולם, אשר לך ים.
73 עתה נחרב ואין; כל אלה בהיות ההיכל.

rounded off with a concluding doxology.[74] In this way the enemies of an authentic tradition, which they had forged into an artificial one, had to acknowledge the authority of their opponents in poetry and ritual. Just as, more than three hundred years ago, Levi ibn Ḥabib[75] stated that the Karaite liturgy consisted of no more than poems and biblical verses, so would he today similarly deny it any historical basis and dynamic organism, and at best—like {Isaac} Reggio[76]—he might admire the biblical compositions.

74 אל אלהים יאזין.

75 Responsa no. 79.

76 *Oṣar Neḥmad* part 1 {1856} p. 150.

Pp. 162–78

Piyyuṭ may have survived and developed among the Jewish people, but it was nevertheless deprecated at times by important personalities. Although

P. 163

such attacks were too isolated to have any effect, and the degree of their effect was indeed next to nothing, they do deserve our attention, not only out of respect for the critics and a passion for historical truth, but also because they adumbrated later developments and explain subsequent phenomena. The earliest opposition expressed by the Geonim attacked only the *qerovah* as something new, added by unauthorized prayer-leaders to the statutory *tefillah*, but did not object to the *'avodah, azharot, hosha'na, pizmon* and *seliḥah*. In versions of Amram's *Siddur* the *qerovah piyyuṭ* is already authorized, and soon afterwards, the Gaon Sa'adya, who was the leading halakhic authority of his day, made an appearance with *piyyuṭ* and incorporated into his order of prayers poetic compositions in the style of Qalir. In transmissions of the Pesiqta[1] the payyeṭanim were equated with the presenters of *aggadah*. The isolated concerns expressed by Ḥananel[2] and others were set aside not only by way of the rulings of Tovelem and {Rabbenu} Tam but also by the general usage, which could no longer be rejected, and by the prestige of such personalities as Meshullam b. Qalonymos, Simeon b. Isaac, Benjamin b. Samuel, Abitur, Tovelem, Shabbethai b. Moses, and Isaac Ghiyyat. The greatest poets, respected rabbis, deep thinkers and learned linguists (Gabirol, Moses b. Ezra, Yehudah Ha-Levi, Ibn Ezra, and Zeraḥiah Ha-Levi) soon joined in. In France the halakhic objections had lost ground so that R. Jacob of Marvège could declare that the number of hymns recited, even within the body of the *tefillah*, could never be enough.[3] When Maimonides was writing, the poems had become common property and the freedom granted to those leading the prayers had meant that unspeakable individuals operated as such and that inferior poetry was publicly presented, as adequately documented in the derisive comments of Ḥarizi. Just as Sa'adya had attacked Dunash and Hayyuj had done the same to Menaḥem, Ibn Ezra, who composed *ma'amad* poetry, criticizes not *piyyuṭ* as a whole but examples of inaccuracy, obscurity

1 See above p. 7, note 32, but the word פייטנים is lacking in Yalquṭ Hosea 533.
2 Maimoniot תפלה 6.3. 4 תניא f. 8b. שבלי 11.
3 תשובות מן השמים § 57.

P. 164

and excess. Mysticism and excessive prayer were repugnant to Maimonides; he approves of Sa'adya's liturgy,[4] not in order to lengthen the statutory worship but only for domestic devotion. He also criticizes the hasty recitation of the מאה ברכות, presumably the result of a taste for chanting at a later point which led to the neglect of the preceding items of prayer. Since at the time the prayer-leader alone recited the *piyyuṭ*, and only a few, or often nobody, had a text in front of them, such an insertion, which led to disruption and inattention,[5] seems worthy of censure. Maimonides and his colleagues prayed the *shema'* in their study centre without the addition of any *piyyuṭim*; his son Abraham[6] regards חזנות as an unwelcome alteration of what is legally prescribed. When people recite so many *seliḥah*'s during the penitential nights and the night of the Atonement festival, they are tired in the morning and sleep through the *shema'*. He states that the *qerovah*'s and the *ma'amad* are unnecessary and that the poetic items inserted into the *shema'* are inappropriate. A similarly strict viewpoint is found in the comments of Meir Ha-Levi[7] and Naḥmanides,[8] although the latter himself did compose a *piyyuṭ* for the New Year festival, while David Qimḥi and Shemtov Falquera disapprove of frequent and inappropriate prayers. With such a large and varied mass of poetry and the unrestricted production of prayers and *Maḥzor* manuscripts, it was inevitable that individual notes of warning would be sounded. Among those was that of Menaḥem b. Zeraḥ[9] who composed *vidduy* prayers for *shaḥarit* and *minḥah* in which angels and Sefirah's were summoned up. He approves the relocation of the *qerovah* to the end of the *tefillah*[10] and is of the view that one should not insert after the *tefillah* any of the specific prayers (*baqashah*'s, *yehi raṣon* and similar private entreaties) but only the Psalms. Yomṭov of

---

4 Communicated by Steinschneider, citing codex Uri 243.
5 Compare Isaac b. Sheshet Responsa 75.
6 Codex Uri 316 ff. 56a and 58b [Steinschneider].
7 *Ṭur* I 68.
8 שהמוסיפים בפיוטים וזמירות אינן נוהגין כשורה (לקוטות f. 2c).
9 Sedah La-Derekh I, 1.36, IV, 5.17.
10 Ibid., IV, 5.7.

P. 165

Seville[11] and Ibn Shuaib[12] do not criticize the insertion of *piyyuṭ*, only the omission of a section of the *magen* benediction. One should not overlook the fact that the learned legalist disparaged the prayer-leader and viewed poetry as an activity that could not be compared with the halakhah that he studied and expounded. Meanwhile the sermon, *piyyuṭ* and chanting penetrated dynamic usage as part of the divine service, and custom established itself counter to the established halakhah and its aristocratic guild. There were those who even looked askance at metre and acrostics and Joshua b. Shuaib[13] recommended the poetry of Qalir because the later poets paid more attention to verse structure than to content and transmitted coinage that looked beautiful but was counterfeit. Brevity and conciseness are the attractive characteristics of the early prayer formulas and, where there is no long-established custom, one should refrain from *qerovah* insertions in the first three benedictions of the *tefillah*. Although Nissim does not say anything about *piyyuṭ* in the *shema'*, he, as well as Isaac b. Sheshet,[14] disapproved of individual worshippers who stepped out of the congregation and prayed the *shema'* by themselves. In a work that he wrote in the year 1468[15] Joseph עלילי attacks the *yoṣer*, the *ofan*, calling upon angels, and various departures from talmudic regulations, as well as the sevenfold repetition of the phrase ה' הוא האלהים.[16] Unless it is a false attribution, the author must have been from Provence or Italy. The rabbis, especially from France, Germany and Italy were so far from taking a stand against the poetry of the festival prayers that even those who considered *piyyuṭ* as insignificant or the interruption {of the statutory prayers} to be forbidden never did more than abstaining from participation in the *yoṣer*. Moses Mintz did recite the *piyyuṭ* with the congregation and excused only those who were worshipping alone from its recitation,[17] while

11 On 'Avodah Zarah f. 8.
12 דרשות f. 79d.
13 On שמיני 45c, ואתחנן 79b.
14 Loc. cit.
15 אגרות ישר part 1 {1834} no. 19. Compare החלוץ 1, pp. 158, 160.
16 Compare Tos{afot}, Berakhot 34a.
17 Responsa no. 87. The citation in *gott. Vortr.* p. 417 [and from there in {A.} Wolff, {*Rabbinen uber die*} *Stimmen der*. . .*Pijuthim* p. 19] is incorrect.

P. 166

insisting that the prayer-leader should devote the time necessary for mastering both the texts and the interpretation of *piyyuṭ*, *zulat*, *ma'ariv* and *seliḥah.*[18] It was such halakhic caution that led in Spain and in some regions of Provence to the postponement of the *qerovah* until after the *tefillah.*

As scientific knowledge increased, there remained only one objection to certain *piyyuṭim* in the public worship, and this related to the incomprehensibility of some early items in the German and Roman *Maḥzor*. Abraham Farissol[19] was among those who complained: the worshipper did not understand the author and if the latter was a מקובל {a kabbalist} that was even less helpful to him. "In order to adhere to an alphabetical order", notes Yoḥanan Trèves,[20] "the authors of these *pizmon* poems and responses chose whichever expressions they wished and I think it would have been wiser had they kept silent" [that is to say, they would not then have erred in interpreting the difficult passages]. Isaac Shalem expresses his dissatisfaction even more powerfully, especially with regard to the *yoṣer* for Pesaḥ by Shabbethai and Solomon, by opting not to comment on incomprehensible items and by approving the omission of festival *qerovah*'s and various other compositions.[21] Archevolte[22] evaluates *piyyuṭ* in terms of its linguistic accuracy and offers a degree of justification of unusual forms if they have biblical precedents while warning against the imitation of problematic models. He himself, however, like most Italian poets, composed prayers only on the basis of syllables and metre. Unlike certain kabbalists who respected only the early prayers, these poets[23] asserted the rights of every age and every poet and saw specific advantage in the profusion of poetic prayers. Only a few items of Qalir's poetry were excluded from this. The objections that originated in Poland are even less significant. R. Löw in Prague discontinued the recitation of the hymn of unity in the same way that Samuel of Medina[24]

---

18 Op. cit. no. 81.
19 Commentary on Qohelet ms. on 5:1.
20 Maḥzor Bologna 1540 part 1 on the *qerovah* for the Ninth of Av.
21 Roman *Maḥzor* 1587 part 1 ff. 247b, 309b. Part 2 f. 229a.
22 *Grammar* {of Samuel Arkivalti} chs. 28 and 32.
23 Introduction to כנף רננים {of Joseph Yedidiah b. Benjamin Yequtiel} Venice 1626, ff. 7 and 8.
24 Lonzano דרך חיים ed. Constantinople f. 21b.

P. 167

treated the metaphysical investigations in Baḥya's Duties of the Heart. The translator, Anshel of Posen, excuses Qalir's difficult and obscure expressions as part of the contrived structure of his poems and apologizes himself for having reproduced only their basic sense.[25] The grammarian, Shabbethai of Przemysl,[26] mocks the rhymes of his contemporaries that have neither metre nor rhythm. Even more severe is the criticism of the outspoken Ephraim Luntschitz.[27]

These statements of disapproval of one sort or another, at times contradicting each other, were even less influential in leading to change than the opinions based on the halakhic doctrines of J. Karo[28] and of some later authorities. When, already many years earlier, scholars were said to have studied during the recitation of *qerovah*'s and *seliḥah*'s, this was criticized as arrogance,[29] while two centuries ago Yehudah del Bene[30] defended the festival prayers against the criticism of David Qimḥi which he claimed to have been expressed only in connection with some *yoṣer* poems for Purim, items for the Ninth of Av, *ma'aravim*, as well as some *seliḥah*'s and *pizmon* poems. For him, the Spanish poetry, as in its *pizmon*, lamentation and *hosha'na* compositions, is outstanding, and the *qerovah*'s for the festivals are irreproachable. Joseph del Medigo[31] is sharply critical of Qalir and the later poets, and especially of the German *Maḥzor*; some of such statements perhaps belong to Karaite authors.[32]

During the tumult created by the followers of Shabbethai Zevi, there were (from 1667) some transitory trends that occurred in the matter of prayers. In some places there was a desire to omit the poems of lament from the early devotions, while in others some thought about abolishing the Ninth of Av and about changing the prayers for that day. The {Sabbatean} party

25 מחזור for the three [pilgrim] festivals, Prague 1600 f. 44.

26 {שבילי דעת} מהלך {of Moses Qimḥi} Hamburg 1785, appendix.

27 Hebrew in *gott. Vortr.* p. 477, German in Plessner *Die kostbare Perle* p. 177.

28 Ṭur I 68 and 112.

29 Maharil 79a. שלטי הגבורים {of Joshua Boaz}, Berakhot ch. 1. Compare חמדת הימים for י"כ {Yom Kippur} 103a, לבוש א"ח 90, Elijah Wilna in מעשה רב § 57.

30 כסאות לבית דוד {of Judah b. Eliezer David del Bene} ch. 9.

31 אחוז p. 15; in {his} נובלות חכמה f. 200b he is referring to his contemporaries.

32 See my communication in Steinschneider's מפתח האוצר {1848}p. 333 and *Bodleian Catalogue* p. 1511.

P. 168

even had its own תקון printed in Amsterdam and Venice.[33] Although it survived among individual followers, this offensive left no serious effect. Meanwhile, the example set by some scholars, the influence exercised by Spanish poetry and the comments made in various books of ritual, none of which were conducive to the gabbling of incomprehensible prayers, produced those who mocked the *yoṣerot* and the *seliḥah*'s. They were opposed by Elyaqim b. Jacob (1688)[34] when he provided a new translation of the *seliḥah*'s. Hayyim Bacharach[35] expresses the view that the poetic interruption of the *tefillah* is not an issue since it occurs only during the repetition by the prayer-leader. He recommends that the individual should not depart from the congregational usage, should at best recite the "*bikkur*" after the benediction, and should on no account ridicule any of the customs relating to the festival prayers. Rightly ascribing the animosity towards the prayers to a failure to educate in the mother tongue, Aaron b. Samuel composed his {Yiddish} *Kräftige Arznei* {*Powerful Medicine*} (1709), hoping that this would bring the contents of the prayers closer to the hearts of the youth. With the same purpose in mind, Joseph Koschman compiled his new commentary on the *seliḥah*'s with an appendix,[36] and, in the summer of the year 1729, Isaiah Romanin produced a Hebrew translation and exposition of the *seliḥah* תא שמע. For grammatical reasons Solomon Hanau[37] expressed his disapprobation of *piyyuṭ*. The impetuous Jacob Emden[38] was very displeased with the changes to the prayer texts that the grammarian {Hanau} had deigned to make. Although he himself had composed his own *piyyuṭim*[39] that would have done credit to Solomon Ha-Bavli, he does in a number of places in his works take strong objection to *piyyuṭ*, sometimes because of his preference for the Spanish *Maḥzor* and sometimes out of halakhic considerations. Among other things, he criticizes

33 באר עשק {of Shabbethai Baer} no. 29. תורת הקנאות {of Jacob Emden} 71b describes the *Siddur* edition כתר יוסף [Berlin 1700] and that of Michel Epstein [Frankfurt a. M{ain} 1704] as infected with Sabbateanism.

34 Preface to סליחות ed. Amst{erdam}.

35 Responsa 225, 238 [incorrectly by Wolff {n. 17 above}on the *piyyuṭim* pp. 22f.].

36 קנה 31a.

37 קורות ארזים 31a.

38 עמודי שמים (1745) ff. 177a, 368a. שערי שמים (1753) ff. 50a, 64a, 87b. ברכת שמים (1748) f. 206a.

39 שי למורא, see שערי שמים 47b.

P. 169

the interruption of the biblical reading with the Aramaic אקדמות which was only ever attached to the Targum and never to the biblical text itself and which Jacob Heilprun had already defended in the year 1621. That said, this bitter enemy of the philosophers is no ally of the modern detractors of *piyyuṭ*. Aaron Emmerich[40] regards most *baqashah*'s and *piyyuṭim* as having been written not for the public divine service but for prayers composed by the authors for their own use; at least with regard to the poetry of *yoṣer*, *qerovah*, *'avodah*, *hosha'na*, *ma'ariv*, *rehiṭim*, the *seliḥah*'s for fast-days and the laments, this is an erroneous claim.

When taste began to be more refined in the age of Moses Mendelssohn, and when language and science were given their correct place, at first among the German Jews and then gradually among their Polish counterparts, midrash and *piyyuṭ* were pushed into the background; as world literature became familiar to them, it towered over midrash and the torch of freedom put the *piyyuṭim* into the shadows. At first secretly but then openly, grammar, poetry and philosophy vitiated the medieval forms, in particular the German-Polish divine service. Joyous at the fall of arbitrary domination, such a one as Hirz Wessely could in Berlin greet the news of the storming of the Bastille with the words of the New Year *tefillah*: "when you remove the arrogant power from the earth." Such a statement complemented that of the ancient sage Eliezer b. Nathan who had once applied the expression וכל הרשעה in that same prayer to the Roman apostolic rule. In the soil that had already been prepared, and readied for improvement, by Mendelssohn and Wessely, Isaac Satanow[41] seeded his attacks on synagogal poetry[42] in the guise of textual emendations, pious glosses and facetious remarks, borrowed from earlier sources.

P. 170

He was concerned not so much with the elimination of errors but with the removal of the talmudic aspect in its totality. The bitterness against the representatives of Talmud and Zohar at that time may be explained by the latter's hatred of science and grammar, and the voices of the enlightened authors, who openly recommended reforms, inevitably drowned out those of the earlier writers, especially of

---

40 מגלה סוד Hamburg 1765 f. 7, cited in קנאת האמת {of Judah Löb Mieses} p. 104.
41 ס' המדות 88b. מגלת חסידים ch. 35 where there is a new *Kol Nidrey*; הולך תמים end; compare his editions of כוזרי (2.39), גדרים (46b, 54a, 77a), מאור עינים and especially the סליחות of Berlin 1785 f. 4b and on nos. 6, 9, 12, 17, 54, 96. אגרת בית תפלה § 339, 406.
42 In no. 9, f. 5b לברר מלין etc., compare Ibn Ezra on Qohelet 5:1.

the *piyyuṭ*. Isaac Euchel, in his translation of the prayer-book (1786) criticized the festival *piyyuṭim* especially with regard to the expressions used there for God.[43] In this he was merely following the strict philosophy of Maimonides; nevertheless, he omitted that passage in the second edition and contented himself with saying that the *piyyuṭim* were full of wordplays, tautologies etc.[44] He is the first one to use the expression "the *piyyuṭim*" to discredit, on the basis of some individual compositions, a rich literature on which thousands of poets and thinkers had laboured for a millennium. In the same year (1799), David Friedländer[45] portrays the Jewish prayers as progressively deteriorating, written in a language that offends the ear, logic and grammar, and that fortunately is not understood by most people, and with content that is, for the contemporary world, meaningless and even misguided. L. Dohm[46] and A. Muhr,[47] whose writings were prompted by Friedlander's *Ein Wort zu seiner Zeit* {*A Word in its Time*}, also aimed their arrows against medieval poetry; in order to save the Hebrew language for the divine service, Dohm gives up on the *piyyuṭ* because it is poor and unauthoritative Hebrew. On the other hand, Muhr's call to "get rid of them" seems to be directed only at the kabbalistic items in the weighty liturgical editions. {J. L.} Benzeev[48] associates himself with the well-known statements of Ibn Ezra (on Qohelet) and David Qimḥi (in his Dictionary

P. 171

s.v. עתר): the items in the German *Maḥzor* have nothing of poetry other than rhyme, they have incomprehensible content, and their commentaries should not be consulted during prayer. The voices of Joseph Bamberger (1807),[49] who wishes to abolish the *zulat* and the Gemara, and of A. Bock (1823),[50] who sees a way to reform the divine service by granting his sermons priority, went unheeded, since both of them were later baptized. Of greater importance was the decision of the Westphalian Consistorium, supported by Mendel Steinhart, to delete certain prayers and *piyyuṭim* since this was the first time that such a step was taken by

43 In § 28 of the annotations, see *Meassef* 1786 p. 205 ({בכורי העתים} בכה"ע 6.45).
44 Preface p. XVII.
45 {D. Friedlander} *Sendschreiben* {1799}p. 42. *Ein Wort* etc. 1812 pp. 8 and 20. *An die Verehrer* etc. 1823 p. 152.
46 *Etwas ~~über~~ zum Schutz . . .der ebräische{n} Sprache bei den Gebeten*, Breslau {1812}, pp. 7, 8.
47 *Jerubaal über religiöse Reform*, Breslau 1813 p. 23.
48 *Hebr. Wörterbuch* {Vienna 1807} introduction and entry עתר.
49 *Beiträge {. . .}zur Verbesserung* etc published by Paulus, Frankfurt a. M{ain} 1817 p. 13.
50 *Vorschläge zur Verbesserung* etc Magdeburg 1823.

the German rabbinate. Several more recent individuals have borrowed weapons against *piyyuṭim* from his treatise.[51]

Meanwhile, in Poland *yoṣerot*, *ma'ariv* and similar *piyyuṭim* were abolished, especially by the Ḥasidim, and in Germany improvements were made in various places; in various orders of prayer most items and many *seliḥah*'s and poetic laments have now disappeared from the *Maḥzor*. In the religious struggles that broke out from around 1817, those who were abolishing such items were not very circumspect in their statements. For Peter Beer,[52] the *Maḥzor* is a hotchpotch, a labyrinth of inconsistencies, that should disgust everyone; the *piyyuṭ* is a rhymed noise and those who say it are the mob. He[53] and Solomon Cohen[54] define the *Maḥzor* as "beneath all criticism"; the latter also wishes to abolish the poems of lament.[55] He nevertheless assisted[56] the Orthodox party with the publication of their book דברי הברית and even arranged the publication of a *seliḥah* booklet. S. Fränkel[57] speaks about the

P. 172

gibberish of the "litanies". What we hear from J. Auerbach[58] are familiar things already stated by Benzeev; David Caro[59] contents himself with the remark that the divine service is overloaded with *piyyuṭ*, and with רב"שע and "*yehi raṣon*" prayers. Jost's contemporary criticism (1827)[60] and {J. }L. Mi{e}ses's statement (1828)[61] that the later prayers, *seliḥah*'s and *piyyuṭim* have content that is mostly foolish and blasphemous, seem exaggerated.

There was also no shortage of pleading on behalf of the persecuted *piyyuṭ* and the traditional prayers. Ḥayyim Köslin[62] already opposed Satanow's interference with the liturgical text; later (1808) Solomon Pappenheim remarked that the

---

51 {Steinhart} דברי אגרת 1815 p. 12.

52 *Geschichte der Secten* {1822–23} part 1 p. 347, *Reminiscenzen* 1837.

53 *Skizze einer Geschichte der Erziehung* 1832 p. 58.

54 *Historisch-kritische Darstellung des jüdischen Gottesdienstes* 1819 p. 275 (from which the expression "au dessous de la critique" used by Holländerski: *Les Israelites de Pologne*, Paris 1846 p. 177).

55 Loc. cit. p. 272 and ff. Preface p. XX.

56 D. Caro ברית אמת p. 43. The expression Verfassung (for Abfassung) is in דברי הברית p. 121 and in {*Historisch-kritische*} *Darstellung* p. 274.

57 *Schutzschrift* etc {Hamburg 1819} p. 8.

58 *Sind die Israeliten verpflichtet* etc {Berlin 1818} pp. 19–22.

59 Op. cit. {n. 56 above} p. 112.

60 *Geschichte der Isr[aeliten}*. part 7, pp. 221, 240.

61 קנאת האמת {Vienna} 1828 pp. 102–104.

62 באר רחובות [{in} *Meassef* 1786 p. 51] Berlin 1814.

content of *piyyuṭ* was precious, even if the language was often cumbersome.[63] Especially noteworthy in this context are the commentaries of Moses Büdingen[64] and the level-headed W. Heidenheim. For about the past thirty years, as Jewish self-confidence has increased, an unprejudiced view of ancient Jewish life has gained ground; it is the belief in what is true rather than true belief that should prevail in matters both dated and modern. Plessner does indeed prove this in his five lectures on *piyyuṭ*.[65] Distinctions began to be made between the reform of institutions and the assessment of poetry and national ideology, and drew lines between what was motivated by morality and what by taste.[66] Presentations in the periodicals[67] sometimes touched on the early authorities but more often on the inadequacy of *piyyuṭ* for contemporary needs, although they have their share of superficial and trivial items.[68] The intention was to meet modern needs by way of new German prayers, religious hymns, "purely German" *teḥinnah*'s for women by Peter Beer (1815,

P. 173

and again in 1843 in German transliteration), by Heidenheim and by many others, as well as by the creation of new melodies. Thus *piyyuṭ* and *seliḥah* items, and indeed the מענה לשון {booklet for the cemetery}, were given new {German} translations—from 1770 the German and Portuguese *maḥzor*'s were also translated into French, English and Dutch—and the "Israelite" prayer-book published in Breslau in 1854 included an arrangement that was not part of the {standard} text. As a result of synagogal arrangements and such prayer-books, the existing German rite was split up into various branches, in which even the statutory prayers were no longer the same. The above-mentioned Breslau prayer-book included in the translation six *seliḥah*'s and Meir of Rothenburg's poetic lament שאלי שרופה. The prayer-book of the new London synagogue, with scant respect for the *qaddish*, included nine *seliḥah*'s from the Spanish *Maḥzor* and had a similar number from the German rite, of which only two had not undergone abbreviation.[69] Barukh {b. Samuel}'s

63 Commentary on the *seliḥah* כי הנה כחמר, Breslau 1808.

64 On the *Maḥzor* (Metz 1817) and on the *seliḥah*'s (Metz 1822).

65 *Die kostbare Perle* 1837 lectures 8 until 12 (pp. 159 ff).

66 Compare Jost, *Gesch{ichte}. d{es} Judenthums* vol. 2 pp. 270ff.

67 Compare Geiger's *{Wissenschaftliches} Zeitschrift* 1.393, *{Allgemeine} Zeitung des Judenthums* 1838 p. 235, Jost's *Annalen* 1839 pp. 363, 379; 1841 pp. 161, 172, 322, 330.

68 כוכבי יצחק part 13 (1847) p. 22; *{Der} Orient* 1849 *L{iteratur}b{latt}* p. 393; *Archives Israél{ites}* 1857 and 1858.

69 אנא השם and אנשי אמונה אבדו.

piyyuṭ אני הוא forfeited twelve stanzas. The "striking difference between usages, that has a disruptive effect on the liturgy as a whole",[70] has therefore increased rather than decreased among those who follow the German rite, and what the distance between countries did in early times now leads to freedom on the one hand and slackness on the other.

The fate of the *piyyuṭ* was also affected by grammatical and critical revisions, especially in the modern period. The effort to arrive at an authentic text of the prayers goes back as far as the works of the Geonim. Even if initially the main concern was for what was halakhically valid, Sa'adya's work is also at the same time a restoration of {what he saw as} forgotten or corrupted prayer formulas. The earliest commentators searched out good copies in order to deepen their understanding and the vocalisers, who themselves worked on {the production of} many manuscripts, followed the rules of grammar, authoritative sources, or appended commentaries, and added their own

P. 174

marginal glosses.[71] We have information about individual corrections to the prayers and to the *piyyuṭ* already made by Joseph Tovelem, Meir b. Isaac[72] and Rashi. The first-mentioned of those read, in the *'alenu* prayer, ואנחנו (not ואנו), and the last-mentioned read, in Qalir's *musaf* prayer for New Year, תכריע (instead of תעוטר). R. Elijah corrected, in the grace after meals, רועינו to רענו.[73] An anonymous writer objected, in the the *ofan* for a wedding Sabbath, to the word אופד which he corrected to אפוד;[74] Zalman of Breisach read, at the beginning of the *yoṣer* for the Day of Atonement, הודיתה and not הוריתה. In the margins of a French *Maḥzor* there are some twenty suggested readings by הרי"ח, several by הר"ם, one by Meshullam and one by Yose. We also have specific readings by Meir b. Barukh[75] and Jacob

70 *Würtembergische Gottesdienst-Ordnung* (1838), beginning.

71 E.g. Samson (Geiger, {*Wissenschaftliches*} *Zeitschrift* 5.423), Jacob Ha-Levi ({Zunz} *zur Geschichte* p. 114).

72 Readings in the prayer ישמח משה (excerpts from Maḥzor Vitry ms., compare הפרדס 55d), in the poem for Purim אספרה אל חק (Opp. 1074F), in the *seliḥah* אם עונינו רבו (that is, in the penultimate stanza reading לכלי for לבלי, as in the printed commentary, ed. Cracow, and incorrectly in the prayer-book שער השמים {Amsterdam 1717} f. 40a).

73 באר מים חיים {Hayyim b. Jacob Obadiah. Saloniki 1546} ch. 27.

74 Qalir in the *musaf* for New Year has אופד, and Eliezer has אפוד in the *ḥatanu* אודך ה' כי אנפת.

75 Tashbeṣ § 254, 316. Responsa 507. Compare Heidenheim's *Commentary on the Maḥzor* (*qerovah* for סכות) and on the *seliḥah*'s ed. 1833 section 1 f. 150b.

Mölln[76] in both the statutory prayers and other places in the *Maḥzor*. It is to such revisers that we probably owe the insertion of the word הוה in the *piyyuṭ* האוחז and in other items.[77] Several accurate emendations made by modern scholars are owed to manuscripts, and that source could have been behind particular emendations made *ex ingenio* as, for example, the reading הַרהוֹר as in an early *seliḥah*,[78] although the verbal noun הִרהוּר should not be ruled out. From the sixteenth century, various publishers and exegetes, including Gershom Soncino, Yoḥanan Trèves, Benjamin Ha-Levi and Isaac Shalem extended their attentions to the text. Corrections were made by Meir Benveniste of Salonika (1564) to the Spanish siddur,[79] by Solomon Luria to specific items,[80] and by Shabbethai b. Isaac (1603) to the Polish prayer-book. During the seventeenth century that was so fateful for German and Polish Jews, the prayer-books were full of unwelcome additions and errors, and it was not until a century after Shabbethai that Azriel and Elijah

P. 175

of Wilna proposed their corrections. Solomon Hanau,[81] who followed them soon afterwards, was bolder and even rejected many items that had long been common in *tefillah* and *piyyuṭ*, including the *nitpa'el* form that had been used by Maimonides and innumerable authors, as well as by Yehudah Ha-Levi himself in his Zion poem, while nevertheless making a significant contribution to the creation of an accurate text. Mordechai Düsseldorf and Jacob Emden tried to refute him; the latter, as similarly Isaac of Przemysl, did much for the correction of the prayer-books. It is true that their activity did not extend to the festival prayers; in the meantime, however, a taste for grammar had been awakened and the first light of the Mendelssohnian era had dawned. In the year 1773 the אגרת בית התפלה of Isaac Satanow appeared, to be followed twelve years later by his emendations and explanations for the prayer-book, the Pesaḥ Haggadah and the *seliḥah*'s. In these works numerous corrupt words were corrected but many unjustified corrections were also made; particularly prominent is the elimination of the word שנשתלחה in the *musaf* prayer, the

76 Maharil ff. 49b, 50a, 62a.
77 Note VII [below].
78 In אוילי and אלי אלי אזון.
79 אות אמת ed. 1 ff. 173b–181b, ed. 2 ff. 86–90.
80 Responsa no. 64.
81 בנין שלמה {Frankfurt am Main} 1708 ff. 9a, 45a, 91a, 106b; שערי תפלה Jes{s}nitz 1725, Amst{erdam} 1766. יסוד הנקוד {Amsterdam} 1730 ff. 61b, 62a, 67a, 69a; some individual items in his grammar book.

removal of which was still approved by Solomon Hanau,[82] and its replacement with השלוחה,[83] which has since then wrongly been retained in that prayer.[84] Many of his corrections in the *seliḥah*'s are faulty and the case for a justified emendation is often spoiled by a conjectural one. Since he did not consult any manuscripts, his battle is frequently being waged against phantom foes.[85] There is greater and more lasting value in the works of W. Heidenheim who may be called the Mendelssohn of the *Maḥzor*: he promoted the text and meaning, as well as the structure and appreciation of the *piyyuṭ* and has remained the driving force behind a large number of publishers and exegetes.

Towards the end of the Middle Ages, the Christian world became aware of the Jewish payers, at first only the daily ones but later, mostly with hostile intent, also the poetic ones. The first leaders in

P. 176

this field were apostates such as Böschenstein,[86] Margaritha,[87] Wolf,[88] and Hess:[89] the first is convinced that the Jews who have been so long known as graced by God will again be enlightened and blessed; the second cites examples from the daily prayer, from some table hymns, and from seventy-two Bible verses, clearly demonstrating that the prayer of the Jews is not acceptable to God; the third copied the second, while the fourth reveals that the content of those prayers concerns the eradication of Christianity in its entirety. From their successors until {H. B. X.} Cleve,[90] hardly anyone can be named who touched on the Jewish prayer system and advanced beyond ולמשומדים and עלינו. From the time of Buxtorf's *Synagoge*, scholarly knowledge was indeed more extensive but the same cannot be said about the level of evaluation; the motive for their studying was hatred and they were interested in the *Maḥzor* only for the curses that would lead to auto da fé's and atrocities. Only Rittangel[91] constitutes an exception; he explains the obscure language

82 See לוח ארש {Altona 1769} 57a.
83 Appendix VIII [below].
84 See Luzzatto מבוא p. 19.
85 Appendix IX [below].
86 *Precatio et confessio jud{aeorum}* Augsburg 1521. *Vil gutter Ermahnungen*, no date and Nürnberg 1525, *Birchat Hamason*, Augsburg 1536.
87 *Der ganze jüd. Glaube* {*Der gantz Jüdisch Glaub*} Augsburg 1530.
88 *Spiegel der Juden*, Danzig 1544.
89 *Judengeissel*, Fritzlar 1589.
90 {*Der*} *Geist des Rabbinismus*, Münster 1823; *Soria*, Köln 1823, pp. 42–51.
91 *Hochfeierliche Sollenniteten*, Königsberg 1652, compare pp. 103ff, 156.

of the *piyyuṭ*, as also the aggadic items about God, Leviathan and similar matters, which are still mocked in our own century, as parabolic. He was the first to defend the Jews against the accusation of worshipping the saints, and to translate the *Maḥzor* of the first day of the New Year festival and indeed Qalir's *teki'ata* which in several places is barely discernible. Hottinger[92] states of the *Maḥzor* that it is understood by few and that it is recited in the way that the Latin Psalms are recited by the nuns. Wülfer uses his knowledge of an early *Maḥzor* for no other prupose than to denounce several *rehiṭim*; Bartolocci[93] sprays poison, and Eisenmenger can find nothing else in the *seliḥah*'s but material for the eighty-two terms of abuse that he lists. Wagenseil wrote prescriptions for *'alenu* and *Kol Nidrey* ailments.

P. 177

For the hymn דודי ירד לגנו in *Sha'arey Ṣiyon* a Prague Jesuit persecuted the publisher and the bibliographer Shabbethai b. Joseph in the year 1712, and he was arrested eight days before Pesaḥ. Basnage draws on Buxtorf, Leo de Modena, Vitringa and the Spanish translation of the *Siddur* (*orden de las oraciones*); von der Hardt makes a whole performance of the Lurianic midnight lament;[94] Schudt devotes thirty-three quarto pages[95] to listing—apart from the prayer for the King and the *seliḥah* of a contemporary—nothing but hackneyed anti-Jewish accusations; Willemer[96] introduces *teḥinnah*'s; in his humility Wähner[97] says only a little about ritual variations. There appeared in the year 1745 a selection of *seliḥot* to which was attached the name of Leser Wolf of Fürth who had since 1733 been called Christlieb. The Jews were defended against this hostile book by Chr. B. Michaelis[98] and S. J. Baumgarten;[99] the son of Michaelis, Johann David, defended his father against an attack in a learned periodical in Regensburg, noting, among other things, that an apostate Jew was not unbiased. Scholarship {by non-Jews} in this branch of Jewish literature ends with Bodenschatz[100] who provides details of the daily prayers, individual items from the Haggadah, the grace after meals and *Kol Nidrey*, but not from the *qinnot*, *Maḥzor*

92 {*Promptuarium sive*} *Biblioth. Orient* {Heidelberg 1658} p. 25.
93 *Biblioth*{*eca Magna Rabbinica* Rome 1693} I, 192, II, 728.
94 *Officia judaeorum antelucana*, {Helmstedt} 1706.
95 See ch. 33 of book 6 {in *Jüdische Merckwürdigkeiten* Frankfurt 1714–18}.
96 סדר תחנות, in Latin, Leipzig 1734.
97 *Antiquitates* {Göttingen} 1742 vol. 2 § 1355.
98 *Bedenken* etc. Halle 1745.
99 *Theologisches Bedenken*, Halle 1745, 80 quarto pages.
100 *Kirkliche Verfassung* etc (Erlangen 1748) part 2 pp. 40–85, 146, 151f, 155, 169, 188, 299, 306ff, 369. Part 3 pp. 4ff, 84. Part 4 pp. 65, 125ff, 179.

or *seliḥah* texts. Würfel devotes a whole chapter to a description of the Nürnberg Maḥzor that is so artfully done that one learns not an iota about its content. For obvious reasons, no account at all needs to be taken of Anton's *Jüdische Gebrauche* {*Jewish Customs*}and Selig's *Jude.*[101] A. F. Büsching still prides himself on the claim that he had deliberately not read the work of Basnage nor even looked at it when he wrote his *Geschichte der jüdischen Religion* {*History of the Jewish Religion*} (Berlin 1779). There (ibid. § 56 p. 192) he has one lone paragraph about the public divine service of the synagogue

P. 178

where it is stated: "The Jews are guided by the regulation of Moses, son of Maimon, who requires that where there are ten Jews" etc. No further information is offered there. On p. 205 it is claimed that the title "*Rosh Avot*" or patriarch probably dates from the time of Nerva. Four years later[102] he put in print that the Jews had a man, called the angel of death, whose task was to tie up the deceased's neck before burial. Wünsch[103] copies from Eisenmenger; Remer[104] copies from Büsching[105] his seven lines about the religious position of the Jews in the course of five hundred years (where the comment about the "*Rosh Avot*" also appears); the preacher in Berlin[106] copies from Basnage, and he is in turn copied by the author of Charlotte Sampson (1800, p. 135) who is even ignorant of Euchel's prayer-book. Herder, with a loving soul, also gave consideration to midrash and to more recent Jewish poetry.[107] No hint of such love is, however, to be seen in the book *Levi und Sara* by J. Niemczewicz (Berlin 1825) which misrepresents Abuab's Candelabrum, relates foolish nonsense,[108] and utters the most thoroughly dishonest items plagiarized from Wünsch's *Rabinismus*. Only Delitzsch, whose *Jüdische Poesie* {*Jewish Poetry*} (1836) reflects advances in the scientific study of Judaism, represents a glorious exception. More recent studies of poetry have taken no account of the synagogal variety. Such works as Oettingen's *Die synagogale Elegik des Volkes Israel* (Dorpat 1853), which exploits Yehudah Ha-Levi's Zion poem to propel readers towards conversion, do not

101 See part 2 pp. 233, 276, 363, 365.
102 *Der Sammler* {המאסף} 1784, first addendum p. 15. בשמים ראש 102c.
103 *Rabinismus* {*oder Sammlung* Amsterdam} 1789 pp. 153, 275.
104 *Handbuch der mittlern Geschichte* {Braunschweig} 1798 p. 309.
105 Pp. 189, 190, 192.
106 *An einige Hausväter jüdischer Religion*, Berlin 1799, pp. 23, 24.
107 לכה דודי in *Adrastea* (vol. 10, p. 118); Judah Ha-Levi's Zion poem.
108 Compare pp. 41, 73, 83.

stand in the way of the progressive spirit of humanity; undeterred by short-sighted enemies of *piyyuṭ* and by anti-Semites who protect it, it {i.e. that spirit} pursues its course towards the destination indicated by genuine science, and towards the goal at which the freedom, knowledge and love expressed by the poets become popular notions and the various rites are united.

Annotations

Pp. 179–83

1. [p. 3] The section וילך was not counted as a separate entity and the early authorities (Ha-Pardes 19d, 20a) deal with only one division called נצבים; hence also in a manuscript of יד שערים the undivided section is called נצבים שלמה and one part of it חצי נצבים. Otherwise, there would have been fifty-four pentateuchal sections rather than the fifty-three (op. cit. and Raziel {Ha-Malakh} 15a) that are expressly indicated by the name גן that is given to the commentary. Both Abraham b. Ḥiyya (ס' העיבור p. 70) and Abudarham testify to the fact that שלח and קרח are joined up, rather than חקת and בלק. As the former reports, there were some places where they divided משפטים, כי תשא, וירא: Baḥya and Aaron Ha-Kohen (27b § 63) refer to the division of משפטים at אם כסף תלוה which then constitutes an independent *parashah*; כי תשא is divided at the verse Exod 32:15 or at 33:12. In Constantine וארא was divided at Exod 9:13 while in other places מקץ was divided at Gen 42:19 ({Issachar} Even Shushan 33a). According to R. Asher the order of the lectionary is a custom and not a halakhah and each legal authority in his own place can either divide or join the sections as desired (חזה התנופה no. 54).

2. [p. 22] A book of customs for the whole year by Abraham חילדיק is held in Parma; from de Rossi (codex 1233 no. 2) we learn no more than that the author is wholly unknown. It seems to me that he may be identifiable with the teacher of the מהרי"ח who is cited as Abraham חילדיק in the Haggahot Asheri ([Bava] Batra, ch. 3 § 14, compare ch. 1, § 36).

3. [p. 32] Joseph Karo regarded the Kol Bo as a digest and counted it with the Semaq and האגור {of Jacob b. Judah Landau} (introduction to the בית יוסף). Its compiler brought together, from both parts of the ארחות חיים, sometimes in a different order, what he regarded as necessary for his reader; all discussions were omitted, especially relating to those topics, like *Kol Nidrey*, that were regarded as authorized usage in his time and in his native location: hence the section dealing with the evening of the Atonement Festival (Aaron Ha-Kohen 105d until 106c) is shrunken into half a column. Likewise, a whole column (ibid., 17cd) between the words שלם עמו and מי שלא is lacking. For other examples, see above p. 28,

https://doi.org/10.1515/9783111142500-003

P. 180

note m {172}, p. 31, note e {187}, p. 125 note b {89}. The expression ובמקום אחר (f. 1b) makes sense only in Aaron's original text where it is preceded by the phrase ובשם רשי זל (5c § 16); the Kol Bo, which deletes this phrase, has to insert afterwards the words ברבינו שלמה that were not at all in the original. He often moves individual items to other locations, as, for example, when he transfers כתב ה"ר אשר from Aaron's text 3a to a later place at the end of 5b § 5. Aaron's allusion in 69d § 2 is lacking at the beginning of 43 in Kol Bo which includes there instead the text from תפלה § 103f. 19d. Especially noteworthy is the fact that in the Kol Bo some authorities have completely disappeared, such as Aaron Ha-Levi, as noted by Benjacob (*Kerem Chemed* 8.168). Some items are corrupted, such as the middle of f. 9a where כתב ה"ר is taken from Aaron 17b § 73; and in 1b where הריא"ף appears instead of הרי"ף (Aaron 5d top). Whatever the editor could not use for his purpose has disappeared, as for example most of the French translations, and the calculation made by Ariençο (f. 76b at the foot, in no. 62; compare Aaron 105a); and the note that the *hosha'na*'s are not everywhere identical (no. 52 f. 57c, compare Aaron 78b, top). In other cases, the Kol Bo is not consistent: references to Catalonia are mostly deleted, as twice in 10b no. 20 (Aaron 22b § 7, 8), 41c no. 41 line 6 from the foot (Aaron 66d § 6), no. 42 f. 42c (Aaron 69b), 45d (Aaron, 120b § 26) replaced with בהרבה מקומות, 46a (Aaron 120c no. 31), twice in 78b (Aaron 108a § 44, 46), in one of which there is a retained reference to Narbonne, about which much is said in the section dealing with mourning customs. On the other hand, there are instances (no. 21, f. 14b and no. 35, beginning) in which place names are provided that are lacking in Aaron's text (7d § 17, 61b), and in those cases the text of the ארחות חיים needs to be emended on the basis of the Kol Bo; compare above p. 19, note d, p. 28 note a, and below Appendix III. Of a similar nature are the two examples of the phrase ואני כותב (2a) which should already be read in Aaron's text (6bc § 30, 31) together with the phrase מצאתי בקונדריס א' מלקוטות; perhaps also to be preferred are Kol Bo's readings of וה"ר יצחק חסיד in no. 11 f. 5c for Aaron's והר"י חסיד [14b § 16] and יצחק בר יהודה חסיד in פסח f. 49d where Aaron (75c § 100) has only רבינו יצחק חסיד. The French word גאנץ (*gands*) in Kol Bo 16a line 8 is lacking in Aaron's text (1b § 6), and Aaron similarly lacks (in 3a line 13) the reference to הראב"ד ז"ל which Kol Bo has at the end of no. 23. The תחנות מפויטות were retained in 10b (in Aaron 22a) but deleted in 42c (Aaron 69b); the omission of Aaron's original headings (Aaron 5b § 11) may be explained by a change in the planning of the book by Kol Bo. The view that Aaron Ha-Kohen had himself written the Kol Bo at some earlier period is wholly untenable; a thorough discussion cannot, however, be entertained, as long as the second part of Aaron's work is lacking.

P. 181

4. [p. 39] The reading קוניהם in the morning prayer is found in: Amram, Abuab (section 131), Abudarham, the *Maḥzor* of Spain, Catalonia, Avignon, Rome, Greece and Burgundy. Likewise in the lunar benediction in: tr{actate} Berakhot 59b according to ms. evidence cited in the בית נתן, Halakhot Gedolot, Amram, Alfasi, Maimonides (ברכות 10.16), סמ"ק 150, שבלי 46, Aaron Ha-Kohen 69d, Abudarham 80c, Ṣedah La-Derekh 1.3.28, Spanish *Maḥzor* 1519 f. 120, Roman *Maḥzor* 1540, Burgundian *Maḥzor* ms.

The reading קונם in the morning prayer is found in: the German *Siddur*, Algerian *Maḥzor*, and is preferred over קוניהם in מעשה רב {Elijah of Vilna} § 34; it is found in the lunar benediction in Sanhedrin 42a, the Roman and German *Maḥzor,* Roqeaḥ 229, Semag, positives 27, Asheri, Ṭur I 426, Joḥanan Trèves {in his commentary on Maḥzor Roma}. This benediction is incompletely transmitted in Yalquṭ Exod. 58b, Ha-Manhig 46a, Candelabrum section 132, Kol Bo no. 42, f. 43b, Mordechai Berakhot section 4, end; the whole item is lacking in Tractate Soferim 20.

קוניהם, which occurs in Bereshit Rabbah 10 end, and Yosippon p. 711, is rare among the liturgical poets. Benjamin אדיר has לקוניהם. The phrase רצון קוניהם, which almost all the rites have in the *piyyuṭ* אל אדון, is also used here and there by a commentator, as for instance in an anonymous ms. on Ezra 4:19. Incidentally, in the cited prayers, the word רצון always precedes קוניהם or קונם and parallel idioms are familiar in talmudic texts and are common among the poets, e. g. רצון קוני (Sifrey נשא, Yalquṭ Isa. 45c, Ḥullin 7a), רצון קוֹנֶךָ (Ḥullin ad loc., Midrash Va-Yosha' 1.3, in ברכת Cochin 43a), רצון קונך (*Maḥzor* ed. 1587 part 1, f. 86a, Eleazar's poem איומה for the New Moon), רצון קונהו (Midrash "Three Things" cited in Kol Bo, the *yoṣer* אדיר ונאה), רצון קונו (Tanḥuma 45a, 73d, Isaac Ghiyyat's מה אמונה, an early translation of {האמונות והדעות, section 9 end, Isaac Seniri's שנה, Immanuel 54b), רצון קונה (Bereshit Rabbah ch. 5, Yalquṭ Gen 8, *yoṣer* אדיר ונאה), רצון קוננו (Eliezer's אלהים זדים). The form קונם is just as common, both in prose (B. {d. R.} Eliezer 25, Tanḥuma 26b, Nissim in בית האוצר {Luzzatto} 1{1847} 57b, Eldad {Ha-Dani} beginning, לקח טוב ,מגלת סתרים 4a, 89d etc.), and among the poets such as Solomon's *'avodah*, Simeon's איחד שם, Gabirol's לשוני חוד, Shabbethai's עד שוכן, Moses Ibn Ezra's החרשים, the hymns שחק אלי and אין מספר, the *'aqedah* אזרחי הוער, the *seliḥah* אל עבדיך, the *yoṣer* אחר שלישים and אומנות, the *zulat* אלהי בך, the *tokheḥah* הרוחות אל אלהי and documented in many other texts.

5. [p. 76] The Roman rite is called after its main centre (קהל קדוש רומה in *Mahzor* ed. 1486 and later editions), or, since it is in Italy, the Italian rite (טלייאן in Jos{eph} Colon responsa 83, טלייאנו in Gedaliah {ibn} Yaḥya 65b, איטלי in Roman *Maḥzor* ed,

1559 in the epilogue, also in ed. 1587 part 1 f. 86a, איטאליאני in Steinschneider, *Catal. Bodl.* no. 2077). Another way of describing

P. 182

that rite arises out of a meaning given to the word לעז. Among the eleven expressions that can be used in Hebrew literature for “translating”, the word לעז refers to the vernacular form, the translation into the local language as distinct from Hebrew; thus the translations of biblical words are known as לעזים (*zur Geschichte* p. 198). Those who reside on the other side of the Alps are known to the Germans as Wälschen (“foreigners”) and as late as a century ago Italy was called Wälschland. So among the Jews: ארץ לועז (Or Zaru‘a cited by Jonah אסור והיתר 20.14); and לשון לועז by Ibn Ezra (at the beginning of Genesis) perhaps refers to Italian. לועזים is used to describe Italians in the works of Parḥi (35b, 58a), Qalonymos (Purim Tract), Joseph Colon Responsa no. 9, Abravanel (עטרת זקנים 33a) and others. In the Roman *Maḥzor* of Rimini 1521 the title page includes the words כפי מנהג הלועזים.

6. [p. 144] The two stanzas זכר באי and זכר בחוני were inserted before the prayer או"א זכרנו in the *musaf tefillah*; an Oppenheimer *Maḥzor* has only one stanza זכר באי באש בחוני. The stanza זכר בחוני occurs in a Bodleian manuscript in Yose’s אפחד במעשי after the stanza רם and in another *Maḥzor* in Qalir’s זכר תחלת before the stanza זכר אמונה.

7. [p. 174] In the {*piyyuṭ*} האוחז the concluding stanza was called היה ויהי which constituted its opening two words, as they already appear in ed. Bologna 1540 [ויהיה] and ed. Cracow 1599. The phrase היה ויהיה also occurs in תאיר נגה, in Simeon’s *qerovah* for the Feast of Weeks (no. 2), Isaac ibn Ghiyyat’s *musaf qerovah*, the hymn אז עד לא (Tripoli), in the book העיון p. 10. In the Alphabet of R. Akiva the text is הייתי ואהיה and Ephraim in the hymn אשר אין לו has: יהיה והיה. The notion [of divine eternity], which is based on the expressions in Isa 41:4, 43:10, 44:6, and on the phrase מעולם עד עולם in Psalms (90:2, 103:17, 106.48), is well expressed in the Hebrew linguistic forms of the עבר and עתיד.

The inclusion of הֹוֶה was the result of {philosophical} speculation. In the linguistic usage of the Bible the word הוה has the sense of “becoming” “happening”, including the non-divine notion of mutability (compare Sa‘adya cited by Yoḥanan Trèves {in his commentary on Maḥzor Roma} on that passage), and this meaning was not retained in its entirety by the thinkers; besides the philosophical sense of “becoming and passing away” (הוה ונפסד), the word הוה also conveyed the sense of what was always present, that which existed without accident. Thus, God is הוה (Naḥmanides Exod 3:14, 20:2), הוה בכל (Eleazar in the Letter of Naḥmanides), הוה

לעולם (Hymn of Unity), קים והוה (codex H h 205 f. 7a), קדוש ההוה (Moses ibn Ezra, *silluq* for *minḥah* {on the Day of Atonement}, or ההוה (Eleazar cited in פרשנדתא {by Abraham Geiger 1855} p. 50) with the addition of והוא יהיה (Nehemiah's מלך האחד, {rite of} Tripoli. As expressly noted (Commentary on אדירי איומה, Ha-Manhig 15b and Aaron Ha-Kohen 4d § 3),

P. 183

three tenses were now appropriate—in Baḥya כד הקמח entry מציאות: הוא יתברך שליט בשלשה זמנים העבר וההוה והעתיד—and the saying ה' מלך ה' מלך ה' ימלוך made use the analogy of היה הוה יהיה for explaining the nature of the divine name, compare Bekhor Shor on Exod 3:14, Roqeaḥ 5c, כתר שם טוב p. 41, Baḥya loc. cit., Aaron Ha-Kohen 36b. The idea also transferred to poetry (אדון עולם, האדיר בשמי, אתניה שבחיה, Eleazar Ha-Kohen's המלך אל); the Hymn of Unity (Day 3) declares: היית והוה ותהיה. Yehudah (יה אלי) has היה ויהיה הוה והויה. Joḥanan Trèves {in his commentary on Maḥzor Roma} recommends reading הוה in the *piyyuṭ* האוחז and this is the text in the French manuscripts and in the German *Maḥzor* editions (Saloniki, Cremona, Venice), while the early Polish *Maḥzor* remains with the original reading. That the noted additions are early emerges from the *qedushah* כבודו אמוניו for *minḥah* {on the Day of Atonement} which has in the mss. אני הייתי ואני עתיד להיות, while a *Maḥzor* from the thirteenth century {cited by Heidenheim} similarly has in the *piyyuṭ* האדיר for *shaḥarit* אני הייתי והוה ועתיד אני להיות. There is a like occurrence in the *piyyuṭ* תאיר נגה in which the earlier text has only היה ויהיה (Luzzatto מבוא p. 23). The Karaite poet Aaron writes היה והויה ויהיה (*Siddur* part 1 pp. 179, 203); for such somewhat affectatious deviations, see above p. 157.

Appendices

Pp. 184–93 Appendix I

Appendix I
[P. 16]
An inventory of geonic decisions and statements concerning ritual

Saboraim: Alfasi Megillah ch.4. Maimoniot תפלה 12. Isaiah {di Trani} המכריע 31. שבלי 19. Ha-Manhig 28a § 30.

Samuel: Mentioned in the Halakhot Gedolot f. 34a (לולב), also 84b, 85b. Aaron Ha-Kohen 39c ברכות § 38. Two Geonim with the name Samuel preceded Yehudai.

Yehudai: Siddur Amram ms. 50a (Purim reading), 64b (cited by Ha-Pardes 44b). Responsa שערי צדק 22b no. 12. Ha-Pardes 39a (קדוש), 42a (the same in Maimoniot שופר beginning). ספר הישר 75b. Ha-Manhig 105a § 150. שבלי 13, 15, 81. Candelabrum ch. 297. Aaron Ha-Kohen 7a, 40c § 58. Kol Bo 155b. ʿIṭṭur {of Isaac b. Abba Mari} cited by Ṭur II 265. Ṭur I 582 (New Year prayer). The citations in Halakhot Gedolot (10a, 41d, 137c) seem to refer to those halakhot.

Mordechai: Alfasi ברכות ch. 5 end (cited by Sol{omon} Adret Responsa part 1 no. 675).

Nisi b. Samuel: Amram ms. f. 21 cited by Ha-Pardes 38c, ליקוטים ms. f. 39 and לקוטי הפרדס 6a where the editions have יוסי for ניסי. Cited without the mention of his name in הרקמה {of Ibn Janaḥ} p. 13, Tos{afot} Berakhot 49b, Asheri Berakhot 7 § 25, Yeruḥam {Toledot Adam} 16.7 f. 148b, Aaron Ha-Kohen 33a, Abudarham 74d. He is nowhere designated as a Gaon.

Joseph b. Abba: He is mentioned by Sherira (חופש p. 40) and Asher b. Ḥayyim in הפרדס ms. Zedekiah (שבלי 17c) refers to: מר רב יוסף גאון ומר רב אבא while תניא 31b has only "R. Joseph Gaon". Isaac Ghiyyat in הלכות פסחים refers to יוסף בר מר רב (ר' אבא is abbreviated to רב), as also in Ṭur I 483 which has in another passage מר רב יוסף בר מר רב יהודה which is also the name given to this Gaon by Abraham Ha-Levi; the same topic is mentioned

P. 185

anonymously (שדרו ממתיבתא) by Alfasi Pesaḥim ch. 2 towards the end. He is cited merely as "R. Joseph" by Aaron Ha-Kohen 41b § 70 and Nissim Pesaḥim ch. 10. ס' המאור {of Zeraḥiah b. Isaac Ha-Levi} (Pesaḥim 154a) cites from Is{aac} Ghiyyat: מר רב יוסף בר רב מארי גאון where מארי —unless we have to emend to ורב מארי—is

https://doi.org/10.1515/9783111142500-004

a textual error, as is also {the naming of R. Joseph's father as} עמרם in שבלי 69 and תניא 68a.

Joseph b. Ḥanina: a question was addressed (שבלי 34 f. 17b) to him and to his father (מורינו רב יוסף בן מורינו רב חנינא ואביו) and he seems to be the same as מר יוסף בר חיננא whose *pesaqim* were included in an early set of rulings from the academy cited by 'Iṭṭur {of Isaac b. Abba Mari} 95c. He may perhaps be identical with the Gaon Joseph b. Ḥiyya who was a contemporary of Joseph b. Abba.

Ṣadoq: In Amram ms. f. 62 [אדוננו מאור עינינו מר רב], from where it is cited in אבן העזר 78b. Also in Maḥzor Vitry and שבלי 35 f. 17c, where an earlier Ṣadoq Gaon of Sura is also mentioned. The Gaon Ṣadoq is cited together with the Gaon Jacob by Eliezer b. Nathan (אבן העזר §§ 243, 325), Barceloni in {Isaiah di Trani} המכריע 88, Nissim and {הגבורים} שלטי {Joshua Boaz} on Hullin ch. 3 (והני מילי שלא כסדרן), Tashbeṣ § 325, Kol Bo 116c where he is Isaac [instead of Ṣadoq] Gaon. Amram ms. f. 85 (מביאין לפנינו מים) also has Isaac while Ha-Manhig (98b) has צדק; Isaac Gaon who is cited in Pisqey Recanati 342 is called Ṣadoq in Meir of Rothenburg's Responsa, quarto, n. 82. Yeruḥam (מישרים 31.2 f. 95a) and Haggahot Asheri, {Bava} Batra ch. 8 § 22 write צדק while Sherira p. 41 has צדיק. In the Geonic Responsa ed. 1848 (8b and 41a) Naḥshon states כך פירש בה אבא מרי מר (בר) רב צדוק ראש ישיבה (compare Rapoport {תולדות רבנו} נתן p. 26, Introduction to the Responsa f. 9a); we should therefore also attribute to him the words cited in the 'Arukh (ed. 1531) entry וכן פירש אבא מרי גאון מר רב יצחק ראש ישיבה :עד. The same Gaon Ṣadoq appears in Responsa ed. 1802 n. 217, Responsa שערי צדק 21a, 29a, 31a (from where Recanati op. cit. 462), Ha-Pardes 26a, Maimoniot שבת ch. 3, Tos{afot Bava} Meṣi'a 71a. In Maimoniot שבת ch. 29 the name "Isaac b. Ṣadoq" probably originated in a conflation of two text versions.

Moses: Responsa שערי צדק 20b no. 14 concerning mourning obligations. Amram f. 29 (morning prayer): so also in Maḥzor Vitry § 64, 'Arukh entry תפל, לקוטי הפרדס 8d,

P. 186

Semag, positive precepts 19, 3 שבלי, Ṭur I 268. Amram f. 31 (Sabbath eve), from which Ha-Manhig 24b, Semag loc. cit., 17 שבלי, Ha-Pardes 56a, Abudarham 32d. Amram f. 49a, from where Ha-Manhig 42b (מגלה § 19). Amram ff. 55 and 57 (eve of the Pesaḥ festival); so also in אבן העזר 74d, Ha-Manhig 85b § 78, 87b § 89, Maimoniot פסח end, Ṭur I 481. Isaac Ghiyyat הלכות ms. פסחים (concerning the fifth cup of wine in the evening) and ר"ה. 'Arukh entry ד or דד from which Tos{afot} Soṭah 40a. Siddur of Solomon of Sijilmasa. Ha-Manhig 53b § 11 (*musaf* prayer for the New Year festival), from where Aaron Ha-Kohen 100a § 9 and Ṭur I 591. Isaiah {di Trani} המכריע 84 concerning קלף.

Palṭoi: Amram ms. f. 20a. Dispensation from the obligation to recite the benediction שהכל; also in Ha-Manhig 37b § 6, Meir Rothenburg in ברכות מהר"ם {= סדר הברכות} 3a. Amram 52a, from which Ha-Pardes 60b, לקוטי הפרדס 19b, and, without any specification of the source, in ʿArukh הזיו לך. Compare שבלי 100 f. 44c. Amram 64b, from which Ha-Pardes 44b top, Ha-Manhig 52b § 5, Ṭur I 582 [New Year]. Concerning the leaved booths and the palm-branches {of Sukkot} in Amram f. 81, הלכות ms. by Isaac Ghiyyat and in Ha-Manhig לולב § 8, 13, 18, 33. Isaac Ghiyyat on the Festal Day of Atonement (from which Ha-Manhig 61a § 62, Ṭur I 621) and the Ninth of Av (from which Ha-Manhig 50b § 27). Ha-Pardes 44a (insertions in the New Year prayer). Siddur Solomon {of Sijilmasa}. Isaiah {di Trani} המכריע 24 (heated wine), 85 (שרטוט {scoring of ms. lines}). שבלי 9, 11, 19, 38, 94. Mordechai Yoma. Yeruḥam {b. Meshullam} 6.1. Ṭur I 235, 619. Nissim on Alfasi תענית ch. 1 f. 172b.

Kohen Ṣedeq: Responsa שערי צדק 22b no. 11 (circumcision). Amram 64b, from which Ha-Pardes 44b [where צדק is omitted] and Ha-Manhig 53a § 6 [New Year]. R. Gershom rulings in מעשה הגאונים 172, compare שבלי no. 11 line 6. Isaac Ghiyyat הלכות ms. in תשובה and פסחים. ʿArukh entry אמן 2. Siddur Solomon{of Sijilmasa}. מעשה הגאונים 216, compare שבלי 92. שבלי 94. Aaron Ha-Kohen 27b top. Ṭur I 124, 474, 484, 581.

Sar Shalom: Responsa שערי צדק 19b no. 2 and 21b nos. 19, 20, 21 (mourning rites), 22a no. 4 (circumcision benediction); Responsa ed. 1802 nos. 205, 330 (Targum recitation);

P. 187

perhaps also Responsa ed. 1848 no. 8, complementing what is cited by Ha-Manhig 92b § 112. Amram ms. ff. 16, 26, 30, 37, 40, 47, 56, 57, 84, 85. Isaac Ghiyyat הלכות פסח. ʿArukh entry ראש. Ha-Pardes 38d, 46c, 56bc, 57a. לקוטי הפרדס 16c. אבן העזר 69d. ס' הישר 720 f. 73d. Ha-Manhig תפלה § 32, 78, 84. שבת § 3, 15, 30, 63, 65. תעניות § 5, 6. לולב § 18. פסח § 91. Tos{afot} Menaḥot 30a. שבלי 11, 17, 67, 118, 119. Asheri Rosh Ha-Shanah end, Sukkah 3 § 5. Maimoniot ברכות 5 § 6, סדר תפלה f. 136b, חמץ ומצה 8 f. 265a, שופר ch. 1. Aaron Ha-Kohen 61c § 2, 63c § 12, 66b § 4, 69a § 33. Ṭur I 146, 237, 273, 292, 295, 481, 552, 566, 582. Isaac b. Sheshet Responsa 412.

Menaḥem: Isaac Ghiyyat הלכות ms.: אמר רב נחמן גאון קדש ושתה כוס של קדוש. Compare Responsa 21 in ed. 1802.

Matathiya: Responsa שערי צדק 20b no. 9 (*qaddish* in the burial place). Isaac Ghiyyat op. cit. לולב. Solomon {of Sijilmasa}'s Siddur. Joḥanan's ms. commentary on Aḥa's Sheiltot. Ṭur I 458. Abudarham 48a (Haggadah).

Naṭronai: Responsa שערי צדק 20a nos. 3 and 4 ibid., 20b no. 12, 21b no. 22 (mourning rites). Amram's Siddur cites him in twenty-seven passages. Isaac Ghiyyat op. cit. פסחים and סוכה. Alfasi Megillah ch. 4. Ha-Pardes 6d, 7b, 39a [concerning two loaves; the Gaon's name is lacking there but becomes clear from Amram f. 33 and Maḥzor Vitry], 55d, 56a, 57b. Maḥzor Vitry §§ 63 until 66. Ha-Manhig 7b, 8b, 11b, 12a, 19b, 23b, 24b, 25b, 28ab, 33b, 34a, 42a, 44b, 46b, 50a, 51b, 53b, 58a, 59b, 61b, 63b, 66b, 67ab, 69a, 82b, 88a. Yehudah Barceloni cited in Aaron Ha-Kohen 106a. {Isaiah di Trani} המכריע 31, 88. מעשה הגאונים 11, 172. Semag positive precepts 19. Ṭur I 46 (concerning the order of the daily hundred benedictions that was sent to Lucena, cited from Amram's Siddur), 52 [according to the Semaq § 11 f. 7b, cited from Amram; anonymously in לקוטי הפרדס 8d], 59, 128, 131, 135, 145, 267, 268, 269, 281, 298, 442, 461, 474, 483, 556, 566, 591, 597, 609, 619, 620, 621, 622, 649, 651, 690. These citations, as well as those in Mordechai, Asheri, Maimoniot, in Meir of Rothenburg (Responsum 603), Zedekiah {b. Abraham Anaw}, Aaron Ha-Kohen, and Abudarham have as their sources the geonic responsa [compare ed. 1802

P. 188

no. 245], Amram's Siddur and the works of Isaac Ghiyyat and Yehudah Barceloni.

Amram: is cited in his Siddur ms. six times, namely at the beginning and then in *qiddush* (both items also in שבלי 9c at the foot and 10a: מצאתי בשם רב עמרם גאון, compare Ha-Manhig 26a § 19); Purim (compare Ha-Manhig 43a § 23 and 24, שבלי 54 f. 24c in the middle: דתניא א"ר חנינא וכו' although this last-mentioned is cited in Amram's name only in Ṭur I 688); קדוש for Pesaḥ evening (Ha-Manhig 82b § 58, Aaron-Ha-Kohen 80c § 21 end); and hand-washing (Ha-Manhig 87b § 88). Luzzatto mentions the responsum that Amram sent to Barcelona (בית האוצר {Luzzatto} 48a). Compare also 38 שבלי towards the end, {Isaiah di Trani} המכריע nos. 85, 87, Yeruḥam {b. Meshullam} 5.4 f. 45b.

Naḥshon: Responsa שערי צדק 19b no. 14, 22a no. 5 (Kol Bo 153a, compare Rapoport {תולדות רבנו נתן} p. 37). Siddur Amram f. 6 concerning the knee-bowing in *qaddish* (also Maḥzor Vitry § 12, Ha-Pardes 58a, לקוטי הפרדס 7d, where no name is mentioned, Ha-Manhig 11b). The entry תפל in the 'Arukh perhaps originates in Naḥshon's lexicon that is cited in מעשה הגאונים § 103. Responsa שערי צדק 90b no. 34 (מלקות beatings). שבלי 5 (morning prayer, *yoṣer* for an individual), 101 (concerning חמין on the day before the Festival of Atonement: it occurs neither in Siddur {Amram} ms. f. 80 nor in Aaron Ha-Kohen 108d § 49). Aaron Ha-Kohen 11d § 4 (the *amen* of the individual; apparently this was not known to Naḥmanides in his לקוטות 4c top). Yeruham b. Meshullam} 6.3 (against fasting on the New Year festival); the parallel passages make no mention of Naḥshon; he is however mentioned in Mordechai Rosh Ha-Shanah ch. 1; but there one should read Sa'adya {and not

Naḥshon} not only because of the style of the ruling but also as is clarified in שבלי 93 and תניא 102b.

Ṣemaḥ b. Ḥayyim: mentioned in Zedekiah {b. Abraham Anaw} אסור והיתר ms. § 66.

Ṣemaḥ b. Palṭoi: Alfasi Shabbat ch. 22; mostly cited only as "Ṣemaḥ", as in Amram's Siddur f. 20 (from which לקוטי הפרדס 9a, where both editions read יצחק צמח, Ha-Manhig 20b § 76, Ṭur I 132); 'Arukh entry מגל (abbreviated in the editions; the parallel passage is in 56 שבלי f. 25c. In Ha-Pardes 47bc and Ha-Manhig 42a

P. 189

§ 12, there is no mention of Ṣemaḥ's name). Isaac Ghiyyat op. cit. סכה and פסחים; Roqeaḥ 306 (*musaf* for the New Moon that occurs on the Sabbath); Semag positive precepts 41, Ha-Manhig 51a, 69a, Asheri Sukkah ch. 4 § 3 (Ṭur I 643); 'Iṭṭur {of Isaac b. Abba Mari} cited in Ṭur II 265; Ṭur I 473, 559; Aaron Ha-Kohen 80b (Pesaḥ evening, as also in שבלי 65). שבלי (6 *yoṣer*).

Ṣemaḥ b. Solomon: is cited by Isaac Ghiyyat in הלכות לולב; furthermore, his ruling is in מעשה הגאונים ms. § 87 and his responsum in Maimoniot (יום טוב 2 § 30) where he is called "the Head of the Academy" while in the 'Iṭṭur {of Isaac b. Abba Mari} (79c) he is mentioned as דיינא דבבא. R. Ṣemaḥ דיינא דבבא is mentioned by Amram (see {Luzzatto} בית האוצר 48a) and by Joḥanan in a ms. commentary on the Sheiltot. That same title is applied to Sama (Sherira p. 38), Joseph b. Ḥiyya (ibid., p. 41), Ḥaninay (Responsa שערי צדק 3a), Hai (התחיה p. 41), and is found in *yequm purqan*, in Solomon's *reshut* אלהא מקמא and in the Responsa just mentioned 91b. The expression בבא דמתיבתא appears in Naṭronai, see Iṭṭur entry שומא f. 32d.

Hai b. Naḥshon: is mentioned concerning "*Kol Nidrey*" by Barceloni and in Responsa ed. 1802 no. 143; see Asheri Yoma end, Ṭur I 619 [where the patronym בר נחשון is lacking, Rapoport in his supplements to Hai {תולדות רבנו האי גאון} p. 11], Aaron Ha-Kohen 106a, Kol Bo 68.

Sa'adya: compare the passages cited above, p. 19 note a {n. 97}.

Aaron the Gaon: mentioned by Hai according to Kol Bo 154a.

Sherira: Isaac Ghiyyat לולב (concerning the Sabbath of the Feast of Tabernacles, so also Ha-Manhig 70a § 42, Ṭur I 660) and פסחים (Naḥmanides on Alfasi, 158b). Solomon {of Sijilmasa}'s Siddur. Ha-Manhig 59a § 53, 61b § 67, 26b § 21. Naḥmanides לקוטות f. 5a (sent to Fez, to which city were also directed the texts mentioned in the 'Iṭṭur {of Isaac b. Abba Mari} 20b and {M. Isserles} תורת העולה 39b or Responsa ed. 1802 no. 122, compare התחיה p. 41). 5 שבלי [also in Ṭur I 59] and 34. Asheri Sukkah ch. 3 § 31. Ṭur I 120, 286, 589, 594, 609, 630, 658. Aaron Ha-Kohen 18a § 78 and 79, 18b § 84 (from which it is cited by R. Aboab on the Ṭur I 127), 103b § 4. Pisqey Recanati 595. Tos{afot} Menaḥot 42b. Often mentioned in joint projects with his son Hai, e.g. Ha-Pardes 38d [on Jacob b. Nissim of Qayrawan, compare above p. 19, note d {100}], Isaac Ghiyyat and Naḥmanides on פסח, 'Arukh entries הלקט and צץ (מילה) {Barukh b. Isaac} Ha-Terumah § 206 (תפלין),

P. 190

Ha-Manhig 25a § 13 (קדוש) 30a, no. 43 (*musaf*), 53b § 12 (New Year); Semag positive precepts 22; Ṭur I 474, 591; Abudarham 17c (אהבה רבה).

Eleazar Ha-"Alluf" from Spain: a contemporary of the Geonim Palṭoi and Naṭronai (Responsa שערי צדק, 25a, 'Iṭṭur {of Isaac b. Abba Mari} 16d) who had seen Anan's Law-book, as reported in Amram's Siddur. He is perhaps identical with Eleazar ריש כלה whom Naṭronai mentions in connection with Samuel (cited in the 'Arukh as גמע {Ibn Jam'a}) and whose responsum is included in מעשה הגאונים 425. Living at the same time was the proselyte Eleazar who moved to Saragossa.

Ḥefeṣ Ha-"Alluf" or Gaon: is mentioned by Isaac Ghiyyat on יו"כ and לולב, from which Ha-Manhig 61a § 62, 67a § 18.

Daniel Gaon: שבלי 6, תניא 5a, Kol Bo 9; occurs also in Pisqey Recanati 476. In the time of Benjamin of Tudela that was the name of the leading scholar in Rome; a later scholar of this name is mentioned in the commentary on ארעא רקדא (*Oṣar Neḥmad* 2 p. 199).

Nathan Gaon or Head: is mentioned in Siddur Amram ff. 46 and 49, and these same references occur in Joseph Migash Responsa 83 and 193, אבן העזר 78d top and 79a foot. Ha-Manhig 42ab, 47b, שבלי הלקט 11, Mordechai on Megillah chapter 3 beginning, Ṭur I 565, Abudarham ed. Ven{ice} 54d [the error "Naḥman" in ed. Prague is corrected by Rapoport in Responsa {תשובות גאונים קדמונים} 1848 f. 9b], Simeon Duran חדושי 21a, Solomon Duran Responsa 101. In addition, there is a mention of Nathan in Meir of Rothenburg Responsa 122, and in Ṭur I 566 [for which in Kol Bo 155a, as Joseph Karo noted, the reference is to Yehudai], and {Ṭur I} 690 is perhaps a reference to the Gaon or "Alluf" Nathan b. Yehudah, Sherira's uncle. There is also mention of a R. Nathan of "Africa" in an early Responsa of the Geonim (Tashbeṣ ms. § 73 codex H h 184), in Aaron Ha-Kohen [in the unpublished second part] and from there into Kol Bo 85c. "Africa", or more correctly "Afriqiya" is Qayrawan, as is clear from the words of R. Nathan Ha-Kohen in Yuḥasin (ed. Cracow f. 120b) and from ס' הקבלה f. 44a; R. Ḥananel was also from "Africa" (ספר הישר 72d) and is counted as one of its scholars (ibid. 382 f. 38d). Belonging to that same group of scholars is

P. 191

Yehudah b. Yehudah b. Saul, to whom Naṭronai writes ({Luzzatto} (בית האוצר 59b) and who is probably to be identified with the same Yehudai b. Samuel to whom, as well as to Nathan, that same Naṭronai wrote (Responsa {in} ס' הפלאה, no. 4). Consequently R. Nathan and R. Yehudah flourished in Qayrawan in the same period, as indicated by the ruling in {Responsa} שערי צדק 84a no. 3, where they are both mentioned together as judges. It could be that the pupils and the sons of that departed R. Nathan (רב נתן), to whom Sa'adya refers (ibid. 18b no. 12, belong to that scholar {Yehudah b. Saul}.

Hai [compare Sherira above]: Amram's Siddur at the beginning. Responsa שערי צדק 22b nos. 6 and 13. Responsa ed. 1802, no. 38, 47, 55, 56 etc. Nissim in המאור {of Zeraḥiah b. Isaac Ha-Levi} Beṣah f. 182b; Ha-Manhig 81b. Alfasi Shabbat ch. 19. Isaac Ghiyyat op. cit. פסחים, ר"ה, לולב, as well as in {Shemtov ibn Gaon} מגדל עוז on סכה 6, 12, Jos{eph} Colon Responsa 9, Ha-Pardes 22c, 38b, 44a, 58b and d. תמים דעים 119, 172. הישר 331. Isaiah di Trani on Alfasi Megillah 266a. Aboab Candelabrum ch. 290. Abudarham 2b, 53b, 73a, Ha-Manhig 8a, 21b, 23a, 42a, 44a, 48a, 49b, 50a, 51ab, 52b, 53a, 55a, 59ab, 60b, 61ab, 62a, 63b, 64a, 68b, 70a, 71a, 72a, 97a. Often mentioned by Zedekiah {b. Abraham Anaw}, Asher, Jacob b. Asher, Maimoniot, Aaron Ha-Kohen.

Samuel b. Ḥofni: Among his works, called שערים (Rapoport Hai {תולדות רבנו האי גאון} p. 86 § 8), שערי הברכות also belong (שבלי ms. § 159, Maimoniot ברכות ch. 11, § 2, חמץ ומצה ch. 3. Compare Azulai *Lex.* {שם הגדולים} Part 1 p. 175 no. 106, Dukes {נחל קדומים p. 62). He is mentioned in codices Uri 280 and 298 (the Siddur of Solomon {of Sijilmasa}), אבן העזר 69d, Asheri, end of Rosh Ha-Shanah, שבלי 41, 42, 45, תניא 39b, 40a, 41a, Maimoniot ברכות ch. 5, Ṭur I 582, 664, Abudarham 9c. In the 'Iṭṭur {of Isaac b. Abba Mari} he is called "the wise" "from Fez" or "in Fez" (חכם פאס, see Rapoport loc. cit.), and here and there he is referred to as Kohen; is he perhaps to be identified with the Samuel Ha-Kohen who lived in Fez around the year 1000 (ס' הקבלה 42a) and was later Gaon in Sura? See S. Sachs התחיה p. 45. A Samuel Ha-Kohen is mentioned by Isaac Ghiyyat in the halakhot of פסח,

P. 192

העומר and לולב; the last mentioned passage is also in Aaron Ha-Kohen 116d § 35.

The honorific title of "Gaon" originally belonged exclusively to the leaders of the Persian academies but, once {North-}Africa and Europe could also show that they had notable talmudic scholars, it was also transferred, from about 900, to those rabbis; thus it was that those who held the title included Ḥefeṣ (in 'Iṭṭur {of Isaac b. Abba Mari} and Ha-Manhig), Donolo (by Rashi, as demonstrated by Sen{ior} Sachs in *Kerem Chemed* 8.101), Meshullam b. Qalonymos, Shemariah (see Steinschneider, ibid. 9.39; perhaps {the Shemariah} from Bari), Nissim, Mevorakh (in Or Zaru'a and in the Small Or Zaru'a; in Tashbeṣ, mss. and editions, the title of Gaon is given in that passage only to Nissim, while in its citation by Abr{aham} Klausner 9a neither Nissim nor Mevorakh is accorded that title), Dosa, Moses of Pavia (ספר הישר 362 and Semag), Samuel Ha-Levi (Ibn Ezra on Lev 16:8), Eleazar b. Isaac (Rashi on Ps 76:11), Samuel b. David (Ha-Pardes 23a), Isaac Ha-Levi (Ha-Pardes 48c and לקוטי הפרדס 18c, where the printed text has אביתר, probably corrupted from אביו הר', compare Maimoniot אבל ch. 10 § 5), Rashi (codex H h 63), Joseph of Narbonne (Ha-Manhig 86a) and others. In the writings of the twelfth century the earlier scholars are often called Geonim, and their rulings are included in the geonic responsa, so that Zedekiah (שבלי 114) cites as one of the תשובות הגאונים what is in fact a ruling of Solomon of Worms (Ha-Pardes 44d). The title of Gaon was effectively synonymous with רב, חכם; they wrote לפני גאון פלוני (Hai cited by Parḥi 44), ומפי גאון (Rashi Ḥullin 46a), אם יש גאון (ס' האשכול cited by Aaron H-Kohen 24c, Kol Bo 11b). Every outstanding Talmudist was counted among the Geonim, as Maimonides specifically notes in the introduction to his work (A. Fuld in {Azulai} שה"ג ed. 1847 p. 280). Consequently, גאון or שו"ת הגאונים in the citation of an anonymous teaching refers to the Babylonians only in the early sources, for example, in the Halakhot Gedolot 12d, 42a, Tanḥuma Genesis beginning, in Alfasi Megillah 3 and 4 (Ha-Pardes 59d), Rosh Ha-Shanah 3 (שבלי 100 beginning), Isaac Ghiyyat, or wherever the terms הבבליים (Rashi

P. 193

Ḥullin 47a, Berakhot 49b, Meir of Rothenburg Responsa 866) or ראשי ישיבות (Ha-Pardes 44b) are added. With regard to other citations, for example Barceloni in Parḥi 8 f. 34a and Aaron Ha-Kohen 106a, Ha-Pardes 41d, Semag positive precepts 27, Ha-Manhig 17a, 28b, 37b, 64a, Mordechai Yoma beginning, the use of the designation "gaon" or "geonic" does not indicate the specific historical source, unless it can be proven from elsewhere. Even the attributions to specific names in the regular editions of collected responsa are not always to be trusted. As stated in Ha-Pardes 22bc, "Although this responsum is also cited in the name of R. Yehudai, the attribution cannot be relied upon." With regard to an expert opinion cited by Ghiyyat in the name of Hai, Naḥmanides regards this very suspiciously and is of the opinion that one cannot at all rely upon the existing collections (ר"ה מלחמות 214b, סוכה 246b). Shemayah describes one responsum as corrupt (משובשת), see Mordechai

Pesaḥim end; Abraham b. David states that the responsa are no longer as accurate as when they reached the early scholars (as against המאור {of Zeraḥiah b. Isaac Ha-Levi}, Pesaḥim 31d). Sherira Gaon ({Responsa} שערי צדק 18a) already explains that some items in Sa'adya's book are actually interpolations. It may be stated, in general, that such interpolations reach far back into an early period and that one must be especially careful when using the geonic responsa in the collections of Saloniki 1802 [Lepizig 1858], in which such numbers as 43, 99, 122, 143, 187, 268, 299 and 339 have no claim to be authentic.

Pp. 194–201 Appendix II

Appendix II
[P. 23]
The medieval commentators on *piyyuṭ*, alphabetically arranged {in original German}.

Aaron b. Ḥayyim Ha-Kohen wrote the *Maḥzor* codex Uri 255 in the year 1227 and enriched the commentary every now and then with his own additions, as for example with regard to Purim, the Feast of Weeks and the New Year Festival. He was the nephew of Samson of Coucy and of the martyred R. Jacob of Corbeil (compare *zur Geschichte* p. 77). There is no such commentator as David b. Menaḥem (Wolf {*Bibliotheca*}1.321, 4.809).

Aaron b. Mordechai. There is a note by him in the commentary Opp. 1073 folio size, f. 160.

Abba Shalom is the name that the commentator calls himself a number of times in cod. Opp. 1483Q, for example, before *barukh she'amar* and Ps 100. Since he cites R. Eleazar of Forchheim (*zur Geschichte* p. 104), he seems to be from the fourteenth century.

Avigdor. The commentator in cod. Opp. 1074F—who is not, as claimed in the printed catalogues, Elijah b. Benjamin, which is actually the name of the copyist—cites in the poem זכר תחלת what he heard from his uncle, R. Avigdor. In the above-mentioned codex Opp. 1483Q on ויושע a comment is communicated from the book of R. Avigdor. Similarly, in the marginal notes of a defective *Maḥzor*, on vellum in folio size, for the Day of Atonement, which I viewed on 7 October 1854, it is stated at the beginning of the *yoṣer*: מספר הר"ר אביגדור ומיסודו נעתק זה. In early manuscripts there is sometimes mention of an Avigdor הצרפתי (*Kerem Chemed* 7.69, 8.160). In a letter to Beziers, Naḥmanides mentions R. Isaac and R. Avigdor; the latter is perhaps the one mentioned in a ms. of the Niṣṣahon

P. 195

(*zur Geschichte* p. 86). A disciple of Eleazar of Worms is also called Avigdor (codex Mich. 615). In the margin of codex de Rossi 694 there appear explanations of a few words in the prayer-book by Avigdor b. Solomon b. Yehudah, to which de Rossi adds the superfluous comment: “cujus auctoris nulla iterum in Wolfio extant indicia”.

Abraham. Mention is made of רבנא אברהם in a fragment of a commentary on אז שש מאות before the beginning of codex Opp. 1159Q (communication from Steinschneider).

https://doi.org/10.1515/9783111142500-005

Abraham b. Yequtiel, mentioned in a commentary on {the poem} אשרי העם (for the Torah Festival) in codex H h 132.

Asher b. Jacob Ha-Levi, perhaps from Osnabrück, occurs many times in codex Opp. 1483Q, for example on the שמע, before the *tefillah* and in the *qedushah*.

Azriel b. Nathan [*zur Geschichte* p. 48] is mentioned in the commentary on {the poem} ואתה אזון קול (New Year) of his contemporary Eliezer b. Nathan.

Barukh b. Isaac, who is probably the author of the ס' התרומה, is cited at the end of the Ḥanukah *yoṣer* in H h 17.

Barukh b. Meir, the father of Meir of Rothenburg, is cited by his son (in H h 17) on Purim, {Shabbat} Parah, at the end of the Haggadah, before the *yoṣer* אור ישע, and on the *seliḥah* אין כמדת בשר, תפלה תקח. Also there is the abbreviation במז"ל which is on his tombstone ({L.} Lewysohn *Epitaphien {von Grabsteinen}* p. 27).

Benjamin b. Abraham {Anaw} commentated on the prayer-book, the Haggadah, the Aramaic ארעא רקדא and probably also on other *piyyuṭim*; there are samples in the works of his brother Zedekiah. Compare Dukes in *Oṣar Neḥmad* 2.199.

David b. Moses Ha-Levi mentions in the margin of codex Opp. 1073F f. 144b on שבתי וראה (Second Day of New Year) that he looked through many commentaries and finally found an explanation in an early manuscript.

David b. Moses Yehudah is supposed to be the commentator on the *seliḥah*'s in the Vatican codex 308; compare Bartolocci {*Bibliotheca*} vol. 2, p. 277, Wolf {*Bibliotheca*} vol 1 p. 321.

Eleazar b. Isaac in cited on {Shabbat} Parah in H h 17.

P. 196

Eleazar b. Yehudah: His commentary, which was used by Hirṣ Trèves {Thiengen 1560}, is in codex Opp. 1010F and covers the daily prayers, individual Psalms, Avot, *hosha'nah*'s, Haggadah, grace after meals and the אתה הראית passage for the Torah festival; in codex Opp. 1073F there are annotations on this *Maḥzor* commentary, some individual items of which are included in codex H h 17, specifically explaining several *seliḥah*'s and *piyyuṭim* of the Atonement Festival.

Eliezer b. Nathan: Codex H h 61, though defective, includes explanations that conclude with the *qerovah* for the Ninth of Av and that deal with the daily and Sabbath prayers, notable Psalms, Haggadah, wedding benedictions, New Year prayers, *Kol Nidrey*, *hosha'na*'s, five *yoṣer* poems, three *zulat* poems, three *ofan* poems, and two *ma'arivim* for ליל שמורים. Other manuscripts have more or less complete versions, or sometimes the insertion of some additional items of his commentary on the *Maḥzor*, especially on the *rehiṭim*, the four Sabbaths, the Sabbath of Ḥanukah, New Year and the prayer for rain on the concluding festival {of Tabernacles}. Some specific items from that commentary are printed in the editions of סדור נהורא and קרבן אהרן; in the commentary on the second *ma'ariv* {for Pesaḥ} (MS ff. 44a–45d) in the *Zionwächter* {*Watcher over Zion*} (שומר ציון Altona 1852, nos. 128, 129) and several passages in החלוץ 2.121. Related material is also to be found in העזר אבן § 12, 204 and ff. 74a, 128a.

Eliakim Ha-Levi: explains one passage from את חיל (New Year) in codex H h 17.

Elqanah: Codex Opp. 1075F has, at the end of the New Year prayers, the words כה אמר אלקנה. He was a commentator in fourteenth-century Germany.

Ephraim b. Jacob of Bonn: a *Maḥzor* is cited in his name. Codex H h 17 includes various items from his commentaries; he often raises objections to the views of Menaḥem b. Seruq.

Ephraim b. Menaḥem: is mentioned in codex Uri 255, on {*Parashat*} Sheqalim and New Year (את חיל).

Friedel of Erfurt: has transmitted in codex Mich. 656 some comments by a *seliḥah* exegete.

Hillel b. Jacob; is cited by his brother Ephraim of

P. 197

Bonn and by Eliezer b. Nathan in their commentaries.

Isaac b. Ḥananel: offers some interpretations in אמל ורבך (H h 17).

Isaac Ha-Levi: Rashi's teacher, is mentioned several times in manuscripts and editions, as for example on Yose's אהללה, and on Sabbath Zakhor [תכלית שבעים]. He praises Meir b. Isaac for his presentation of the *selihah* תעלת צרי (codices Opp. 1073F and 1606Q).

Israel b. Yeḥiel: cited in אמתי שמו (Feast of Weeks) in codex H h 17.

Itiel b. Meshullam; is cited for {Sabbath} Parah in codex Opp. 1074F.

Jacob b. Yaqar: is cited from Rashi on a *piyyuṭ* for {Sabbath} Sheqalim.

Jacob b. Meir [Rabbenu Tam]: is mentioned several times in H h 17.

Jacob Nazir: is cited in the *hosha'nah*'s and {the poetry for} the New Year. In תפלה ed. 1525 the word נזיר is lacking.

Jacob b. Nehemiah Ha-Levi: is mentioned in the *zulat* אהבוך נפש (first day of the Pesaḥ festival). In the printed commentary הלוי is lacking.

Yaqar Ha-Levi: Marginal notes by him are preserved in codex Opp. 1073F at the end of the eighth day of Pesaḥ. His additions to Vitry's commentary on Avot are in codex Canon. 83 and in a Roman *Maḥzor* from the year 1441.

Yeḥiel: There is an annotation in codex Mich. 652 before the *'avodah* אמיץ which reads: "This is what I, Yeḥiel, found, written by my father R. Moses Saltman." There was a Moses Baltman who lived in twelfth-century Regensburg, and a later one of that name in Zürich in 1393.—In codex H h 17 for the Feast of Weeks there is the statement: “This is what my relative (קרובי) R. Yeḥiel told me.” This seems to me to be a note by Ephraim of Bonn who in another passage mentions the communal leader Samuel and his son Yeḥiel. In ס' הישר 70b there is also a reference to קרובו הרב ר' יחיאל.

Yeḥiel of Paris: An explanation of his appears in the printed commentary for New Year (at the end of תפן במכון).

Yehudah of Paris: His explanation of יטידוך is cited in a manuscript commentary on the *rehiṭim*.

P. 198

He is probably the רבנו החסיד who is described in codex Canon. Orient. 1 as the author of several Aramaic clarifications of the Decalogue. He is also mentioned in *Meged* {*Yeraḥim*} part 1 p. 7, compare *zur Geschichte* p. 35 and הדר זקנים {on the Torah} 39b (where he is designated חסיד) with פירוש ר"אש 37b (where {he is cited as} מפריש).

Yehudah b. Moses Ha-Darshan: who is cited by Menaḥem b. Ḥelbo (*Oṣar Neḥmad* 1.106. The printed commentary also has that passage but cites the source only as “midrash”) is probably the same Yehudah Ha-Darshan who explained a passage in the *teqi'ata* אנוסה in Opp. 1074F.

Yequtiel Ha-Levi: [*zur Geschichte* p. 51] the communal leader who is cited by the father of Meir of Rothenburg on the *yoṣer* אור ישע is certainly that Yequtiel b. Jacob Ha-Levi who died in Worms in the year 1261 ({L. Lewysohn} *Epitaphien {von Grabsteinen}* p. 26).

Yomtov the martyr [*zur Geschichte* pp. 52, 86]: whose explanations of אריא וגנבי are mentioned in codex Canon. 1.

Jonathan: it is not clear from de Rossi’s description of codex 653 what this commentator had explained in that *Maḥzor*.

Joseph of France: known as מולעין is cited in Opp. 1073F f. 79.

Joseph Qara: Items from his commentary on the *Maḥzor*, large parts of which are transmitted in manuscripts, are also sometimes cited in the printed commentary, e.g. in the *zulat* אהבוך, אלים ביום (*Ṭal* {prayer for dew}).

Joseph בדוס: Commentator on the Haggadah, cited by Aaron Ha-Kohen 83b (*Kol Bo* 56c), perhaps identifiable with “Joseph, the expounder of prayer” who occurs there on f. 65c (*Kol Bo*, 40a).

Joseph: making the note אני יוסף הכותב in H h 17 (*yoṣer* אור ישע, end).

Qalonymos b. Yehudah: is cited in Opp. 1073F in a *qerovah* for the Ninth of Av.

Qalonymos b. Shabbethai of Rome: occurs in a *silluq* for {Sabbath} Sheqalim (also in the editions), a *qerovah* for the Ninth of Av, a *teqi'ata* אשא דעי, and a *seliḥah* אז קשתי.

Menasseh b. Levi: Towards the end of a Michael manuscript he is described as the author of explanations of

P. 199

various synagogal items (the *yoṣer* אור עולם, the *ma'ariv* שמיני אותותיו, the hymn ברוך ה' יום).

Meir b. Abraham: According to codex H h17, the explanation of the word הצנוע in the *piyyuṭ* האחד בעולמו is by him and this is also noted in Hirṣ Trèves ({Thiengen 1560} before *ne'ilah*). In an early commentary on New Year [prayers] the author states: "by my brother-in-law R. Meir b. Abraham" (Opp. 1073 F).

Meir b. Barukh of Rothenburg: is cited several times in H h 17 which includes individual items by him [compare Barukh]; he also mentions there his brother Abraham (Feast of Weeks).

Menaḥem b. Ḥelbo: His explanations deal with the *silluq* for {Sabbath} Zakhor (also in the editions), the *yoṣer* items אור ישע, אבן חוג, תפן במכון (also printed), the *teqi'ata* זכר תחלת, and Qalir's *qerovah* שושן.

Meshullam b. Moses: probably to be identified with the Meshullam who often occurs, who is called המורה by Eliezer b. Nathan, and who is often named as the commentator in mss. and sometimes also in print. He is cited in poems for {Sabbath} Sheqalim (אלה אזכרה and a *silluq*), {Sabbath} Zakhor (Opp. 1074F), {Sabbath} Ha-Ḥodesh, (אדון מקדם) אז שש מאות (Opp. 1159Q), אנסיכה, and the *seliḥah* תעלת (H h 17).

Moses: Commentator on the *reshut* אציתו למימרי in codex Can. Or. 1.

Moses Ha-Darshan: He explains the expression תכלית שבעים (also in editions), the astronomic content in רבות עשית for Sabbath Ha-Ḥodesh (Luzzatto in *Kerem Chemed* 8.37), and סלוף דינה (New Year) in codex H h 17. Contrary to what is suggested in {S. J. Rapoport's} *The Life of R. Nathan* p. 47 and {Jost's} *Geschichte des Judenthums*, vol. 2, p. 388, הדרשן in the lament איכה ישבה is not this Moses but R. Akiva (compare Eliyahu Zuṭa ch. 1 and *syn. Poesie* p. 139).

Moses b. Itiel; is cited in the *yoṣer* for Ḥanukah in H h 17.

Nathan: H h 17 and the printed commentary include his explanations on אלים (Ṭal {the prayer for dew}).

Nehemiah: is mentioned is Asher's commentary on the *yoṣerot* (26b), at the end of the *yoṣer* אור זרוע.

Obadiah [*zur Geschichte* pp. 90, 101] Ha-Sefardi (codex Opp.

P. 200

260F): is probably an earlier contemporary of Bekhor Shor (see his commentary on Gen 2:2, 18:5, Exod 4:13, 10:2, 15 end, 22:19 and 23:25) and is identical with the Obadiah b. Samuel who is mentioned in his ms. commentary on Prov 28:16 and 30:31 and later in the book גן, and in the "*dibra*" מישך (Codex Can. {Or.} 1). Compare Geiger פרשנדתא p. 39. The Obadiah mentioned by Israel Brünn, Responsa 245, is later.

Otniel b. Ephraim: is mentioned in H h 17 as the commentator on Qalir's *qerovah* שושן.

Zalman of Speyer: He is cited on אומץ אדירי (H h 17) and is perhaps the Solomon, son of Yehudah He-Ḥasid, who is mentioned is ס' הגן {Venice 1606} § 4 and studied with R. Yedidya in Speyer. Asheri on Berakhot 3 makes reference to a ר"ז Ha-Levi from Speyer.

Solomon b. Isaac [Rashi]: What have come down to us are his explanations of the *zulat* אהבוך נפש, of the *meḥayyeh* for *musaf* on New Year, of two passages in the *teqi'ata* of Qalir and of יהויד and ובכל וכל in the *rehiṭim* (later also in the *Maḥzor* edition of 1712). His explanations of the statutory prayers are in Maḥzor Vitry and Ha-Pardes.

Solomon b. Isaac: Codex Opp. 1073 F on אנוסה לעזרה has the comment: ואני שלמה בן הרב רבי יצחק שמעתי מאת דודי רבנו יעקב שמצא במחזור ישן מדויק דלג וכו'.

Solomon b. Yaqar: is mentioned in a manuscript commentary on מלך אזור.

Solomon b. Meir: shares something from an early *Maḥzor* of R. David (Opp. 1073 F); on the same passage in codex Mich. 656 (on the *seliḥah* תערוג) he is called Samuel b. Meir.

Solomon b. Samson: is mentioned in Opp. 1073 F (on the *seliḥah* ארכן) with the words: "I, S. b. S., have found in the Arukh".

Samuel of Bamberg: the son of R. Barukh of Mainz who is called שמריל in the printed Tashbeṣ (§ 465) is cited by Meir of Rothenburg on the *seliḥah* תפלה תקח (H h 17), anonymously (ואני הכותב) on אור ישע (codex Opp. 1073 F), by the expounder of the

P. 201

prayers in codex Opp. 1483 Q, who mentions several times his conversations with him and that he is a relative. In the former codex it is reported (f. 177a) on the *seliḥah* אל באפך that R. Samuel had told him etc. I relate the expressions שמואל הכותב (same ms. on the lament איכה ישבה) and ולי שמואל נראה בעיני (same ms. on the *rahiṭ* כי תודה) to that same Samuel, whose decisions are in Maimoniot שבת ch. 6 and in a ruling in {the novella} Aggudah ע"ז § 73.

Samuel Ḥazan: was murdered in Erfurt. An item of his is transmitted in codex H h17 before the *zulat* אין צור חלף.

Samuel b. Isaac Ha-Levi: A contemporary of Rashi, he is noted in the *teqi'ata* אנוסה (Opp. 1069 F, H h 17). He is perhaps the one cited on {the *piyyuṭ*} אדר והוד in the phrase ולר' שמואל נראה (H h 17); compare, however, the entry above on Samuel of Bamberg.

Samuel b. Qalonymos: A contemporary of Eleazar of Worms, he is cited in Opp. 1073 F on והחיות אשר. An earlier namesake is mentioned in אבן העזר § 116.

Samuel b. Solomon of Falaise: is noted in the comments in de Rossi's manuscript catalogue p. 217 as "comment. prec." {liturgical commentator} but furnished a commentary only for Tovelem's אלהי הרוחות. See my *Additamenta* and *zur Geschichte.*

Shemayah: In Opp. 1074 F on מלך במשפט several items are by R. Shemayah, and there identified as ליקוטין.

Shemayah of Soissons: commented on the *Maḥzor* (compare my *Additamenta on Leipzig Codices* 1; Munich codex 5 in פרשנדתא p. 20); there is in H h 17 a passage from his explanations of the *seliḥah* אמרנו נגזרנו.

Simeon b. Abraham Kohen: is cited in codex Opp. 1483 Q.

Zedekiah b. Abraham {Anaw}: His commentary on the Haggadah has been copied from a manuscript of שבלי הלקט into תניא.

Pp. 202–3 Appendix III

Appendix III
[P. 23]
On the book מחכים

The catalogue of the Hebrew manuscripts of the Vienna Library lists an item on p. 78 as ס' המנהגים, reporting that it is not by the Maharil, and that some poetic verses written by the scribe occur at the end and are perhaps by the author. These verses, which are noted on p. 23 and assigned to the scribe (Ḥayyim b. David) could have indicated to the editor of the catalogue the name of the author and the work; the verses conclude with the following:

על כי לא (?) מחכים פתאים הוא, מחכים לעיני כל קראתיהו, נתן שמו נקרא ואביהו, לביא אשר צרפו ועשהו Thus, what we have here before us is the מחכים of R. Nathan b. Yehudah [Leo] which is cited in the commentary on the prayers in ed. Trino 1525 dealing with the Sabbath *tefillah*'s (quoted by Hirș Trèves {Thiengen 1560} on תכנת), in the שלטי גבורים {Joshua Boaz}on Mordechai ברכות ch. 4, and in the Responsa of Joseph Colon in the first edition no. 49. Azulai was the first to note the last-mentioned reference; the המחכים was regarded as an error in the second edition of those responsa and corrupted to החכמים. H. J. Michael has now revealed that codex H h 80—originally Uffenbach 126—includes a fragment of Maḥkim [of no less than 17 folios] and that this note has been inserted in the manuscript list drawn up by Dukes which includes Hebrew codices in the Municipal Library of Hamburg.

That discovery led to a comparison of that Vienna manuscript with the numerous citations of R. Nathan by Aaron Ha-Kohen and in the Kol Bo. Where the former has simply הרב נתן (6d § 36), the latter has ה"ר נתן בן הרב ר' יהודה (no. 5); that said, there are rather a large number of corruptions in Kol Bo, as for instance, the sentence וראיתי כתוב מר'ם נ"ע בשם רבי אלעזר זקנו (12 f. 9c, top, ed. Venice)

P. 203

which is correctly recorded by Aaron Ha-Kohen 43b § 4 as ראיתי מא"ם נ"ע בשם רבינו עזריאל זקנינו. R. Nathan refers to his father on two other occasions on the *Kol Nidrey* prayer (in ms.) with the same formula אמנ"ע. Lacking before the words לכל בריה in the Kol Bo (37 f. 39d top) is the phrase כתב ה"ר נתן. In addition, according to the

https://doi.org/10.1515/9783111142500-006

Vienna codex, the work begins with : מעולם לא עברתי על דעת חבירי והם בקשו ממני לסדר סדר התפלה יחד למען ירוץ קורא בו למען לדעת כמה יעבוד בוראו. In the Hamburg codex the first three lines are lacking and it begins [כי] ביוצרי בטחתי ולכבודו הוחלתי כי התפלה. One passage from the Maḥkim occurs in a marginal gloss in a manuscript of Mordechai (ברכות ch. 3) that was written in Piedmont in 1450.

Pp. 204–10 Appendix IV

Appendix IV
[P. 30]
Isaac Abuab, author of the מנורת המאור

Gedaliah {ibn} Yaḥya was the first to identify the author of the Candelabrum (מנורת המאור) as the Castilian Rabbi Isaac Aboab, who had died in Portugal in 1492. The one scholar since then to have begun to express doubts about this identification was Azulai sixty years ago who did so simply on the basis of the way that the author of the Candelabrum is cited by Abraham Zacut. My late friend, H{eimann} J{oseph} Michael, stated to me some sixteen years ago the view that the Candelabrum was earlier than is commonly believed. This question has occupied me since that time and the result is my unquestionable confirmation of this claim: Abuab, who composed the Candelabrum, lived around 1300, and no later than 1320.

In two passages {of the Candelabrum} R. Asher is cited (no. 94, his responsum, no. 97 a brief note of his, compare Ṭur I 239). If these sources are authentic, the author cannot be later than the above-mentioned time. Apart from that, there are no names or works mentioned in the Candelabrum that are later than the thirteenth century. Those who are cited are Isaac Ghiyyat, Yehudah Barceloni, Isaac Laṭif (no. 237, compare no. 292), the Malmad (no. 93)—works that were barely accessible in a later age; as to those who had written about providence, he knows only Maimonides and Laṭif, and he cites geonic responsa by number (293, 297, 103), as well as from מגלת סתרים (preface and nos. 95 and 133). What he cites in no. 297 as from the geonic responsa actually belongs to Isaac Ghiyyat, as is clear from Abudarham (נעילה), and it can be compared to Aaron Ha-Kohen 108a where it is attributed to וי"א. In thirty passages

P. 205

he cites from the Pesiqta, which the later scholars were no longer accustomed to do, and he invokes the midrash השכם (see *gott. Vortr.* p. 281, footnote f), a knowledge of which ceased with Israel Naqawa (1360). The citations as well as their style belong to an early period. References to the Talmud and the Midrash occur with the word וגרסינן, which later became less common, and indeed with וגרסינן עלה, as is written by Zeraḥiah Ha-Levi, Abraham of Lunel, Naḥmanides, Isaiah of Trani and others from that era. Abuab refers to the parts of what was later called Midrash Rabbah according to the individual books {of the Pentateuch} so that, apart from Bereshit Rabbah and Wa-Yiqra Rabbah, he also makes references to Exodus (86, 92, 96, 101,

https://doi.org/10.1515/9783111142500-007

224, 248, 297, 312, 329), Numbers (133, 170, 313) and Deuteronomy (51, 96, 111, 192, 222, 223, 225, 247, 296). Similarly rare among the later authorities were mentions of the halakhic introductions to aggadic passages (see nos. 106, 111). Citations from the tractate כלה as they occur in nos. 1, 3, 9, 39, 119, 212, 220, 245, 328, 332, 337 (compare *gott. Vortr.* p. 90 note c, p. 132, note d, J. Reifmann in *Zion* 2.180) are features of an early period; another feature is counting the *pereq* דרכן as part of tractate כלה (332, compare 224), as is done by Zarza {Meqor Ḥayyim} f. 95c and a Yalquṭ manuscript of Luzzatto (*Kerem Chemed* 7.216). Abuab, in an independent fashion, identifies (no. 106) the source of the eighteen *tefillah* benedictions in Hannah's prayer and in the Palestinian Talmud, mentions the longer and shorter versions of the חופת אליהו (201, 247), acquaints us with various midrashim (113, 171, 176, 180, 278, 330, 332; compare the last-mentioned which also occurs at the end of ch. 3 in the book המוסר {of Judah Kalatz}, *gott. Vortr.* p. 286), mentions the sixth chapter of Avot "Pereq R. Meir" (27, 244, 245, 253; the words מאבות בפרק ששי that follow the word ששנינו in no. 242 are a gloss). His mystical comments on tefillin, fringes and circumcision (see 128) match those of Laṭif, Moses de Leon and Zarza; what he says (no. 99) about אמת appears to have been borrowed from the writings of Eleazar of Worms, compare ילקוט ראובני 157d. The use of the phrase על זה רמזו (238, 258, 260, 267) whenever a philosophical conclusion is based on a biblical or talmudic saying is the same as that used by Shemtov Falquera; he shares with Moses de Leon, David ibn Bilia and others the employment of the word פנימי (67, 268, 338) to describe some secret or deeper truth; the notion of seventy types of interpretation—first found in the Hekhalot (ילקוט ראובני 100d),

P. 206

then used by Simeon (in his *yoṣer* אהוביך) and Ibn Ezra (compare Steinschneider in the {*Zeitschrift der*} *Deutschen-Morgenländischen* ~~*Zeitschrift*~~ {*Gesellschaft*} 4.158)—also occurs in Bekhor Shor (p. 140), Baḥya, Recanati and תקוני זהר chs. 29 and 32 (preface and chs 33, 149); "the sons of Adam" (no. 236) are to be found in Falquera (ס' המעלות in ms. p. 29) and Zarza 8d. The later authorities that he mentions by name are: Ha-Manhig (80, 82; the discussion in no. 153 about the reading of the book of Qohelet is also in {Ha-Manhig} f. 71b), Moses of Coucy (155), Naḥmanides, the author of the חיי עולם (317), and probably that same author in no. 314. One passage that he cites (137) from tractate Megillah matches Aḥa's Sheiltot (21b) and is actually more accurate. Yuḥasin 90b cites זיותאי as one of the amora's and as the son-in-law of R. Meir, and Heilprin (93b) notes that this name does not occur in our text (Shabbat 153a); the Candelabrum still has the name (no. 257) as does the later Yalquṭ Qohelet (f. 188a), with both of them in fact reading זיואי. The reading in the commentary on Avot in Maḥzor Vitry is זיותאי. Here too, then, Abuab accords with the literature of the twelfth century.

Abuab also wrote a halakhic work ארון העדות (preface and nos. 152, 154, 155) that is, like the Decalogue, divided into ten דבור, with each דבור divided into מאמרים and הלכות; besides that work, he also wrote שלחן הפנים which is composed of twelve פנים (preface and nos. 60, 109, 112, 114, 115, 294; compare no. 129, beginning, and 142, beginning). The composition of such works towards the end of the fifteenth century would be totally inexplicable, and even more incomprehensible that it could have been written and then disappeared; and the most inexplicable of all would be that the Castilian Isaac Aboab—if he is the author of the Candelabrum—makes no mention of these two works in either a commentary of his on the Ṭur or in the Candelabrum (compare nos. 109, 115). The passage at the end of no. 95 is word-for-word what appears in Ṭur I 59 and Abudarham 17a, and the source is probably Tos{afot} Ḥagigah 13b; if it is that Aboab who is writing, why is he silent about these authorities? Another passage in no. 113, from the Midrash—which is also in לקוטי הפרדס 10b, תניא 29a and cited by Aaron Ha-Kohen 66a in the name of R. Nathan—likewise occurs in Ṭur I 292; here again complete silence. The beginning and end of no. 110 do not match Ṭur I 122; here too that Aboab should have made a note about this. What the author of the Candelabrum (95) and Aaron Ha-Kohen (10a) cite from the Yerushalmi,

P. 207

Zedekiah {b. Abraham Anaw} from the Aggadah, Abudarham (15a) and after him Joseph Karo (Ṭur I 56) from the Midrash, the Tanya and the Castilian Aboab on Ṭur I 125 cite from Derekh Ereṣ Zuṭa: clearly there are two different people speaking here.

The author of the Candelabrum notes that he has composed his book at a time which is not rich in yeshivahs and scholars (244, 270) so that it will be useful for the preparation of addresses, especially since the Aggadah is being unduly neglected (preface and nos. 142, 338); the style, contemporary outlook, manner of thinking and the way of arguing fit the common literature of the thirteenth century; he cites excerpts from the dietary instructions of Maimonides, says of the pious that their spirit kisses the active intelligence (שכל הפועל), from which thought reaches the wise (143, 184, 236, 258), cites (49, 59) from the morality books the merit of maintaining secrecy and silence (compare Mivḥar Ha-Peninim ch. 32), disapproves of the sterile disputations in the talmudic material (preface) that are useful only for scholars, explains the reading of the *shema'* on the basis of Anatoli's Malmad (93), which, other than in his book occurs only in Abudarham, relies (128, 236) on the agreement of Aristotle and Plato, and uses Arabic in his explanations (131, 155, 183)—proving that in his age and place of residence the Jews spoke Arabic, which is known to have still been the case in Toledo at the beginning of the fourteenth century.

If we look broadly at the activities of {the Castilian} Aboab, we find among them his נהר פישון, which includes his presentations, in which there are citations from: Zohar (pp. 24, 31), Baḥya (86), Yedaiah, whom he, in common with his contemporary, Abraham Seba (צרור המור 137a, 138c), calls Bedersi (116), Gersonides (11, 42, 43, 27, 98, 125), Thomas (84), Nissim [b. Reuben] (33, 55, 84, 88), Zarza's מכלל יופי (71), Ḥasdai (11), Matathyah [Yiṣhari] (41, 43), the book עקרים (96, 136), Joseph Yeshu'ah (42). His presentations are more like novellae rather than sermons and on two occasions the word וגרסינן (24) probably refers to the Candelabrum (257, 146), and that is also the source (no. 128) for the passage introduced by ובזה הסכימו (p. 114). There is not the slightest agreement between the Castilian and his predecessor in the treatment of the same topic, as for example

P. 208

the Feast of Tabernacles; neither does the treatment on repentance (Candelabrum nos. 44 and 275 to 284) match what the {Castilian} Aboab teaches (f. 47), since the latter almost apologizes for having for having to issue a rebuke. The two books belong to totally different eras. Solomon b. Mazaltov and Aboab's own son Jacob list the following works by Aboab: commentaries on Rashi and Naḥmanides on the Pentateuch, notes on the Ṭur, discussions of talmudic passages, responsa and sermons; not a word about the earlier Abuab's three works! Abraham Zacut, a disciple of {the Castilian} Aboab, who refers to his teacher as חכם וחסיד חריף ומחודד כה"ר reports what he has found in the book מנורת המאור האחר שאינו של רבי יצחק אבוהב (f. 28a ed. Cracow). Given that this "other Candelabrum" is that of Israel Naqawa and is at least a hundred years earlier than {the Castilian} R. Aboab, such a way of designating his teacher as the author of the first Candelabrum would have been tasteless and pointless, as well as being an inappropriately brief way of making reference to his revered teacher. This passage alone proves that Zacut knew both books called Candelabrum as earlier works and that the better known one was that of Abuab, from which he indeed cites a passage (45b) without giving its title. Another distinct piece of evidence is provided by Jacob Ḥabib who prepared his work 'Eyn Ya'aqov around 1511. Some sources, he states in the introduction, had set out the Aggadah in a different order from that followed in the Talmud, "as the preachers who lived earlier had done (כמו שעשו הדרשנים אשר לפנינו), such as the author of the Candelabrum and the כד הקמח and various others." This last-mentioned work is known to be that of Baḥya and to have been composed around 1290 and the author of the Candelabrum is mentioned before him so that we can place him in an earlier generation. Abraham Seba, who belonged to those who were expelled from Portugal in 1497, and composed his book in Fez, makes a simple reference (section דברים f. 129d) to the Candelabrum as a known work where the topic on which he has touched is also to be found (no. 305). What is more, the manner in which the son {of the Castilian Aboab} refers to his father's talmudic acumen and the use of the expression החכם המפולפל by David Messer Leon to refer to R. Isaac Aboab in a manuscript

P. 209

text are not appropriate to the author of the Candelabrum (see above p. 207).

Abuab, who regularly makes reference to individuals as חכמי המחקר (143, 236, 326), or חכמי המוסר (49, 316, compare 59) and broadly as philosophers (128), also cites "midrash" without more specific detail, and sometimes appears similarly to refer to early sources. Already in the first chapter in a consideration of the Ten Commandments there is a midrash, which is earlier than Qalir's treatment of the Decalogue, and is based on a story transmitted by Baḥya in the entry חמדה and early commentators on the poetic passage אלה הדברים בלא תחמד תלולים and is probably that found in codex Vat. 285 no. 23. In his comments on the Ten Plagues (140), one encounters Ibn Ezra's ideas on Exod 9:1 and the discussions of the seven types of repentance (277) and of the blowing of the shofar (293) are apparently borrowed from other authors; the ten reasons {for the shofar} (294), also transmitted by Abudarham and Zarza (80c), belong to Sa'adya. Elsewhere, when the Candelabrum and later works have common material that is not known from earlier sources, it is clear that it has been copied from the Candelabrum; this is especially true in the case of Meir Aldabi of Toledo (1360), about whose method of compiling from all manner of books we have already indicated in another context.* The whole study of חבור in {his} שבילי אמונה ff. 39–42 is borrowed from the Candelabrum (182–85). Comparisons can be made of דע כי החבור (37d, 38ab) with no. 181, בזמן העונה (39) with no. 182, במזון הראוי (39c) with no. 183, צריך כל אדם (40d) and אור הבהיר (41c) with no. 184, and everything on f. 42ab with no. 185. What appears in Aramaic in the Candelabrum at the end of no. 183 is there (40a) translated into Hebrew. Perhaps Abudarham (1341) already made use of Abuab; compare his comments on f. 63c (נעילה) concerning the phrase כמו העבדים כשיוצאין לחירות with Candelabrum at the end of no. 297. This is even clearer in the case of Samuel Zarza (1368). What Abuab has to say in nos. 149 and 150 about the four elements, the four rivers and the four major limbs of humans—the last-mentioned also in

P. 210

ספר החנוך section 285—is conveyed by Zarza word-for-word (מקור חיים ff. 81d, 82a) in the name of יש אומרים; in addition, the comment (no. 138) about the three wells of Isaac—borrowed from Naḥmanides—is also cited by Zarza as י"א (op. cit., f. 18c). The discussion of the number seven (no. 143) is not only included in Zarza (43c, 83d) but also already occurs in Yeruḥam {b. Meshullam} who was thirty years earlier (5.4, f. 44d). The arrangement (no. 238) of the expression על שלשה דברים in Avot is similar to the explanation offered by Shemtov (in מדרש שמואל) and an interpretation of Prov 22:6 (no. 85) also appears in the commentary קב ונקי {of Ibn Yaḥya} In a manuscript that contains Moses de Leon's משכן העדות and was certainly written before the year 1500, f. 76b tells the tale of those who arrived on an island and refers to the Candelabrum (no. 278) where it occurs and has been borrowed from a midrash; from there the story was transmitted, with the attachment of moralistic ideas—the latter missing in the book המוסר, ch. 2—to the booklet צרי היגון (Cremona 1557 ff. 11, 12) which exploits Abuab nos. 298, 300–302. In the manuscript just mentioned on f. 96a there is a second reference to the Candelabrum and that passage occurs there in no. 144. It seems that Ḥayyim Obadiah (מקור חיים at the beginning and in ch. 18) also made use of the Candelabrum (258, 92).

The definitive conclusion is therefore that R. Isaac Abuab composed the Candelabrum in around 1300, probably in Castilia and maybe in Toledo itself, and that author identifies himself at the beginning of his introduction by way of an acrostic reading חיבור יצחק אבוהב. There is then no need for the assistance of passages that occur in the book Yuḥasin codex Uri 389, followed in ed. London p. 174, in which Zacut mentions a Joseph חלוטה who had written a commentary on the Candelabrum. Abraham Abuab may be dated more securely in the fourteenth century than the said Joseph (Responsa Yehudah b. Asher 53a).

* Compare my "Wünsche etc" in *Zeitschrift der deutschen morgenl. Gesellsch.*, 10.512.

Pp. 211–21 Appendix V

Appendix V
[P. 35]
The Zürich Semaq

After Gedaliah {ibn} Yaḥya related from hearsay that Moses of Zürich had furnished the "Semaq" (סמ"ק) with extensive annotations and that this book was the Zürich Semaq, Conforte {Qore Ha-Dorot}, Bartolocci, Shabbethai {Siftey Ḥakhamim}, Wolf, Heilprin {Seder Ha-Dorot}, Azulai and more recent authors of the past two hundred years have repeated this without having seen the book or named the library in which it is housed. Scholars have had it in their hands but have not recognized it. The work exists in Oxford, in Vienna, for the past six years in the British Museum, probably also in the Vatican, in Paris and Parma libraries, and available elsewhere.

The copy in the British Museum, a thick folio volume in vellum, provides the text of the Semaq and adds in the margin numerous, extensive excerpts from various works which sometimes constitute large treatises; the section on hired labourers (§ 251) is itself as long as 128 columns. In several places in the text itself the explanations are more detailed than in the editions, as is demonstrated, for example, by § 20, when compared with ed. § 19 f. 11a. Even at a first glance one can distinguish the annotations of a first hand from that of a second one, both with regard to the writing and to the places that they occupy, and often also with regard to the sources from which they emanate. The annotations by the first hand, which constitute the bulk of the work, generally indicate, at the end, the source, but sometimes no information is provided and often only 'תו—where it does not mean Tosafot—standing for תוספת addition, or מצאתי, as for example in § 12 at the end of a gloss that originated in Ha-Pardes.

P. 212

In addition, there are instances in which the names of authors are identified rather than those of their books, as with "in the name of R. Isaac of Corbeil" (§§ 84, 95, 96, 107, 142, 152, 223; f. 306a and elsewhere) where the items are perhaps from Isaac's פסקים in manuscript, or from the לקוטים cited by Maharil (Responsa 188). A gloss on *ḥaliṣah* is identified as "in the name of R. Samuel Cohen." A scholar of that name is mentioned in the pentateuchal commentary of R. Asher f. 37b, as also in the section משפטים of codex Dresden 399. § 250 is a citation from Solomon from Chateau Landon who lived around 1280 (*zur Geschichte* p. 98) and was, as indicated in codex Mich. 854, a contemporary of Moses of Marseilles; § 219 is another cita-

https://doi.org/10.1515/9783111142500-008

tion, this time from Samuel of Falaise. In other places (§§ 181, 192, 202, 222, 211) references are made to the autograph writings of Joseph of Nicola, who was a contemporary of Yehudah of Jumiège [שימוייש, but corrupted into ממייש in § 181] and from whose work there are extracts in the manuscript version of the Semaq: similarly, from an autograph of R. M. of London (§ 180), either Meir, Moses or Menaḥem. More commonly, as for example in § 113, ר"א or ר"א [לשון] 'ל is noted and may be a cipher that could refer to numerous names, compare *zur Geschichte* pp. 44, 84, 92, 102 and 104. Other glosses are from responsa (תשובות) and such items are found in Rashi (f. 189b and § 182), Levi of Narbonne (loc. cit.), Isaac b. Samuel (§ 196), Yeḥiel of Paris (§ 202), R. M. of London (§ 220 and f. 187b), Ḥayyim b. Jacob (§ 180, end) [of Montpellier]. In ff. 198a and 300b, however, only רבי' חב"רי ז"ל occurs and cites Meir of Rothenburg and this may refer to Ḥayyim b. Isaac (old Tosafot on 'Eruvin; Mordechai on {Bava} Batra ch. 9). After the gloss that ends with the words מן הבעל [in the printed Semaq 13a], the ms. reads "Menaḥem b. Samuel", as also to be found in a Semaq ms. and in Aaron Ha-Kohen 3b § 30.

The particular works from which the extracts are borrowed, in addition to the Talmuds, She'iltot (§ 180), Alfasi, Maimonides, Semag, Semaq and Mordechai, are mainly the following:

אבי העזרי of Eliezer Ha-Levi, אור זרוע of R. Isaac of Vienna (§ 33), אסור והיתר of R. Yeruḥam (§ 199), חיי עולם [of R. Jonah, according to Steinschneider, *Bod. Cat.* p. 1426 ff.],

P. 213

החנוכי of Ḥanokh b. Reuben (§ 180), the Book of the Pious (§ 279), Maḥzor Vitry (§ 219), נחמני מחכים (§ 180) of Naḥman Kohen [mentioned in the extract from מנהל § 8, Kol Bo no. 101, Maharil, Commentary on the Siddur ed. Trino 1525, Jos{eph} Colon Responsa 145 and 149]; the Seder {"Order"} of R. Meir of Rothenburg, often, as for example, §§ 144, 148; עץ חיים (§§ 180, 223, 225, 233, 251 and 256), which cites on p. 207a the martyr R. Menaḥem of Dreux and adds that ר"א had also given such a ruling. Four early works are mentioned with that same name עץ חיים: a) by Ḥayyim b. Isaac (Oppenh. 279 Q.) who is, according to שם הגדולים section 15, the Ḥayyim of אור זרוע; b) by Jacob b. Yehudah (cod. Leipzig 17); c) by Ḥayyim b. Nissim (Azulai, *Lexikon* part. II p. 112); d) by Samuel Even Shushan, an abstract of Ṭur I, Paris ms. Other sources are שערים (§§ 199 and 211) [by Isaac of Dueren]; התרומה which in § 181 is noted as סר"ב [ספר רבינו ברוך]; תרומה חדשה (§§ 144, 154, 178, a citation of Rashi's ruling on hand-washing, 181, 191 203 where Joseph of Nicola and the book שערי הפנים [R. Eleazar of Burgundy] are mentioned, 211, 219, 293); תשבץ. In addition to that last-mentioned book, mention should be made of the פסקים of Eliezer

b. Nathan, which are also noted as פסקי אבן הראשה and which occur, next to the extracts from תשבץ, in Aaron Ha-Kohen (in the second part) and, from there, in the Kol Bo, nos. 123 and 124. These פסקים are to be found in the book אבן העזר, in part in Mordechai on Neziqin, in the decisions of Meir of Rothenburg and in extracts in Kol Bo, in all of which works extracts from our manuscript all occur, for example, ms. § 245 (א"ה 93a, Rothenburg 767, Kol Bo § 12), § 250 f. 162a (א"ה 93c, Rothenb{urg} 770, Kol Bo § 14), f. 163a (א"ה 93c and 94a, Rothenb{urg} 769 and 771, Kol Bo §§ 16 and 17), f. 168a (א"ה 95b, Rothenb{urg} 777, Kol Bo § 29), ibid. (א"ה 95a, Kol Bo § 26, Mordechai {Bava} Meṣi'a, ch. 3, § 354), f. 164b (א"ה 92d, 93a, Rothenb{urg} 761, 762, 764, Kol Bo §§ 7, 8, 9), f. 166a (א"ה 94c, Rothenb{urg} 714, Kol Bo § 19, Mordechai {Bava} Meṣi'a, ch. 3, § 345); also § 256 and in other places.

Diverse talmudic commentaries and Tosafot are used and, apart from the standard

P. 214

Commentary {of Rashi} (קונטרס), include the commentary on Tractate Ketubbot by the martyr [R. Solomon] of Dreux (§ 180), on {Bava} Meṣi'a ch. 3 and ch. 5 by Yehudah b. Nathan (§ 258, f. 267 ff., 277b and ff.); also the "Shiṭṭah" of Sens, R. Pereṣ, and תוך (on which compare *zur Geschichte*, pp. 35, 41 and 39): the Shiṭṭah of Sens in §§ 180, 181; that of R. Pereṣ in the section dealing with the wedding benediction; these דינים also occur in relation to divorce documents, *ḥaliṣah*, women's ritual bath etc, including several that are to be found in Kol Bo nos. 142 and 146. The Shiṭṭah תוך is the cited source in f. 183a, and R. Eliezer of תוך is mentioned on f. 207a on {Bava} Batra ch. 1. The Tosafot of Sens are used on Qiddushin, {Bava} Meṣi'a, ch. 2 (f. 123b, where Aaron of Eperny is cited), ch. 5 (§ 258), Sanhedrin ch. 3 (f. 342b, where there occurs in one place וכן הנהיג ר"י מקנפניא). Samson of Sens mentions (§ 219) a certain R. אלע' b. Abraham; this is perhaps the Eliezer b. Abraham who is mentioned in Opp. 764 F. in no. 575; in addition, there is a R. Eliezer b. Abraham Ha-Kohen who occurs in the *Tefillah* commentary of R. Eleazar of Worms. In one passage a note is made about the תוס' of ר"א (see above), and in another (§ 109) the תו' of R. Jacob Ha-Levi, which probably means only addenda.

Some source definitions that are offered only in abbreviated forms deserve special attention. One annotation in a section concerning מזוזה concludes: עכ"ל ס"ג ור"א; perhaps ס"ג is to be resolved as סדר גאונים or סדור גדולים, since such a *Siddur* is cited on this topic in the Kol Bo and in notes on the Semaq. In § 180 f. 74a there is a gloss on the subject of a young man who did not adhere to marital agreements which concludes with ע"כ לשו' ל"ה. A few times (§§ 109, 148, 178) there are extracts from a work called ט"ל the author of which must have lived between the time of {Judah}

Sir Leon and that of R. Meir of Rothenburg, and still cites the Halakhot Pesuqot, and was perhaps a contemporary of Moses of Coucy. There are often comments from בה"ריל (§§ 92, 142, 148, 178, 191, 199, 211, 235 and 242) that cite R. Tam and R. Isaac (ר"י) as well as R. Samson (§ 235), R. Yehudah [Sir Leon] in the name of ר"י (§ 242) and ר"י a grandson of R. Jacob of Orleans

P. 215

(f. 337b), and offer explanations in the French language (f. 327); perhaps the author is Jacob Ha-Levi and ב"ה stands for בעל החלום as he and his grandson are known (see the Maimoniot Responsa קנין no. 31, Mordechai at the beginning of {Bava} Qama; compare Azulai, part I, p. 87 no. 224), and he would then be identified as Jacob of Marvège, although he is mostly referred to as Jacob the Pious and not the Levite. In the ms. comments on Mordechai, one work is referred to as בהר"ד; the ב in both cases may mean ביאורים.

Also in the additions by a second hand, there are citations with only the word מצאתי; most of these originate in רקח, התרומה, סמ"ג, אור זרוע, ראב"ן and מרדכי. The last-mentioned commentator is sometimes called "the Large Mordechai" and this designation also occurs in the annotations of the first hand as in § 118. In § 104 a passage is cited from ערוגת הבושם according to which the ten infinities (Sefira's, see the book of Yeṣira ch 1) are known only to God. Among the earlier sources that I have encountered are: רי"ח or מהרי"ח (§ 202) or the Pesaqim of Hezekiah; a citation from Yeḥiel's Disputation (§ 64) and another from the book מקצועות (§ 80) that ends with קונה שמים וארץ and is perhaps borrowed from the Mordechai; the abbreviated Or Zaru'a (אז"ק) which is called סימני א"ז abbreviated to סא"ז in the Responsa of Maharil (54), Moses Mintz (35), Yehudah Mintz (12 f. 21a), and in the annotations to שערי דורא and there in the הלכות נידה (f. 60a). The other comments are borrowed from works of the fourteenth century, namely: Süsslein's Agudah, the Asheri of R. Asher; סימני אשרי under which description are cited the רמזים of Jacob b. Asher or the summary of Asheri also by the German author of the old שם הגדולים, in the responsa of the Maharil (112), Israel Brünn (163, 182, 211 and elsewhere), Moses Mintz (often abbreviated to א"ס), Yehudah Mintz (5), and in the annotations on the דורא f. 23b; the Ṭurim; Haggahot Maimoniot; the Small Mordechai as well as the annotations to the Semaq, and to the large and Small Mordechai's. The last-mentioned work includes also the so-called Halakhot Qeṭanot, as may be seen from § 1298, which is cited by Jos{eph} Colon (Responsum 149) as being from the Small Mordechai;

P. 216

the expression ולי (ואני) הדיוט—which also occurs in Maimoniot נחלות 9.7, Dura 9a, Haggahot Asheri Giṭṭin ch. 1 § 7—also belongs to that same Small Mordechai (§ 152, 203). In addition, use is made of Pisqey Tosafot (§ 241), פרנס (§ 154, 202), the Commentary of Alfasi (in the section on marital regulations), the 36 gates (§ 199), perhaps earlier than those of Isserlein, תשובות, the responsa of R. Asher, a responsum by Avigdor b. Menaḥem with the cipher ז'ק'ן' ש'מ'י' (§ 9), one by R. M. איגרא (§ 12) and two by Ḥayyim Paltiel (§ 107 and f. 300a). There are citations in § 148 from "our teachers, the kabbalists" and in two passages (§§ 195, 199) a statement by מהר"ם Klausner about ניקור. This is perhaps Mendel Klausner who is mentioned at the end of {Abraham} Klausner's Minhagim and is to be identified with the מהרמ"ק who occurs here and there in the Haggahot Asheri. I have not noticed anywhere in the work such Haggahot by Israel Krems—called חדושי מהררי"ק דאשירי by Israel Brünn responsum 252—; just as rare are mentions of Mordechai text from Rhineland or the Austrian version that differs from it, such as are found among the authors of the fifteenth century, compare Isserlein Disquisitions 76, 84, 213 and 342, responsum 192, Israel Brünn 167, 197, Jos{eph} Colon 21. The latest gloss appears to be located in a comment on the New Moon benediction by a student of the Maharil and begins שאלתי את מה"ר יעקב מולין ס"ל אם יש לברך על חידוש לבנה. On the other hand, there is a remark in § 99, beginning ואני הכותב, in the style of earlier comments, in which the writer—or author—conveys something that he had heard from the physician R. Joshua Eliakim—perhaps he is the physician Joshua who was expelled from France in the year 1395 and who is memorialized on a tombstone in Padua as discovered by Philox{enos} Luzzatto.

Firstly, it is clear from what has been noted so far that our manuscript matches the content of Vienna Codex no. 52 (Catalogue, p. 62) and perhaps differs from it only in the order of the sections, as sometimes occurs in manuscripts of the Semaq. From the confusion about names and works that stuns the reader there (p. 63)

P. 217

through seven rows, it is simple to find the sources and authors listed here. The abbreviation ל' ט' ל' ע' נ' ה' should be understood as ל' ט"ל עכ"ה, that is לשון ט"ל עד כאן הגהה. The phrase התשובות חוזרני לסוף is probably not entirely correct but it has a parallel in our codex f. 315b, 320a, where it reads עכ"ל התשובה חוזרני ללשון סמ"ג; compare נחזור לענין הספר Semaq 184. Perhaps instead of לסוף we should read לל' ספ' (ללשון ספר). There R. Meir of London (see above, p. 212) is expressly mentioned beside הר"ם. The word מפליקא is an error for "from Falaise" which occurs elsewhere as מפלירדא (*zur Geschichte* p. 56) and מפליירא (codex Leipzig 6 p. 277); the same applies to R. Samuel of "Montpellier" who is mentioned there and in a ms. (חידושי ש"ס) of Dr Beer in Dresden; compare Mordechai, beginning of Pesaḥim. Others who are also listed: 1) מהרמ"א [perhaps Moses of Evreux], 2) Samuel b. Menaḥem [see Tos{afot} on Yoma 40b, he lived in Würzburg], 3) Simeon de Coucy [compare my additamenta on codex Leipzig 4], 4) Menaḥem מיגוני, probably M. of Joigny, 5) Yehudah of Strasbourg. There is mention of a R. Isaac of Strasbourg in Maimoniot (חמץ ומצה 8 end) and three times in a ms. commentary on אדיר דר. It is possible that this Yehudah—or Isaac—is that מהרי"ש who occurs in the longer אסור והיתר (ed. Ferrara 11.4, 12.4, 34.25), in the commentary אמרי נועם {of Jacob de Illescas} (*Parashah* שמיני and קדשים) and often in the notes on Tyrnau's Minhagim ed. Amsterdam f. 14a, especially since, according to the reading of the מטה משה § 795 {מהרי"ש}—the Minhagim read מהר"ש—he is definitely the one cited in the Zürich Semaq.

The annotations in different hands, which seem also to be included in the Vienna copy, probably derive from a variety of manuscripts. The Semag was often present; six copies were available to Isserlein but there was no copy of Or Zaru'a in his place (Responsa 172 and 112). The Semaq was even more common and, in accordance with the recommendation of the author, had been copied many times: Jos{eph} Colon (Responsa 137) had three copies and there were even more that were accessible to him. The book already had the annotations of Meir b. Barukh and Pereṣ b. Elijah earlier than 1300; in the fourteenth century

P. 218

glosses were added from various directions and were cited as הגהות or as expansions of the Semaq, so that manuscripts such as Leipzig 18 and de Rossi 583 contain the annotations from Maimonides, Alfasi, and Tashbeṣ. Our codex testifies to a gradual enrichment by way of its report (§ 103) that the treatise on the times of the lunar month had not previously been available in copies of this work. This treatise, as well as one on the four equinoxes, is from 1401, a table of the new moons at the beginning of the codex was written in 1400, and there is a gloss next to it that dates from 1429. There is a wedding document with the date of Friday, 19 Shevaṭ 5149 [the year 1389] in טרנבירק "in the manner of the community of Rheins" (רין), that is, Strasbourg (see {Gedaliah ibn} Yaḥya 62a, Jos{eph} Colon 172 where the text has טראבורק instead of the reading שטרבורק as in the manuscripts). This name appears clearly in the Vienna codex but there the document has the date of Zürich, 21 Ṭevet 5151 [1390] and that city also appears in the Semaq text of codex H h 89 f. 288 from the year 1344. The signature of the scribe Jacob b. Moses has the date קנ"ב [the year

1392] and presumably belongs to the original codex from which our manuscript was copied. From these data and from the age of the works consulted, the period of the latest collector is indisputable; he lived in either Strasbourg or Zürich between 1370 and 1390; this is also clarified by the absence, among the earlier citations, of the Asheri which was still a rare item in the Rhine region around 1370 (Maharil ed. Sabionetta 39b, ed. Frankfurt f. 30). An early owner of the codex also testifies to the fact that the author was from Zürich and is evidently the one who provides information from his time (1494 and ff.), stating: "This book is called 'the Zürcher' because there was a learned scholar who enriched the text by inserting fresh annotations from all the books concerning each precept; he had that name because he was from that city in Switzerland." Elijah Levita says the same thing more briefly (Tishbi, s.v. ויטרי) and all the early authors describe the author as "from Zürich"; only three give him a name: the booklet שם הגדולים by a grandson of Samuel Schlettstadt calls him Abraham; Joseph Colon (Responsum 187) calls him Moses; Solomon

P. 219

Cohen in the order of the *ḥaliṣah* ceremony by Yehudah Mintz (38a) offers: הר"ם. The latter two may match each other and are more meaningful than the first. Incidentally, it may be noted that there was a Rabbi Moses who was living in Zürich in the year 1347 ({J. C.} Ulrich, {*Sammlung jüdischer*} *Geschichten* p. 16) and this prompted me earlier to place our author in 1360. It is hardly necessary to offer a refutation of Conforte's view that he lived about 1300.

The work was often used in the fifteenth century, as indicated by the citations from the time of the Maharil and onwards. To the statement of Israel Brünn that one should not make a decision on the basis of this poorly compiled work, Colon responds ({Responsa} no. 170): "Such a statement seems strange to me and everyone should be astonished by it. Did the author go the trouble of making such extensive annotations not to construct decisions based on them? Should he have adopted what is halakhically incorrect and abandoned what is valid? God forbid that we should espouse such a view!" Citations from the Zürich Semaq, most of which may be traced in our codex, are to be found in: the decisions and responsa of Maharil (no. 142, which is in the {London} codex in § 178 f. 70a as from ט"ל), Jacob Weil (no. 189), Isserlein (no. 172.198; compare ms. § 156), Israel Brünn (no. 121, and in Colon no. 170 ed. Ven{ice} f. 186a at the foot), Joseph Colon (nos. 85, 128, 169, 170, 176 and 187; the last-mentioned passage is in ms. {London} § 246), Moses Mintz nos. 52, 109 f. 163b (neither passage is in ms. {London} § 180), f. 163d, 165 bc (both passages are in ms. {London} ff. 77a and 79a); the order of *ḥaliṣah* f 38a (in ms. {London} f. 87a note 2), the glosses on שערי דורא § 76 f. 38a; Tyrnau's Minhagim f. 2b § 21 (in ms.

{London} § 12 f. 7a note 7 from the *Siddur* of Meir of Rothenburg) f. 3b § 44, f. 8b § 103 (from מטה משה § 795), f. 14b § 40 (in ms. {London} § 154, end), f. 15a § 54 with the added comment: "in הלכות מגילה § 148" (in ms. {London} § 146). The last source to mention the Zürich Semaq is the German *Maḥzor* ed. Saloniki p. 99, copied in the מעגלי צדק of the Maḥzor Sabionetta-Cremona f. 64b (which occurs in ms. {London} f. 131a as from תרומה חדשה).

The manner of referring to this compilation

P. 220

varies and seems to be related to its gradual editorial process. The list in the שם הגדולים and Colon describe it as: "lengthy annotations on the Semaq" or "what occurs in the Semaq" (nos. 176 and 128); Isserlein has in both places ספר המצות בקוצר באורך, that is, an expanded extract of the precepts. The most frequent designations are: the Zürich סמק (Codex Mich. 457. Israel Brünn. Colon nos. 85, 169, 170), ס' המצות from Zürich (Jacob Weil 189, Isserlein Terumat Ha-Deshen 198), ס' הצורך (Colon 170), צוריך (*Maḥzor*); צורכר [Zürcher] is written by Maharil, Moses Mintz, the annotations on Tyrnau, the owner of our manuscript from the year 1494 and Levita: the reading סמק"ג is doubtful (Maharil, ed. Sabionetta 65a).

All traces of the Zürich text were lost for three hundred years. What {Gedaliah ibn} Yaḥya (58b) reports he probably had from Colon's responsa to which he refers; but when one checks there no. 122 which he also cites, one finds merely: Maimonides and Semag explain דצרוך לכרוך [read: דצריך]. Even stranger than Yaḥya's unreliability is that fact that the error—which Azulai avoided—was copied by such men as Shabbethai and Heilprin. Bartolocci's error in making out of the הגהות and the ס' הצורך two different works by Moses of Zürich was corrected by Wolf and also Azulai (שה"ג part 2 f. 104b); the latter correction is missed in the Vilna edition (part 1 p. 143). De Rossi says nothing anywhere about the Zürich volume but he ought to have had more to say about his folio codex 172 from the year 1381 than that it is consistently furnished with many "aliorum auctorum supplementa" {"additions by other authors"}. It is possible that it contains one of the earliest redactions of the Zürich volume if the annotations there are not mostly from a second hand. {J. G. C.} Adler had in his hands the Vienna Codex in which the Zürich Semaq accompanies the pentateuchal sections ({*Kurze Übersicht*...}*Reise* {*nach Rom*} p. 5); naturally he had eyes only for the variant readings so that he describes our work as follows: "In the margins and at the end of the Sabbath lectionaries there are excerpts from the allegorical interpretations [Midrashim] of the Rabbis, and from the works of Maimonides, and at times whole chapters of the Mishnah."

P. 221

These whole chapters are probably the source references at the end of the citations similar to other such items of which the compiler lists four in the *Catalogue* (Vienna 1847 p. 63). That *Catalogue* (p. 75) describes as a liturgical commentary what appears to be a continuation of the Zürich Semaq, as suggested by בהרי"ל and other catchwords.

With regard to a Semaq in the Oppenheimer Collection, marked as סה, 3, the old handwritten catalogue notes: “no text of this has ever been published”; consequently, it is not the same as the edited Semaq. The text of the early printed catalogue reads (part 2 f. 13b): סמ"ק עם ביאור ארוך ונפלא מחודשים מגאונים מלוקטים כמו מרדכי ומביא האגודה נראה שהיה לערך בזמן מהרי"ל חשוב הערך {“Semaq with a long and wonderful commentary with novel items collected from the distinguished scholars such as Mordechai and the compiler seems to have been highly regarded in the time of the Maharil”}. The statement made about this codex Opp. 728Q in that catalogue was fairly accurate but the compiler of the list of 1826 only stated: “Semaq with a long commentary.” The few minutes that I was able to devote to the manuscript were sufficient to establish that it constituted a Zürich Semaq. Codex Leipzig 6—which I have not seen—also deserves to be examined again since, although it was written as early as 1305, it already contains annotations from Alfasi, Maimonides, Seder R. Meir [not R. Moses], the Large Mordechai (מ"ג)* and others which appear to have been added later. The same applies to the Semaq manuscripts of the Vatican and the Paris Library; particular attention should be paid to the manuscripts in folio; a comparison of these with the printed editions of the Semaq would yield no small profit for the history of jurisprudence and knowledge of early times.

* סמ"ג and מ"ג are mentioned next to each other by Eliezer Trèves (Moses Mintz Responsa no. 46 f. 66c at the foot); ה"ג sometimes means הגהות on the Large Mordechai (compare ibid. 43 f. 59b at the top). Neither of these abbreviations is correctly deciphered in the Leipzig Catalogue p. 277, first column line 6.

Pp. 222–25 Appendix VI

Appendix VI
[P. 149]
Examples of Censorship

Censorship, compounded by those who were anxious, gradually expelled words, idioms, lines, biblical verses, stanzas and whole sections from the *Maḥzor* and inserted a large supply of spurious items. The word אדומים is among words frowned upon, sufficient examples of which have been supplied elsewhere.*[1] At first, the letter *dalet* was omitted, leaving the word אומים which satisfied them in the sixteenth century (in the *seliḥah* אתה חלקי). Later, the word אומים was suspected of being synonymous with the suspect word גוים and was corrected to רמים (ed. Vienna 1823). It was even safer to use ישמעאלים instead, especially in the time of the Turkish wars and the rogue states. Gabirol's *Azharot* concludes the prohibition concerning shaving one's head bald with the word ככמרים. The word was deleted from manuscripts, and in editions from 1540 onwards it was changed to כמומרים, כמו זרים, כמצרים (ed. 1587). In the *haṭanu* אשמרה אליך the verses of the stanza consist of three words each, so that the final word of the first stanza concludes with the same letter as that which begins the next stanza.*[2] For example, the first stanza {of that *haṭanu*} concludes with the biblical verse אני אמרתי בחפזי. Is it not truly wondrous that the second stanza בקרנך תרום ענוים, which is not actually part of a biblical verse, forces the following stanza to begin with ע (ענוים ביראתך) instead of the expected ג? It was the Dominicans who performed this wonder, because the author had originally written באף תדוש גוים, גוים תגרש לטעת. It is remarkable

P. 223

that the Saloniki edition of the German *Maḥzor* already adopted this alteration, probably to improve sales in Italy.

Missing from the Sabionetta-Cremona *Maḥzor* are whole stanzas from the *seliḥah*'s ישראל עמך, ארכו הימים, אדברה, אני עבדך (f. 125b, but in a mutilated form in f. 202a), and תא שמע, three *rehiṭim* items for the Day of Atonement, a large part of Simeon's *silluq* חסדי ה', and two stanzas that begin with פ' in Qalir's אשא דעי. The *sel{iḥah}* אזון תחן has been altered. The words רעוץ תרעוץ בכלה ונחרצה as well as the *seliḥah* ה' אלהי רבת are already lacking in an undated Italian edition; the same words

1 *Syn. Poesie* pp. 437–55.
2 Compare ibid. p. 105.

https://doi.org/10.1515/9783111142500-009

בכלה ונחרצה have also been deleted from the *zulat* זולתך. Maḥzor Prague 1529 still has the correct text at the end of the *me'orah* אשר יצר but after the Battle of the White Mountain {in 1620} Prague too had to suffer the yoke of the censor. In the אל תזכור of *musaf* according to the Polish rite, the phrase והשמד הגוי העז is replaced by ושמרנו בכח ועז, and in a Vienna edition the expression וצר הצורר (in the *sel{iḥah}* תחרות) is also replaced by מלכות שנים עשר נשיאים. Other deletions are the stanza ריבה in אשפוך שיחי in ed. Venice, and the two stanzas of מלך אחד in the *seliḥot* edition of 1605, and later editions deleted the sixth stanza of the lament איך נפלה. The prayer-book אילת השחר of Mantua 1612, printed under censorship and then revised by Camillo Jaghel in 1621, complains (f. 24a) about an anonymous individual who had followed up on the activity of the tiger {evidently Camillo Jaghel} by breaking bones; the unnamed individual is referred to as חזיר. In אדון אל the line beginning with פ' is spurious, as are the stanzas 5 and 11 in מקצר רוח; likewise, alterations have been made in three stanzas of בת ציון, in four of מאנה, and in the final six stanzas of אוי נא (f. 51). In the *zulat* אריות of Tovelem a slave mentality has given its attention to the words ונותן מלוכה ומעבירה in spite of its origin in Daniel {2:21}.

The baptized Jew, Christlieb, surpasses all his predecessors in his insolent stupidity. In the *seliḥah* edition of 1737, which appeared under his supervision in Wilmersdorf, attention was given to the words קיסר in אלה אזכרה, פסילים in אתה מקדם, מלכיות in ישראל נושע and גלולים in איך אוכל; almost all the items are equally spurious and mutilated: instead of תתאפק, the reading is יתברך; instead of להסיר צרי ואויבי: להסיר צרי ודאגי; instead of עדלה: עו לה! He changes להמיר, which was offensive to him as a מומר, to להחליף which

P. 224

seemed new to him.*[3] The phrase טמא ומת חדש became טורח כל נושא, {the former phrase} a most appropriate epithet for him and his edition.

The Karaite *Maḥzor*, which appeared in Goslow in 1836, and in Vienna between 1854 and 1857, indicates to us how the Russian censor brought joy to the Crimea after 1804, because the *Siddur* edition that began on 9 September of that year in Kale is not yet fettered by its restrictions. Part 3 f. 36a lacks a complete chapter of Ezekiel that speaks of Gog; part 2 f. 104b [p. 212] omits a large part of Yehuda Hadassi's prayer that begins כן תאבד. The appropriate phrase ובן עולה עלי מלך in ed. 1804 part 1 f. 193a became, in ed. 1836 f. 69a and in ed. 1857 p. 374: ונגרשתי מזבולך; the phrase ערל וגם כושי (*syn. Poesie* 447) became צר ומאדיב נפשי (op. cit. 71a, p. 377).

3 Compare *syn. Poesie* p. 453 at the foot.

In אמולה לבתי one stanza has been altered, as have two lines in Calev's כבודה (part 3 p. 232); איך אזלה ידי is barely recognizable as such in various places. עוילים בהם רדים עקדים וברדים becomes בפקדך על העתודים ותלדן הצאן עקדים (part 3 p. 258); the powerful, concluding stanza of Abraham's אי לך:

קומי ונקמי באח
הרבה בשבר ואח
שמח בששון ואח
בשבות משושנו

has its rhyme ruined and is watered down to קומי ונשא נהי נבכה דמעות כים עד שוב כבוד אל ועד יבנה דבירנו (part 1 p. 378).

For fear of persecution, spurious explanations were written for spurious items, if only to avoid surrendering more material to the censor's scissors. Qalir (ה' קנני) says: "their Temple has become graves"; הכליהם is altered to הבליהם and the translation is: "because of their foolishness people are buried". Heidenheim altered קברי to הפילו and puts into the mouth of the payyeṭan: "their ceremonies are strangling people"; in a note he refers to the Bacchanalia of the ancient Romans. What is more, he admits that he has changed several items "for the sake of peace" (סליחה no. 146). The commentator on the Roman *Maḥzor* ed. 1587 already has peaceful annotations. He changes (*seliḥah* אמרנו) רודיינית into דורינית and states: this word denotes

P. 225

Jews who make gifts generously, that is to say, bribes; the סמלוני רשע are the Babylonian idols; רגז ארבע מחטיאותי (*qerovah* in *musaf*) refers to the four former empires; דומה (in the *hosh{a'na}* אנא אזון) to the angel of death. Here the prize goes to the re-interpretation of the anti-Christian *seliḥot*: בלע בגד (לך ה' הצדקה) are the turban wearers, בני עדינה are the Amalekites from the city of עדנית, פורה are the Ammonites, גוי נבל are the Chaldeans, בלעונו אדונים are the Greeks and the Tartars; the *seliḥah* אלהים אל דמי was composed in response to the Tartar persecutions of 1648! The word ממכעיסיך are the sinning Jews, while שוברי (in ה' אלהי רבת) are Jewish informers. The Sefardi prayer-book printed in Vilna in 1840 follows the same track; wherever the words "yoke" or "enemy" occur, the meaning is evil; the word גוי is altered into כותי and the explanation refers to the ancient star-worshippers. When the Psalmist says that "the gods of the peoples are idols" the commentator defensively refers this to ancient images (p. 29, 88); גרי הצדק means foreigners; צר (in המבדיל) has the sense of צרה. In that case the עובדי כוכבים are widely prominent {as גוים} in biblical sources; תתיר צרורה (pp. 23, 101) refers to sin, that is to say, this edition sins against beauty, learning, history, justice and truth.

Pp. 226–28 Appendix VII

Appendix VII
[P. 159]
The book בשמים ראש

With regard to this collection that purports to be responsa by R. Asher and other early rabbis, some concerns were already discussed by Azulai which he set aside but without solving the problem; consideration for the rabbis tied his tongue. Although one reads in {Geiger's} מלא חפנים p. 58 that it has been proved that the book is not genuine, I know of no such proof. What is more, a letter allegedly by R. Barukh b. Samuel was recently produced as evidence for the view that the Jews of the "German talmudic school" of the time underwent a great change in their opposition to the Karaites, especially as regards marriage with a Karaite who had come over to the rabbis. The more groundless this statement is, the more it seems justified to investigate the source from which it emanates.

Anyone acquainted with the literary style of the German rabbis of that time, especially in halakhic matters, will be surprised to find in those responsa by Asher a novel pilpul style that ranges extensively but does not directly with the topic. One should check the responsum about shaving (18) with the spurious citation from Tosafot Nazir, or another responsum dealing with a passage from the morning prayer (19) which is replete with statements in the style of Isaac Satanow, or where he informs us (24) that R. Dan put on Aramaic tefillin. There he challenges the authenticity of various talmudic passages, which, as he remarks, would not need to be examined more closely. In all his responsa the alleged R. Asher takes a lenient view; Rabbenu Tam would have wished to abolish יין נסך and retracted

P. 227

his view only because of the involvement of R. Samson (36)—which incidentally is seriously at odds with 504 ס' הישר. R. Meir of Rothenburg would have been very content to abolish the Omer counting (122); he himself, Asher, was in a great quandary about whether to recite the benediction before or after the reading of the {Passover} Haggadah. He warmly defends the use of peas and rice on Pesaḥ; abstinence had probably been learned (348) from the Karaites in Monzon (!). Also, travelling on the Sabbath is permitted (375). In the matter of reciting "*avinu malkenu*" on the Sabbath [see above p. 42], responsa by the early Geonim are cited, about which Yehudah Barceloni, who otherwise knows and reports the views of the early scholars, knows nothing (71). He decides against R. Gershom (compare Aaron

https://doi.org/10.1515/9783111142500-010

Ha-Kohen 99c), without even mentioning him. On the other hand, he mentions (344) his teacher Samuel who was a great חסיד, but of this person there is no knowledge in any of the authentic works of R. Asher. In no. 251 there is an edifying discussion of the articles of faith; they were relevant to their time, but for today the most important of them are that we are altogether useless and that we are required only to love truth and peace and to know God and his works. That may be fine, but it represents the style and theology of the eighteenth century and not those of the fourteenth.

In the remainder of the exchanges, characteristics of spuriousness appear even more sharply. Isaiah b. Abbamari is cited for us four times (94, 170, 188, 325) and Conforte was already misled about this (see Azulai part 2 p. 156), since such a person never existed. R. Asher had in the summer of 1320 given a decision (Responsa 18.14) which, according to here (191), Solomon Adret, who had by then been dead for many years, opposes. It is not clear why A. Fuld's remark on this matter in the Frankfurt edition of שם הגדולים (p. 280) was omitted from the Vilna edition. Jacob b. Makhir is transferred (301) to Barcelona and is made into a contemporary of Naḥmanides; the city of Mainz is inserted into a decision of Mordechai and a fictitious responsum is cobbled on (159, 160). Meshulam b. Qalonymos (81), in the style of a contributor

P. 228

to *Meassef*, relies on the practice of Jehoseph Ha-Nagid; this Jehoseph is none other than Joseph ibn Alfaruj who lived at the earliest in 1100, if not later, a whole century after Meshullam (compare ס' הקבלה 46b). Barukh b. Samuel cites (184) Abraham b. David, with whom he was certainly not acquainted, and states literally about the Karaites in his alleged responsum (220): "Not one case is known in marital matters that occurred and would be illegal according to talmudic law. If we wished to pay attention to such a thing—in how many rulings do the talmudic teachers, Tannaim and Amoraim and later scholars until our own day, not have divided opinions? Indeed, whoever investigated it would find greater disagreement among ourselves than between us and the Karaites! The talmudic rabbis already made the statement: the בעלי מקרא are your brethren." No distinguished rabbi wrote such stuff around the year 1200. In the commentary on Avot of the {Maḥzor} Vitry, which includes almost all the passages that מדרש שמואל transmitted from the commentary of Ephraim, it is stated in ch. 1: ועמד ענן ירקב שמו אחד מתלמידיו וכתב להם ספר גזירות רעות וחקי און {"There then arose Anan, one of his students, may his name rot, who wrote for them a book of wicked rules and worthless laws"}. Another commentary on Avot warns about those בעלי המקרא who are walking in the dark. So sound the voices of the contemporaries of R. Barukh,—apart from that, no trace has survived of such a responsum in the ס' החכמה or in any of the many detailed halakhic works of that epoch. The modest scholar, H{eimann} J{oseph} Michael, wrote in his manuscript dictionary, under the entry וספר בשמים ראש הנדפס על שמו טובה השתיקה עליו מפני כבוד ,אשר בית אב {"and with regard to the book בשמים ראש, printed in his name, it is best to be silent about it for the sake of our people's honour"}. In his love of peace, he took no account of the principle "Amicus Plato {sed magis amica veritas: I love Plato but I love truth more}" nor of the principle {במקום שיש חלול השם {אין חולקין כבוד לרב {"in a matter of the desecration of the Divine name, no honour is paid to any teacher"}; but his very silence constitutes condemnation.

Pp. 229–30 Appendix VIII

Appendix VIII
[P. 175]
שנשתלחה in the *Musaf Tefillah*

The *nitpa'el* forms, frequently in *piyyuṭ*, therefore occur with verbs that begin with the letter *shin* as exemplified in: נשתברו (*sel{iḥah}* אדאג), נשתבשו (poem in דברי חכמים {of Eliezer Ashkenazi of Tunis} p. 79 {line -4}), נשתדלה (*yoṣer* אמרת רנן), נשתדלו (*sel{iḥah}* על שאנו), נשתדרו (ibid.), נשתטחה (Levi יום עמדתי), נשתייר (*sel{iḥah}* אומץ יוסיף), נשתכלל (Qalir *qerovah* Feast of Weeks), נשתכר (Simeon Feast of Weeks שעשוע), נשתלם (*me'orah* בבוא גושנה, Benjamin רגובה אדני), נשתמדו (lament תמוז בעת), נשתמעו (Qalir, loc. cit.), נשתמשו (Tovelem אות ומופת), נשתעשע (Qalir loc. cit.), נשתתפתה (*sel{iḥah}* אשתטחה), נשתתפו (Karaite *Siddur* part 3 p. 85). Especially common is נשתנה which even Satanow did not alter, for example, נשתנה (*sel{iḥah}* אני הכרם, ארח משפטיך, אתה הרואה, *yoṣer* אשיחה), נשתנו (*sel{iḥah}* אזכרה מצוק, Simeon *silluq* for seventh day Pesaḥ, Isaac יום צדו, lament איך מפי), נשתנית (*sel{iḥah}* אברהם היה). The form נשתלח, which was very common in later Hebrew (Tosefta {Bava} Batra 10, {Bava} Batra 144b, Giṭṭin 14b, Bereshit Rabbah 50 f. 55d, 52 f. 58b, Eliezer Baraita ch. 20 and Yalquṭ Genesis 10b, Tanna Eliyahu ch. 5, Tanḥuma 8a, 31c, 49b, 65c, Bamidbar Rabbah 266a) and was also in use in the early sources (Nathan Ha-Kohen in Yuḥasin 124b, Rashi on Num 33:1, Shevu'ot 10a, 'Arakhin 13a, Eliezer b. Nathan אבן העזר 88c, 147a, Maimonides זכיה ומתנה 4.5, the scholar of Narbonne cited by Aaron Ha-Kohen 23c, David Qimḥi, Gen 28b) went from the living language into the *tefillah*, and this reading is confirmed by Amram, Ephraim (compare *syn. Poesie* p. 472), Maimonides, Abudarham, all manuscripts and rites. The expression השתלחת יד even seems to have been imported from the *tefillah* into Tanḥuma 51d

P. 230

and Bamidbar Rabbah 265d since Va-Yiqra Rabbah 188a has השלחת. The phrase וידו שלוחה, the source of which (Ezek 2:9) is cited by Satanow (אגרת, § 353) in support, is used by Eleazar (*zulat* אדני מעון) with a different meaning. The earlier emendation אשר שלחה made in the Roman *Maḥzor* (edd. 1540, 1587) did not, strangely enough, affect the *Tefillah* of the New Moon or of the three pilgrim festivals. In *piyyuṭ*, נשתלח occurs in *hosha'na* למען תמים עש, in the poem אז מרחם on the Torah Festival, in the *sel{iḥah}* אם יוספים, and in the *yoṣer* אדיר ונאה where the manuscripts actually read ולנשתלח and not ולמשתלח.

https://doi.org/10.1515/9783111142500-011

Pp. 231–33 Appendix IX

Appendix IX
[P. 175]
Isaac Satanow's Edition of the סליחות

Satanow's unjustified corrections are במוצא for במוצאי (Fürstenthal {מטיב שפה} p. 32), ידידיך for ירודיך (*sel{iḥah}* אויתיך). The word ירוד, also thought to be doubly anomalous by Fürstenthal p. 59, is early Hebrew (Tosefta 'Eduyot ch. 1, Yerushalmi {Bava} Meṣi'a 4.1, Bereshit Rabbah 68 end, Midrash Cant. 6c, Midrash Threni 78a, Yalquṭ Ruth § 608, Large Pesiqta 13.2. Tanhuma 35c. Shemot Rabbah 120b, 146c, 155b. Genesis-Aggadah 7, 14, 58; compare Rashi Gen 1:26, 'Arukh אוכלוסא in Buxtorf *Lex.* p. 981); ירודיך also occurs in the lament אשאג, ירודנו in the *sel{iḥah}* אנא אלהי תהלתי, ירוּדַי in the *sel{iḥah}* אם יתקע. Further, he writes מעפרת for מעברת (*sel{iḥah}* חקר), כקופיץ for כבקוף (אין תליה, see Fürstenthal p. 101), הגנת for הגפת (חננו), אויל for אוילי (incorrectly followed by later scholars), לפלשׂ for לפלש (תורה הקדושה). In the *sel{iḥah}* אנוש עד דכא, the mss. and the earlier editions have חרירה which is explained by R. Nissim (המפתח 35b) and Maimonides (Kelim 13.5) as "the eye of a needle", and by Hai as "the point of a needle"; 'Arukh and Samson {of Sens} are unsure. The words of the poet יען חרירה כמחט פתח יהי שלך כאולם נפתח refer to the passage in Midrash Cantic. 28d (Yalquṭ Cant. 179d) on the Song of Songs 5:2, where we now read כחודה של מחט*; this probably prompted the correction חדידה or חדדה. Barukh b. Samuel perhaps read כחורה since he applies the same logic and states: ואם תחתרי לנגדי כמו מחט נקובה (*sel{iḥah}* בטרם הר). Heidenheim ed. 1833 already has the correct reading. In אמרנו נגזרנו the payyetanic form סטנו is often corrected to the grammatical form סטינו. Regarding שְׁבַעְתָּ

P. 232

for שְׁבַעַת (אתה חלקי), see Fürstenthal p. 330. In איך אשא (see Fürstenthal p. 433), he corrects טריה into רטיה. In the *seliḥah* ה' אלהי צבאות he claims that יהו is only the singular form, compare *syn. Poesie* p. 124, 427. In מלאכי רחמים he alters לוקה into לֶקה (see Fürstenthal p. 553) and in אמוני שלומי—also Fürstenthal p. 592—he takes עינים נלוזות to mean "running eyes" and therefore ridicules the poet for having understood it as נזולות. However, the early commentary had correctly referred to נלוז (Prov 3:31) and to the well-known verse according to which the human heart and eye tempt one to do evil {Num 15:39}. Similarly, Satanow derives the word מהודמים (אני אני המדבר), which also occurs in the lament אבל אעורר, from the word הדום "footstool", and the word ובלולים (loc. cit.) from בלל. He battles (in אבינו מלך)

https://doi.org/10.1515/9783111142500-012

against אלילות and (in אל אמונה) against יסודי since the authors had written משכיות and יסוֹדֵי. In the *seliḥah* אתה חלקי he emends יחשך or ישוך into יחשך with a change of *shin* to *sin* and is followed in this by later editors, while here the correct texts are actually כעס השך (rad. שכך) and אהבה המשך, just as in the subsequent stanza one should read לשבויה קרא ושמטה.

In אכפרה פני מלך, however, Satanow is no more blameworthy than his predecessors although there too his alteration expanded the error. The correct reading is דקרני אילת כהפציל "when the rays of dawn spread out". דקרן or דוקרן meaning "pipe" or "ray" from either דקר or borrowed from the Greek δικραιος or δικραινον occurs in Tosefta Sukkah 1, Menaḥot 11, {b.} Sukkah 13a, Menaḥot 95a, j. Kilayim 4.2, j. Berakhot 1.1, j. Yoma 3.2, j. Sukkah 1.1, Bereshit Rabbah 21 (in the 'Arukh s.v.; ch. 50 has תרתין קרנין). קנים הדוקרנים is in {b.} 'Eruvin 16a; this is indeed the reading of 'Arukh and Rashi in Menaḥot loc. cit. and of the 'Arukh in Sukkah. Our text of Tosefta Kilayim 4 reads קנים מדוקרנין; hence also the participle דקרין "beaming" (Shemot Rabbah 47f. 161b). The expression מופצלין מראשיהן on its own, without דקרנין, occurs in Mishnah Menaḥot 11.6 and in Yalquṭ Levit. 189c; it is also indeed stated with regard to the dawn (אילת): קרניה מפצילות (Yoma 29a), and in the biblical phrase בקעה אורה (y. Berakhot and Yoma, loc. cit., Midrash Ps 22, Midrash Cant. 32d, Yalquṭ Ps ch. 22). The poet has indeed thus availed himself of the talmudic expression and since he had to start with *dalet* he chose דקרני

P. 233

(not קרני), which the Palestinian Talmud in any case needs for the first rays of the sun. The sixteenth-century commentator already explains דקרני as ביקוע, only he was confused by the analogy that some wished to draw between דקרני and קרן. The early Polish editions (Cracow 1584, Prague 1605, 1609, and others) left the word undivided; but the German editions (for example Saloniki 1554, Cremona 1560, Venice 1568 and 1600) wrote דֵי קַרְנֵי which the commentator המסביר (Amst. 1712) made into די קרנֵי, altered by Satanow into די קֶרֶן with די being well explained by later scholars as equivalent to היטב "adequately". There is a perfectly parallel passage at the beginning of a *yoṣer* by Meir b. Isaac: אילת השחר דקרניה כהפצילה. With regard to the participles in the *pa'ul* form (see *synag. Poesie* p. 120, 411) of which Satanow disapproved, one should compare Elijah Levita (זקן אהרן no. 79). Although the form רדומים already occurs in Midr. Esther 127c, it is criticized by Joseph Qimḥi, and Asher of Lunel suggests reading רודמים: doctrinaire correctors of language make poor text critics.

* As also Bereshit Rabba 1 and Yalquṭ Ps 86; Ha-Manhig 9a § 6: כחדודה.

Pp. 246–49 Geographical Index

(This is Zunz's original index, only alphabetically and linguistically adjusted. The pagination follows his original pagination, as marked in the margins throughout the English translation)

[North-]Africa 9, 15, 54, 87, 122, 133, 192
Adrianople 79
Afriqiya 190
'Ain el Saitun 55
Al-ḥara 110
Aleppo 55–56, 108, 110–11, 113, 136
Algiers 43, 47, 49, 51, 88–89, 93, 105–6, 113ff, 116, 128–29, 136
Alsace 71, 136, 138–39
Amalfi 78
Amsterdam 88
Ancona 78, 129
Andalusia 5–6
Apulia 78–79, 146
Arabia 5–6
Aragon 6, 41, 43, 96, 106ff, 119, 141, 146
Arelat 101
Arezzo 78
Arles 63
Armenia 83
Arta 51, 79, 82, 161
Ascoli 78
Asti 64, 119, 138
Austria 67, 70–71, 86, 138
Avignon 10, 12–13, 15, 43, 48, 77, 88–89, 93–94, 96, 105, 110ff, 118ff, 124, 129, 132, 134, 136, 140–41

Babylonia 2, 5, 8, 86
Baghdad 57, 85, 101
Barbary 150
Barcelona 42, 112, 122, 188
Bari 78
Benevent 78
Berlin 152
Bern 71
Bohemia 6, 72, 101
Bokhara 57
Bologna 78
Breslau 73 173
Brindisi 78
Brünn 73, 75
Burgundy 6, 63, 86, 92, 100, 105, 134, 140, 181

Cairo 55–56, 130
Calabria 79, 146
Candia 128
Capua 78
Carpentras 10, 50, 89, 93–94, 105, 111, 127, 129, 134, 140–41
Castilia 6, 13, 39, 44, 89, 107ff, 116, 121, 132, 140, 142, 146
Catalonia 6, 22, 41, 45, 106ff, 116, 119, 131, 136–37, 141, 146, 154, 180–81
Cavaillon 50, 127–28
Champagne 63
China 58
Chios 79
Cingolo 78
Cochin 15, 57, 88
Constantine 37, 52, 92, 105, 119, 179
Constantinople 51
Cordova 41
Corfu 82
Cracow 73, 138
Crimea 82

Damascus 51, 55–56
Dresden 152
Düren 22

Eger 73
Egypt 55–56, 92
England 6, 62, 127
Erfurt 70–71, 127, 201
Evora 146

Fano 78
Fayyum 55
Ferrara 78, 129, 156
Fez 53, 88–89, 92–94, 105, 107ff, 116, 118, 136, 189, 191

https://doi.org/10.1515/9783111142500-013

Florence 78
Fossano 64
Fraga 41
France 10–11, 14–15, 21, 34, 59ff, 85, 87–88, 91–92, 94, 96–98, 100ff, 117ff, 120, 127, 134, 136ff, 140ff, 155
Frankfurt a. M. 85, 127, 129, 139, 152
Fürth 9, 119, 130

Galicia, see Russia
Gallipoli 79
Genoa 76
Georgia 83
Germany 9, 12, 14–15, 66ff, 85, 87–88, 90–91, 95–96, 99ff, 117ff, 122ff. 132, 134ff, 137ff, 140ff, 146, 150, 152ff, 171ff
Gerona 22, 42
Greece 9, 15, 79ff, 88, 90, 97, 99, 119, 132, 146
Guadalajara 110
Gubbio 78

Halberstadt 152
Hamat 56
Hamburg 152
Holland 150
Hungary 70, 77

Imola 78
India 57
Iraq 92
Italy 9, 71, 99, 101, 120f, 124f, 132, 136, 143, 146, 149–52, 181f

Jerusalem 83ff, 89, 150–52
Jubar 55

Kabul 57
Kaffa 38, 58, 82, 118–19, 131–32, 143, 150–51
Karaites 99, 139, 142, 146, 156–62, 167, 183
Kastoria 79
Khazaria compare 16
Köln 69–70, 127, 136, 138
Korassow 83

L'isle 50
Lecce 78
Lemberg 152
Lepanto 51
Lisbon 146
Lithuania 120–21, 135–36, 138, 143
Livorno 9, 130, 150
Lombardy 75, 79
London 173
Lorca 41
Lotharingia 6, 21, 64ff, 101, 123
Lucca 76
Lucena 122, 187
Lunel 13, 45

Maçon 92
Magdeburg 70
Maghreb 54–55
Magnesia 41
Milan 76
Mainz 16, 21, 65–66, 68, 85, 128, 131–32
Mallorca 6, 42, 44, 131
Mantua 76, 151–52
Marca 78
Melfi 78
Meliana 81
Messina 51
Mişr [Fustat] 55
Modena 151
Moncalvo 64
Montpellier 46, 107ff, 119, 121
Moravia 73, 125
Moriscos 55
Morocco 41, 53, 86
Mosul 57
Mostarab 55–56, 86, 130

Naples 78
Narbonne 22, 45, 137, 180
Nehardea 5
Neustadt 138
Nürnberg 70, 128, 130, 138

Oran 52, 128, 133
Otranto 78

Padua 148
Palestine 2, 5–6, 12, 55, 83, 87, 92, 95, 150–51
Pamplona 106
Patras 51

Pavia 76
Persia 17, 57, 89, 92, 122
Perugia 78, compare 144
Pesaro 78
Pforzheim 128
Piedmont 64, 101
Pisa 76
Poitou 65, 72
Poland 6, 73ff, 90, 98ff, 119ff, 125, 127, 135–36, 138f, 140–41, 145–47, 150, 154ff, 166, 171
Portugal 146
Posen 75, 100, 120, 128–29, 135, 138, 152
Prague 73, 120, 127, 129, 135–36, 138, 148, 152
Provence 6, 13, 32, 45, 49, 86, 88–89, 94, 106, 111ff, 124, 129, 140, 146
Prussia 75
Pumbedita 5

Qayrawan 54, 92, 189, 190f

Ravenna 78
Recanati 78
Regensburg 70, 129
Rhineland 13, 22, 67, 127, 218
Rieti 78
Romagna 78
Romania 44, 79ff, 90–91, 96, 98ff, 117ff, 132–33, 136, 143, 154, 160
Rome 12–13, 26, 76ff, 87–88, 90–91, 96, 98ff, 118ff, 128, 130, 133, 136, 140, 143, 146
Rothenburg 69
Russia 72

Safed 55, 85, 151–52
Salerno 78
Saloniki 51, 79, 120, 146, 151
San Severino 78
Saragossa 41, 106, 190
Saxony 67, 101, 132
Sengili 57
Seville 12, 30, 40
Shechem 55
Sicily 6, 51, 92–94, 129, 146
Sidon 55
Sijilmasa 27, 54, 86
Silesia 73
Sinigaglia 78
Siponto 78
Slavonia 12, 66, 72
Smyrna 56
Sofia 79
Spain 9, 13, 39, 86–89, 92–94, 101, 104ff, 117, 124, 130, 132, 136f, 146f, 149, 166
Speyer 21, 69
Strasbourg 218
Styria 71, 77
Sulmona 78
Sura 5, 85
Swabia 71, 120, 136, 138
Switzerland 71

Tarent 78
Tenes 44
Tetuan 54
Tiberias 152
Tlemcen 43, 52, 105, 107ff, 118–19, 133, 137, 150
Toledo 30, 40, 42, 106, 207
Trani 78
Tripoli 52, 55, 105, 107ff, 115, 118, 133, 136–37, 141, 144
Troyes 28, 65
Tunis 43, 52, 105, 109, 112ff, 116, 133, 136–37
Turkey 146, 152
Tyre 56

Ulm 70
Urbino 78

Valona 79
Venice 75, 151–152
Verona 76, 152
Vienna 22, 70

Westphalia 171
Worms 69, 86, 95, 120–21, 127–32, 136, 138, 143
Würtemberg 173
Würzburg 86

Xanten 128

Zürich 218

www.ingramcontent.com/pod-product-compliance
Lightning Source LLC
Chambersburg PA
CBHW020227170426
43201CB00007B/339